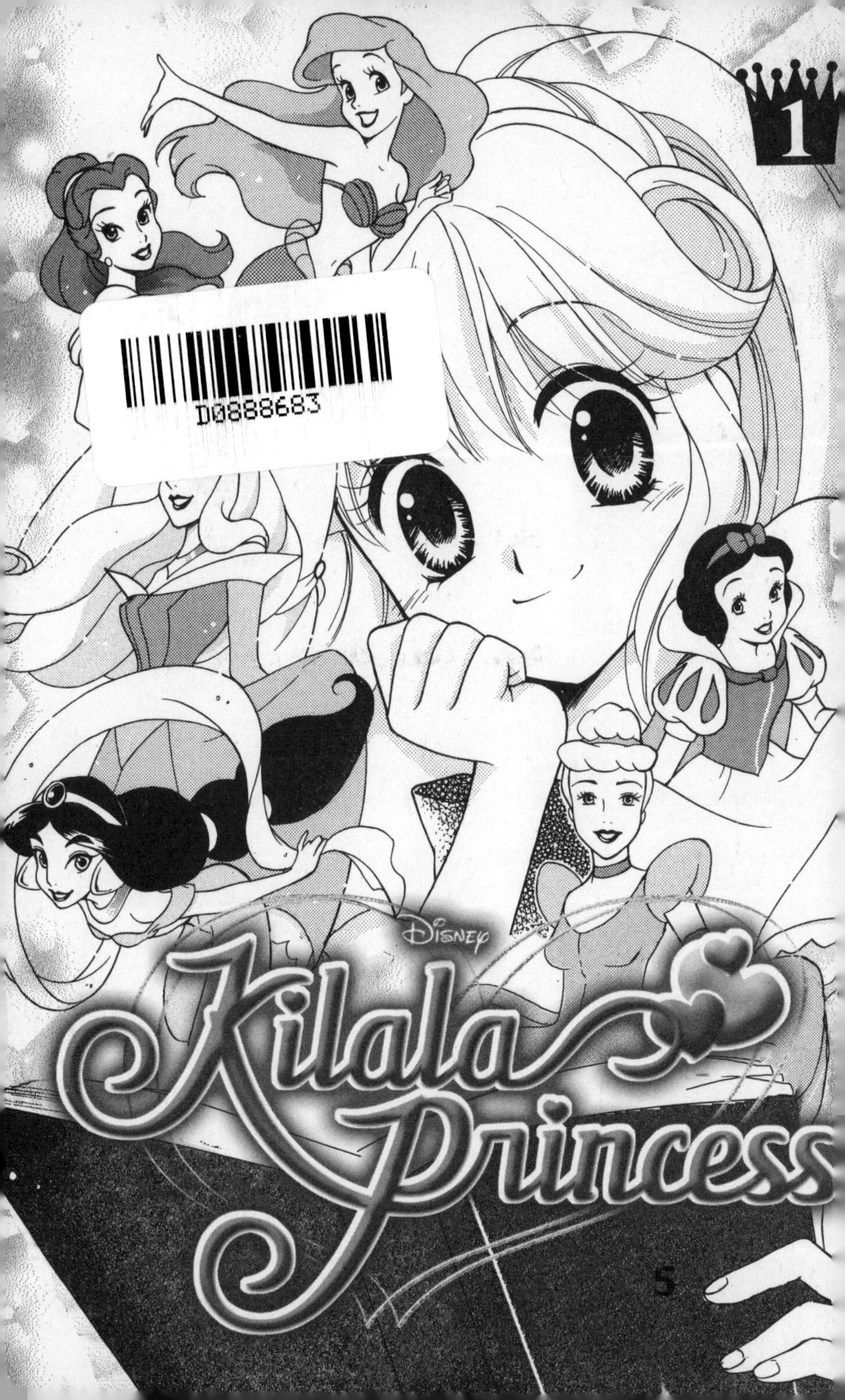
1
DISNEY
Kilala Princess
5

ET

Princess
Aurora

Belle

ey

cesses

Ariel

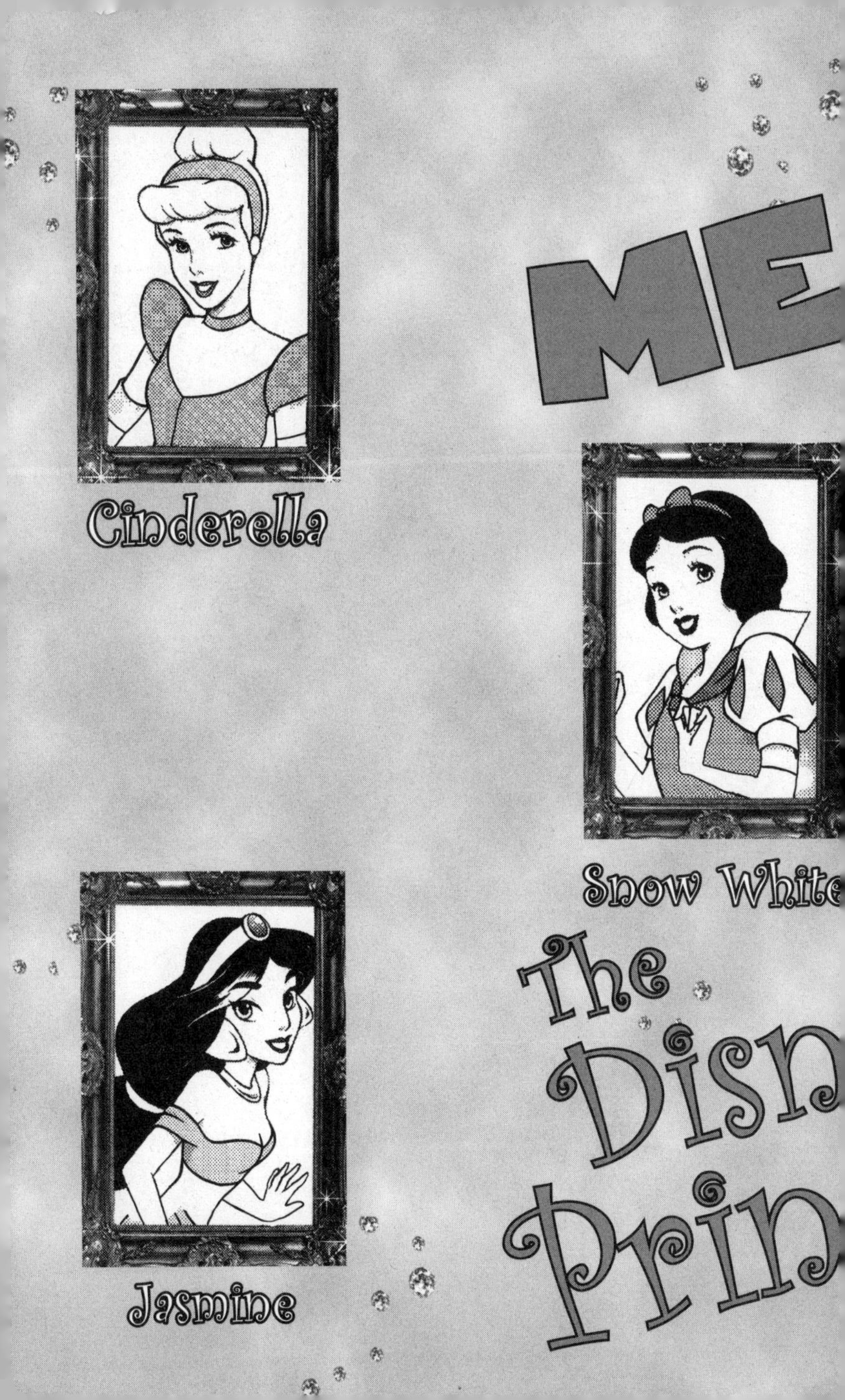
ME
Cinderella
Snow White
The
Disn
Prin
Jasmine

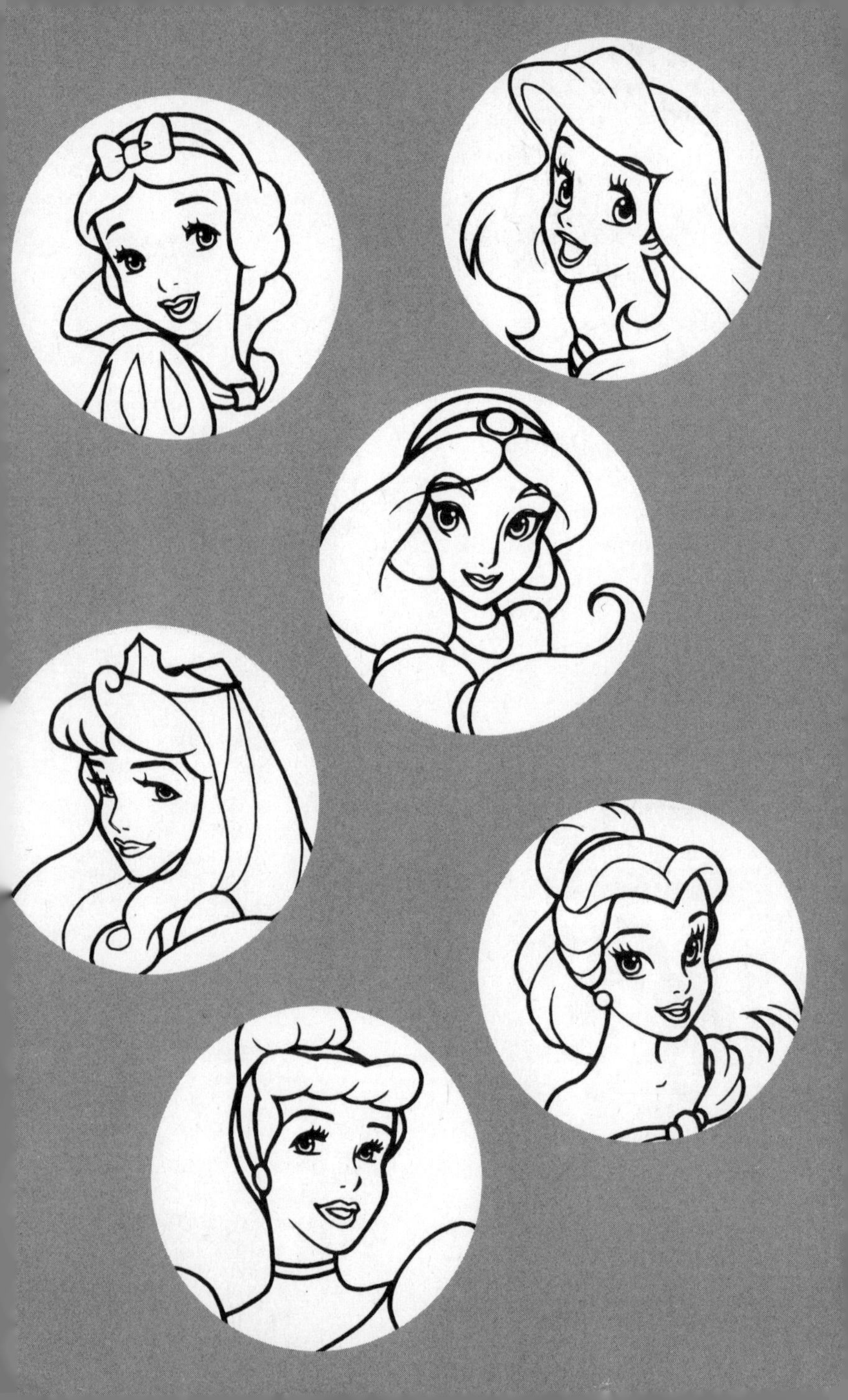

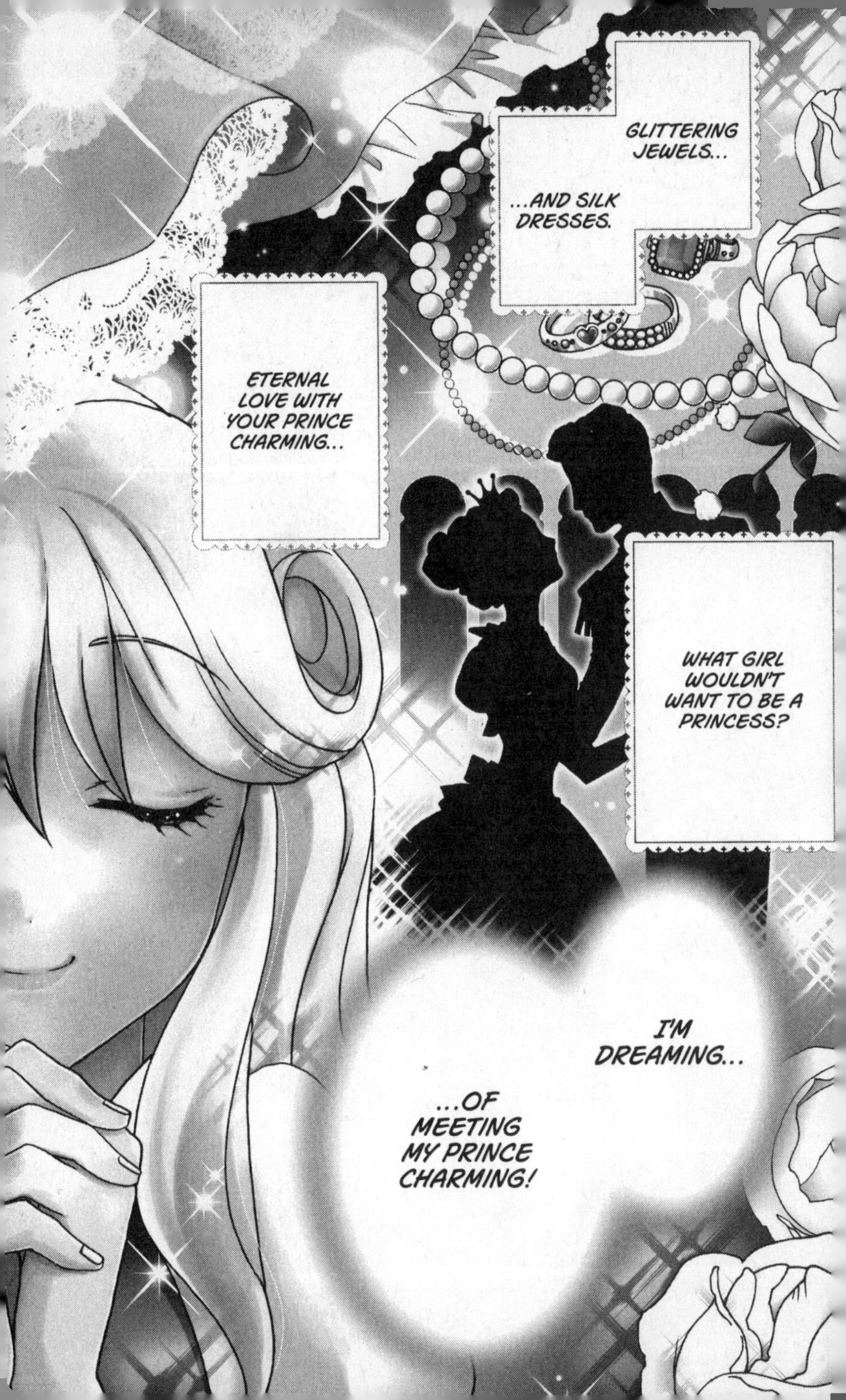
GLITTERING JEWELS...
...AND SILK DRESSES.
ETERNAL LOVE WITH YOUR PRINCE CHARMING...
WHAT GIRL WOULDN'T WANT TO BE A PRINCESS?
I'M DREAMING...
...OF MEETING MY PRINCE CHARMING!

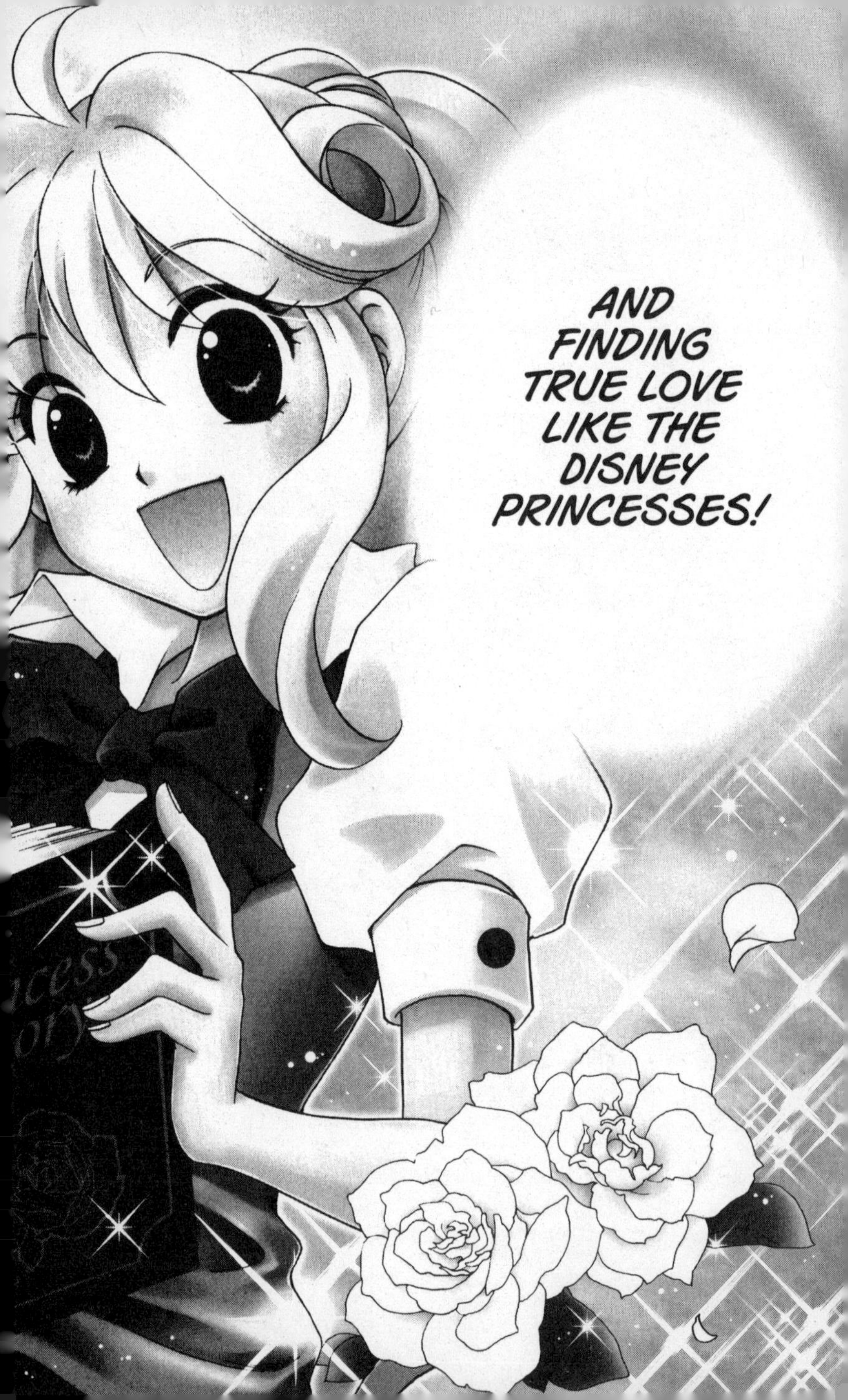
AND FINDING TRUE LOVE LIKE THE DISNEY PRINCESSES!

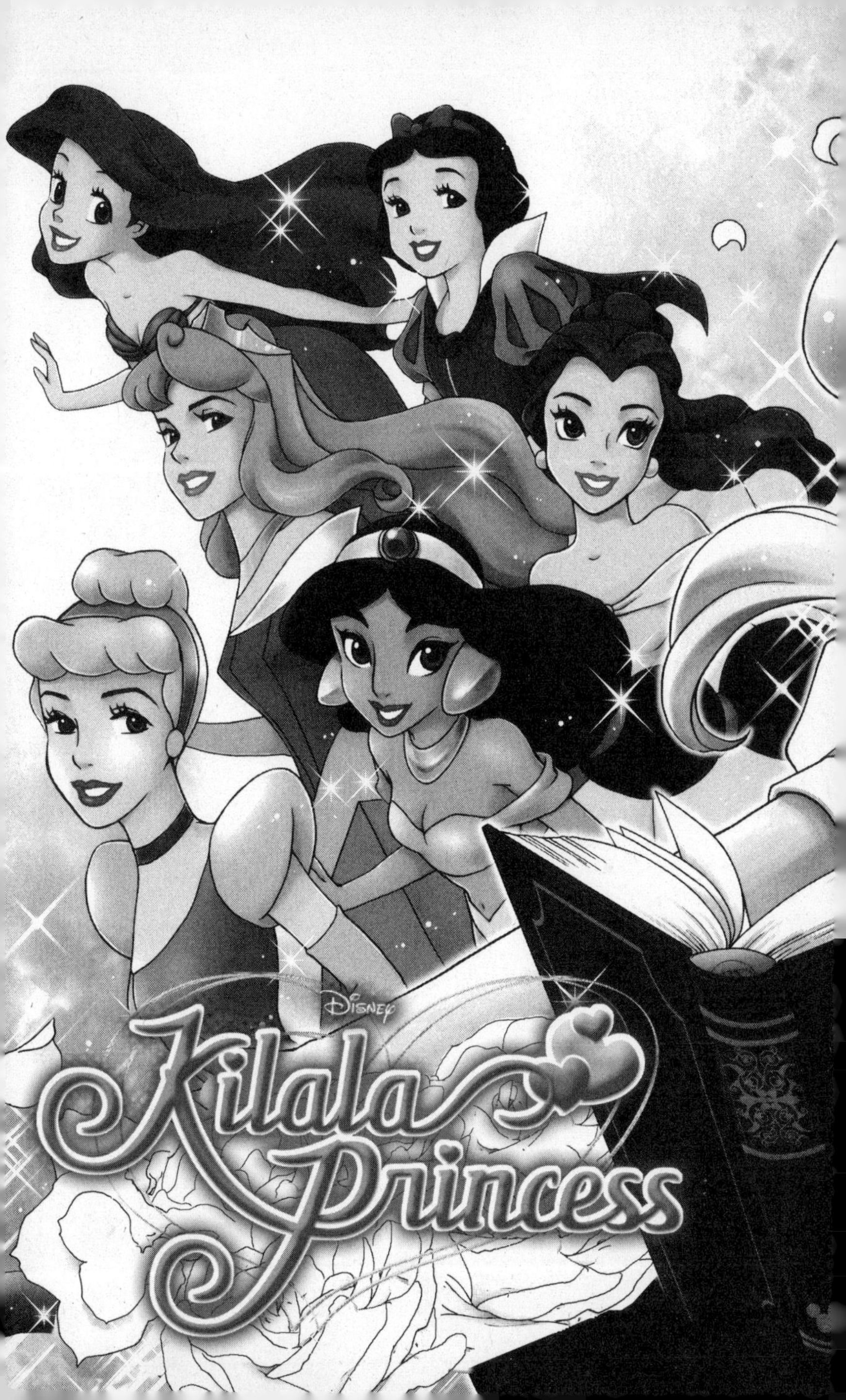
Disney
Kilala Princess

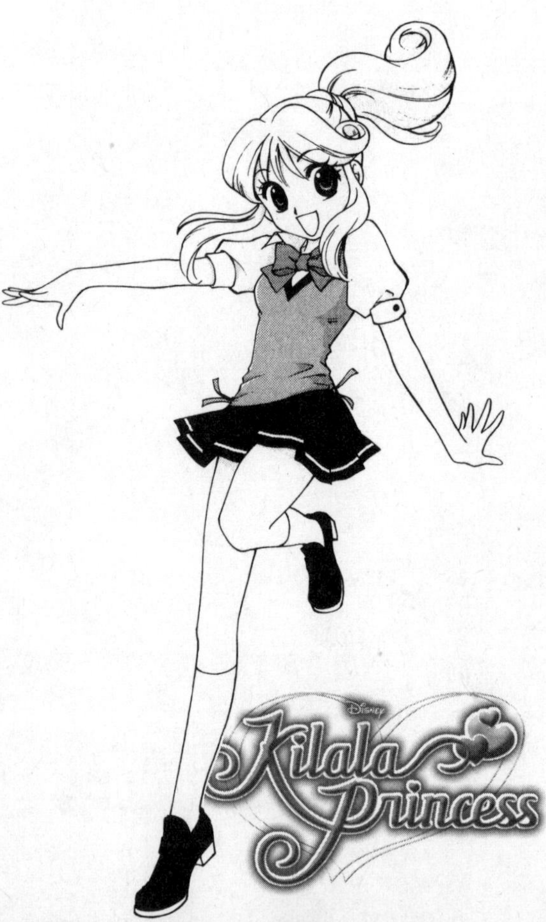
Disney
Kilala Princess

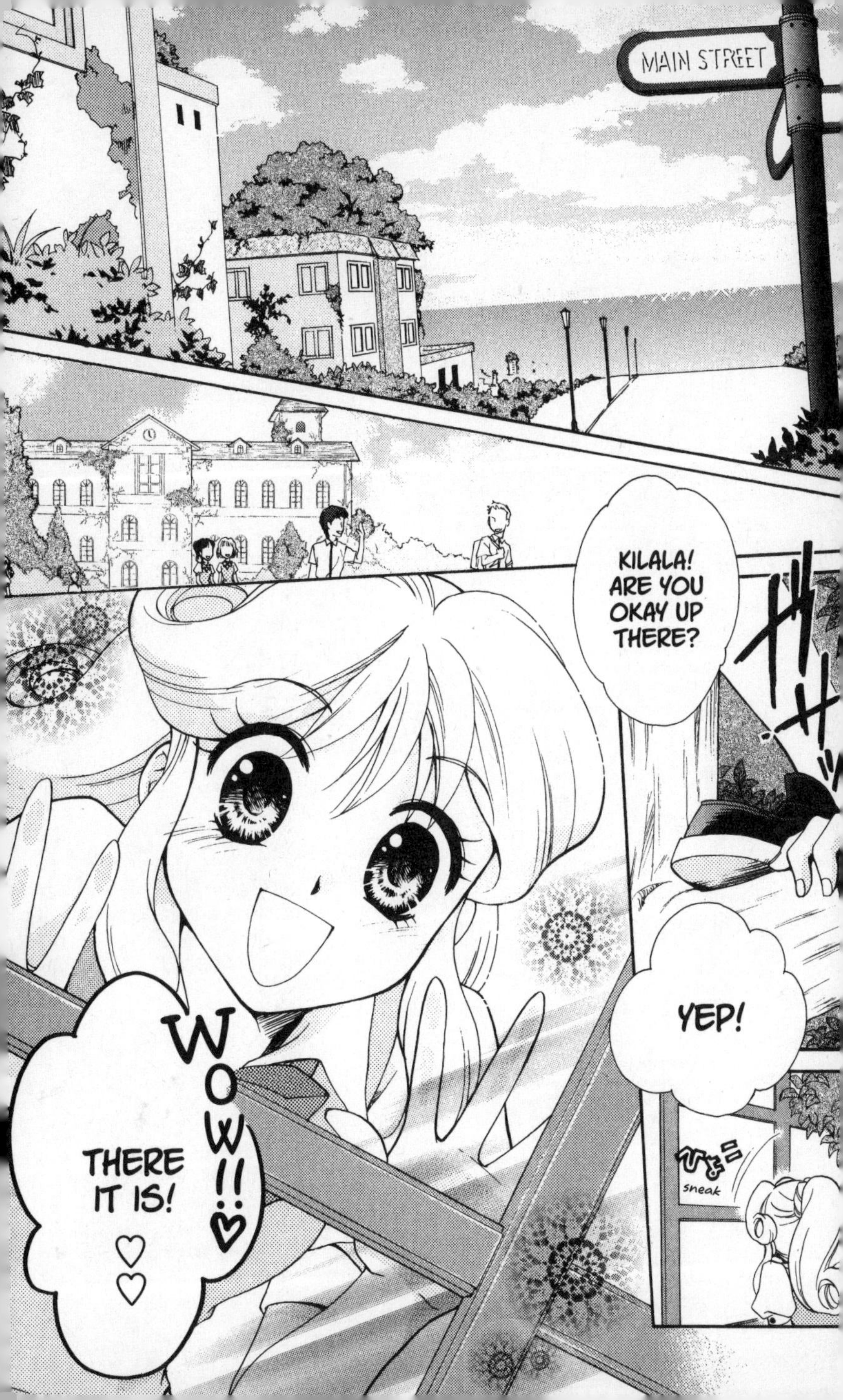
MAIN STREET
KILALA! ARE YOU OKAY UP THERE?
YEP!
sneak
WOW!!♡
THERE IT IS! ♡ ♡

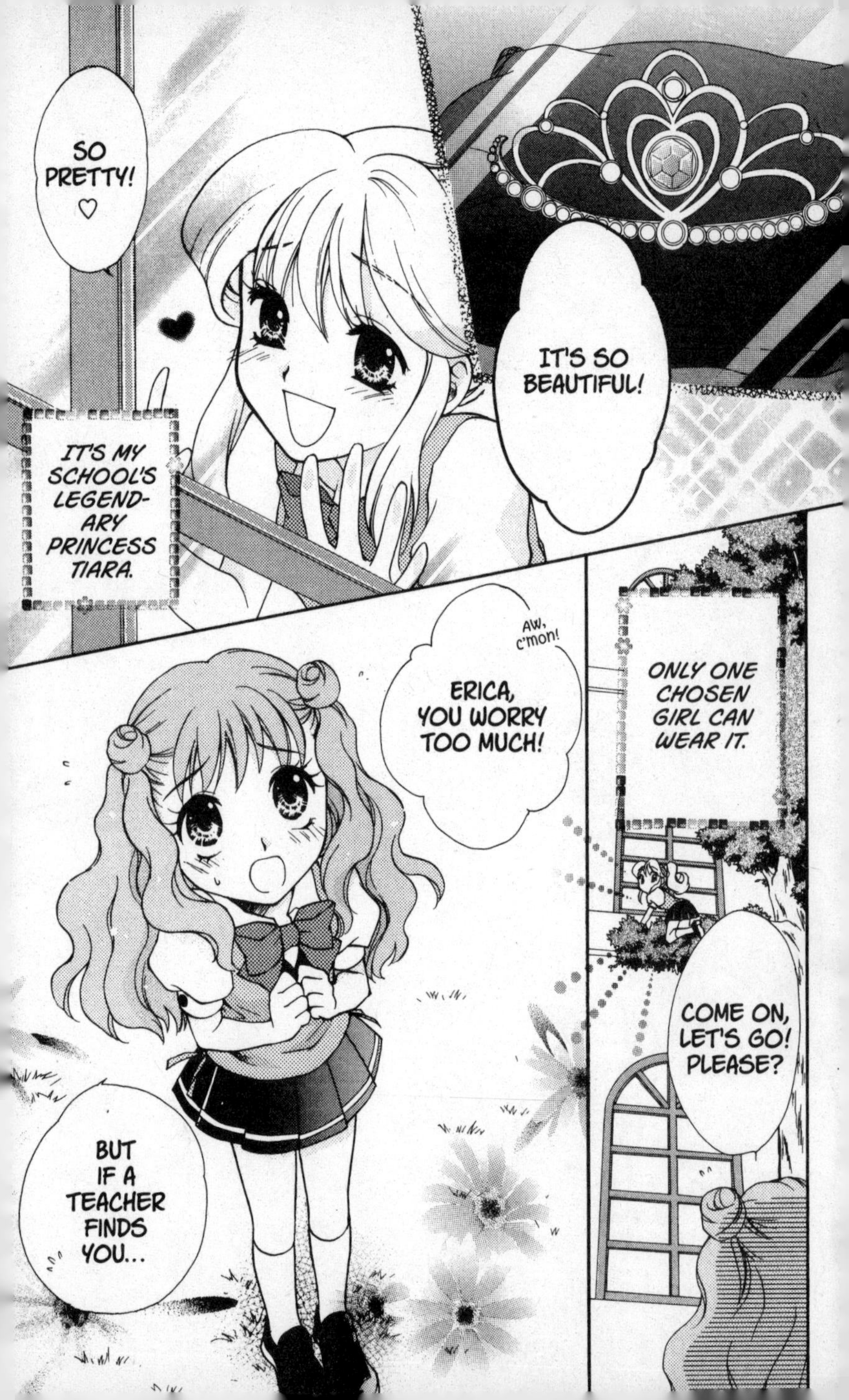
IT'S SO BEAUTIFUL!
SO PRETTY! ♡
IT'S MY SCHOOL'S LEGEND-ARY PRINCESS TIARA.
ONLY ONE CHOSEN GIRL CAN WEAR IT.
COME ON, LET'S GO! PLEASE?
AW, C'MON!
ERICA, YOU WORRY TOO MUCH!
BUT IF A TEACHER FINDS YOU...

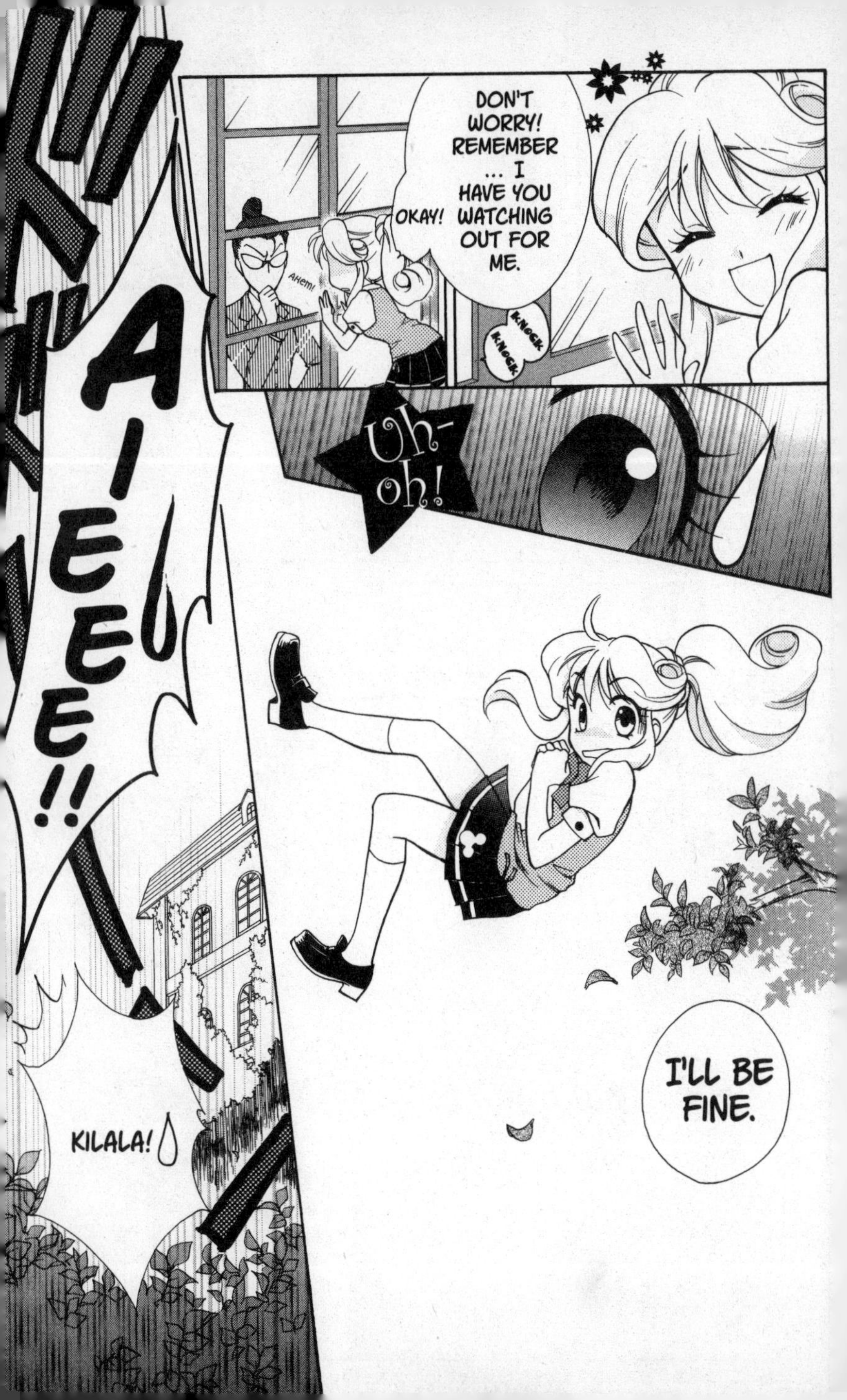

DON'T WORRY! REMEMBER ... I HAVE YOU WATCHING OUT FOR ME.
OKAY!
AHEM!
KNOCK KNOCK
Uh-oh!
I'LL BE FINE.
AI-EEEE!!
KILALA!

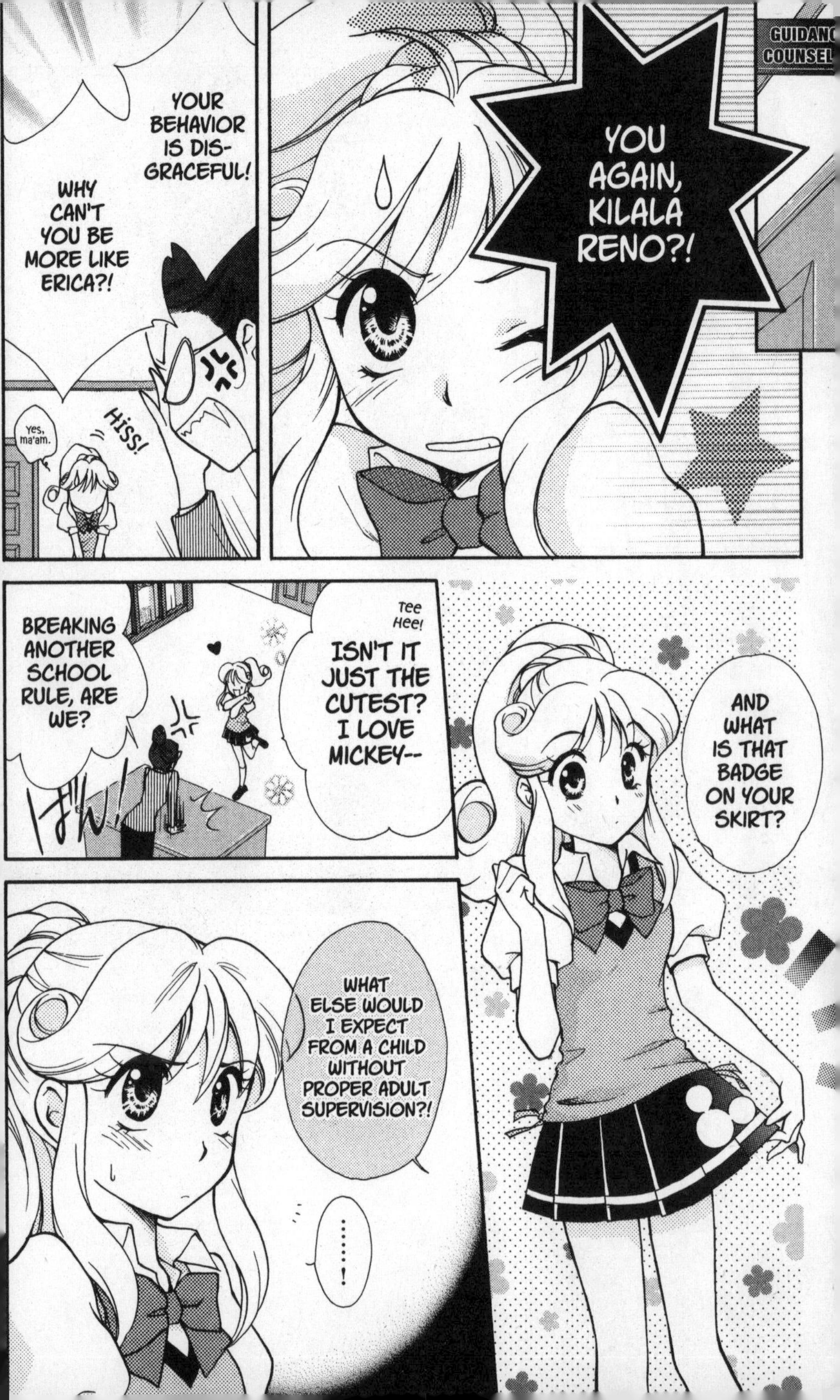
GUIDANC
COUNSEL
YOU AGAIN, KILALA RENO?!
YOUR BEHAVIOR IS DIS-GRACEFUL!
WHY CAN'T YOU BE MORE LIKE ERICA?!
HISS!
Yes, ma'am.
AND WHAT IS THAT BADGE ON YOUR SKIRT?
Tee Hee!
ISN'T IT JUST THE CUTEST? I LOVE MICKEY--
BREAKING ANOTHER SCHOOL RULE, ARE WE?
ばん!
WHAT ELSE WOULD I EXPECT FROM A CHILD WITHOUT PROPER ADULT SUPERVISION?!
......!

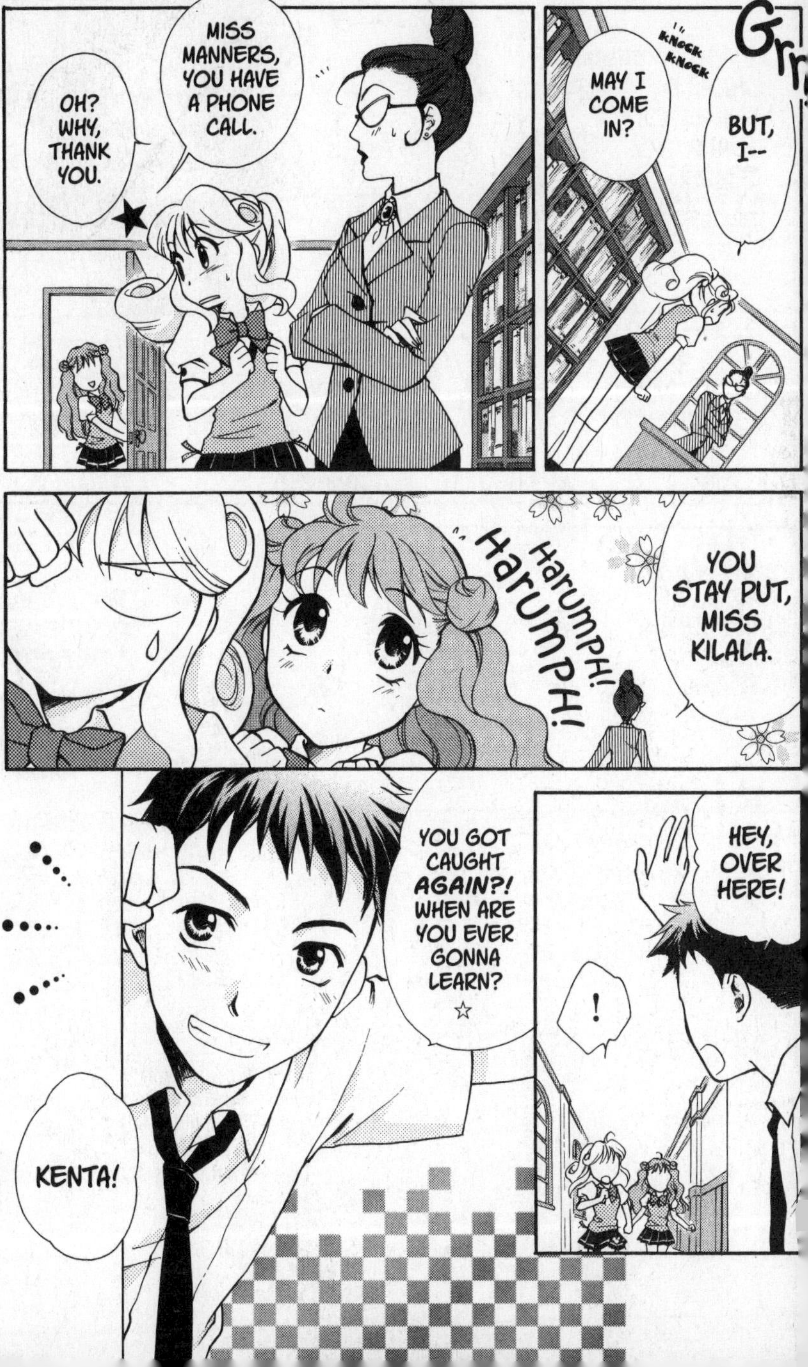
Grr
BUT, I--
KNOCK KNOCK
MAY I COME IN?
MISS MANNERS, YOU HAVE A PHONE CALL.
OH? WHY, THANK YOU.
YOU STAY PUT, MISS KILALA.
HARUMPH! HARUMPH!
HEY, OVER HERE!
!
YOU GOT CAUGHT AGAIN?! WHEN ARE YOU EVER GONNA LEARN? ☆
KENTA!

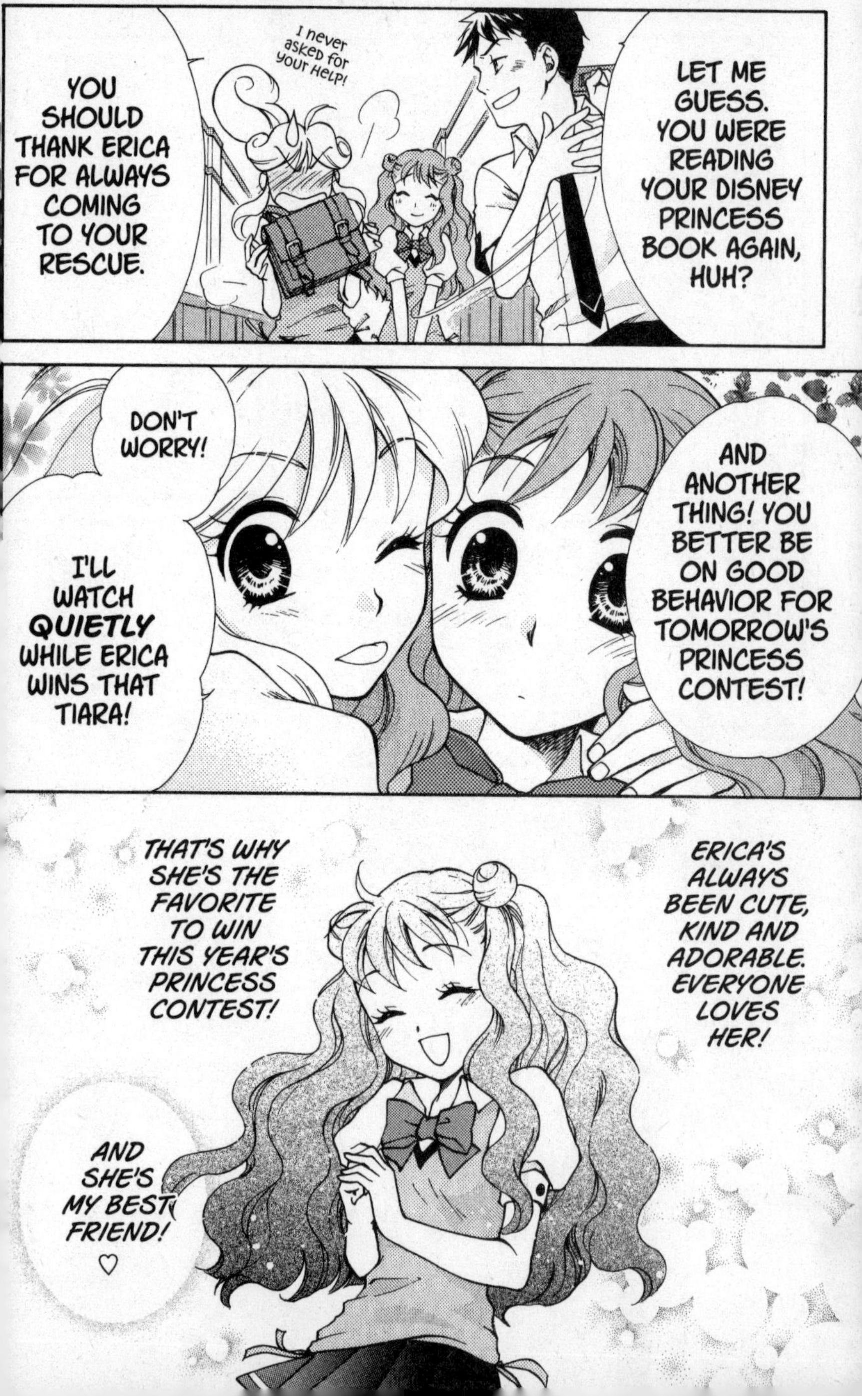
LET ME GUESS. YOU WERE READING YOUR DISNEY PRINCESS BOOK AGAIN, HUH?
I never asked for your help!
YOU SHOULD THANK ERICA FOR ALWAYS COMING TO YOUR RESCUE.
AND ANOTHER THING! YOU BETTER BE ON GOOD BEHAVIOR FOR TOMORROW'S PRINCESS CONTEST!
DON'T WORRY!
I'LL WATCH **QUIETLY** WHILE ERICA WINS THAT TIARA!
ERICA'S ALWAYS BEEN CUTE, KIND AND ADORABLE. EVERYONE LOVES HER!
THAT'S WHY SHE'S THE FAVORITE TO WIN THIS YEAR'S PRINCESS CONTEST!
AND SHE'S MY BEST FRIEND! ♡

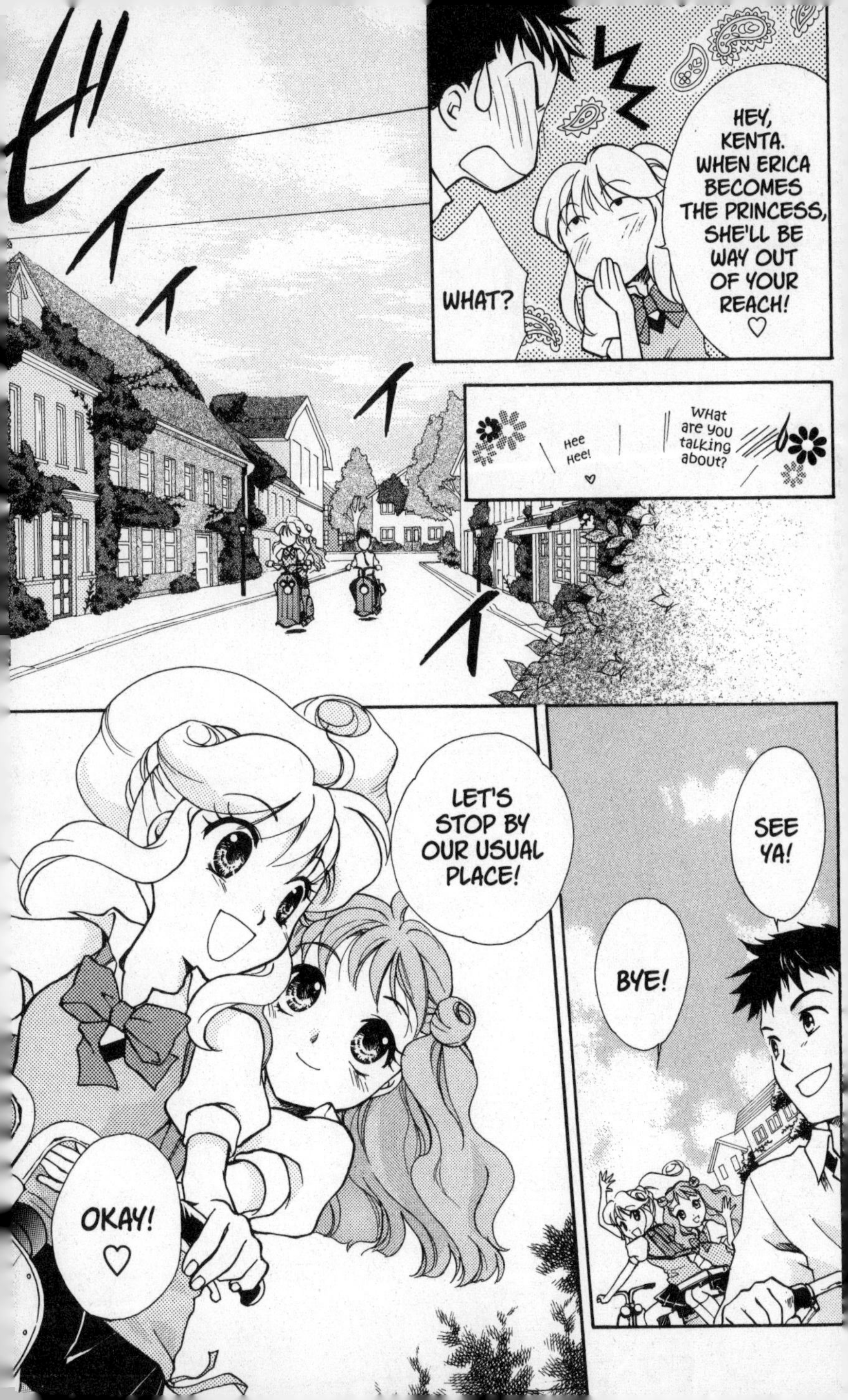
HEY, KENTA. WHEN ERICA BECOMES THE PRINCESS, SHE'LL BE WAY OUT OF YOUR REACH! ♡
WHAT?
What are you talking about?
Hee Hee! ♡
ゼイイイイ
SEE YA!
BYE!
LET'S STOP BY OUR USUAL PLACE!
OKAY! ♡

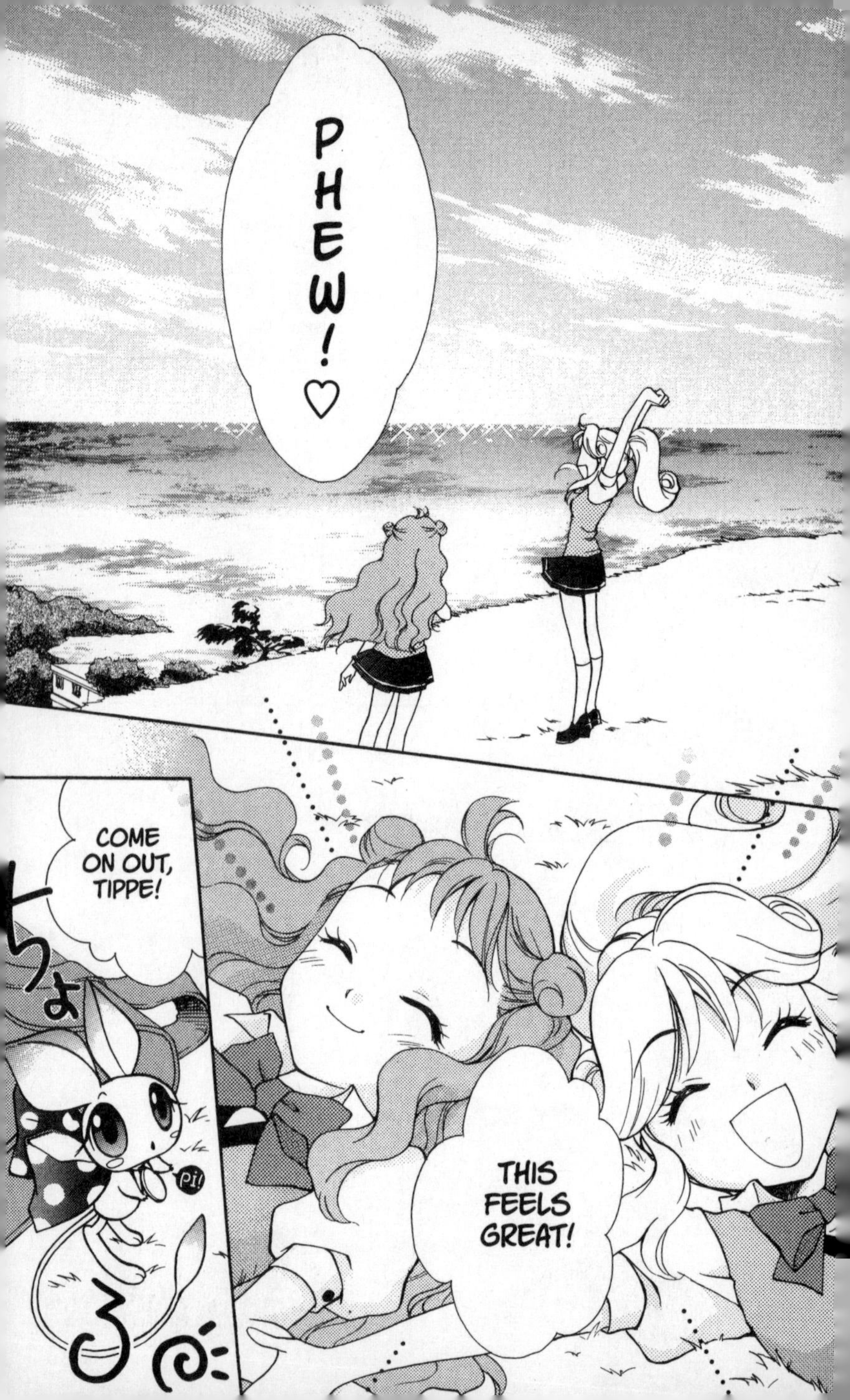
PHEW! ♡
THIS FEELS GREAT!
COME ON OUT, TIPPE!
ちょろ
pi!

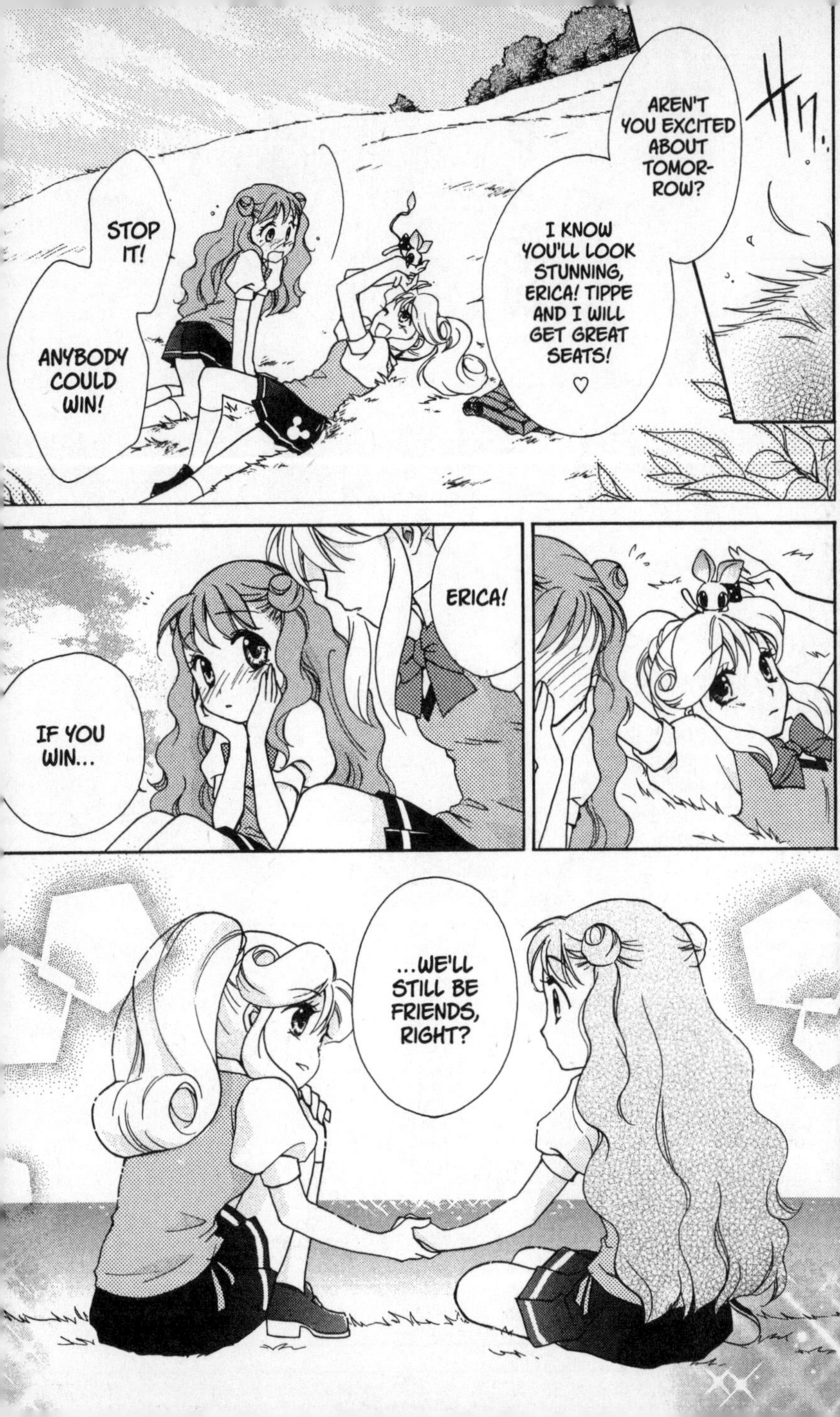
AREN'T YOU EXCITED ABOUT TOMOR-ROW?
I KNOW YOU'LL LOOK STUNNING, ERICA! TIPPE AND I WILL GET GREAT SEATS! ♡
STOP IT!
ANYBODY COULD WIN!
ERICA!
IF YOU WIN...
...WE'LL STILL BE FRIENDS, RIGHT?

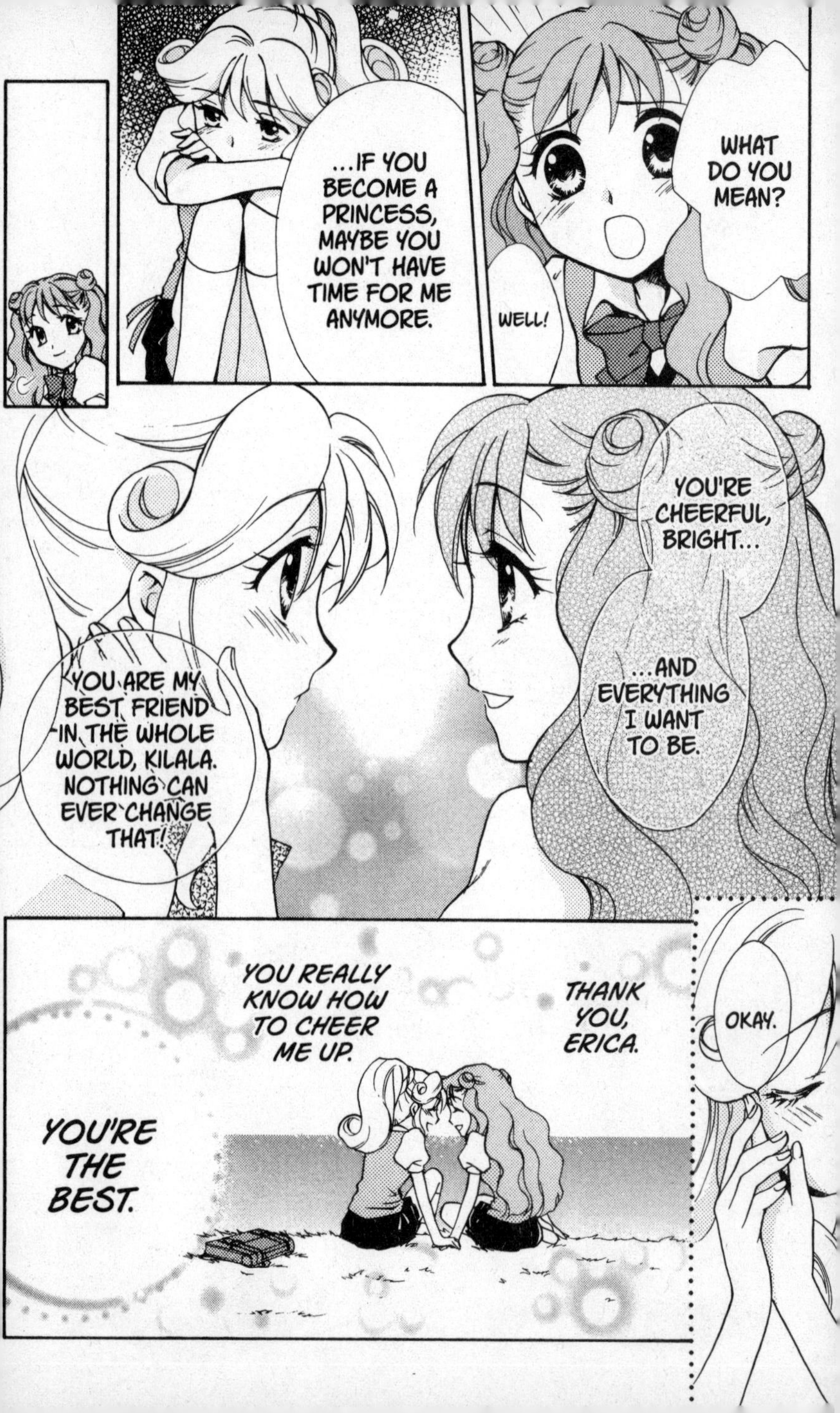
WHAT DO YOU MEAN?
WELL!
...IF YOU BECOME A PRINCESS, MAYBE YOU WON'T HAVE TIME FOR ME ANYMORE.
YOU'RE CHEERFUL, BRIGHT...
...AND EVERYTHING I WANT TO BE.
YOU ARE MY BEST FRIEND IN THE WHOLE WORLD, KILALA. NOTHING CAN EVER CHANGE THAT!
OKAY.
THANK YOU, ERICA.
YOU REALLY KNOW HOW TO CHEER ME UP.
YOU'RE THE BEST.

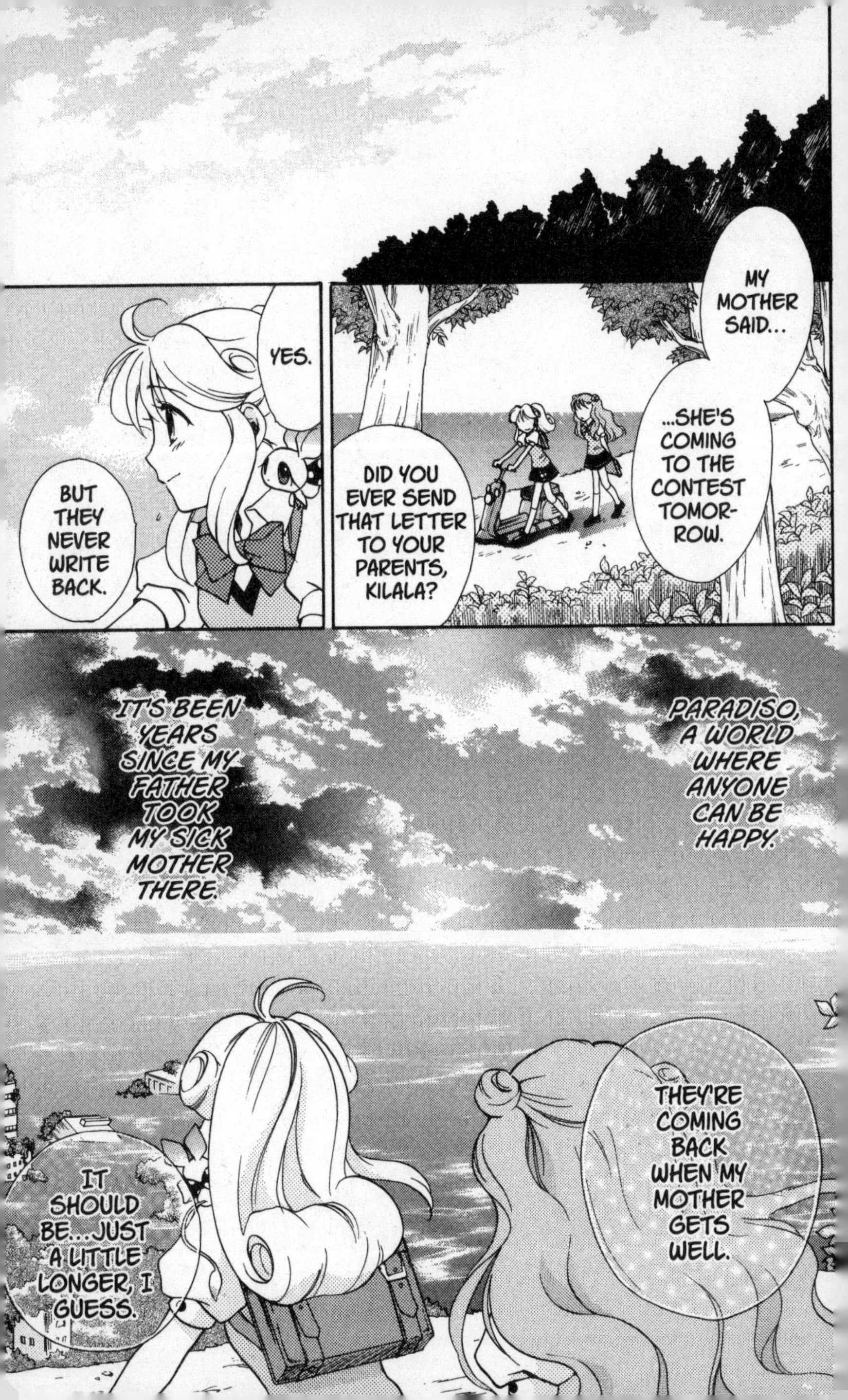
MY MOTHER SAID...
...SHE'S COMING TO THE CONTEST TOMOR-ROW.
DID YOU EVER SEND THAT LETTER TO YOUR PARENTS, KILALA?
YES.
BUT THEY NEVER WRITE BACK.
PARADISO, A WORLD WHERE ANYONE CAN BE HAPPY.
IT'S BEEN YEARS SINCE MY FATHER TOOK MY SICK MOTHER THERE.
THEY'RE COMING BACK WHEN MY MOTHER GETS WELL.
IT SHOULD BE...JUST A LITTLE LONGER, I GUESS.

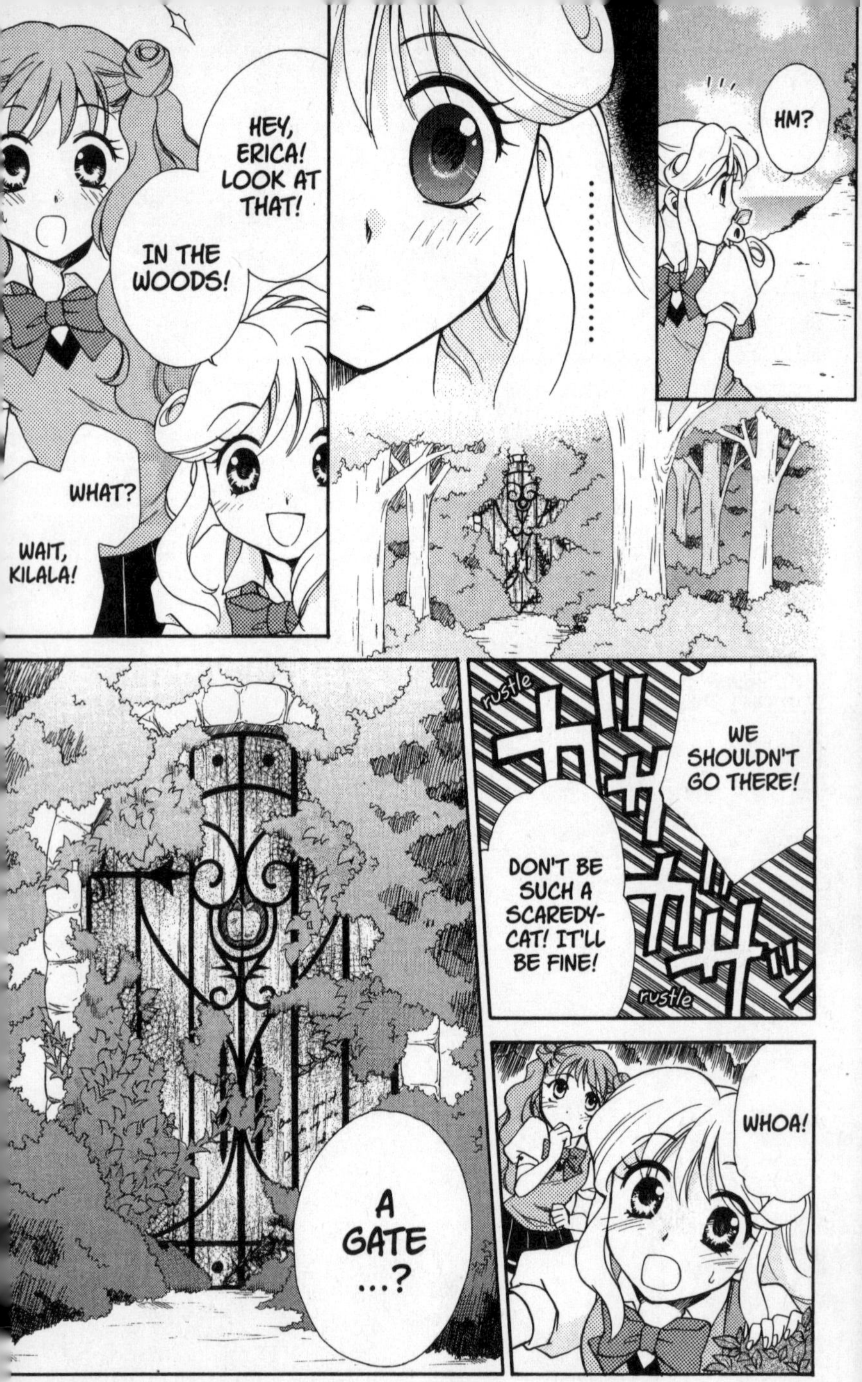
HM?
......
HEY, ERICA! LOOK AT THAT!
IN THE WOODS!
WHAT?
WAIT, KILALA!
rustle
WE SHOULDN'T GO THERE!
DON'T BE SUCH A SCAREDY-CAT! IT'LL BE FINE!
rustle
WHOA!
A GATE ...?

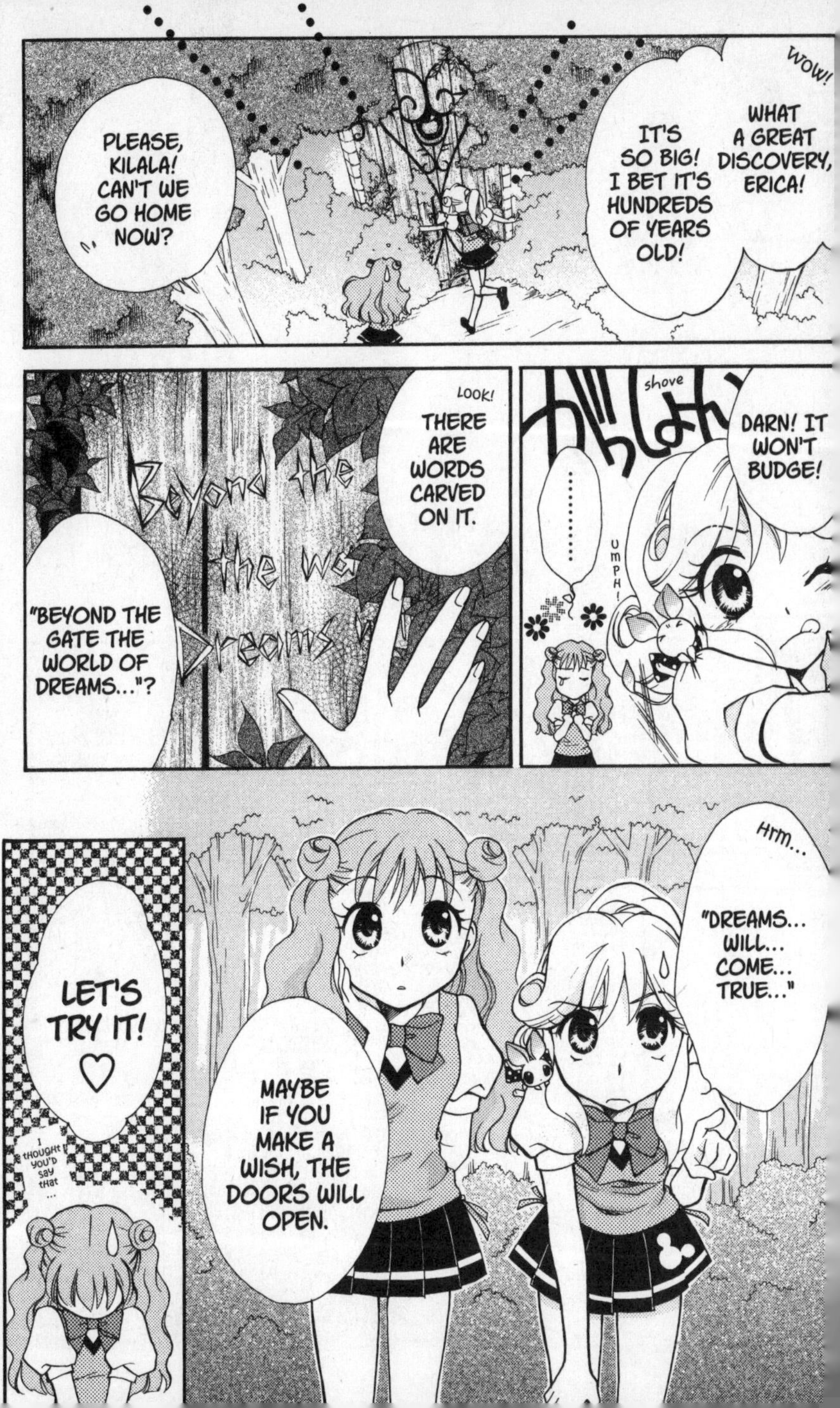
WOW!
WHAT A GREAT DISCOVERY, ERICA!
IT'S SO BIG! I BET IT'S HUNDREDS OF YEARS OLD!
PLEASE, KILALA! CAN'T WE GO HOME NOW?
shove
DARN! IT WON'T BUDGE!
UMPH!
......
LOOK!
THERE ARE WORDS CARVED ON IT.
Beyond the
the wa
Dreams
"BEYOND THE GATE THE WORLD OF DREAMS..."?
Hrm...
"DREAMS... WILL... COME... TRUE..."
MAYBE IF YOU MAKE A WISH, THE DOORS WILL OPEN.
LET'S TRY IT! ♡
I THOUGHT YOU'D SAY THAT...

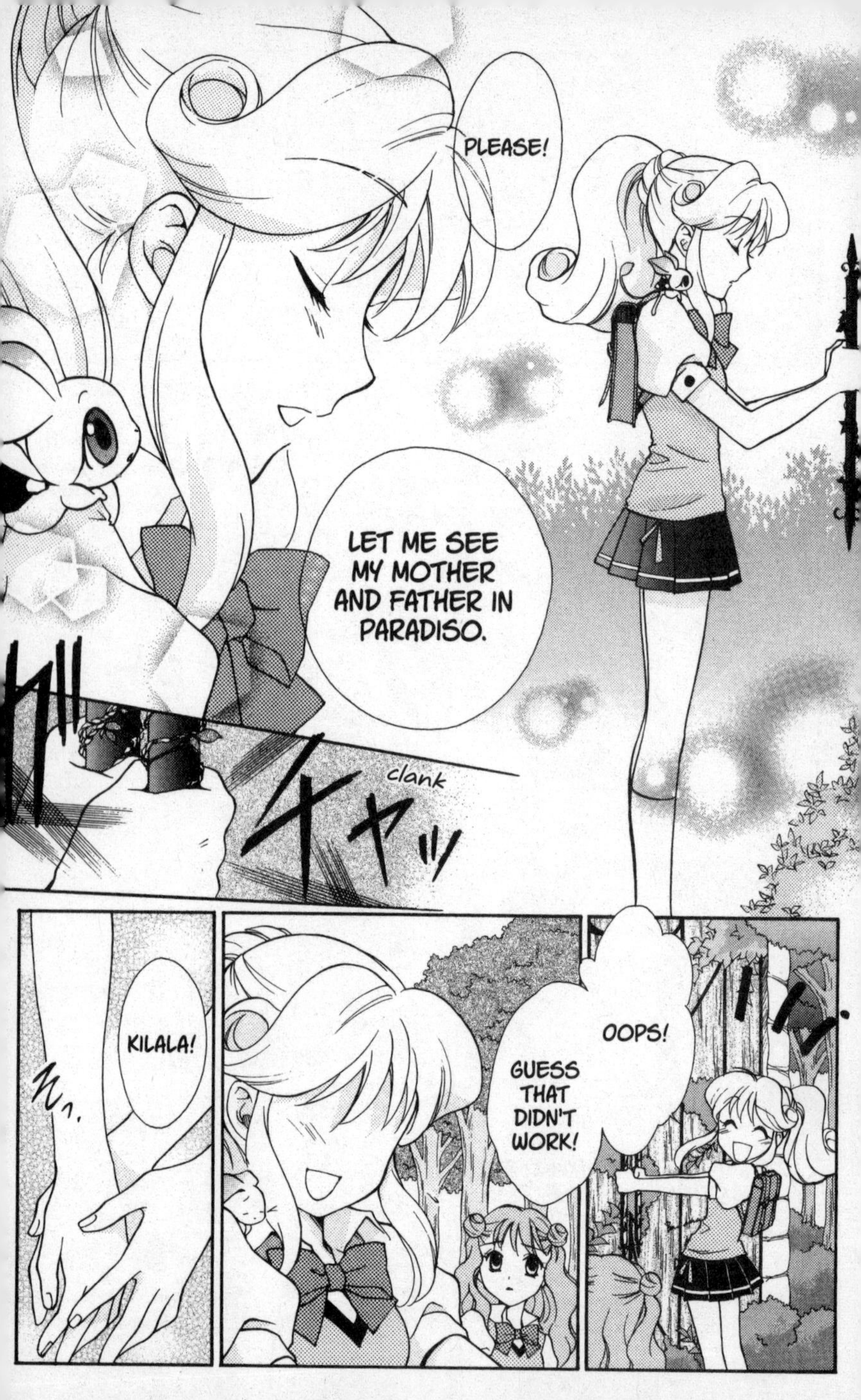
PLEASE!
LET ME SEE MY MOTHER AND FATHER IN PARADISO.
clank
OOPS!
GUESS THAT DIDN'T WORK!
KILALA!

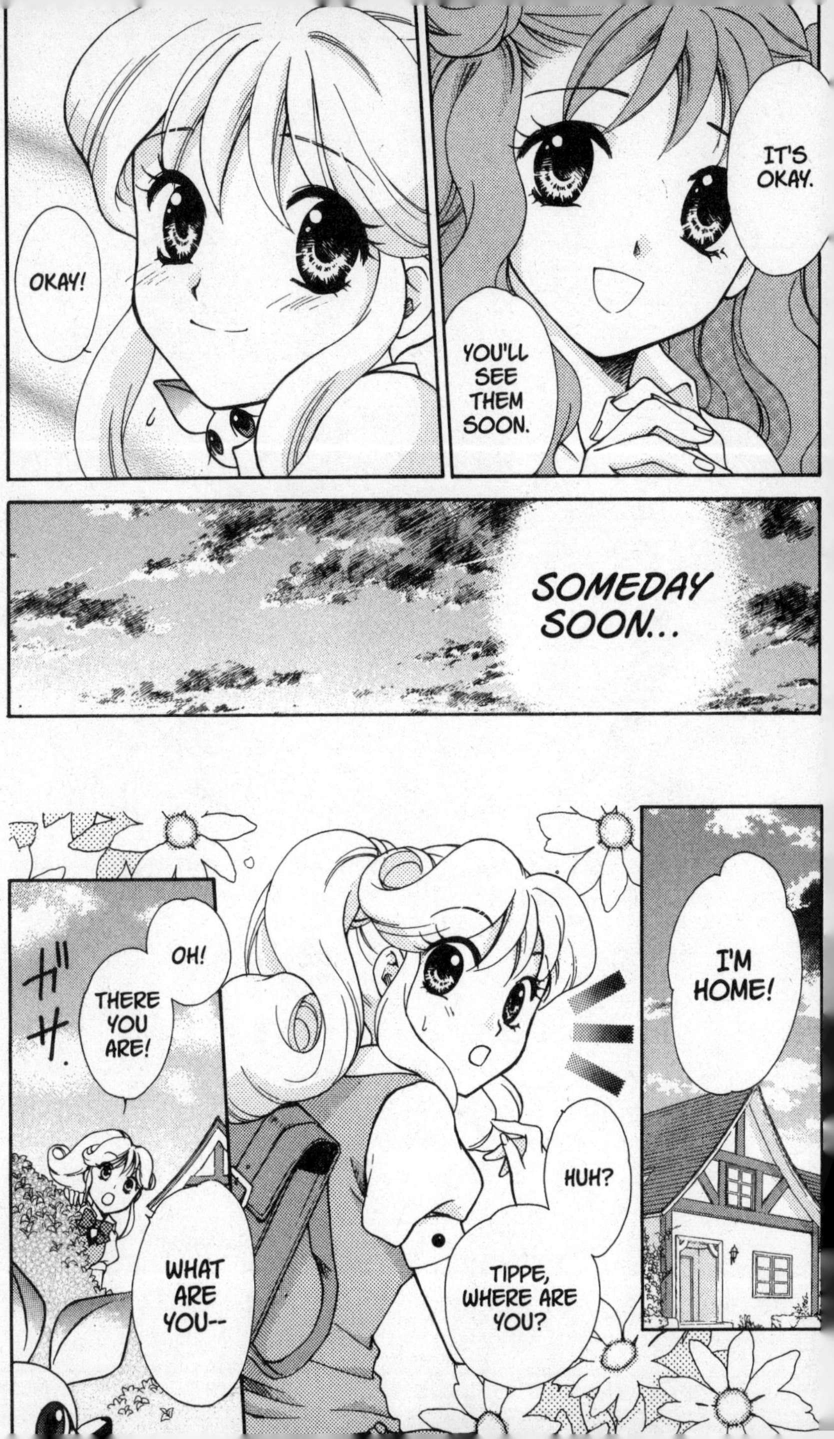
IT'S OKAY.
YOU'LL SEE THEM SOON.
OKAY!
SOMEDAY SOON...
I'M HOME!
HUH?
TIPPE, WHERE ARE YOU?
ガサ
OH! THERE YOU ARE!
WHAT ARE YOU--

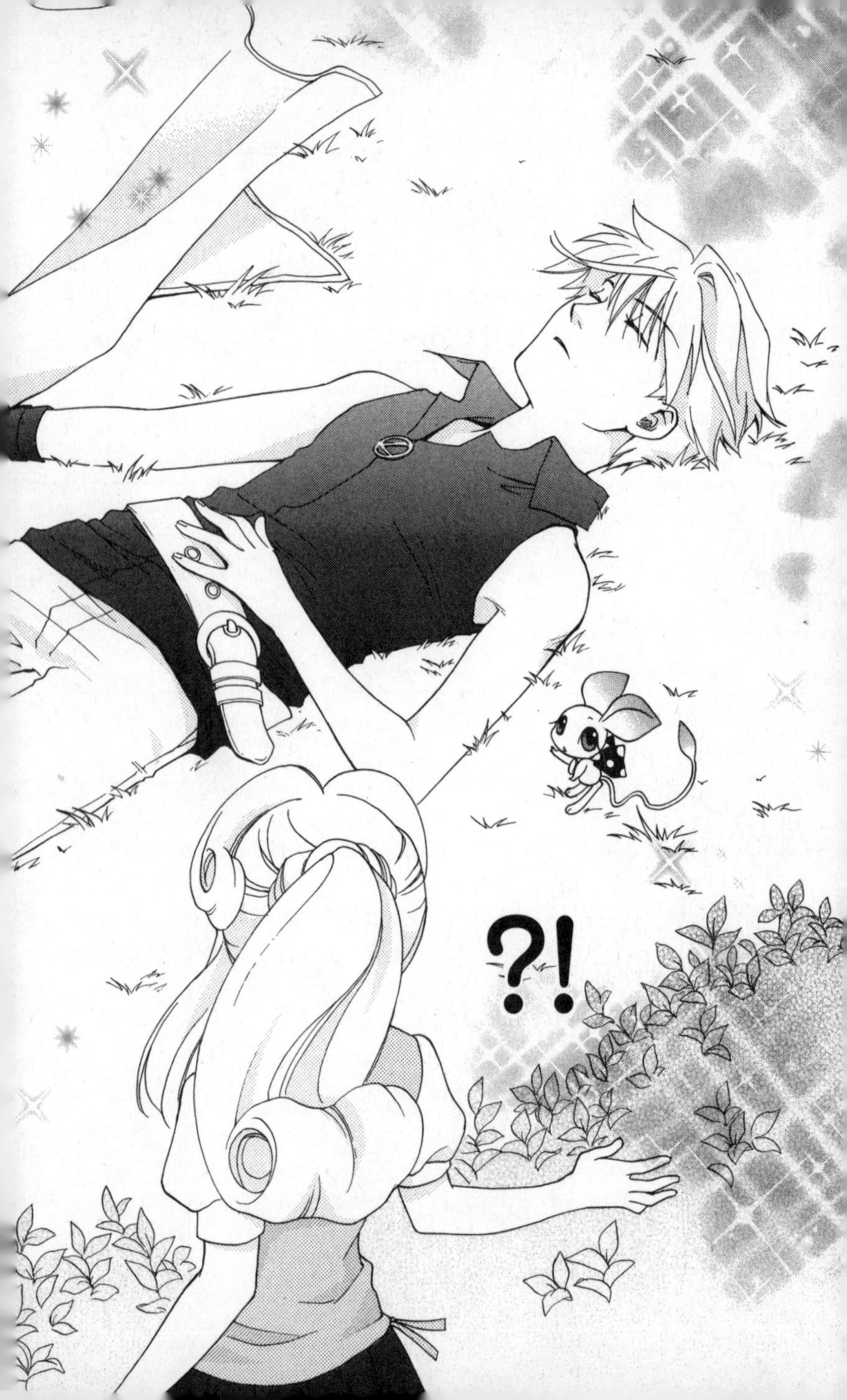
?!

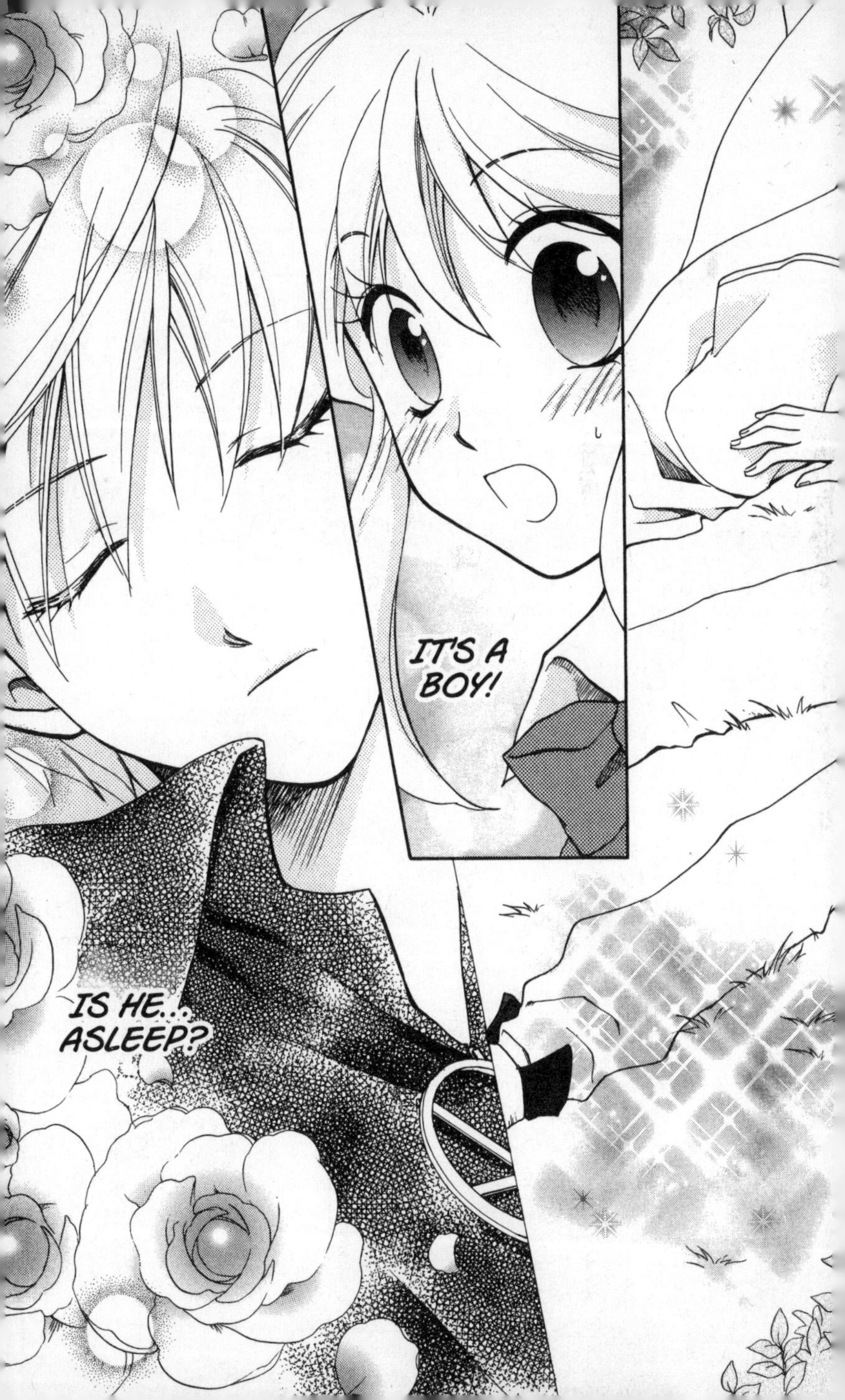
IT'S A BOY!
IS HE... ASLEEP?

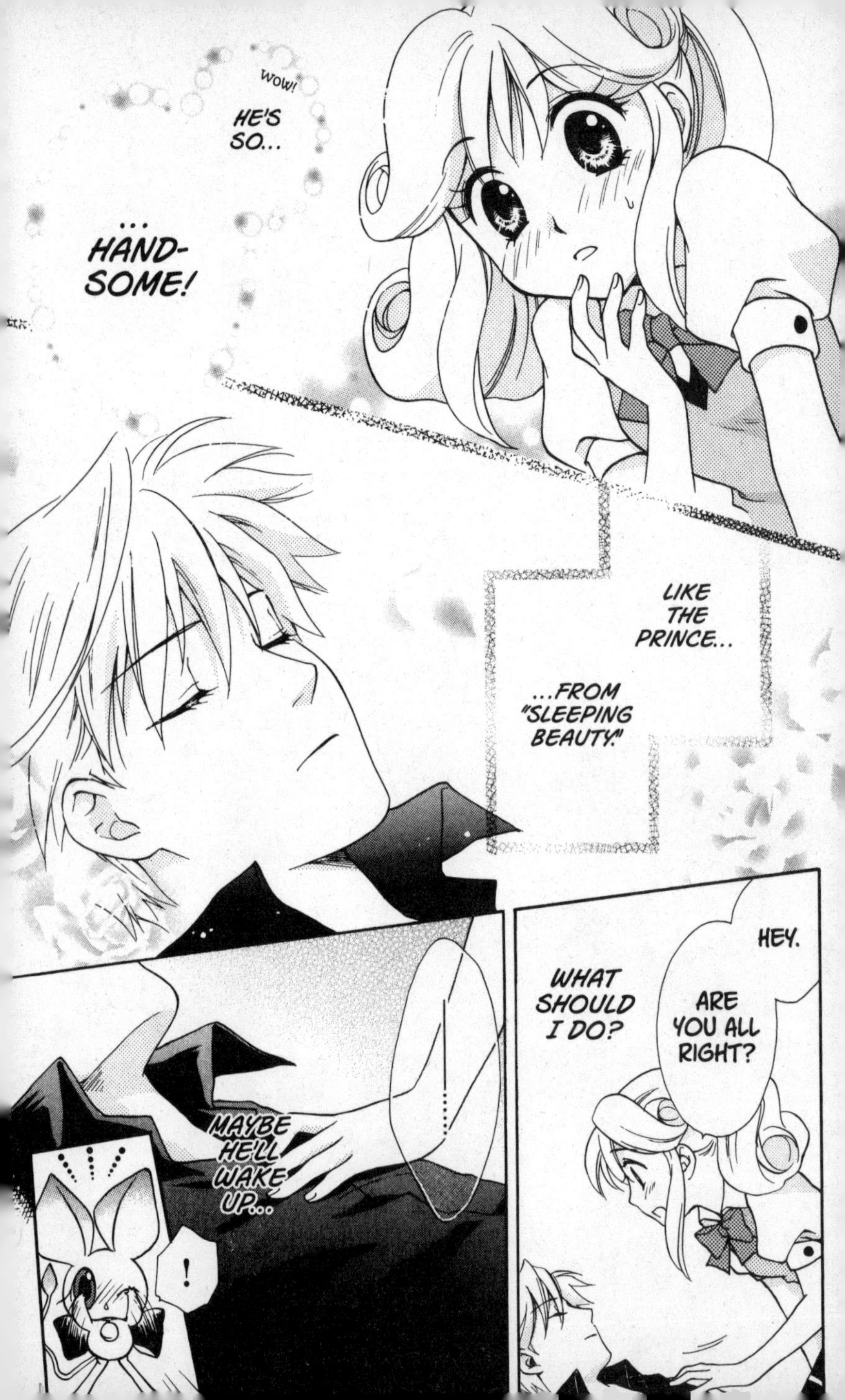
WOW!
HE'S SO...
...HAND-SOME!
LIKE THE PRINCE...
...FROM "SLEEPING BEAUTY."
HEY.
ARE YOU ALL RIGHT?
WHAT SHOULD I DO?
MAYBE HE'LL WAKE UP...
!

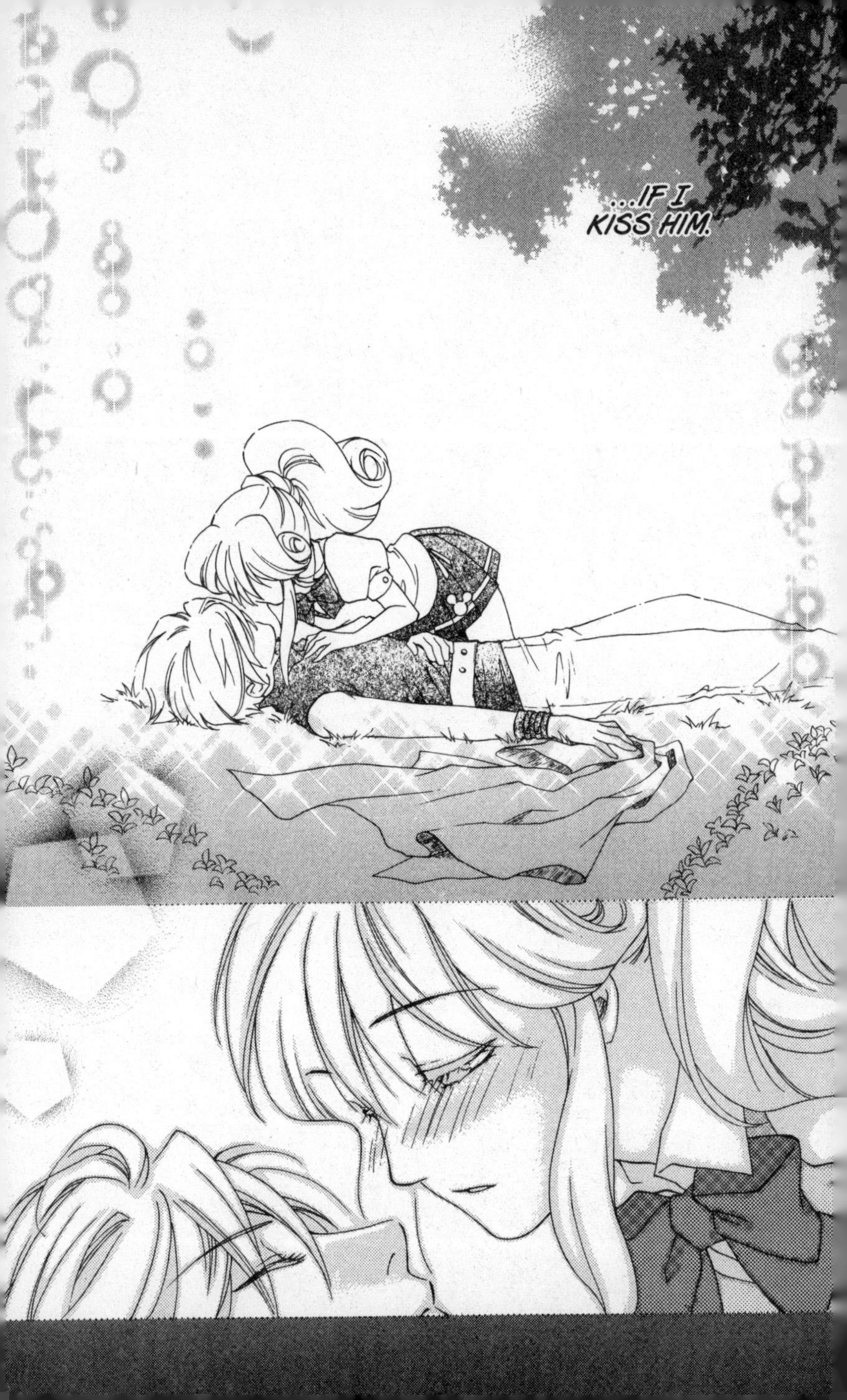
...IF I KISS HIM.

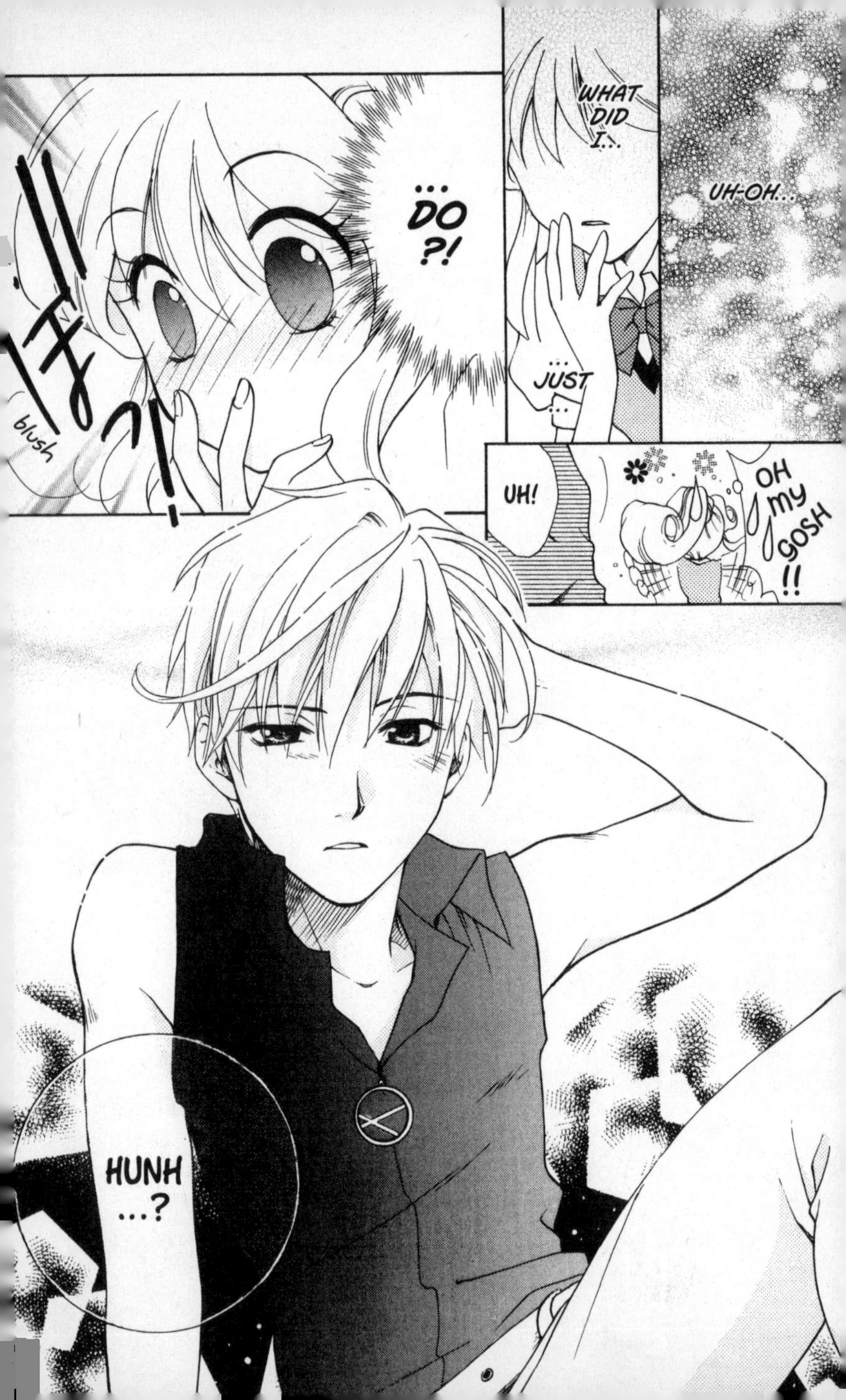
UH-OH...
WHAT DID I...
...JUST...
UH!
OH my GOSH!!
...DO?!
ぽっ!
blush
HUNH...?

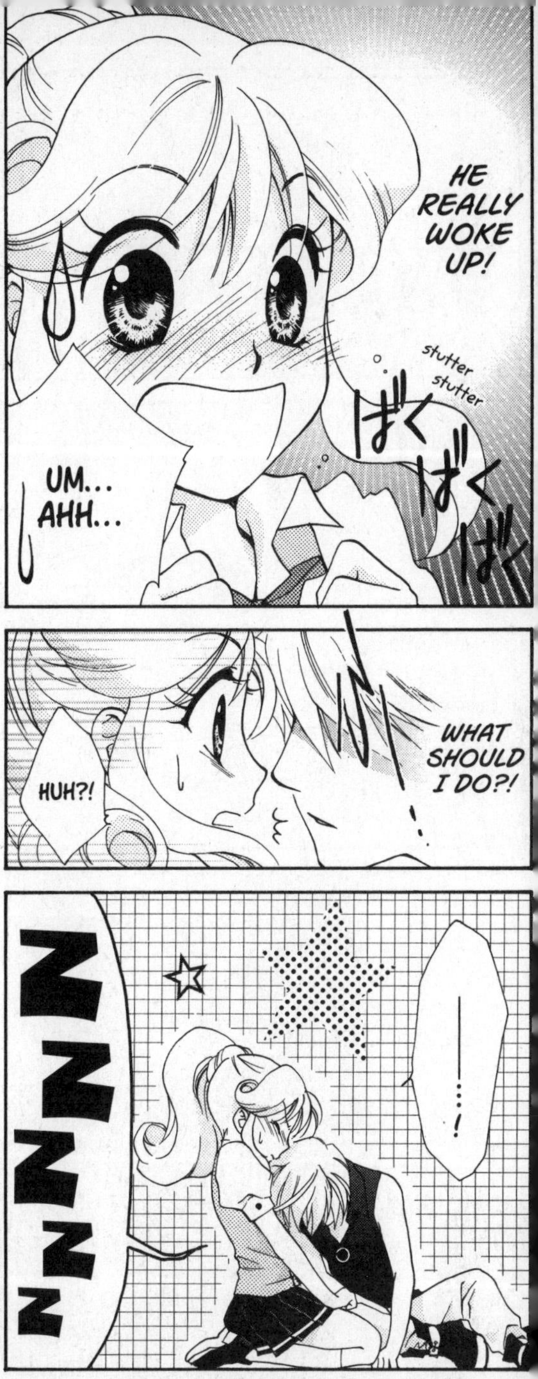
HE REALLY WOKE UP!
stutter stutter
ばくばくばく
UM... AHH...
WHAT SHOULD I DO?!
HUH?!
...!
ZZZZ

Aurora

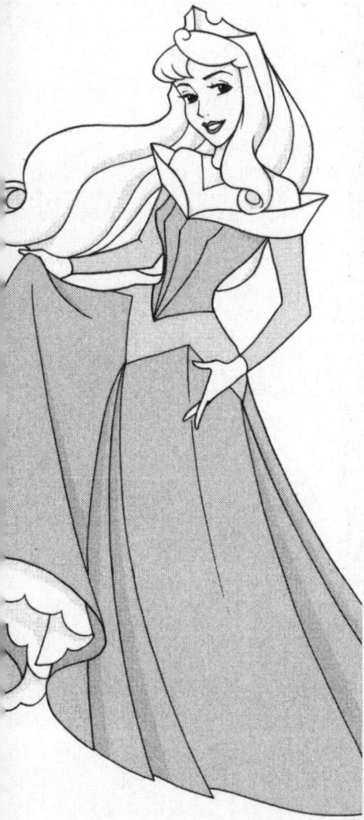

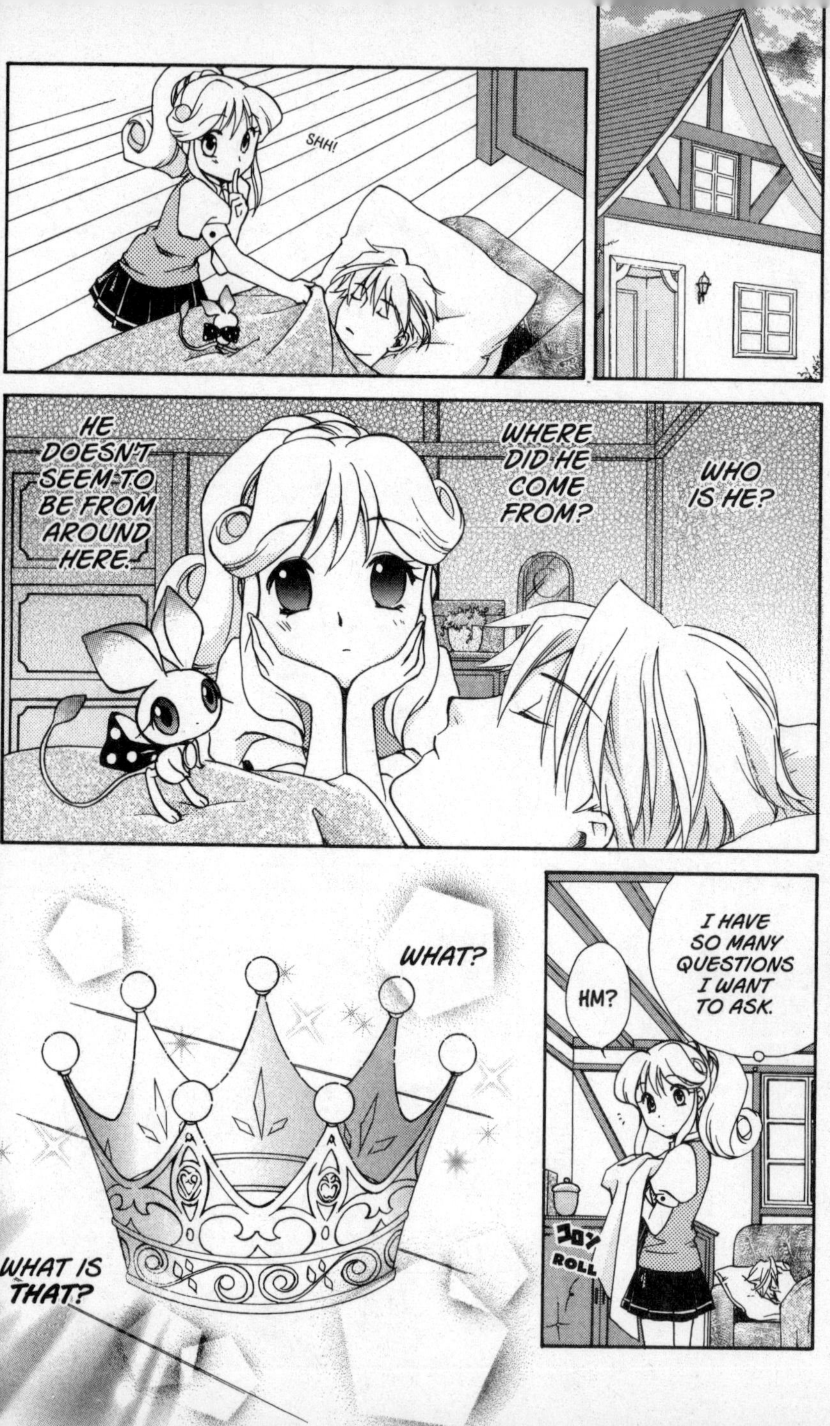
SHH!
WHO IS HE?
WHERE DID HE COME FROM?
HE DOESN'T SEEM TO BE FROM AROUND HERE.
I HAVE SO MANY QUESTIONS I WANT TO ASK.
HM?
コロッ
ROLL
WHAT?
WHAT IS THAT?

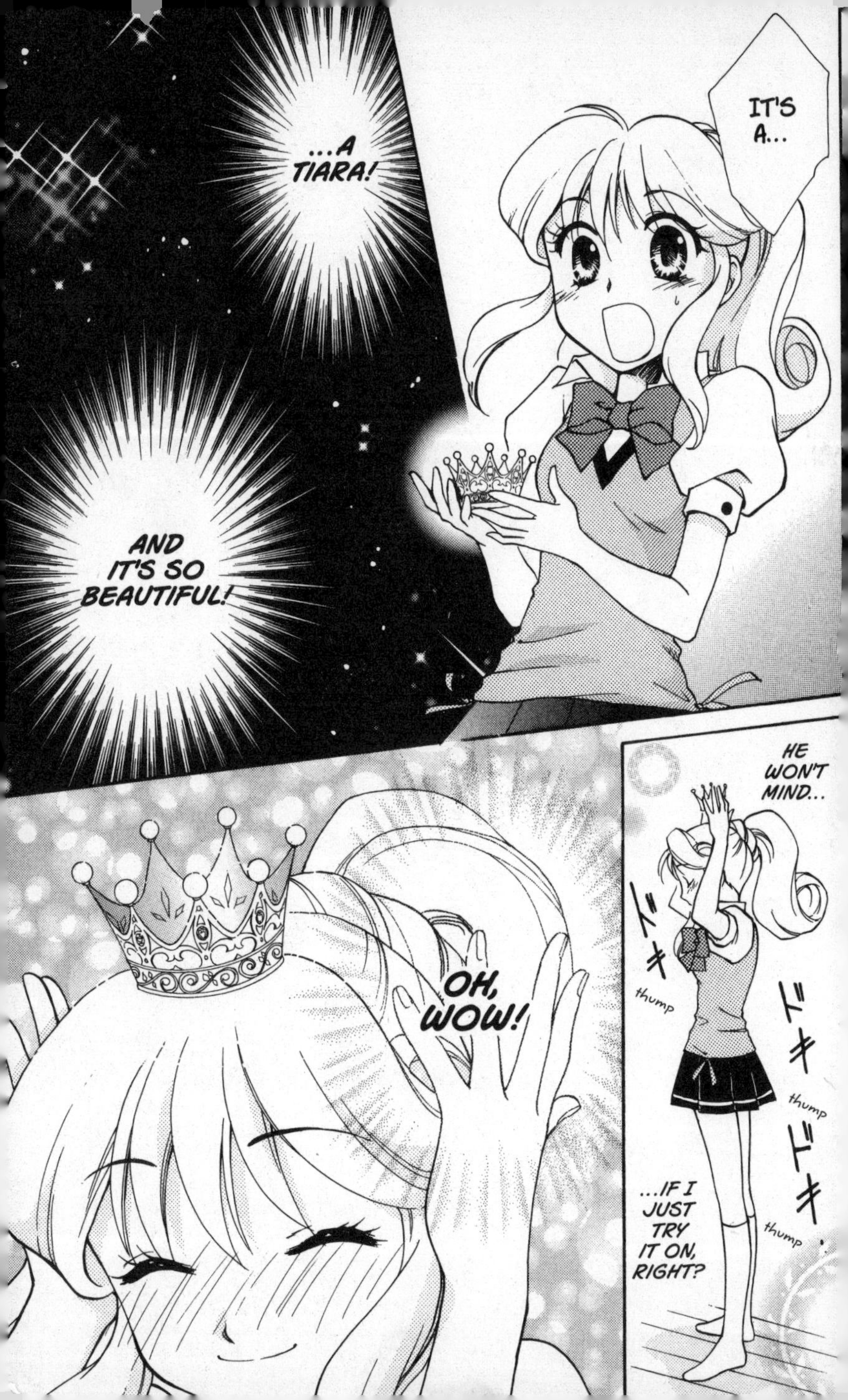
IT'S A...
...A TIARA!
AND IT'S SO BEAUTIFUL!
HE WON'T MIND...
ドキ
thump
ドキ
thump
ドキ
thump
...IF I JUST TRY IT ON, RIGHT?
OH, WOW!

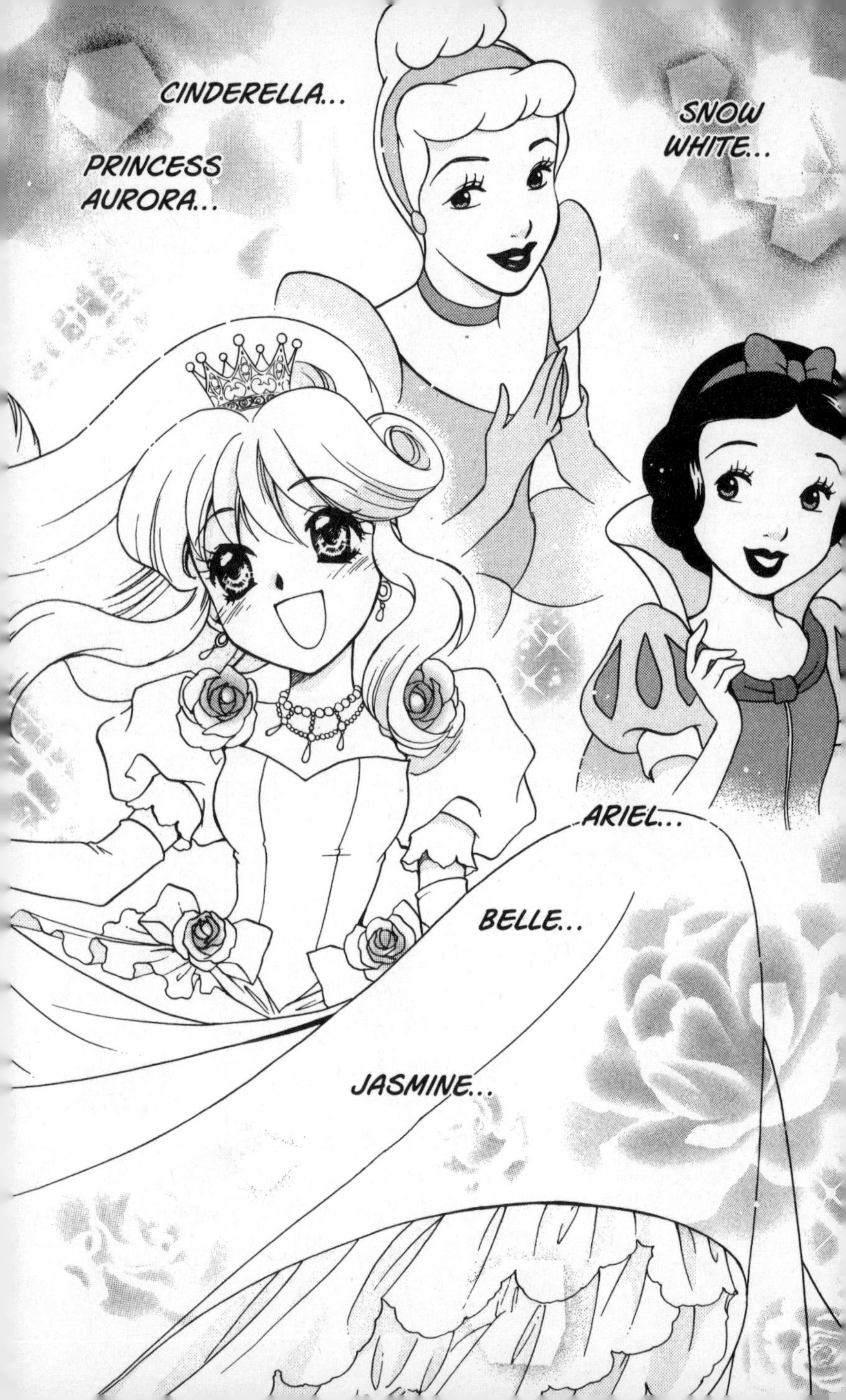
SNOW WHITE...
CINDERELLA...
PRINCESS AURORA...
ARIEL...
BELLE...
JASMINE...

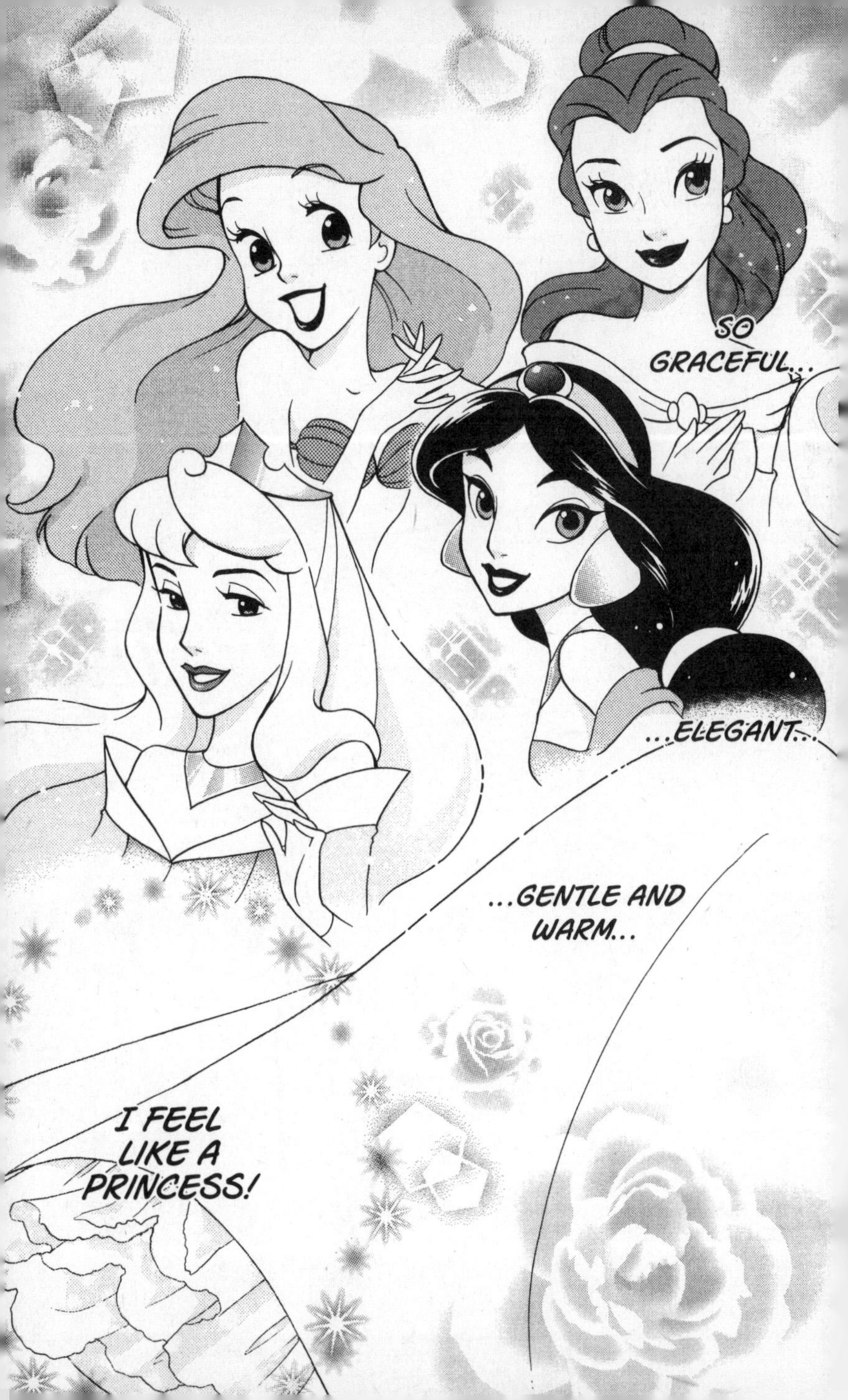
SO GRACEFUL...
...ELEGANT...
...GENTLE AND WARM...
I FEEL LIKE A PRINCESS!

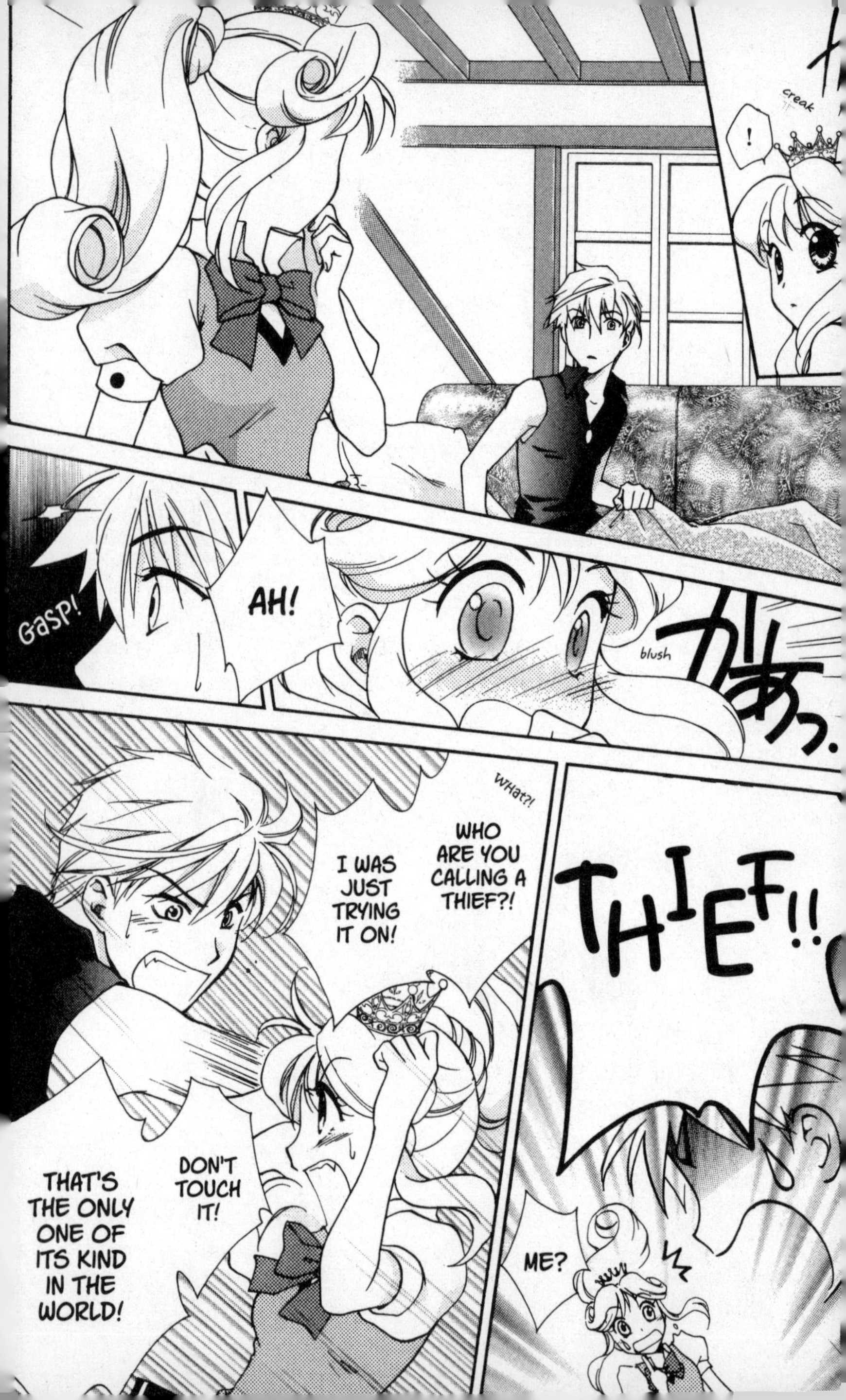
creak
!
blush
かあっ
AH!
GASP!
THIEF!!
ME?
WHAT?!
WHO ARE YOU CALLING A THIEF?!
I WAS JUST TRYING IT ON!
DON'T TOUCH IT!
THAT'S THE ONLY ONE OF ITS KIND IN THE WORLD!

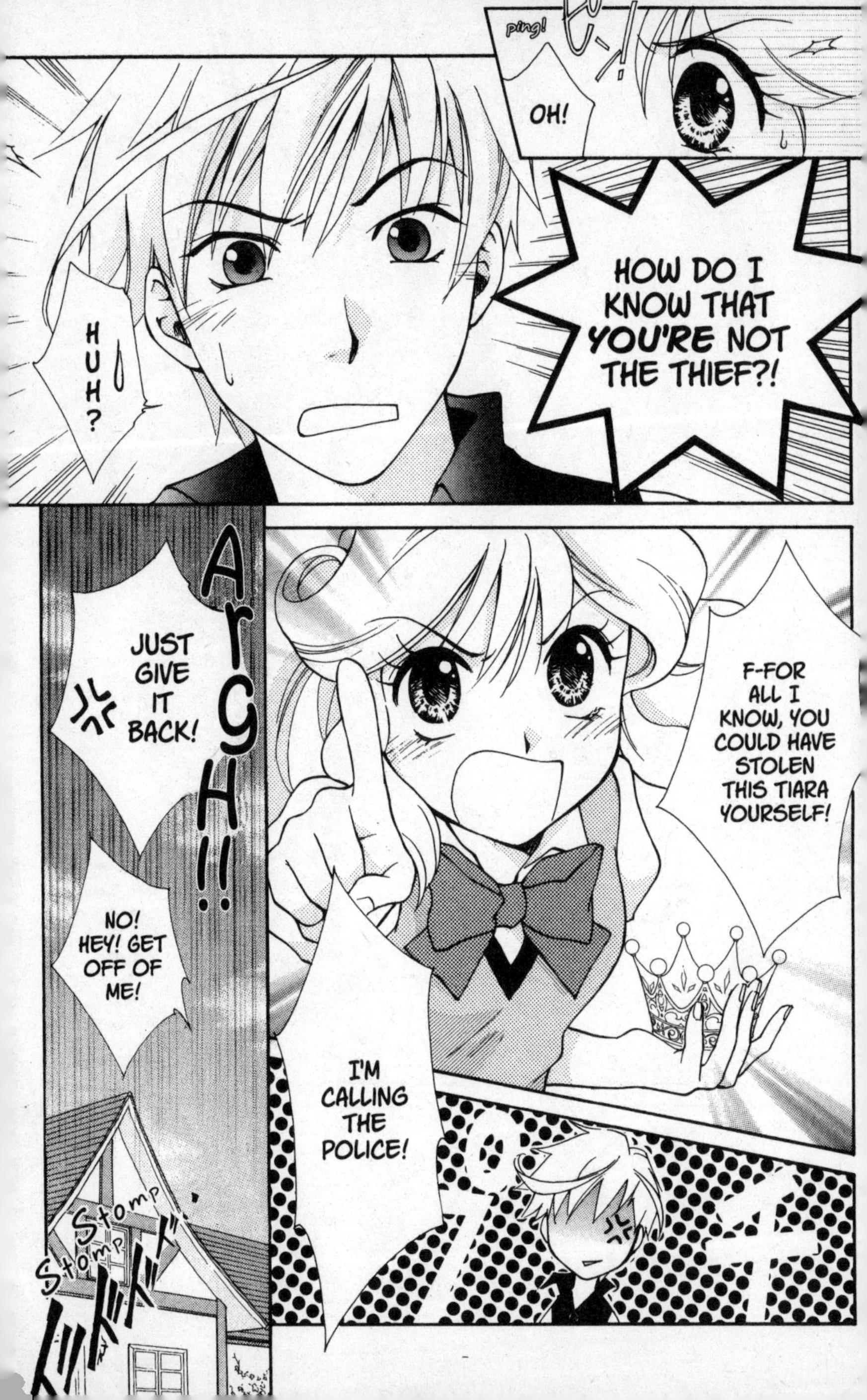
ping!
OH!
HOW DO I KNOW THAT YOU'RE NOT THE THIEF?!
HUH?
F-FOR ALL I KNOW, YOU COULD HAVE STOLEN THIS TIARA YOURSELF!
I'M CALLING THE POLICE!
Argh!!
JUST GIVE IT BACK!
NO! HEY! GET OFF OF ME!
Stomp
Stomp

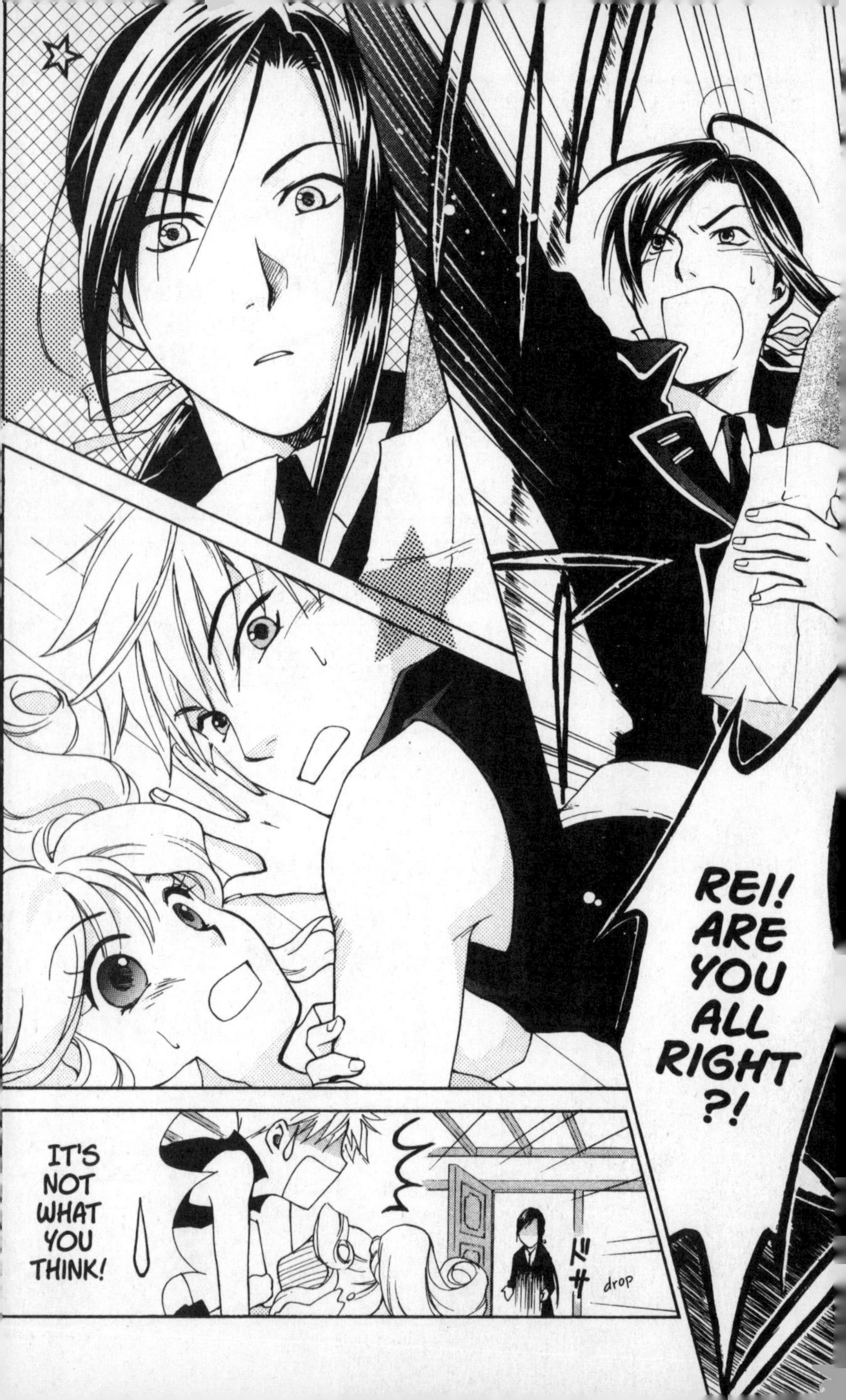
REI! ARE YOU ALL RIGHT?!
ドサ
drop
IT'S NOT WHAT YOU THINK!

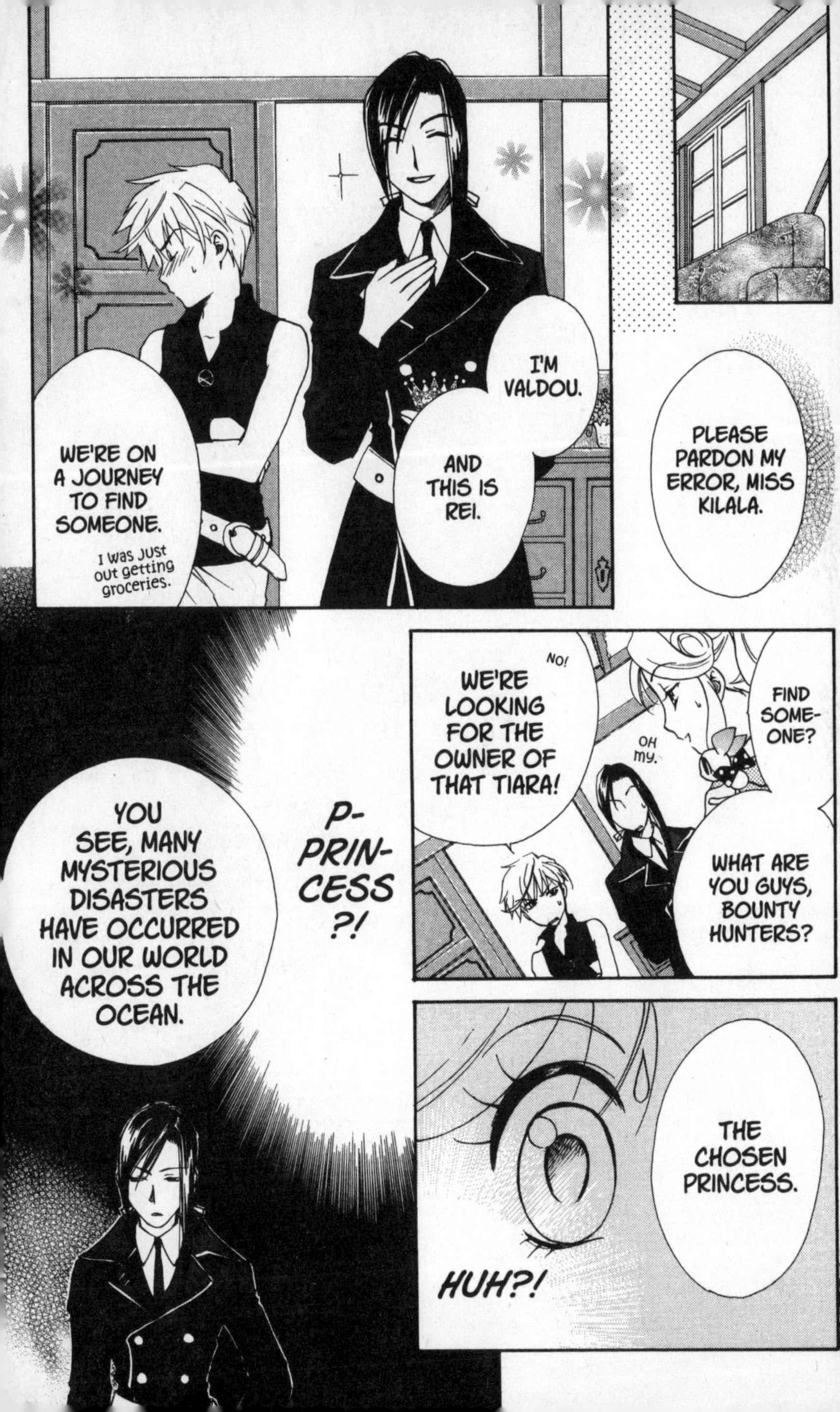
PLEASE PARDON MY ERROR, MISS KILALA.
I'M VALDOU.
AND THIS IS REI.
WE'RE ON A JOURNEY TO FIND SOMEONE.
I was just out getting groceries.
FIND SOME-ONE?
WHAT ARE YOU GUYS, BOUNTY HUNTERS?
OH my.
NO!
WE'RE LOOKING FOR THE OWNER OF THAT TIARA!
THE CHOSEN PRINCESS.
HUH?!
P-PRIN-CESS?!
YOU SEE, MANY MYSTERIOUS DISASTERS HAVE OCCURRED IN OUR WORLD ACROSS THE OCEAN.

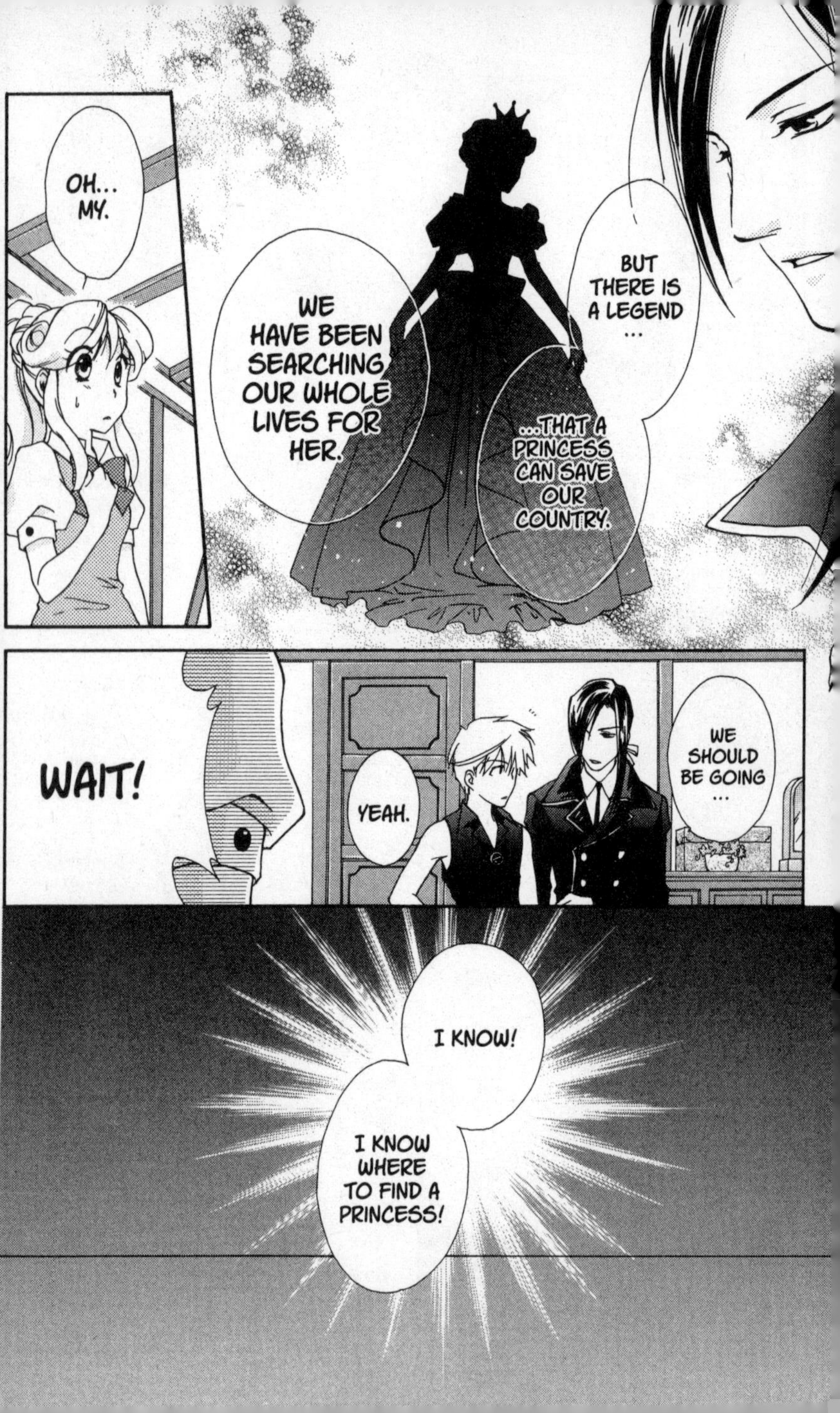
BUT THERE IS A LEGEND...
...THAT A PRINCESS CAN SAVE OUR COUNTRY.
WE HAVE BEEN SEARCHING OUR WHOLE LIVES FOR HER.
OH... MY.
WE SHOULD BE GOING...
YEAH.
WAIT!
I KNOW!
I KNOW WHERE TO FIND A PRINCESS!

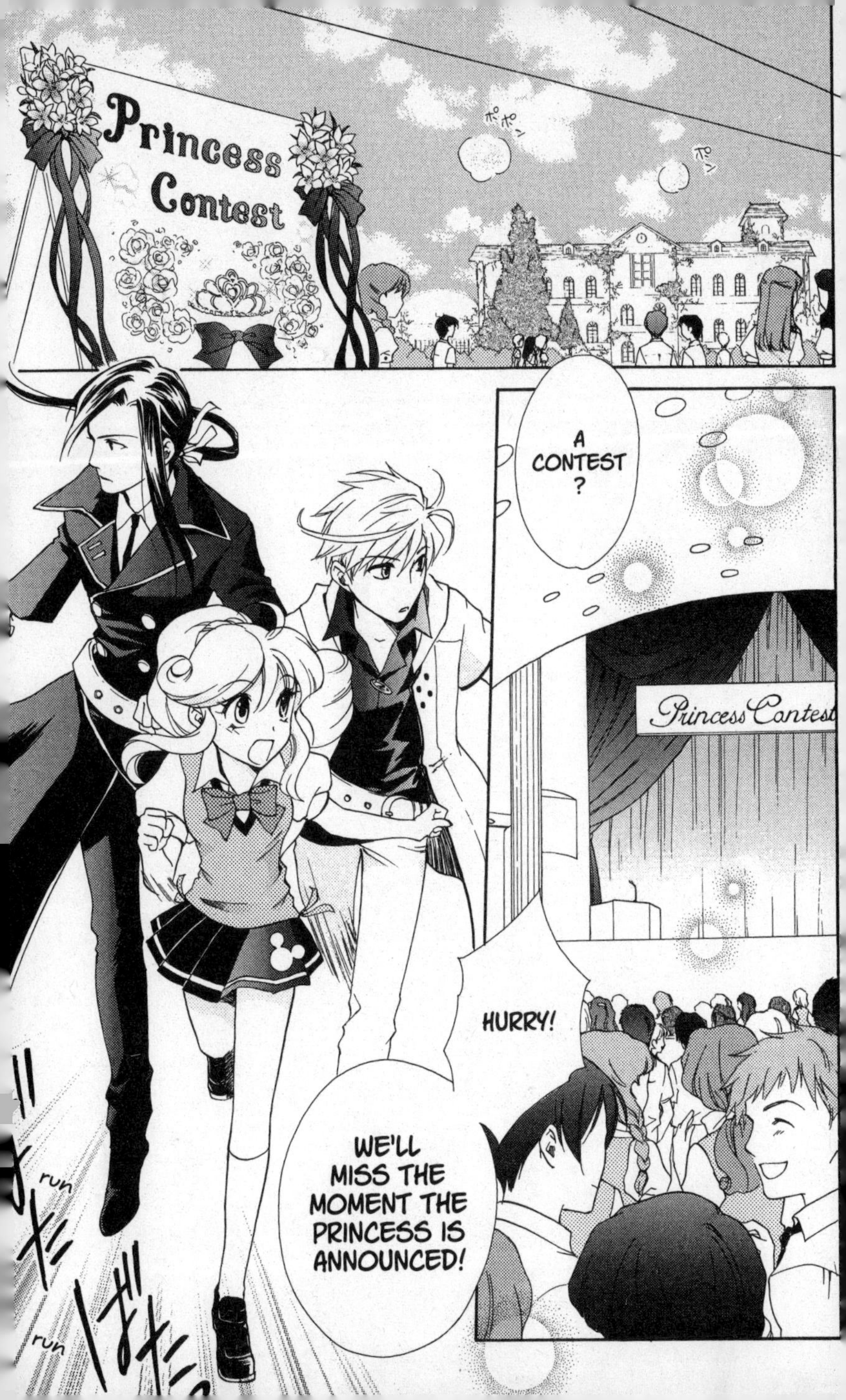

Princess Contest
ポポン
ポン
A CONTEST ?
Princess Contest
HURRY!
WE'LL MISS THE MOMENT THE PRINCESS IS ANNOUNCED!
run
run

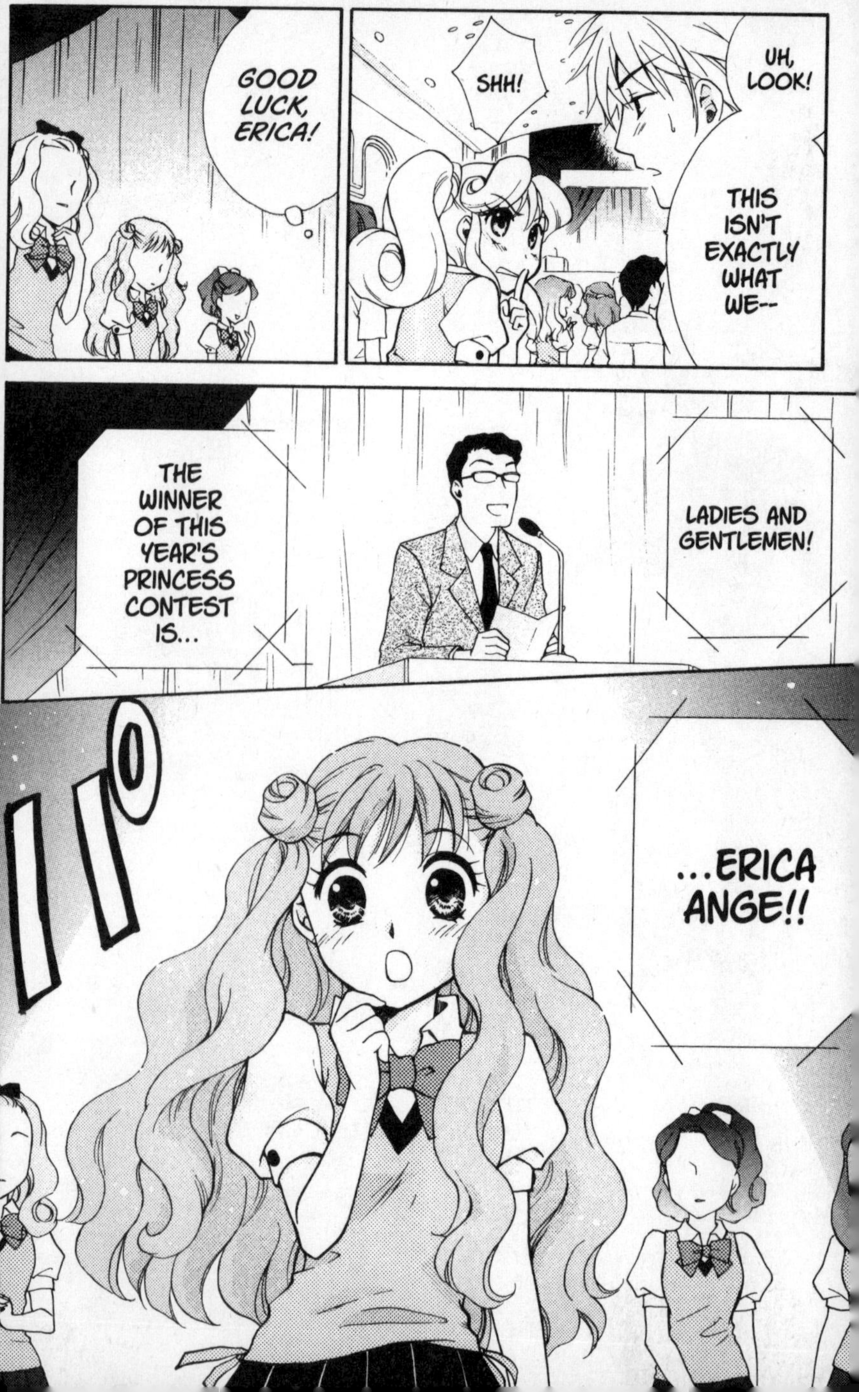
UH, LOOK!
THIS ISN'T EXACTLY WHAT WE--
SHH!
GOOD LUCK, ERICA!
LADIES AND GENTLEMEN!
THE WINNER OF THIS YEAR'S PRINCESS CONTEST IS...
...ERICA ANGE!!

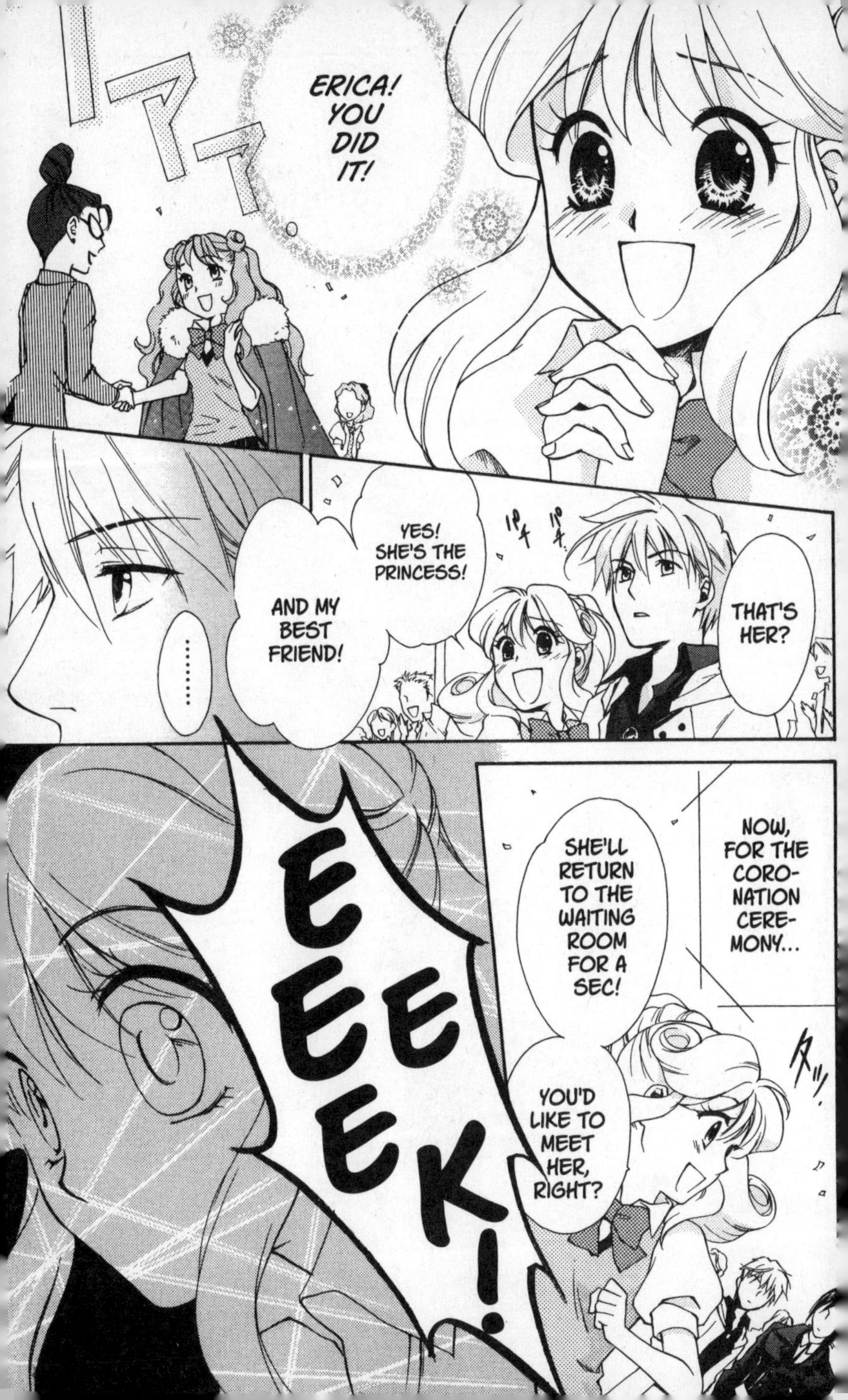
ERICA! YOU DID IT!
THAT'S HER?
YES! SHE'S THE PRINCESS!
AND MY BEST FRIEND!
......
NOW, FOR THE CORO-NATION CERE-MONY...
SHE'LL RETURN TO THE WAITING ROOM FOR A SEC!
YOU'D LIKE TO MEET HER, RIGHT?
EEEEK!

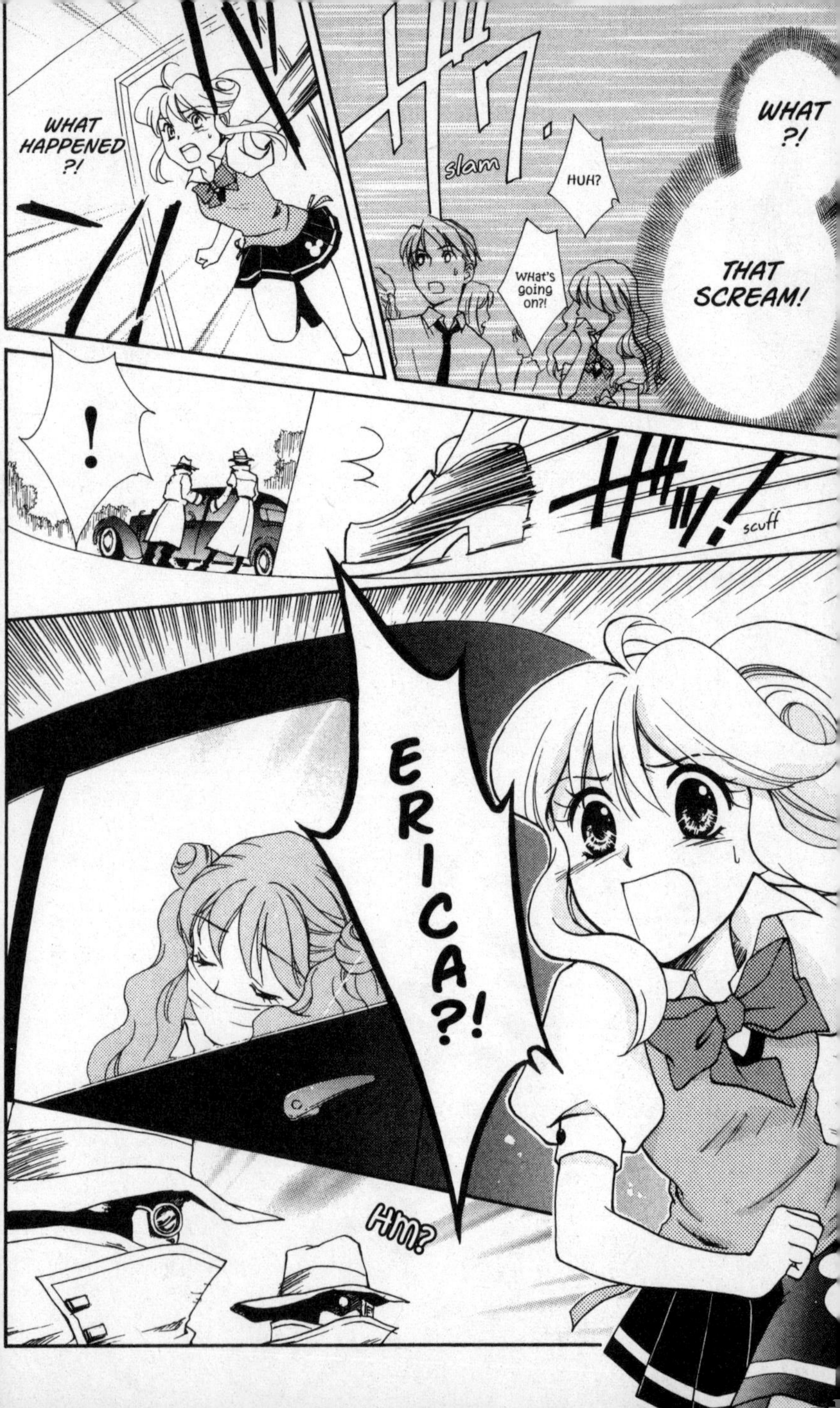
WHAT ?!
THAT SCREAM!
HUH?
What's going on?!
slam
WHAT HAPPENED ?!
scuff
!
ERICA?!
HM?

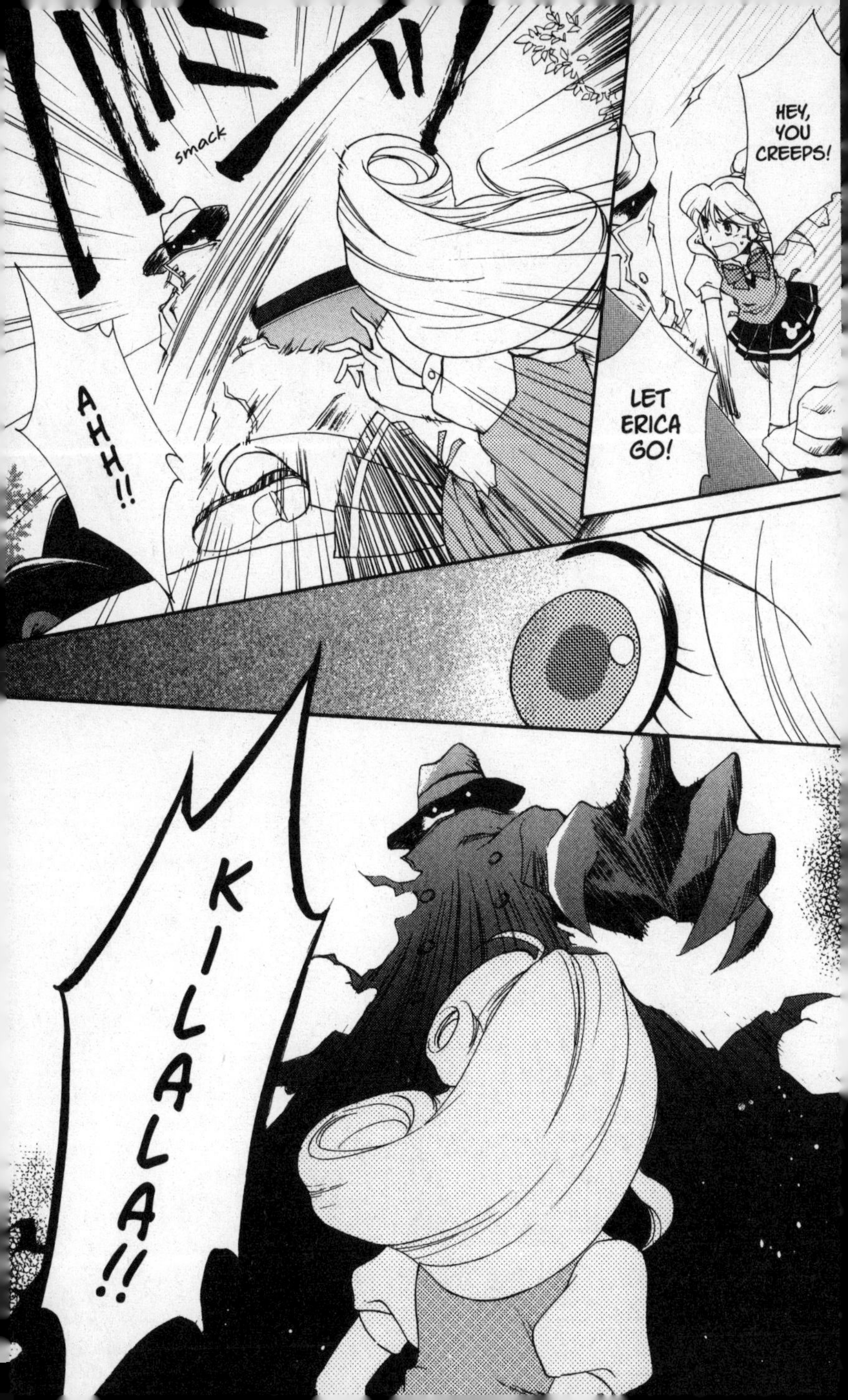
HEY, YOU CREEPS!
LET ERICA GO!
smack
AHH!!
KILALA!!

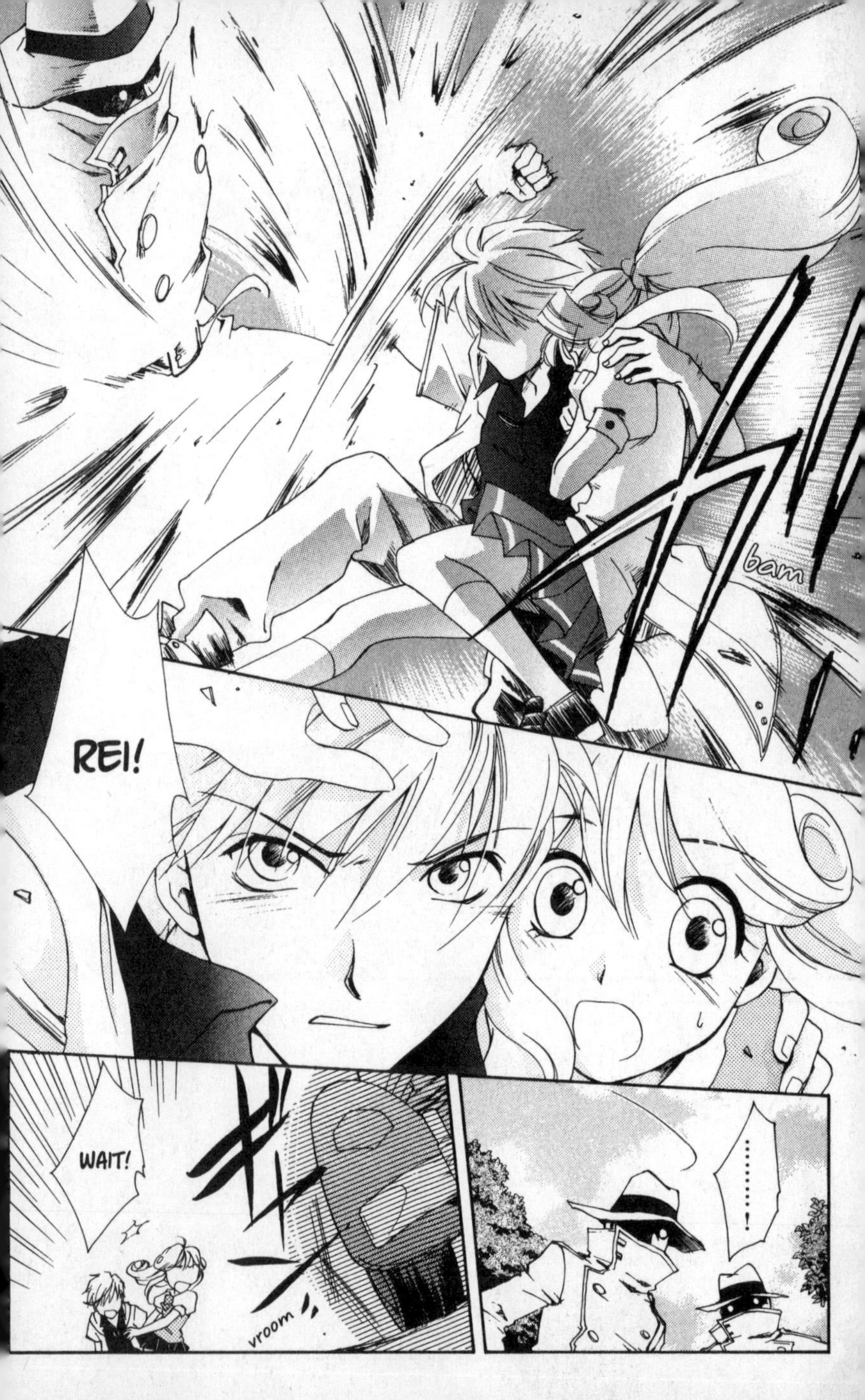
bam
REI!
......!
WAIT!
vroom

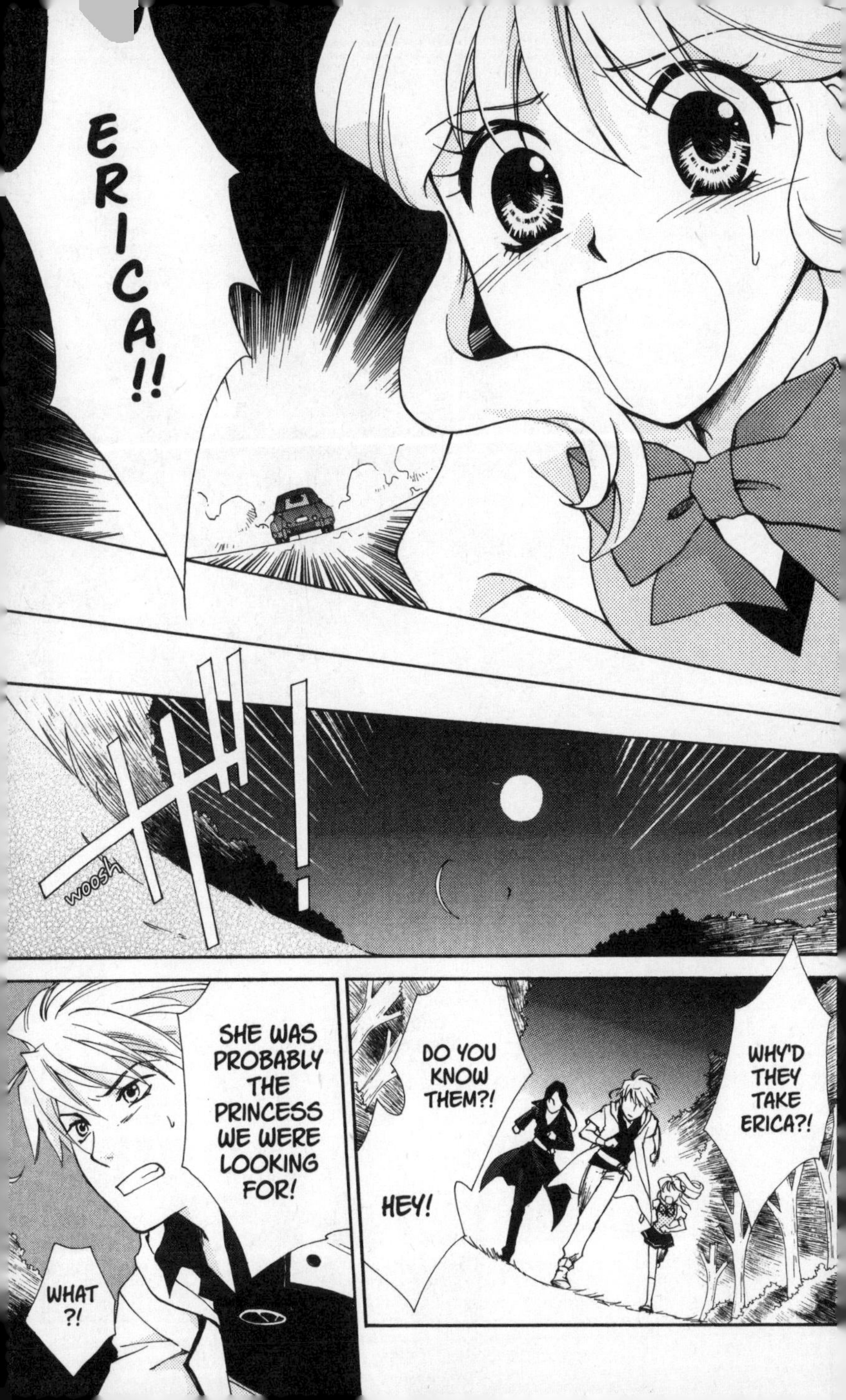
ERICA!!
woosh
WHY'D THEY TAKE ERICA?!
DO YOU KNOW THEM?!
HEY!
SHE WAS PROBABLY THE PRINCESS WE WERE LOOKING FOR!
WHAT?!

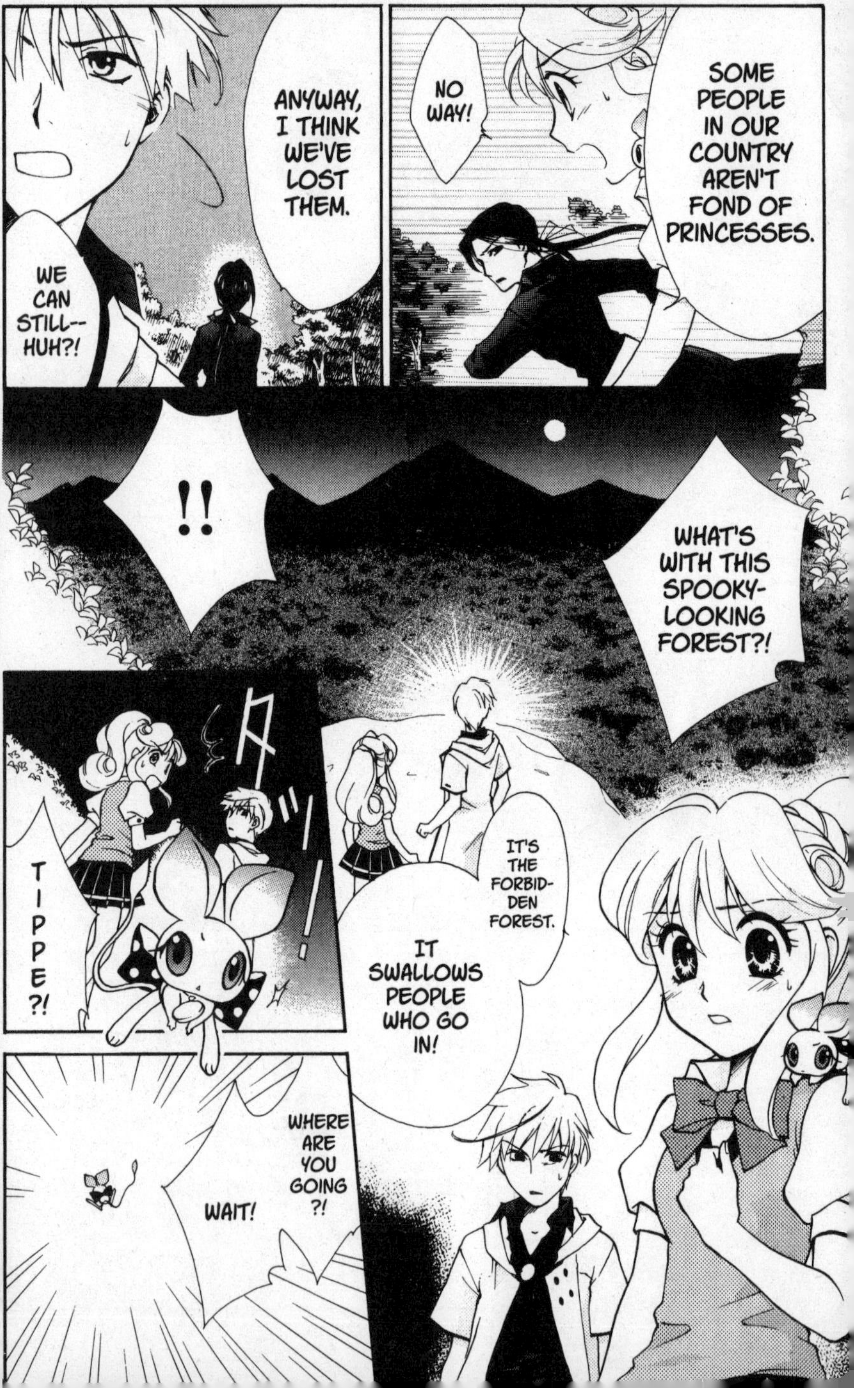
SOME PEOPLE IN OUR COUNTRY AREN'T FOND OF PRINCESSES.
NO WAY!
ANYWAY, I THINK WE'VE LOST THEM.
WE CAN STILL--HUH?!
!!
WHAT'S WITH THIS SPOOKY-LOOKING FOREST?!
IT'S THE FORBID-DEN FOREST.
IT SWALLOWS PEOPLE WHO GO IN!
TIPPE?!
WHERE ARE YOU GOING?!
WAIT!

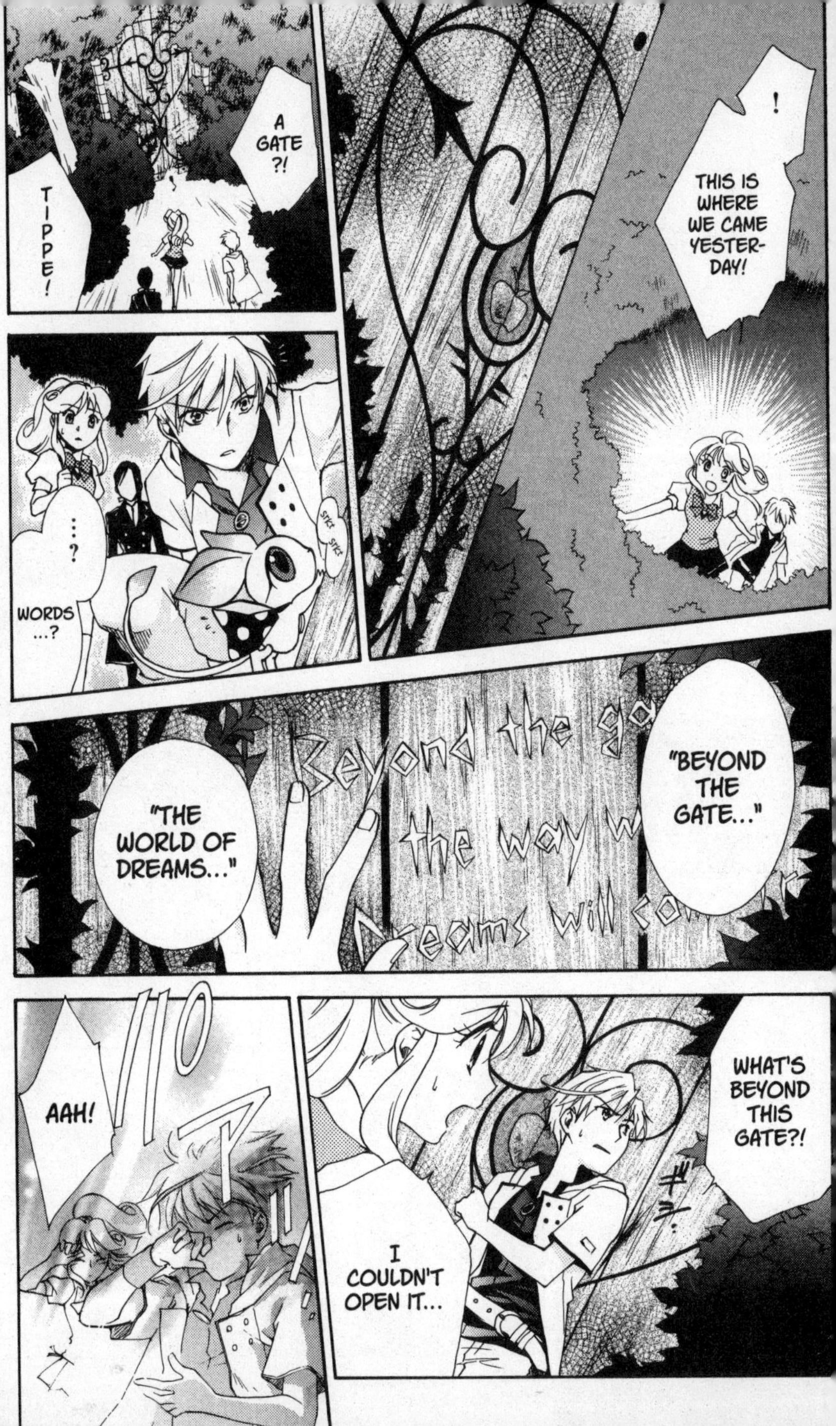
!
THIS IS WHERE WE CAME YESTER-DAY!
A GATE?!
TIPPE!
...?
WORDS...?
"BEYOND THE GATE..."
"THE WORLD OF DREAMS..."
WHAT'S BEYOND THIS GATE?!
I COULDN'T OPEN IT...
AAH!

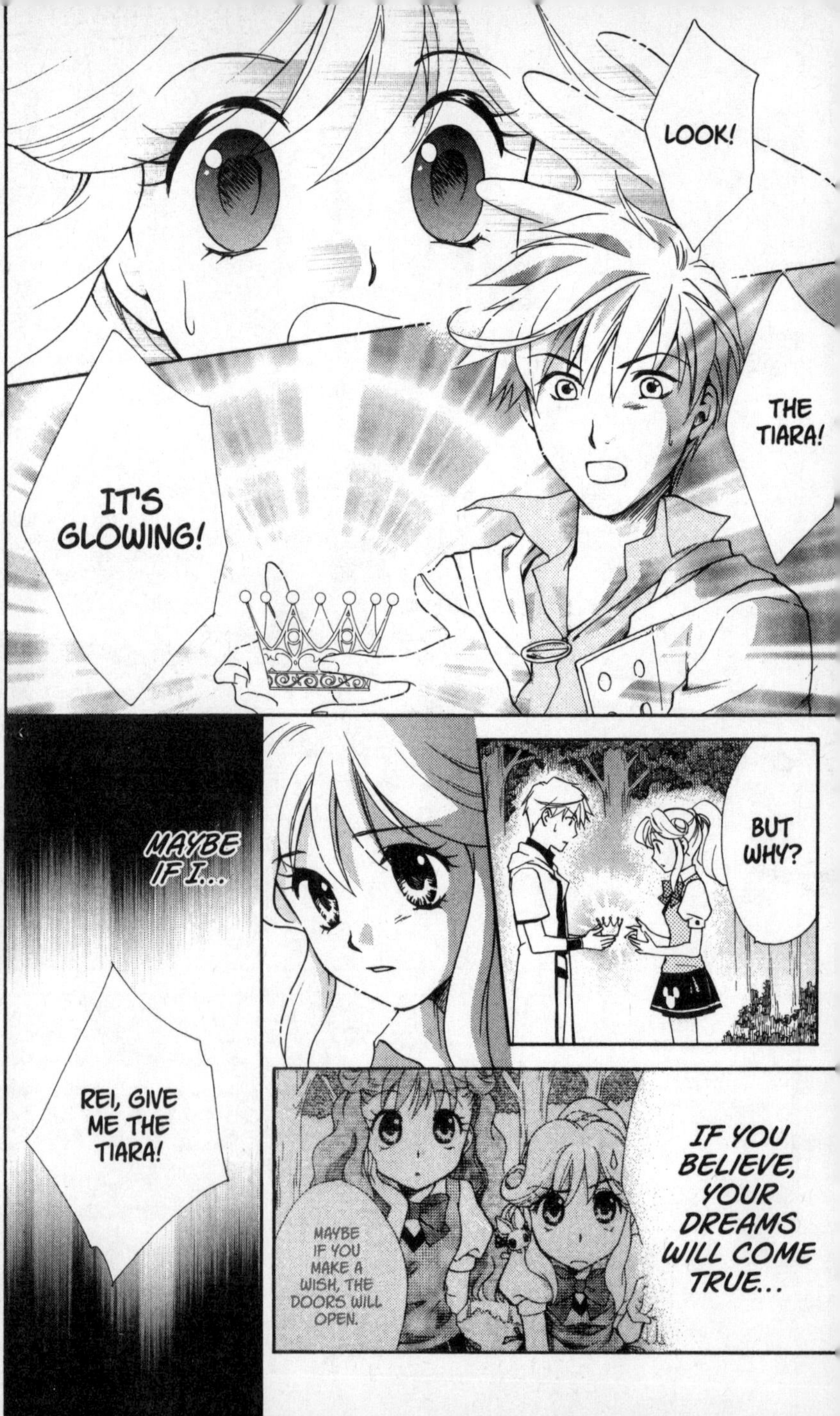
LOOK!
THE TIARA!
IT'S GLOWING!
BUT WHY?
IF YOU BELIEVE, YOUR DREAMS WILL COME TRUE...
MAYBE IF YOU MAKE A WISH, THE DOORS WILL OPEN.
MAYBE IF I...
REI, GIVE ME THE TIARA!

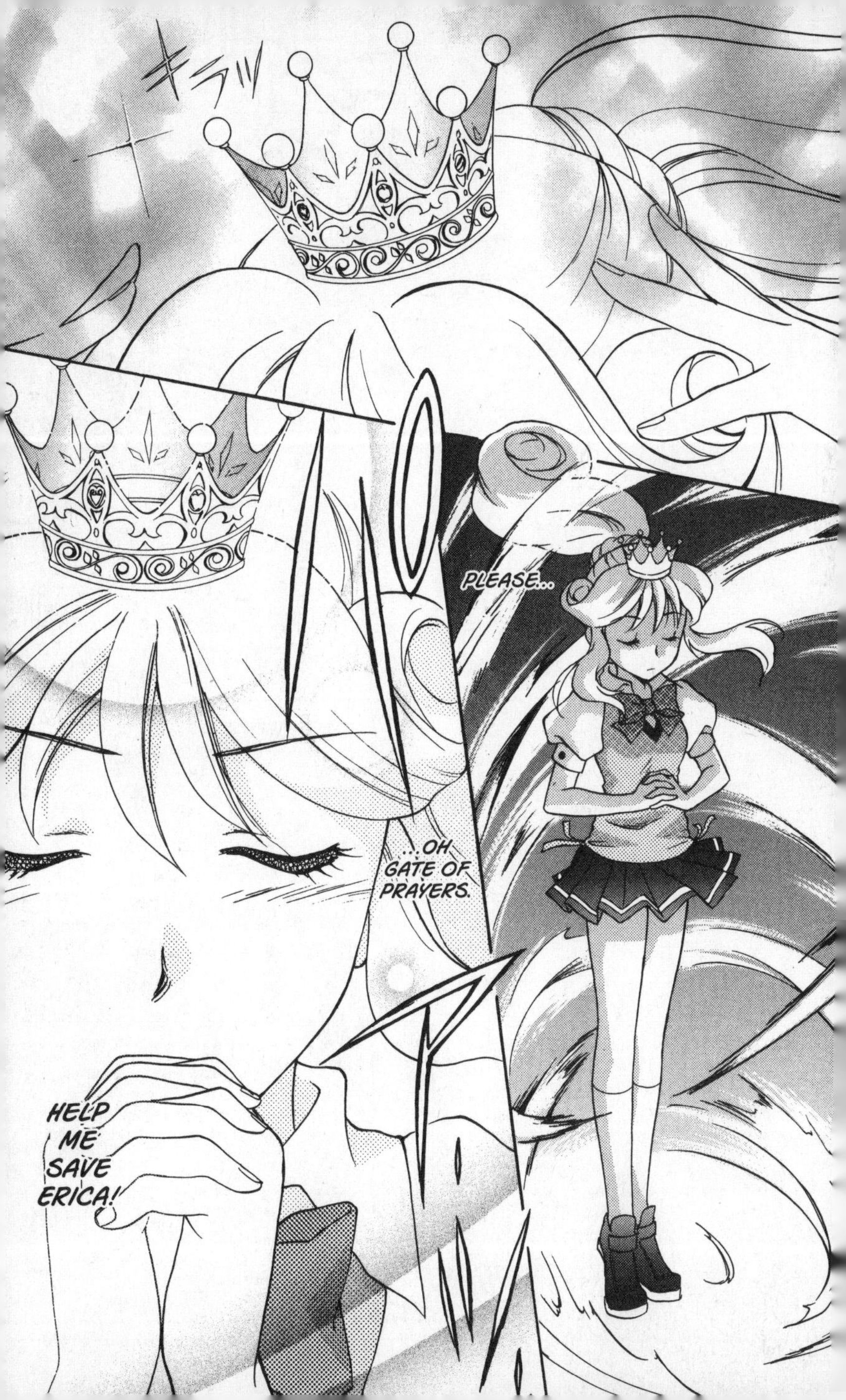
キラッ
PLEASE...
...OH GATE OF PRAYERS.
HELP ME SAVE ERICA!

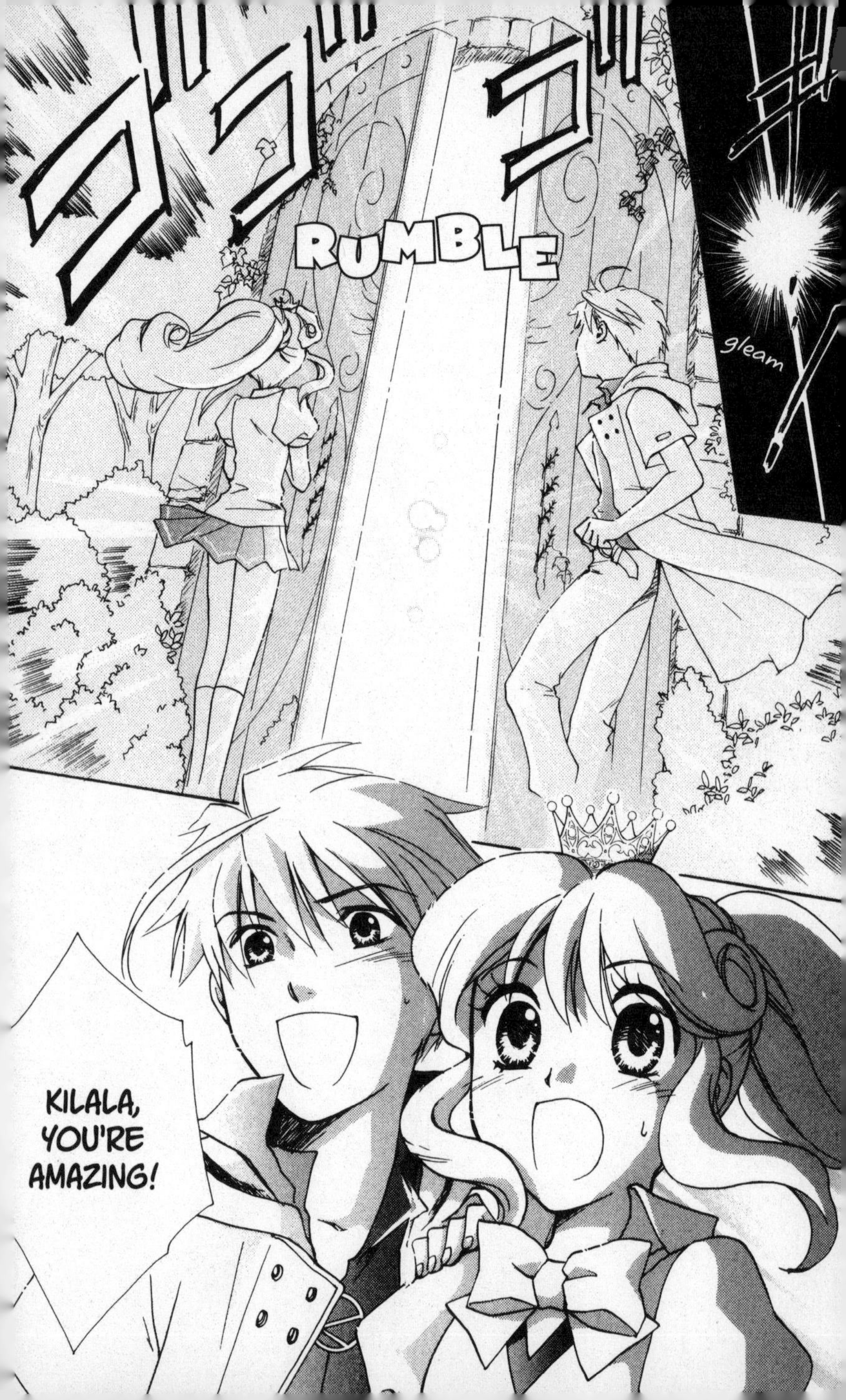
gleam
RUMBLE
KILALA, YOU'RE AMAZING!

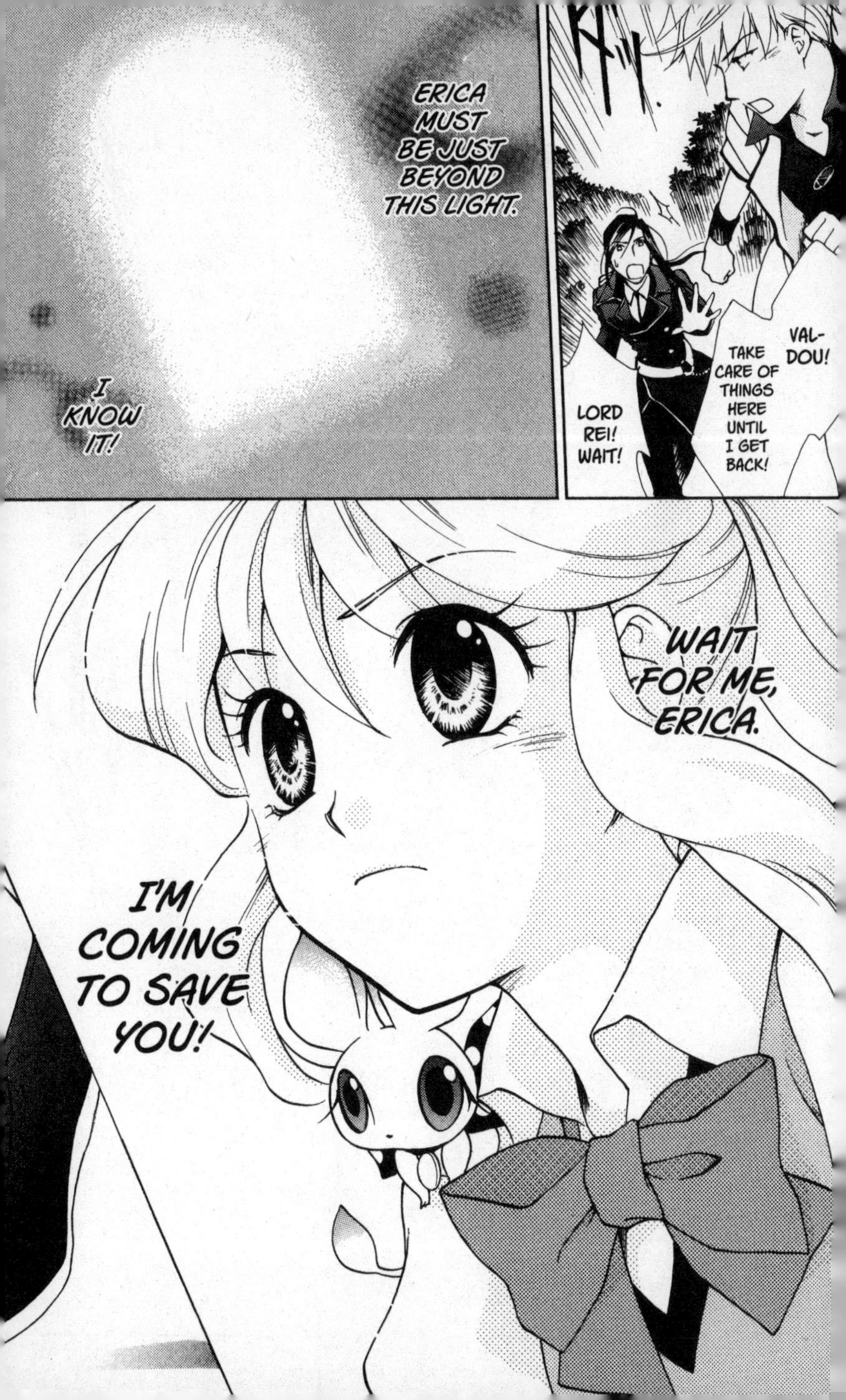
VAL-DOU!
TAKE CARE OF THINGS HERE UNTIL I GET BACK!
LORD REI! WAIT!
ERICA MUST BE JUST BEYOND THIS LIGHT.
I KNOW IT!
WAIT FOR ME, ERICA.
I'M COMING TO SAVE YOU!

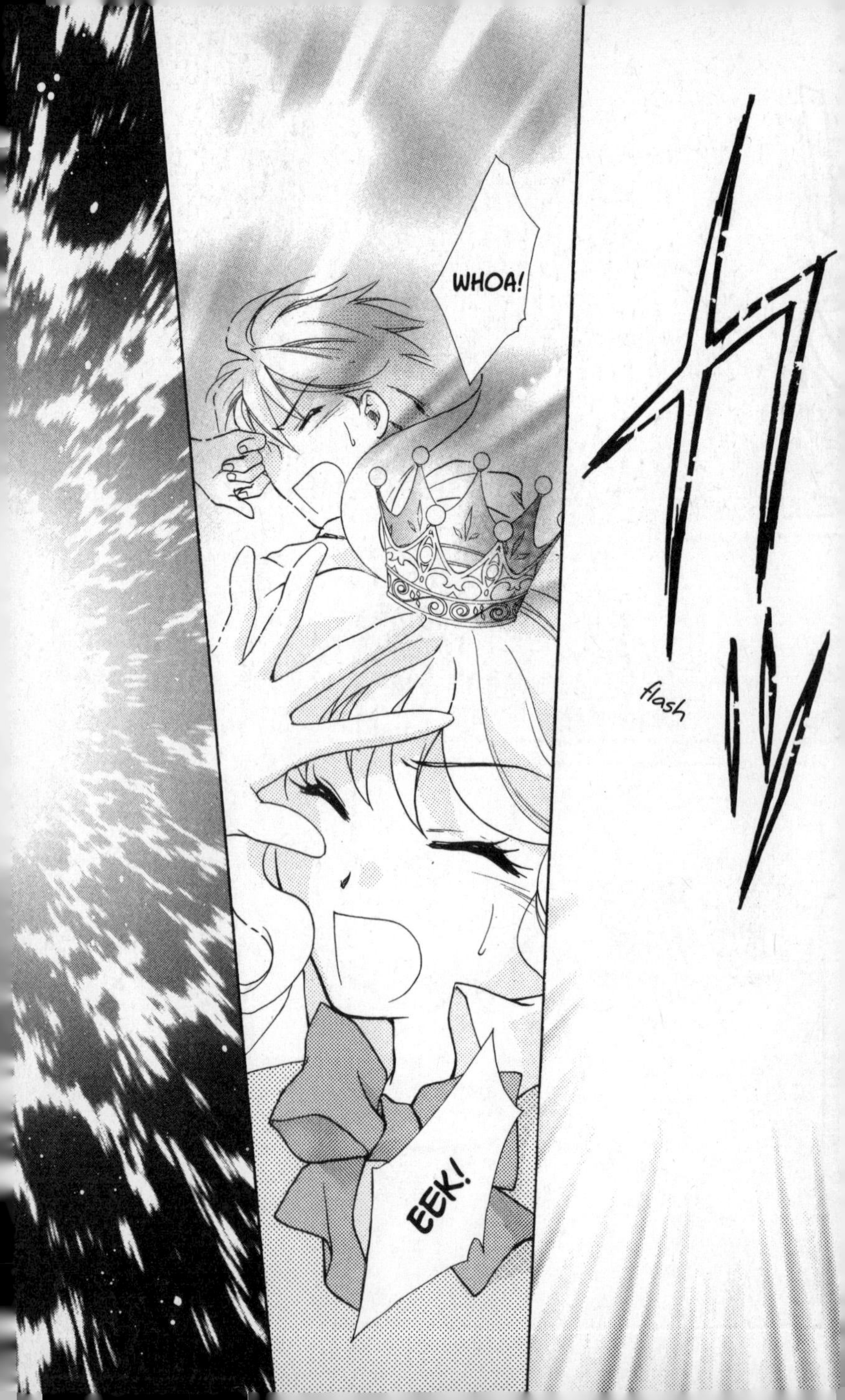
flash
WHOA!
EEK!

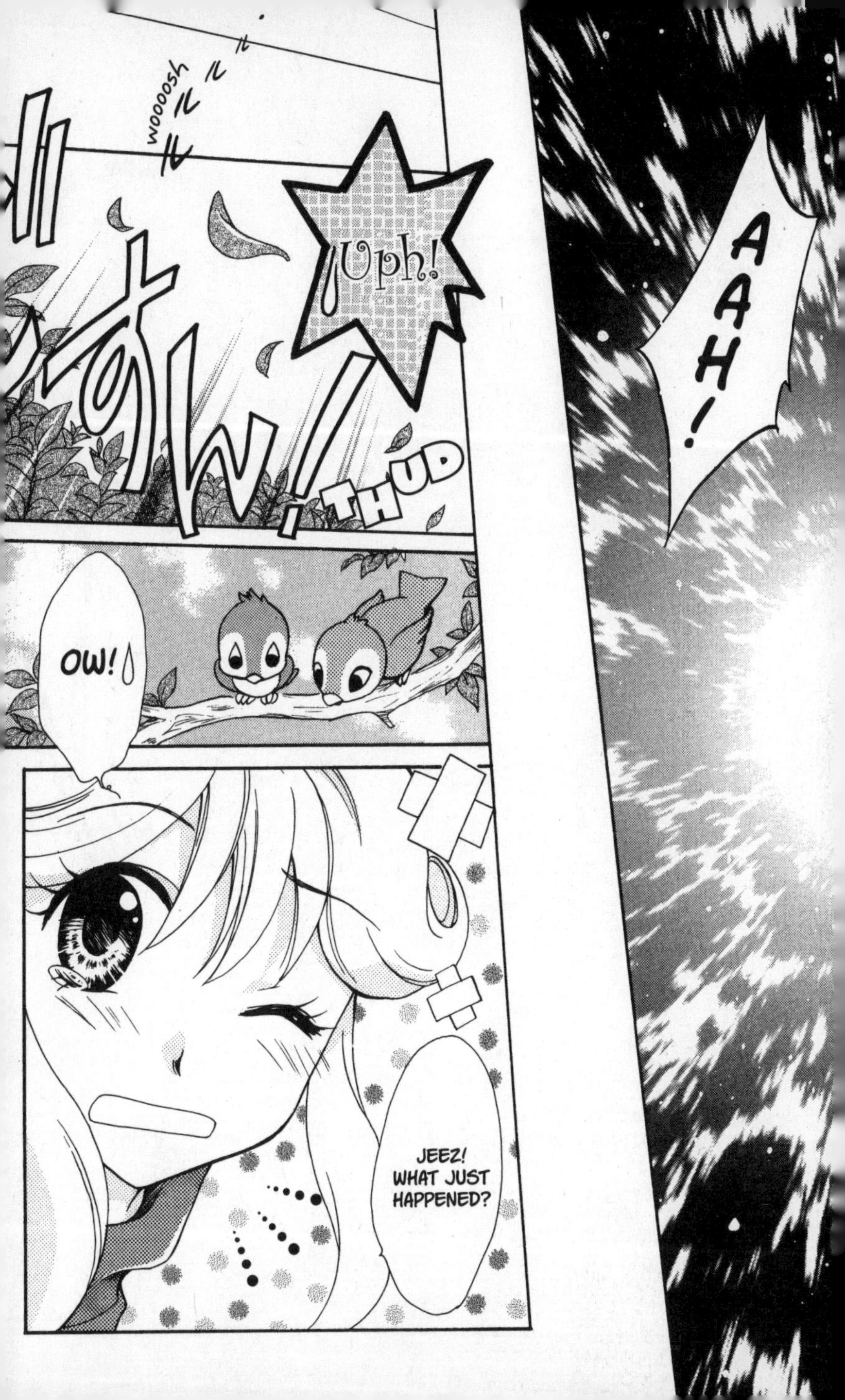
AAH!
wooooosh
Uph!
THUD
OW!
JEEZ! WHAT JUST HAPPENED?

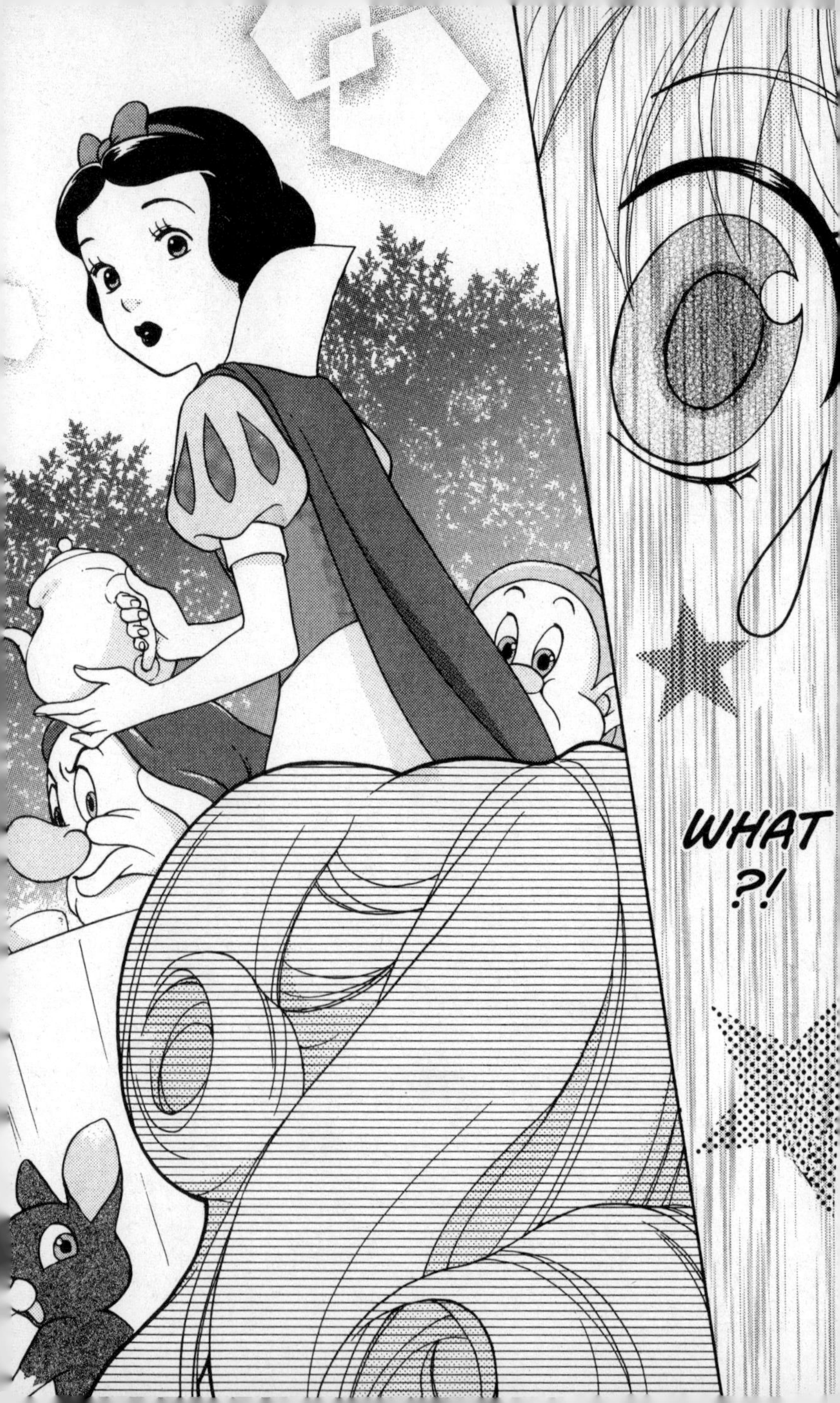
WHAT ?!

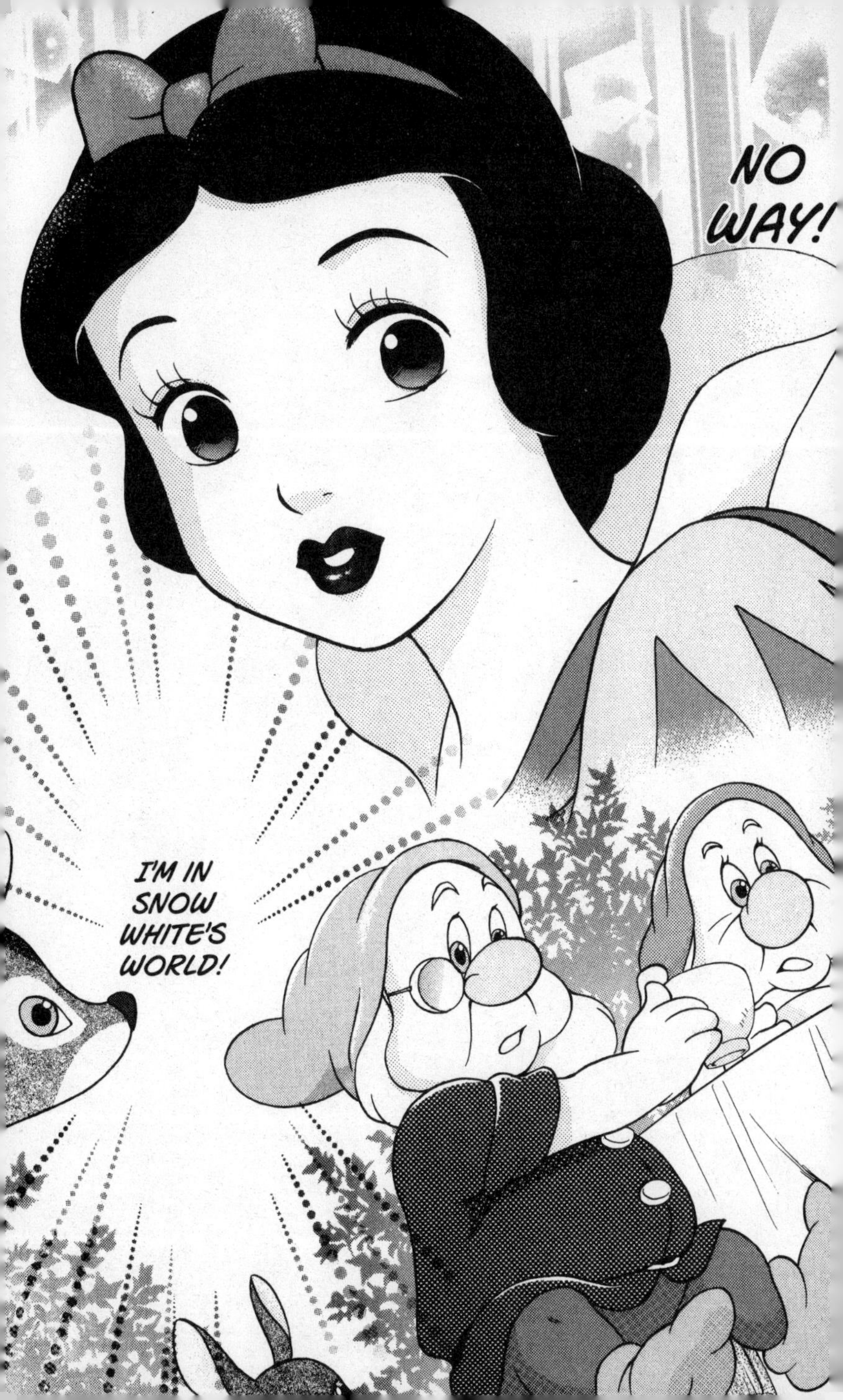
NO WAY!
I'M IN SNOW WHITE'S WORLD!

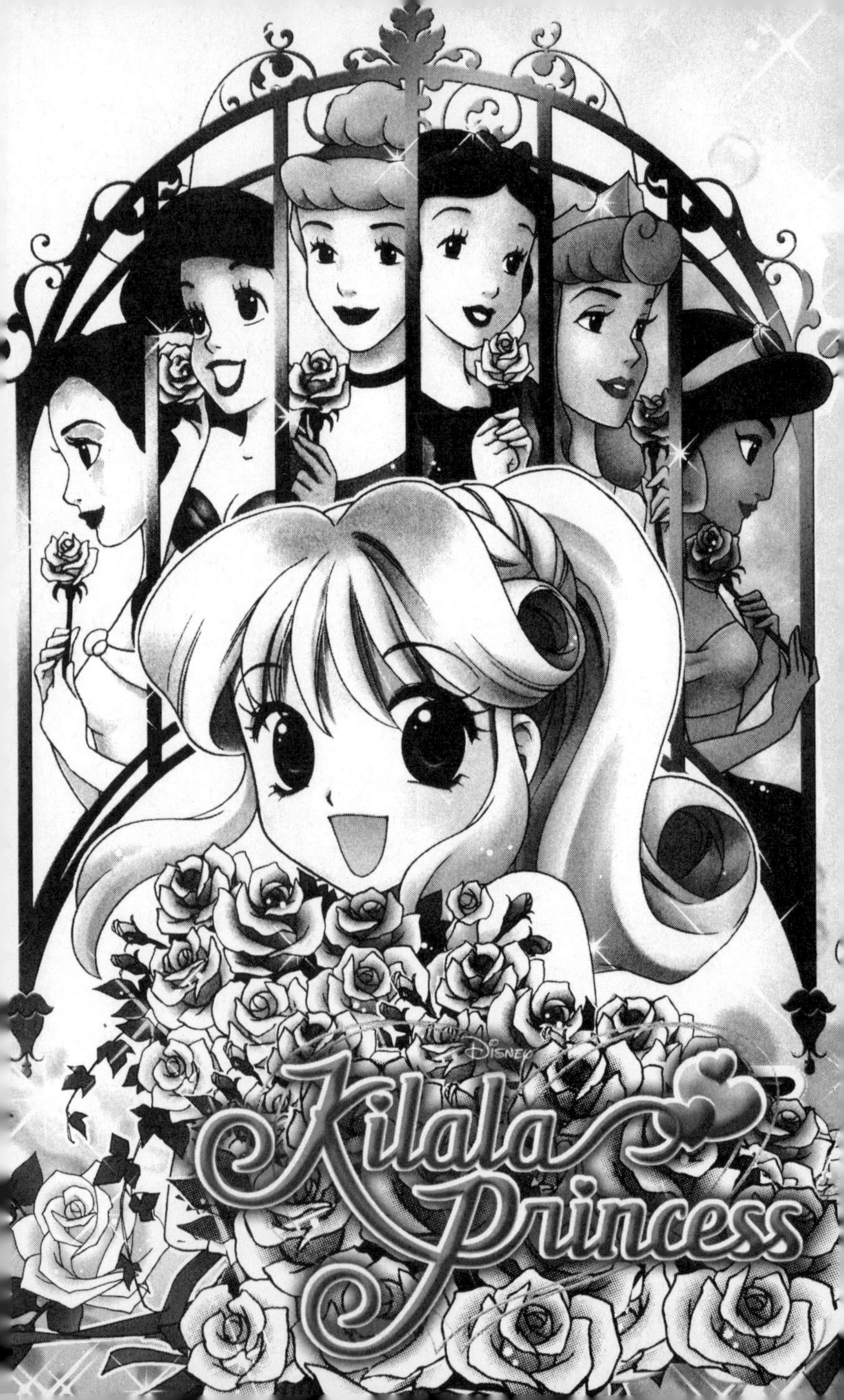
Disney
Kilala Princess

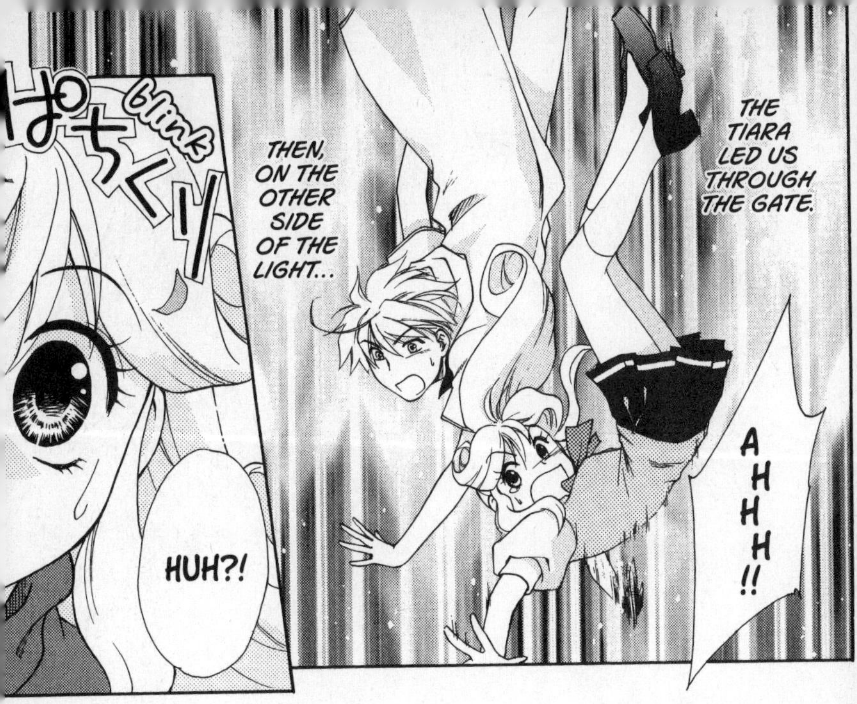
THE TIARA LED US THROUGH THE GATE.
THEN, ON THE OTHER SIDE OF THE LIGHT...
AHHH!!
ぱちくりー
blink
HUH?!

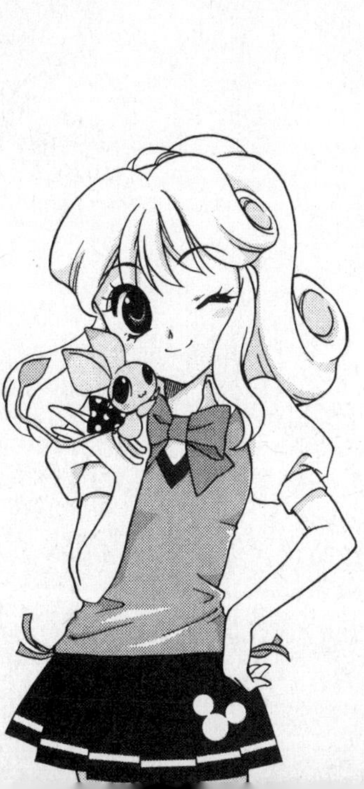

Kilala & Tippe

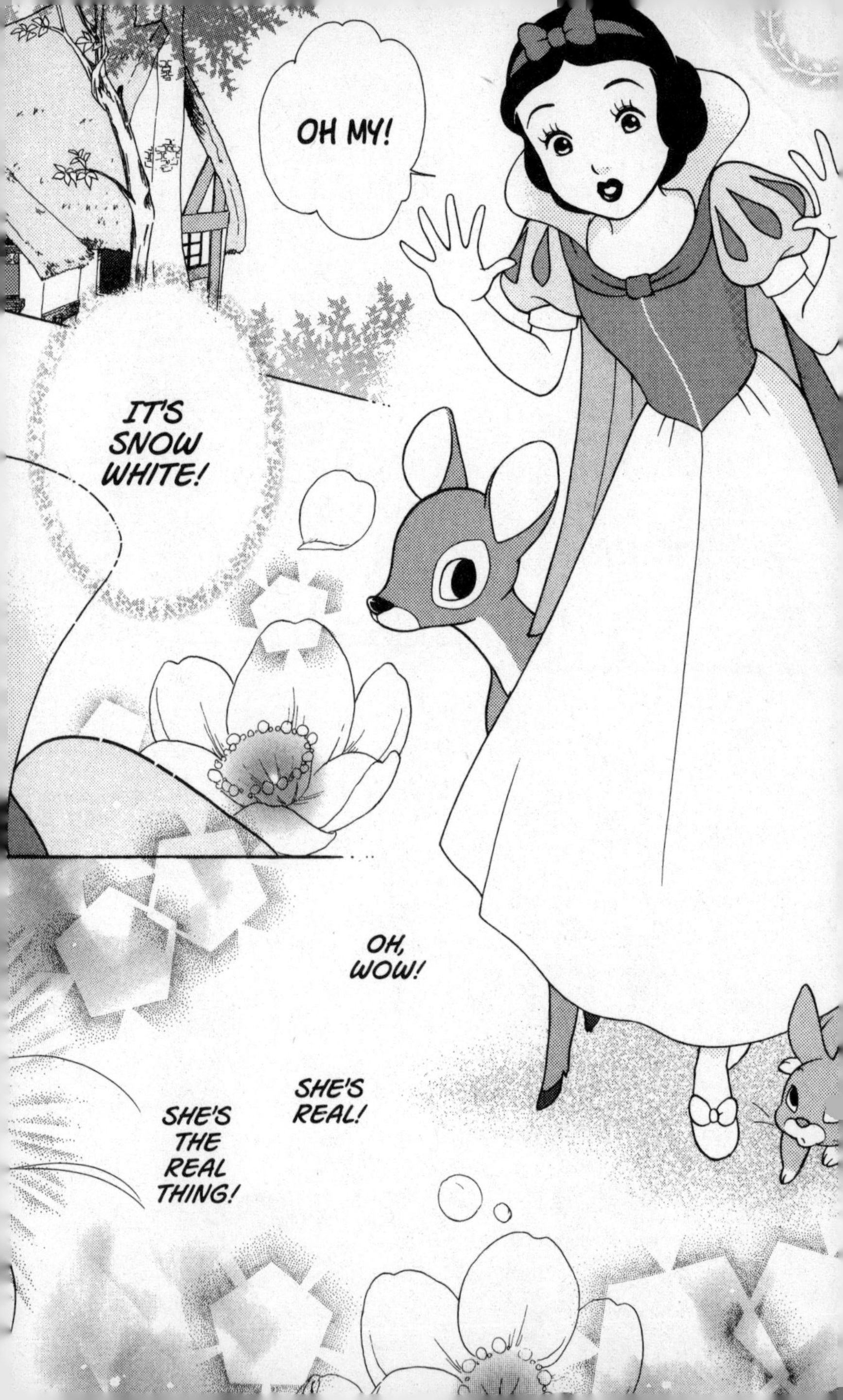
OH MY!
IT'S SNOW WHITE!
OH, WOW!
SHE'S REAL!
SHE'S THE REAL THING!

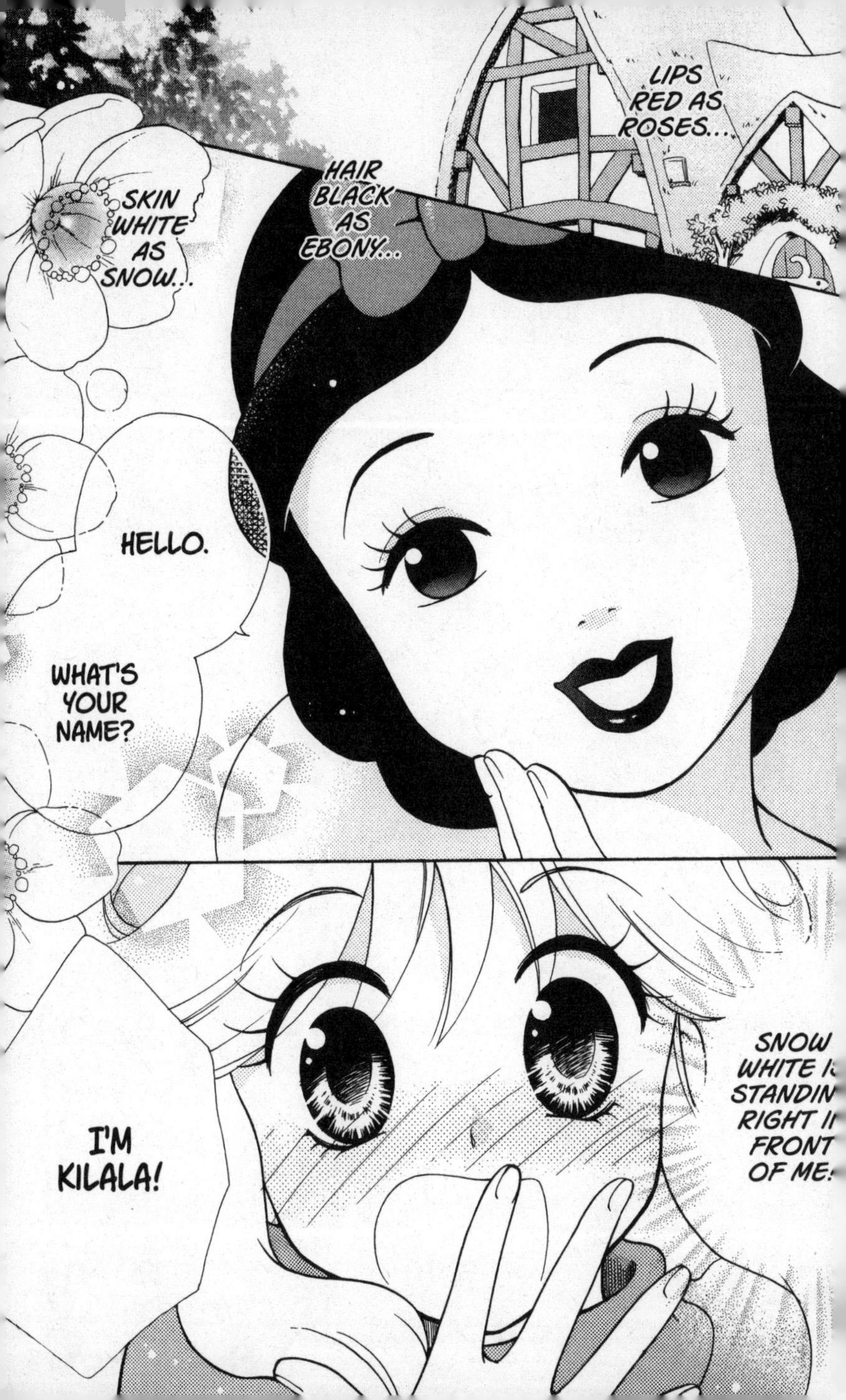
LIPS RED AS ROSES...
HAIR BLACK AS EBONY...
SKIN WHITE AS SNOW...
HELLO.
WHAT'S YOUR NAME?
SNOW WHITE I STANDIN RIGHT I FRONT OF ME
I'M KILALA!

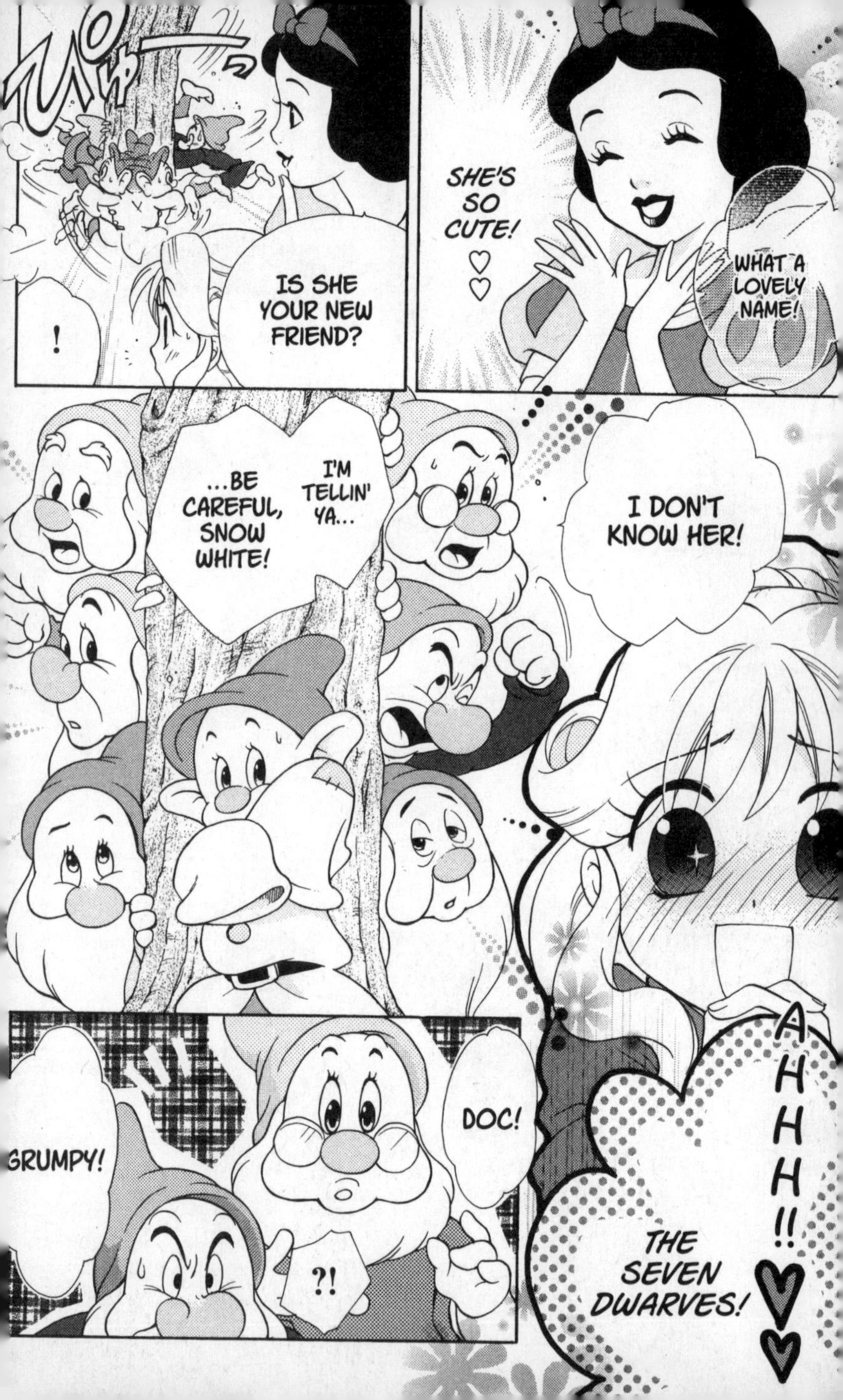

WHAT A LOVELY NAME!
SHE'S SO CUTE! ♡ ♡
ぴゅー
IS SHE YOUR NEW FRIEND?
!
I DON'T KNOW HER!
AHHH!! ♥♥
THE SEVEN DWARVES!
I'M TELLIN' YA...
...BE CAREFUL, SNOW WHITE!
DOC!
GRUMPY!
?!

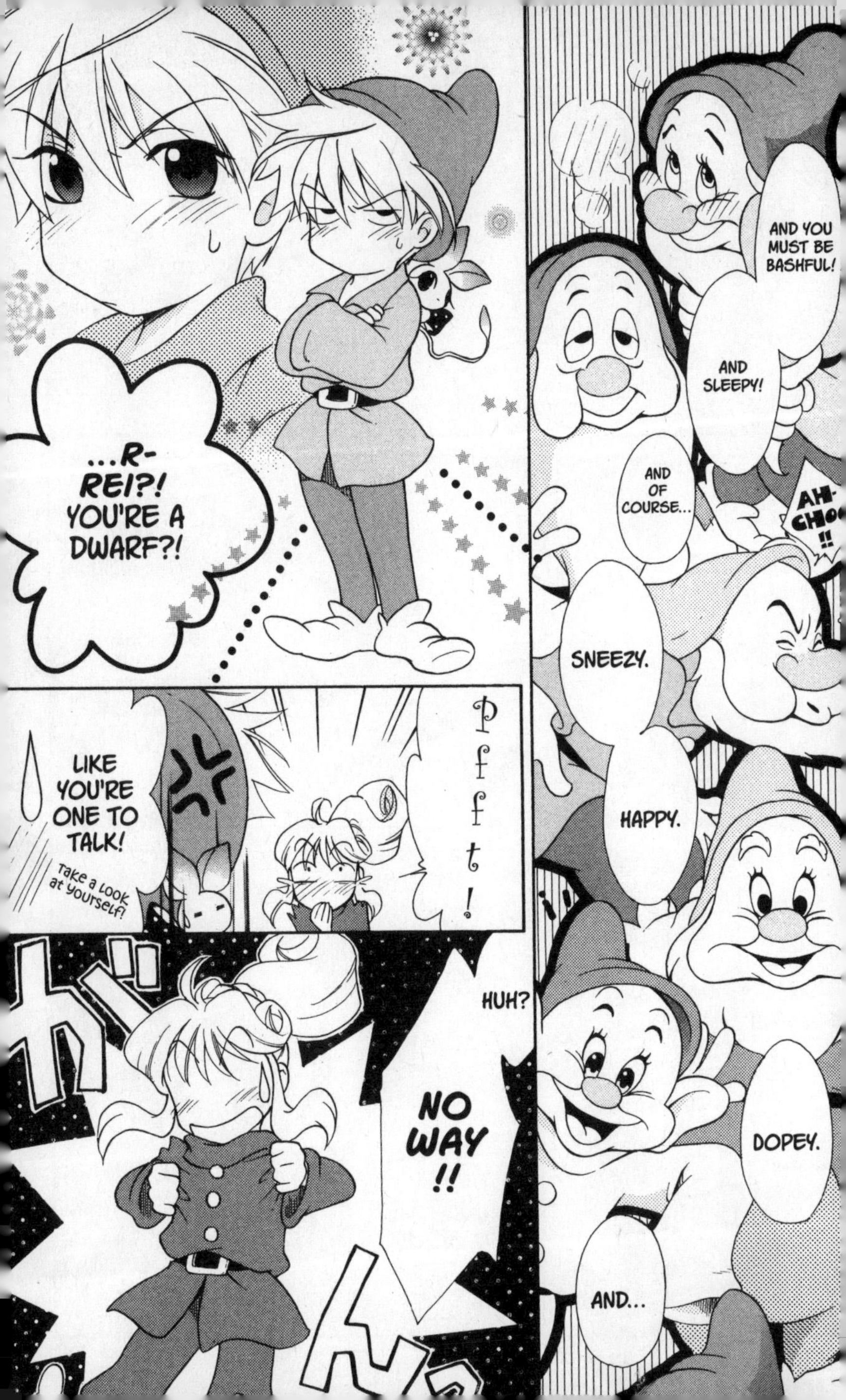
AND YOU MUST BE BASHFUL!
AND SLEEPY!
AND OF COURSE...
AH-CHOO!!
SNEEZY.
HAPPY.
DOPEY.
AND...
...R-REI?! YOU'RE A DWARF?!
Pffft!
LIKE YOU'RE ONE TO TALK!
Take a look at yourself!
HUH?
NO WAY!!

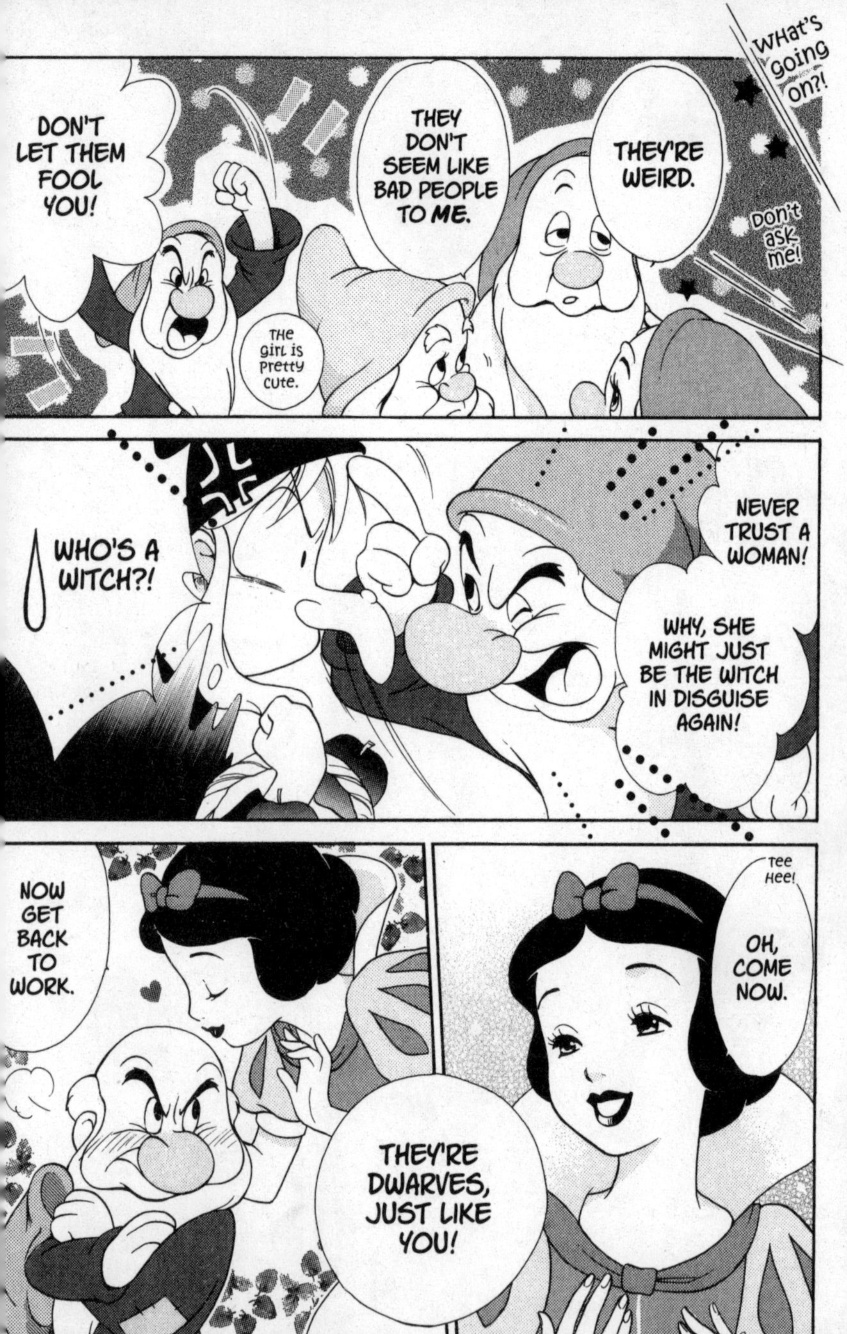
What's going on?!
THEY'RE WEIRD.
Don't ask me!
THEY DON'T SEEM LIKE BAD PEOPLE TO ME.
DON'T LET THEM FOOL YOU!
The girl is pretty cute.
NEVER TRUST A WOMAN!
WHY, SHE MIGHT JUST BE THE WITCH IN DISGUISE AGAIN!
WHO'S A WITCH?!
Tee Hee!
OH, COME NOW.
THEY'RE DWARVES, JUST LIKE YOU!
NOW GET BACK TO WORK.

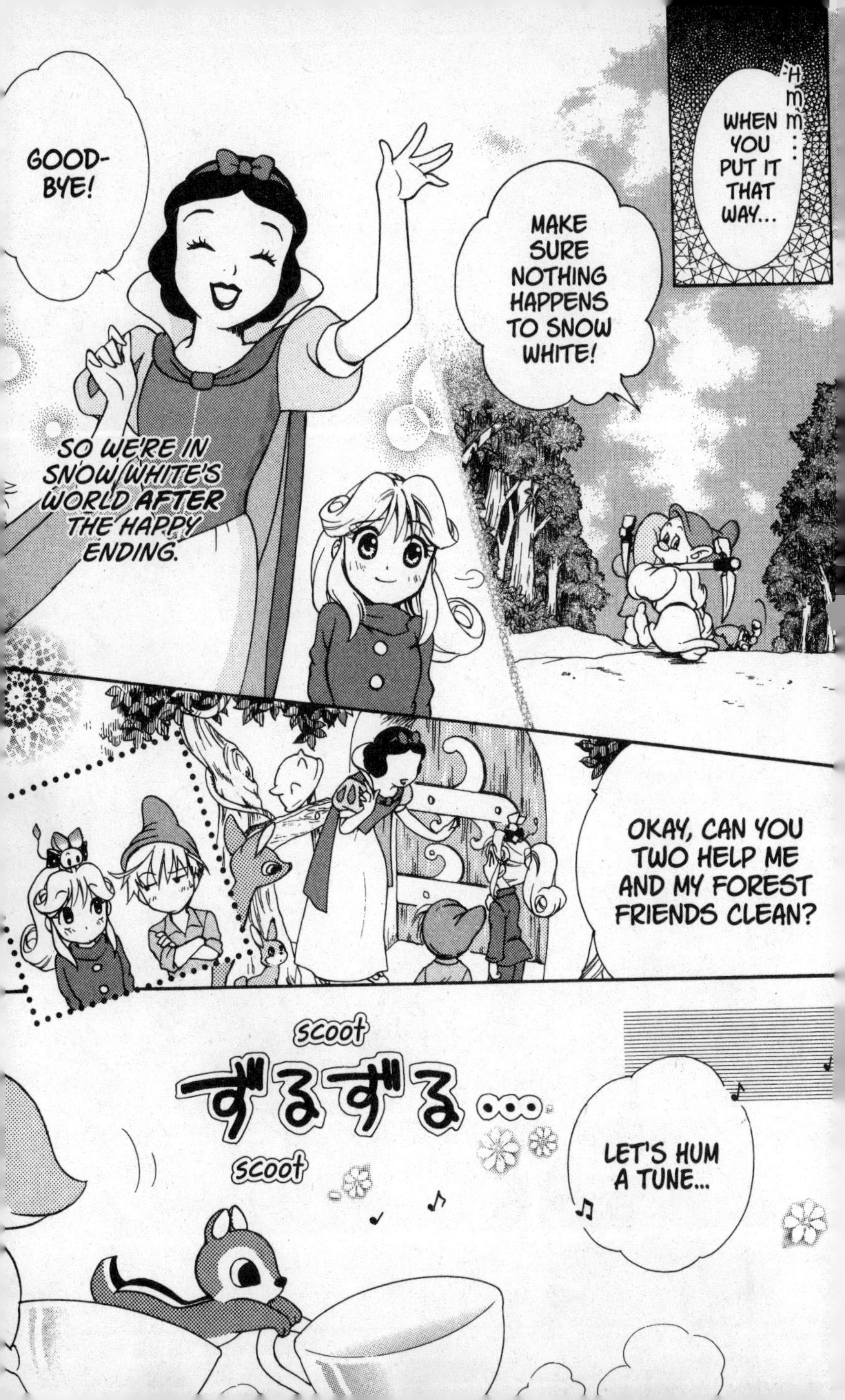
Hmm…
WHEN YOU PUT IT THAT WAY...
MAKE SURE NOTHING HAPPENS TO SNOW WHITE!
GOOD-BYE!
SO WE'RE IN SNOW WHITE'S WORLD AFTER THE HAPPY ENDING.
OKAY, CAN YOU TWO HELP ME AND MY FOREST FRIENDS CLEAN?
LET'S HUM A TUNE...
scoot
ずるずる…
scoot

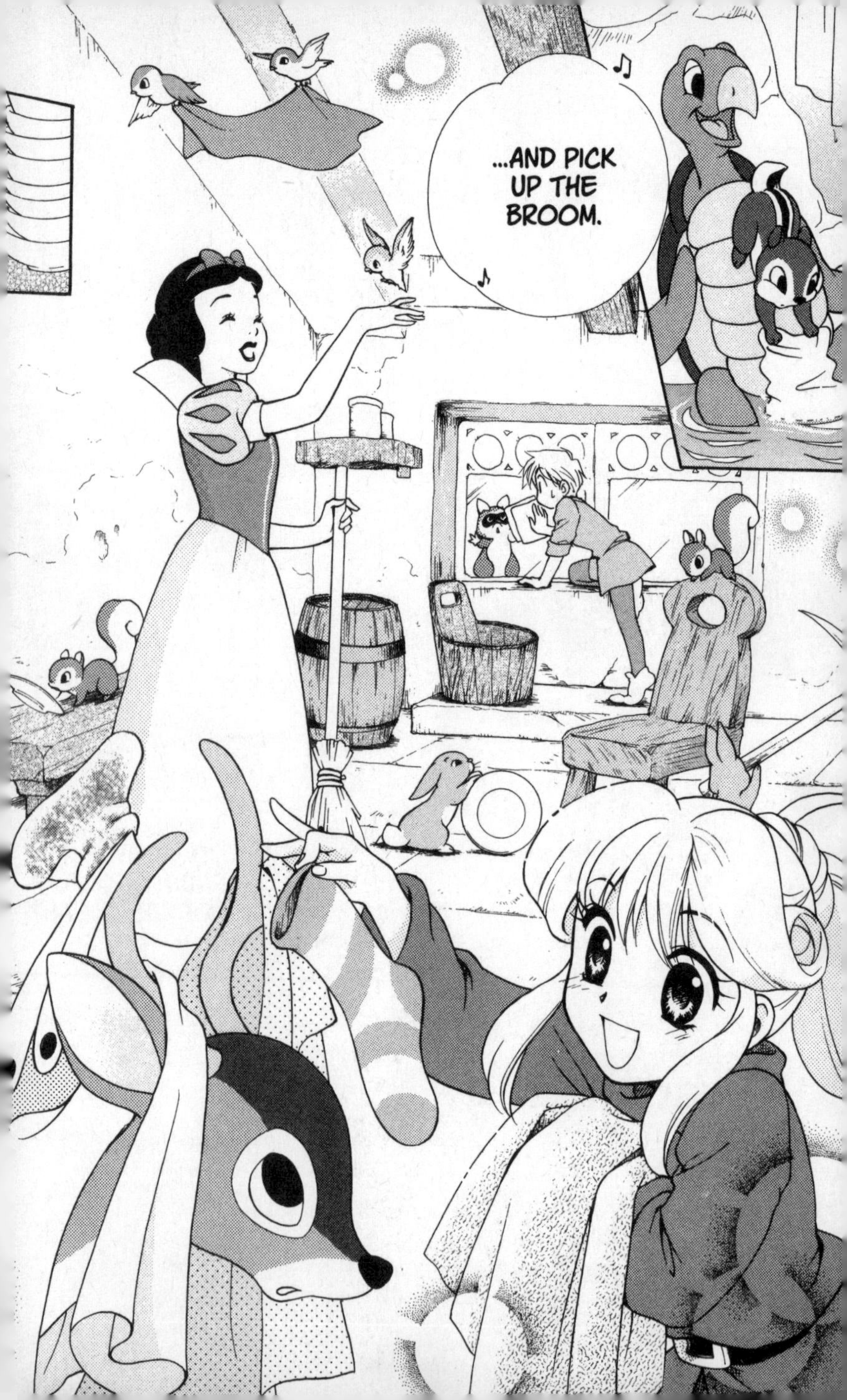
...AND PICK UP THE BROOM.

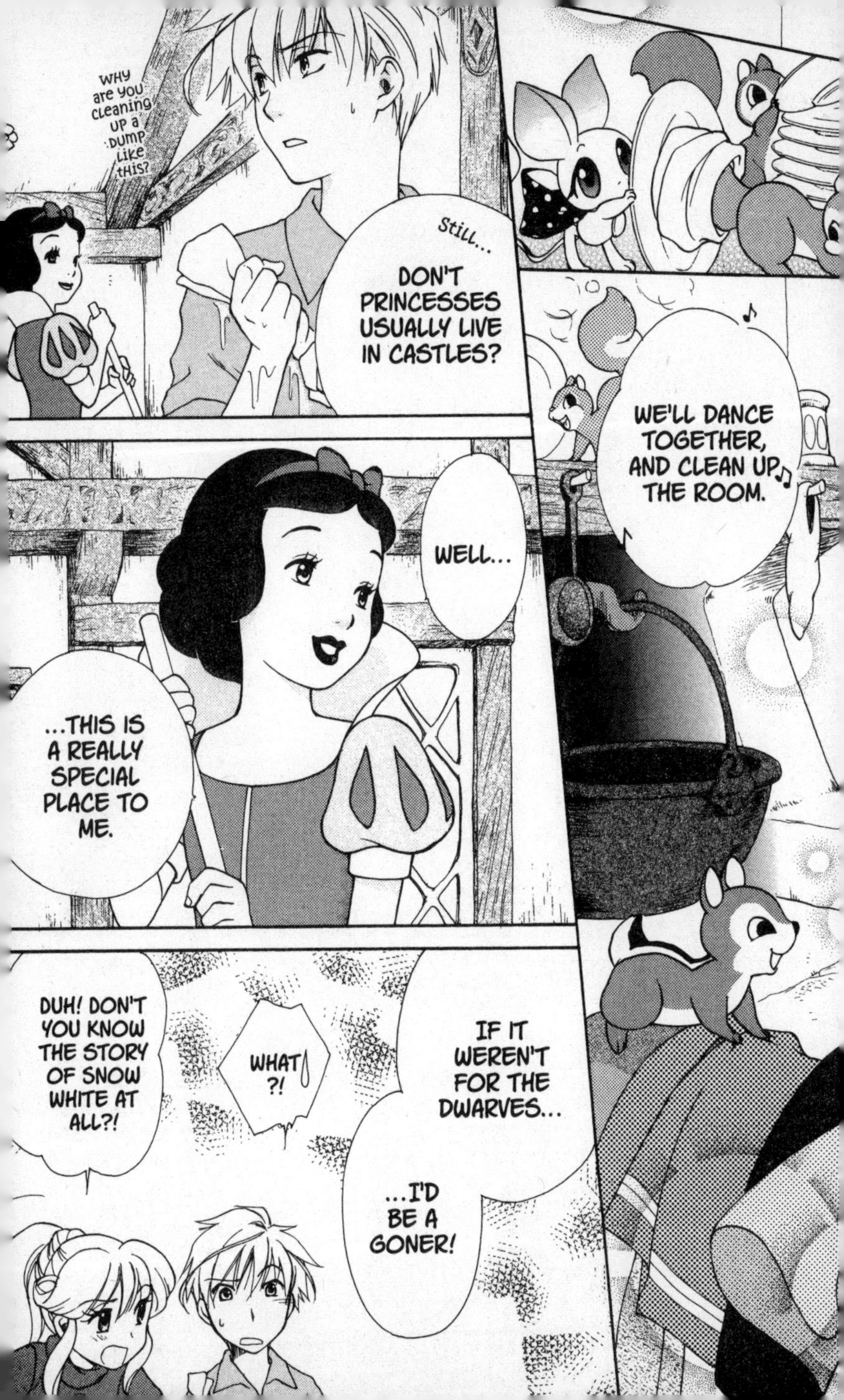
WE'LL DANCE TOGETHER, AND CLEAN UP♫ THE ROOM.
WHY are you cleaning up a DUMP like this?
Still...
DON'T PRINCESSES USUALLY LIVE IN CASTLES?
WELL...
...THIS IS A REALLY SPECIAL PLACE TO ME.
IF IT WEREN'T FOR THE DWARVES...
...I'D BE A GONER!
WHAT?!
DUH! DON'T YOU KNOW THE STORY OF SNOW WHITE AT ALL?!

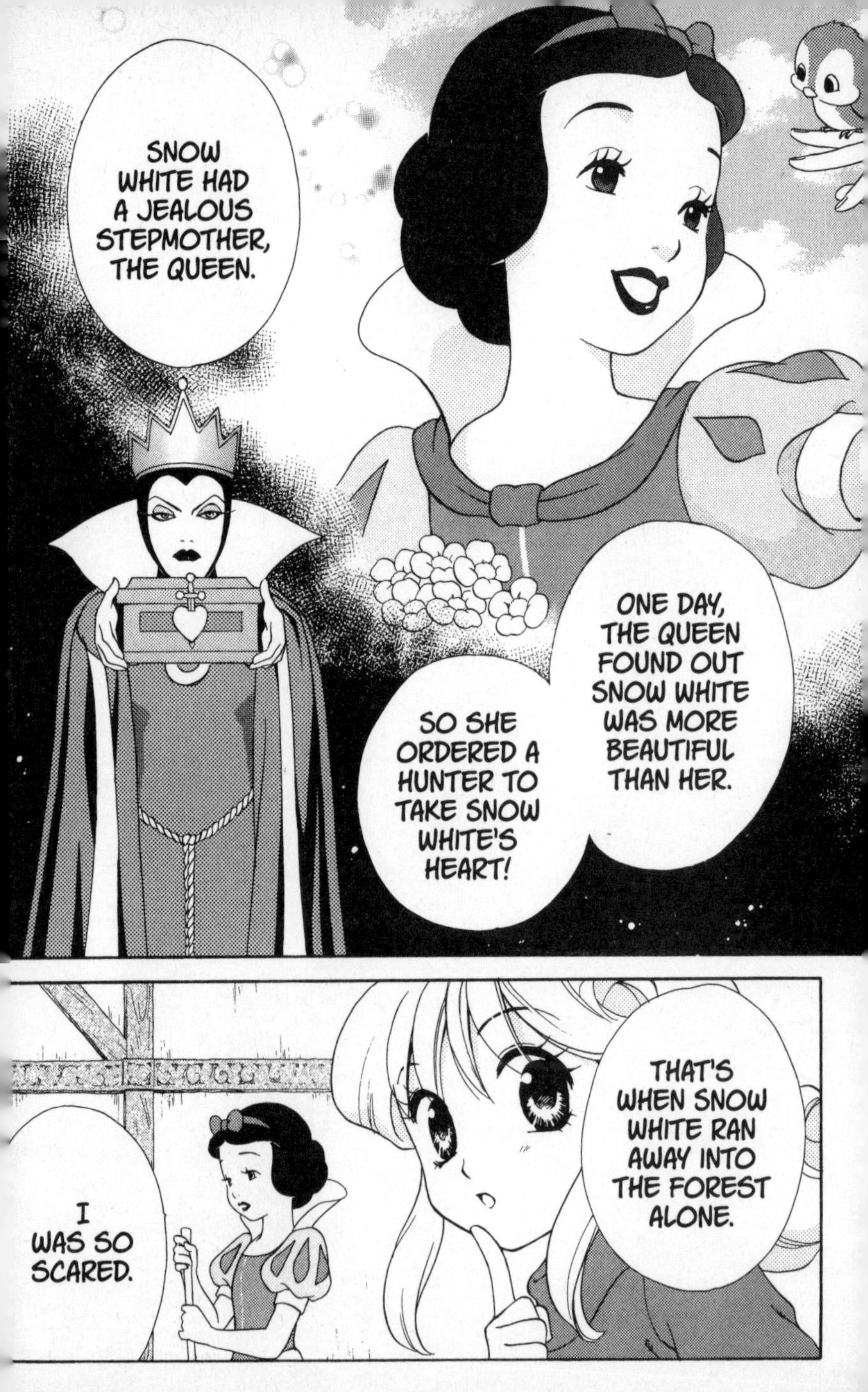
SNOW WHITE HAD A JEALOUS STEPMOTHER, THE QUEEN.
ONE DAY, THE QUEEN FOUND OUT SNOW WHITE WAS MORE BEAUTIFUL THAN HER.
SO SHE ORDERED A HUNTER TO TAKE SNOW WHITE'S HEART!
THAT'S WHEN SNOW WHITE RAN AWAY INTO THE FOREST ALONE.
I WAS SO SCARED.

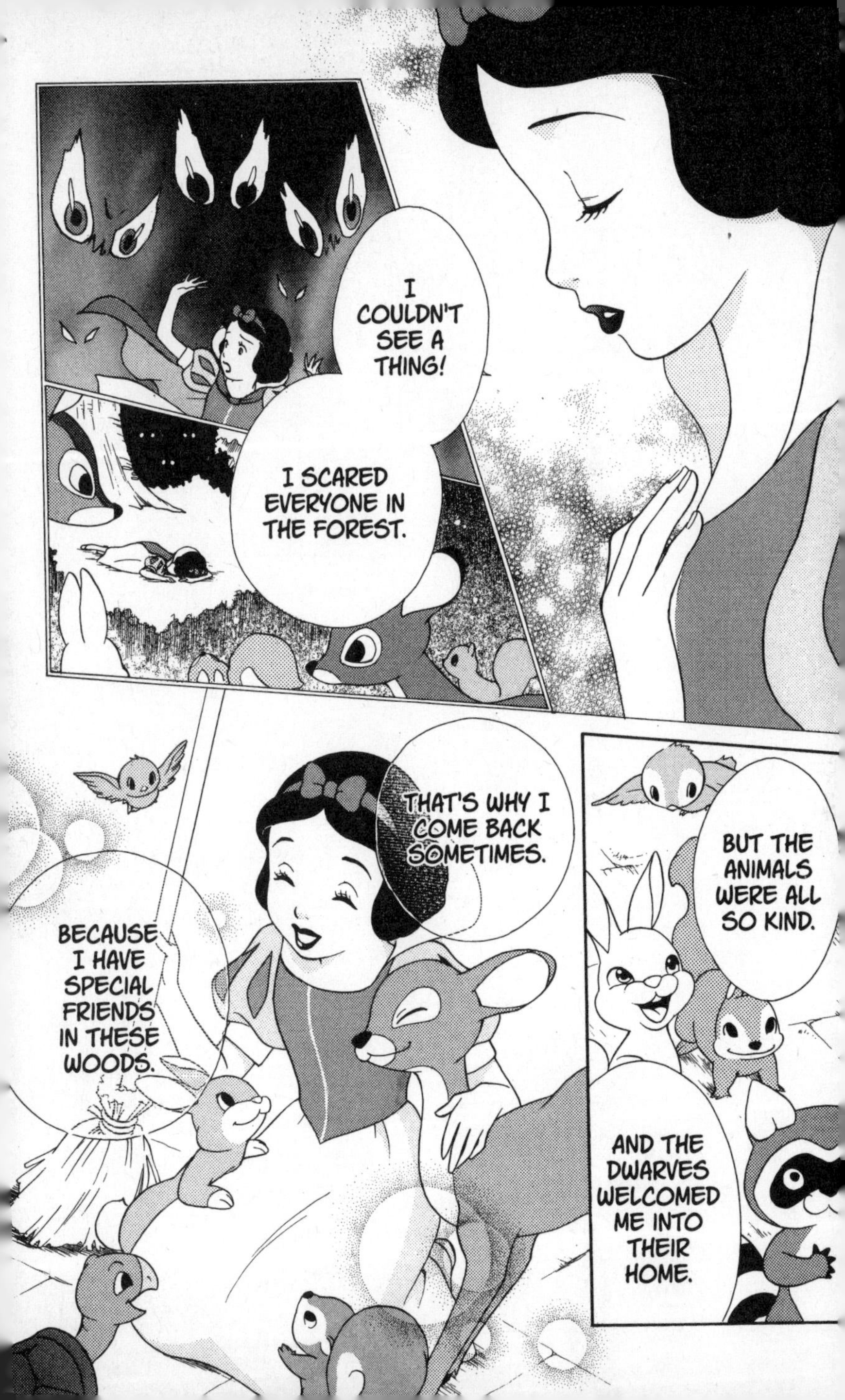
I COULDN'T SEE A THING!
I SCARED EVERYONE IN THE FOREST.
BUT THE ANIMALS WERE ALL SO KIND.
AND THE DWARVES WELCOMED ME INTO THEIR HOME.
THAT'S WHY I COME BACK SOMETIMES.
BECAUSE I HAVE SPECIAL FRIENDS IN THESE WOODS.

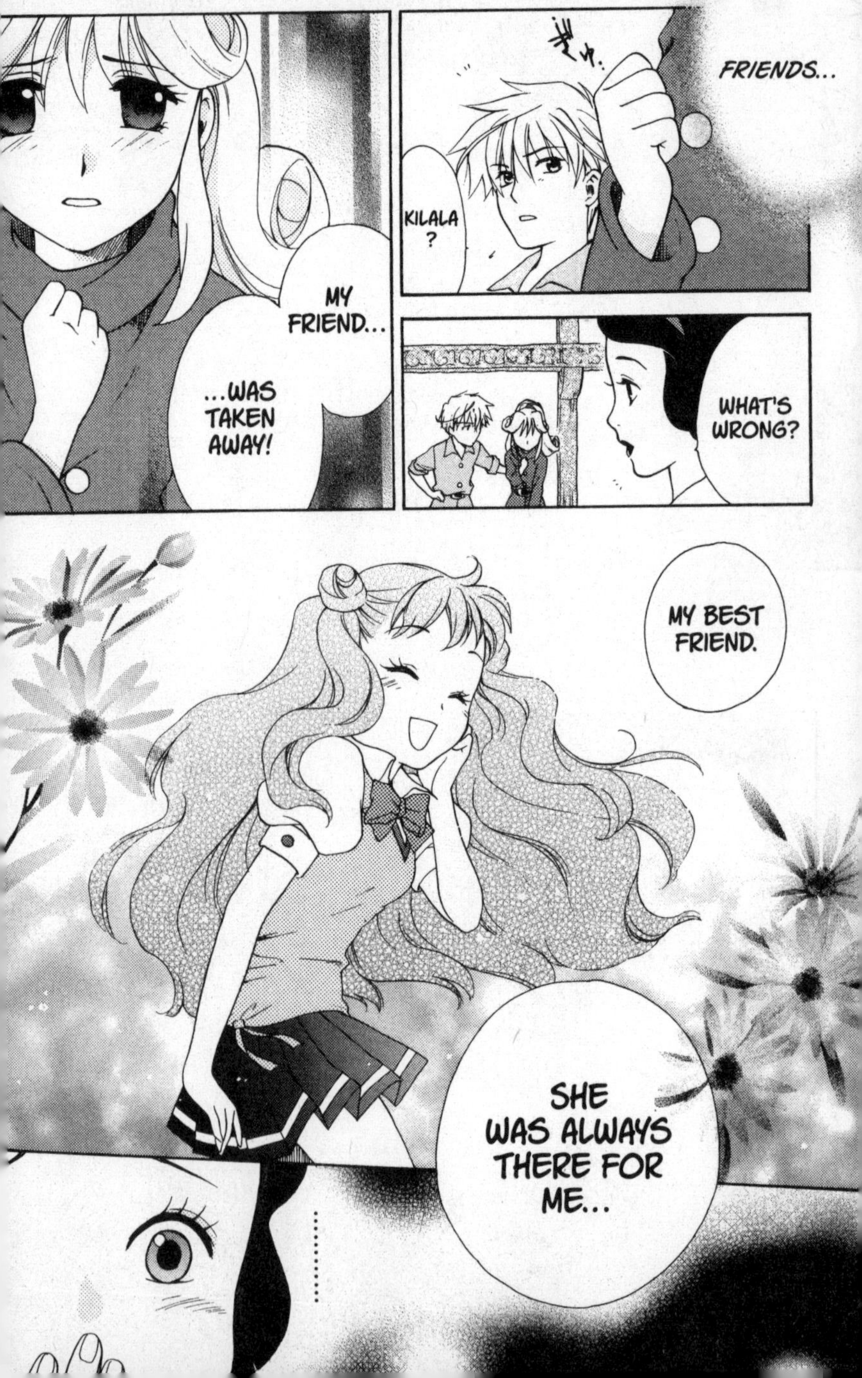
FRIENDS...
KILALA?
WHAT'S WRONG?
MY FRIEND...
...WAS TAKEN AWAY!
MY BEST FRIEND.
SHE WAS ALWAYS THERE FOR ME...

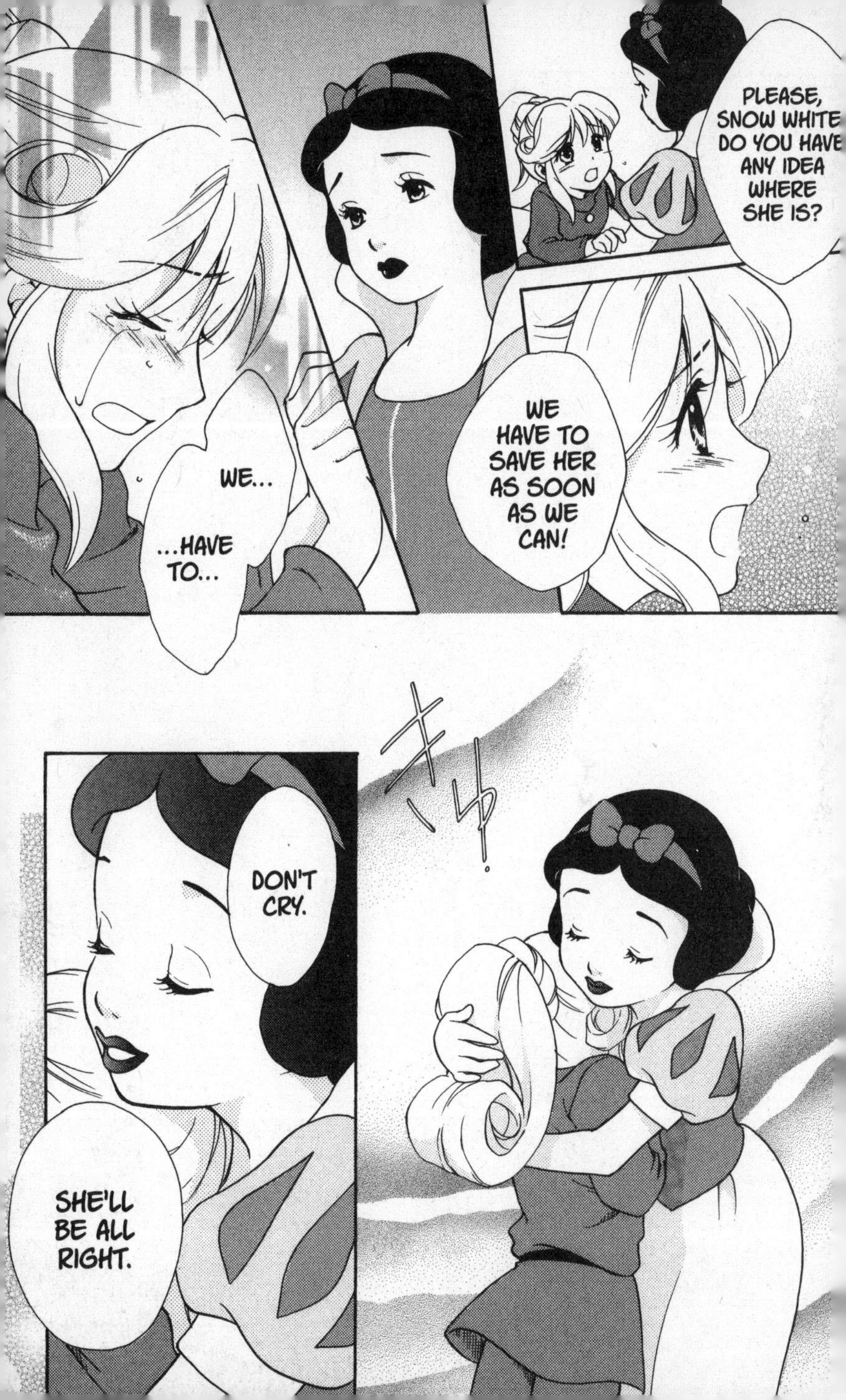
PLEASE, SNOW WHITE DO YOU HAVE ANY IDEA WHERE SHE IS?
WE HAVE TO SAVE HER AS SOON AS WE CAN!
WE...
...HAVE TO...
DON'T CRY.
SHE'LL BE ALL RIGHT.

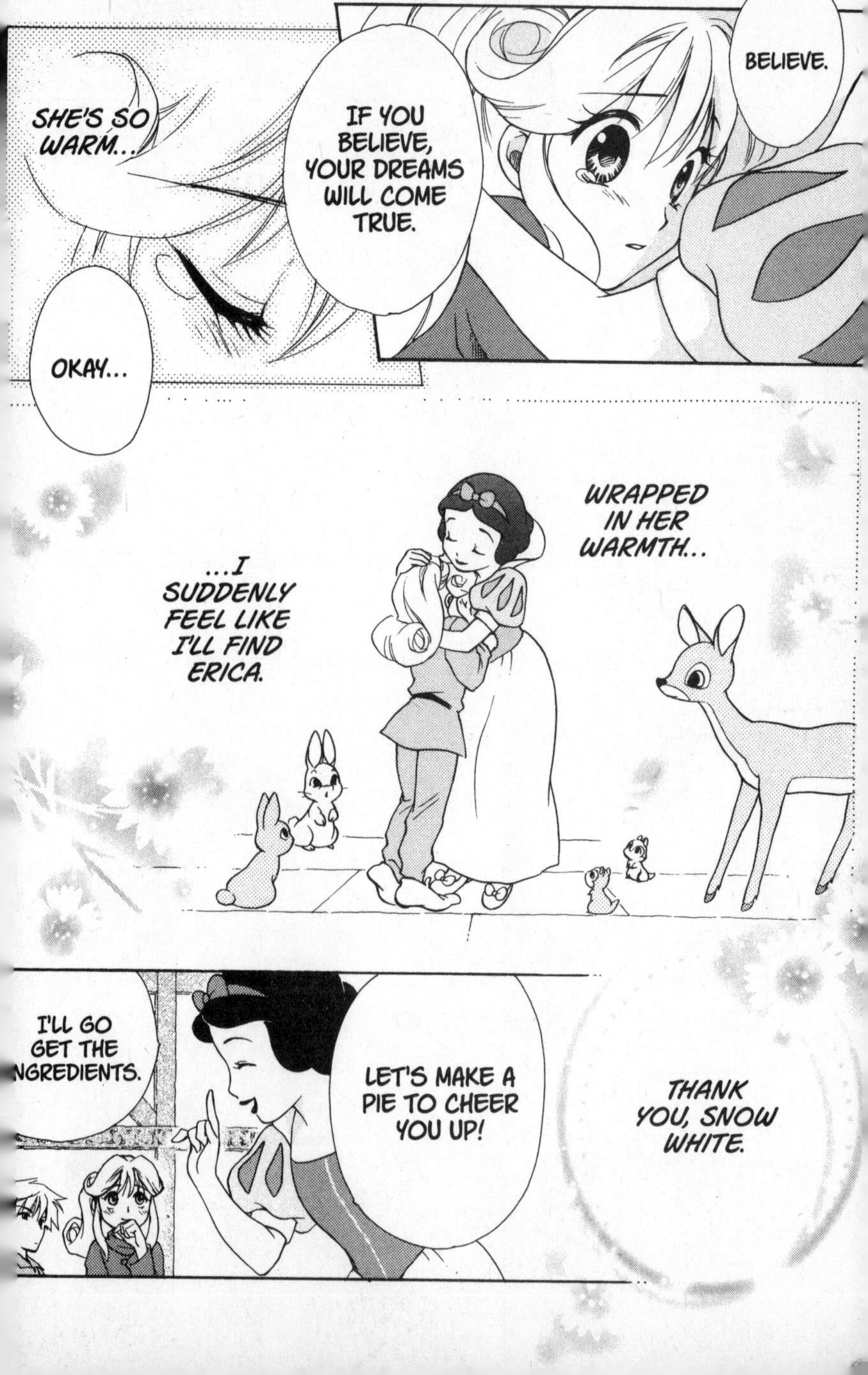
BELIEVE.
IF YOU BELIEVE, YOUR DREAMS WILL COME TRUE.
SHE'S SO WARM...
OKAY...
WRAPPED IN HER WARMTH...
...I SUDDENLY FEEL LIKE I'LL FIND ERICA.
THANK YOU, SNOW WHITE.
LET'S MAKE A PIE TO CHEER YOU UP!
I'LL GO GET THE NGREDIENTS.

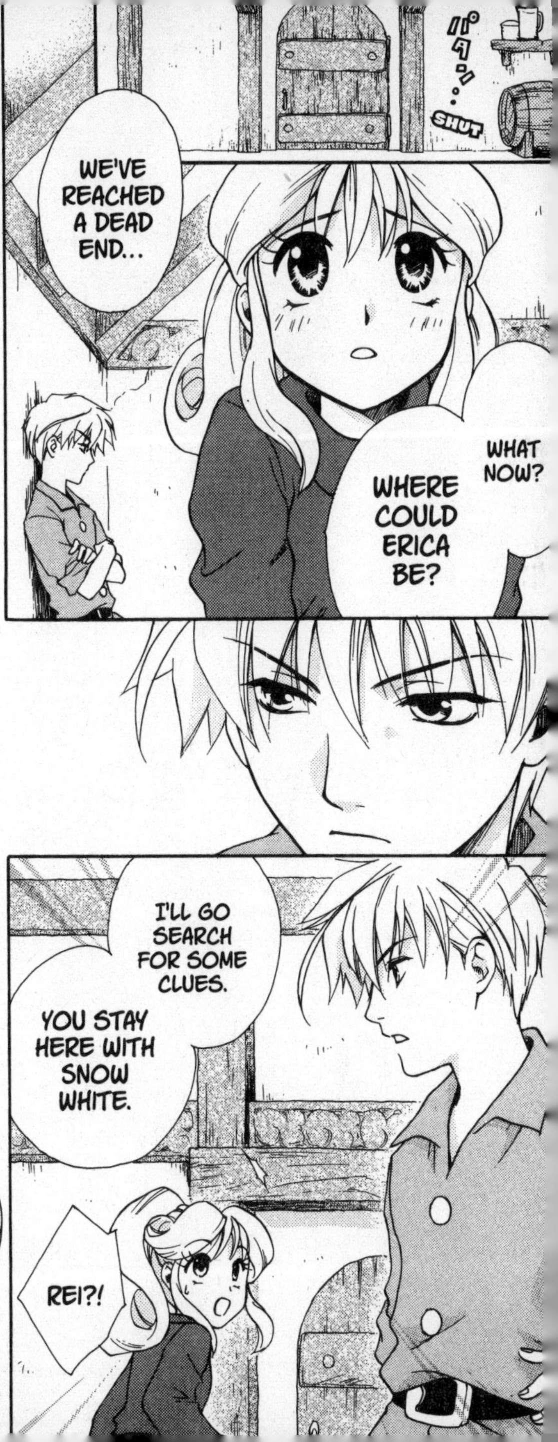
パタン…
SHUT
WE'VE REACHED A DEAD END...
WHAT NOW?
WHERE COULD ERICA BE?
I'LL GO SEARCH FOR SOME CLUES.
YOU STAY HERE WITH SNOW WHITE.
REI?!

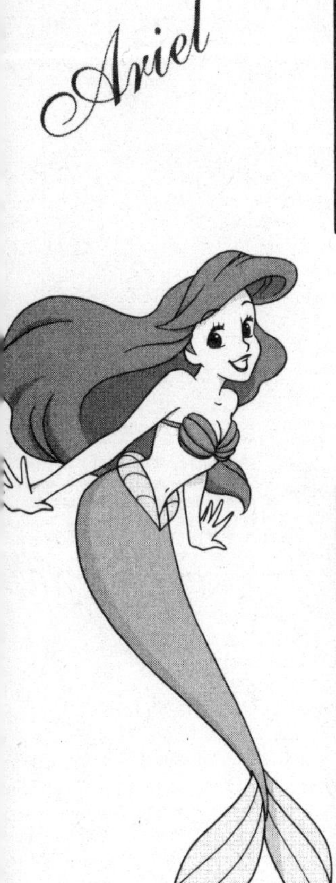
Ariel

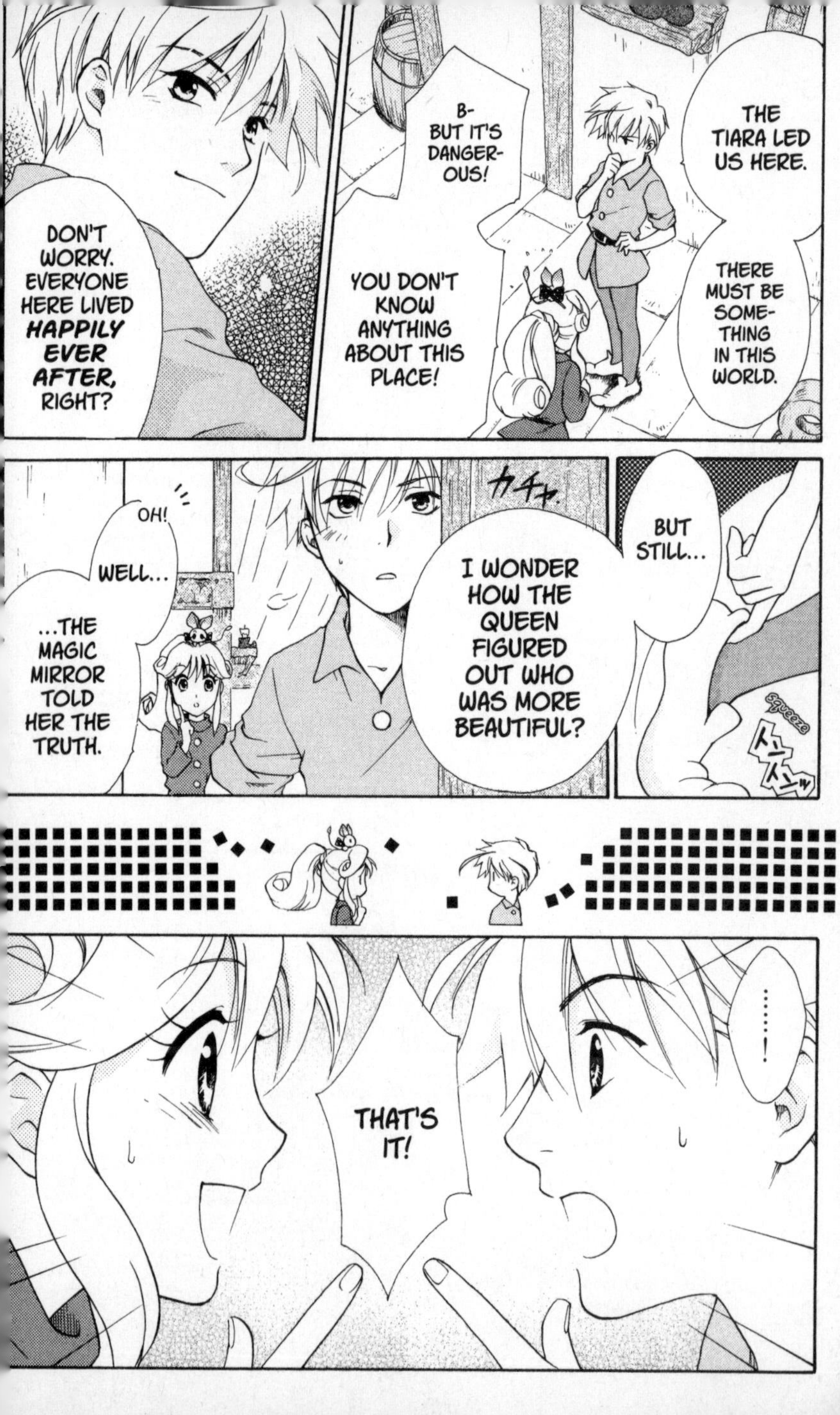
THE TIARA LED US HERE.
THERE MUST BE SOMETHING IN THIS WORLD.
B- BUT IT'S DANGEROUS!
YOU DON'T KNOW ANYTHING ABOUT THIS PLACE!
DON'T WORRY. EVERYONE HERE LIVED **HAPPILY EVER AFTER,** RIGHT?
BUT STILL...
squeeze
トントンッ
カチャ
I WONDER HOW THE QUEEN FIGURED OUT WHO WAS MORE BEAUTIFUL?
OH!
WELL...
...THE MAGIC MIRROR TOLD HER THE TRUTH.
......!
THAT'S IT!

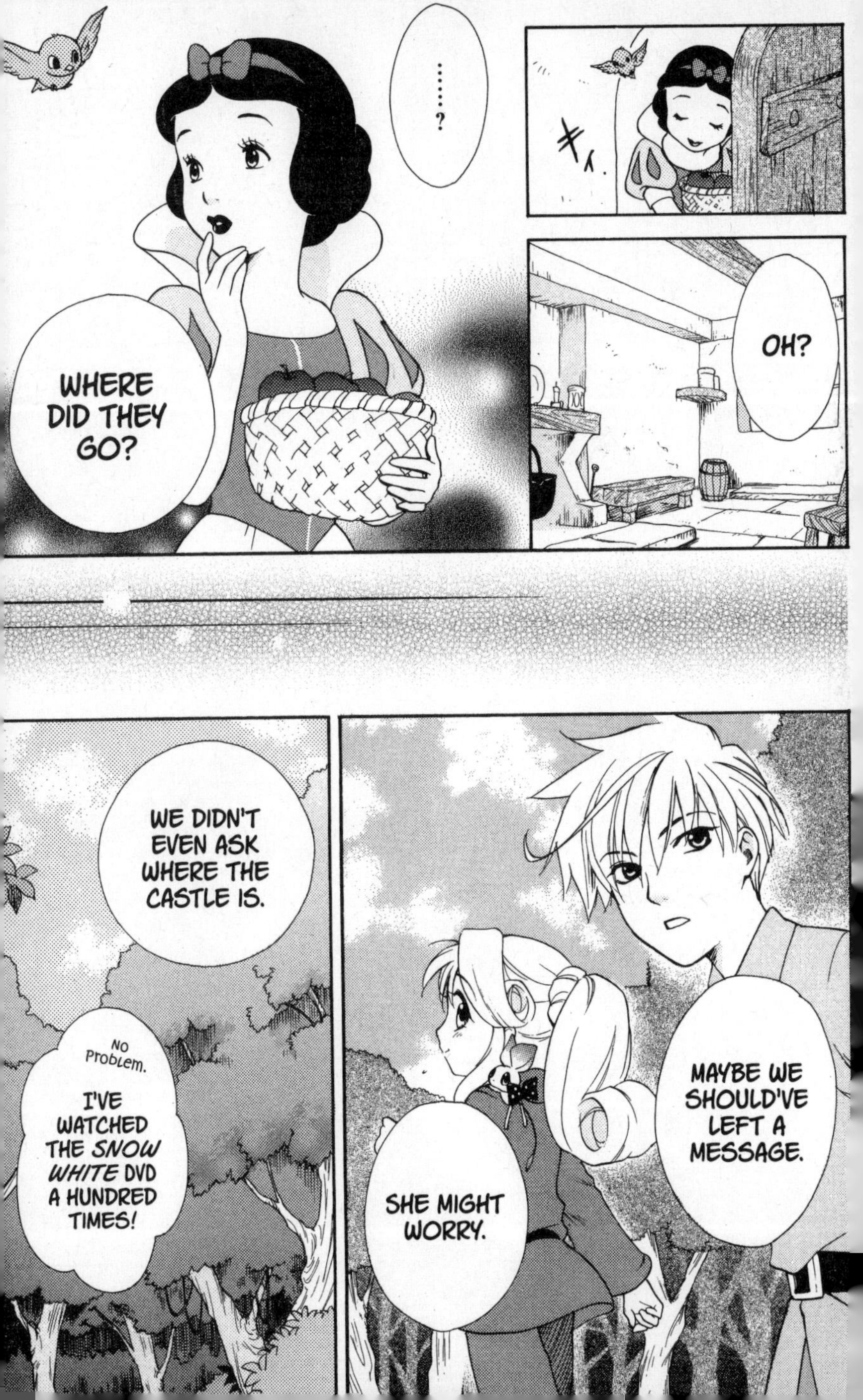
キィ.
OH?
......?
WHERE DID THEY GO?
MAYBE WE SHOULD'VE LEFT A MESSAGE.
SHE MIGHT WORRY.
WE DIDN'T EVEN ASK WHERE THE CASTLE IS.
No Problem.
I'VE WATCHED THE *SNOW WHITE* DVD A HUNDRED TIMES!

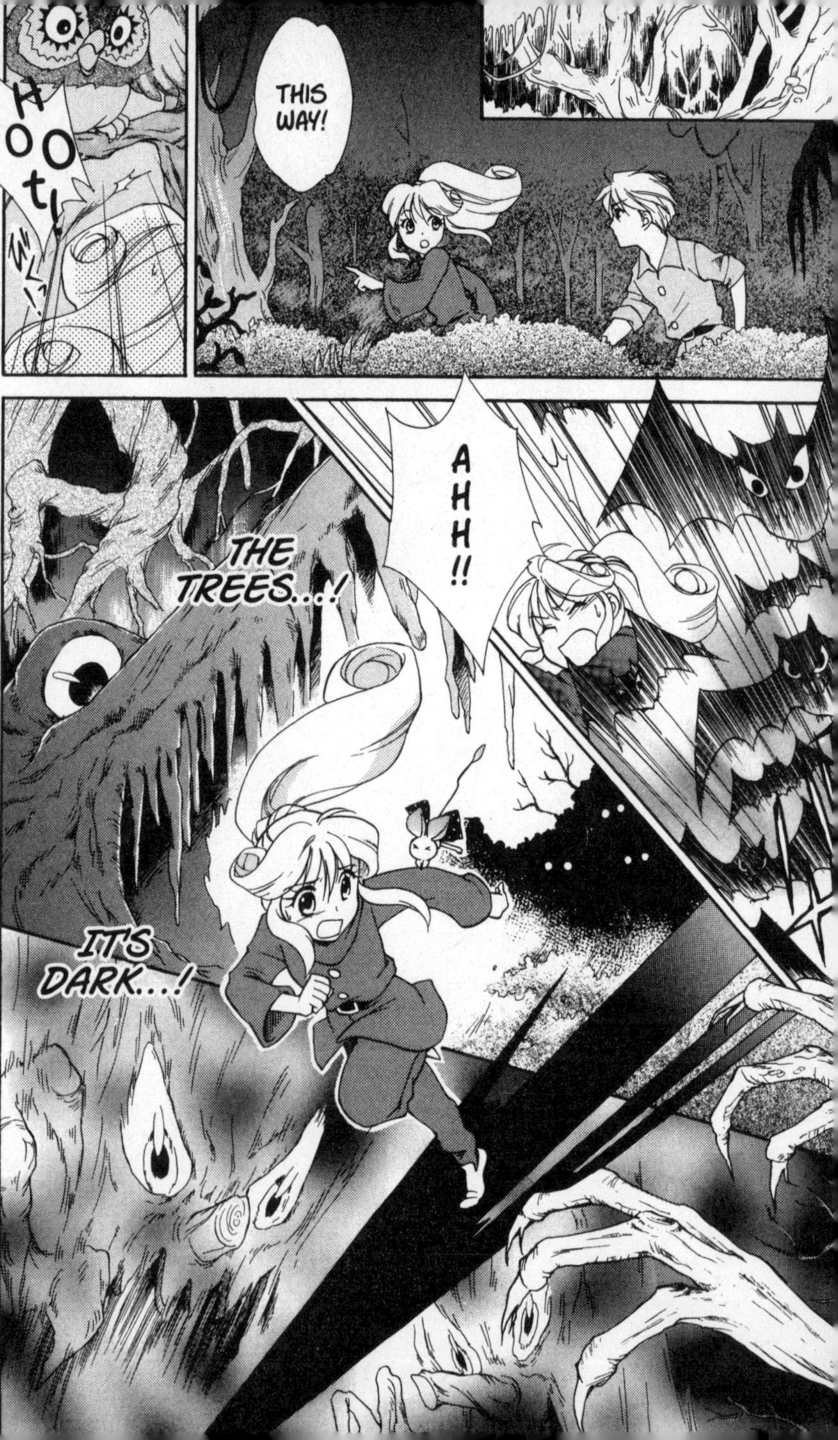
THIS WAY!
HOOt!
びくっ!?
AHH!!
THE TREES...!
IT'S DARK...!

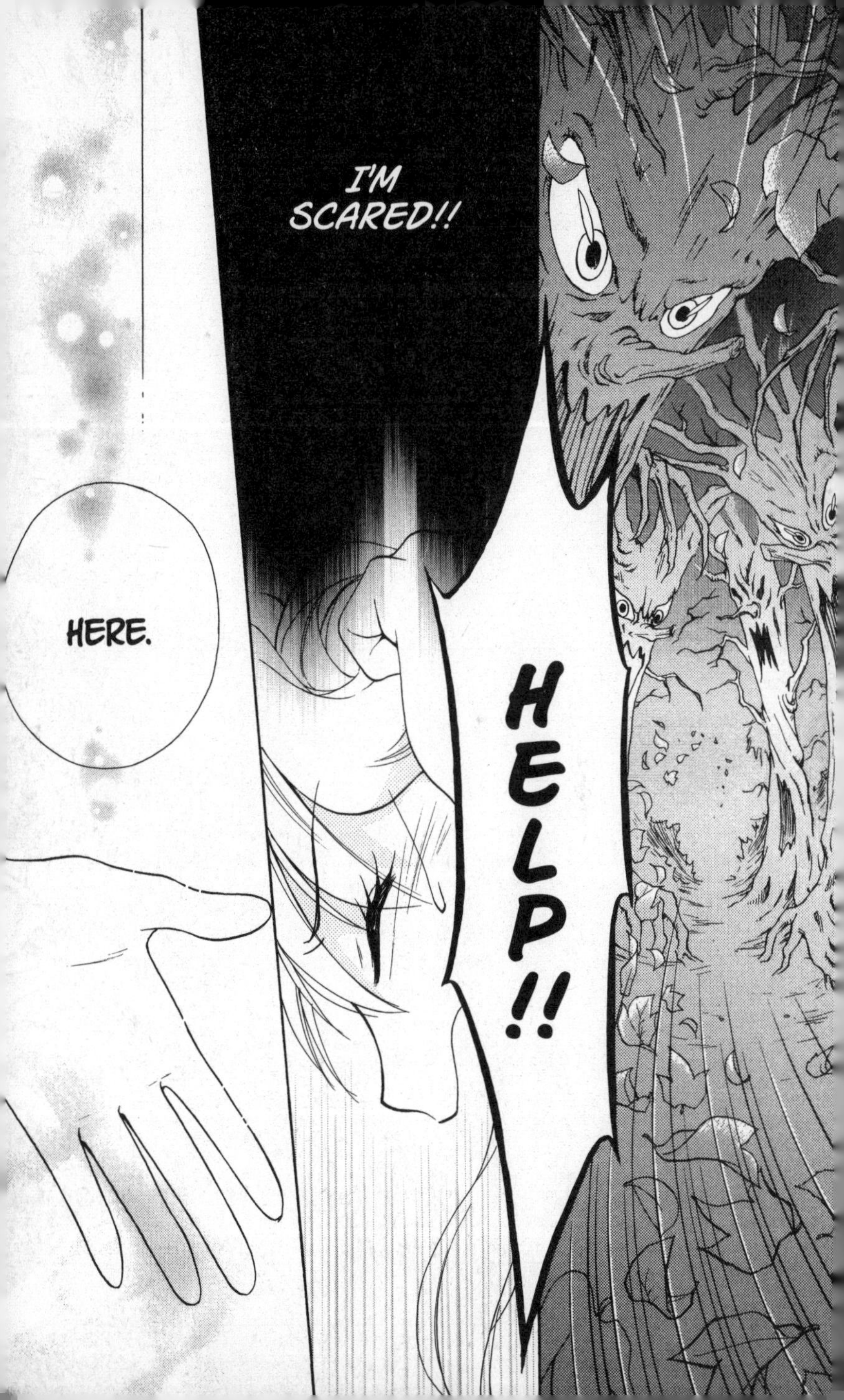
I'M SCARED!!
HELP!!
HERE.

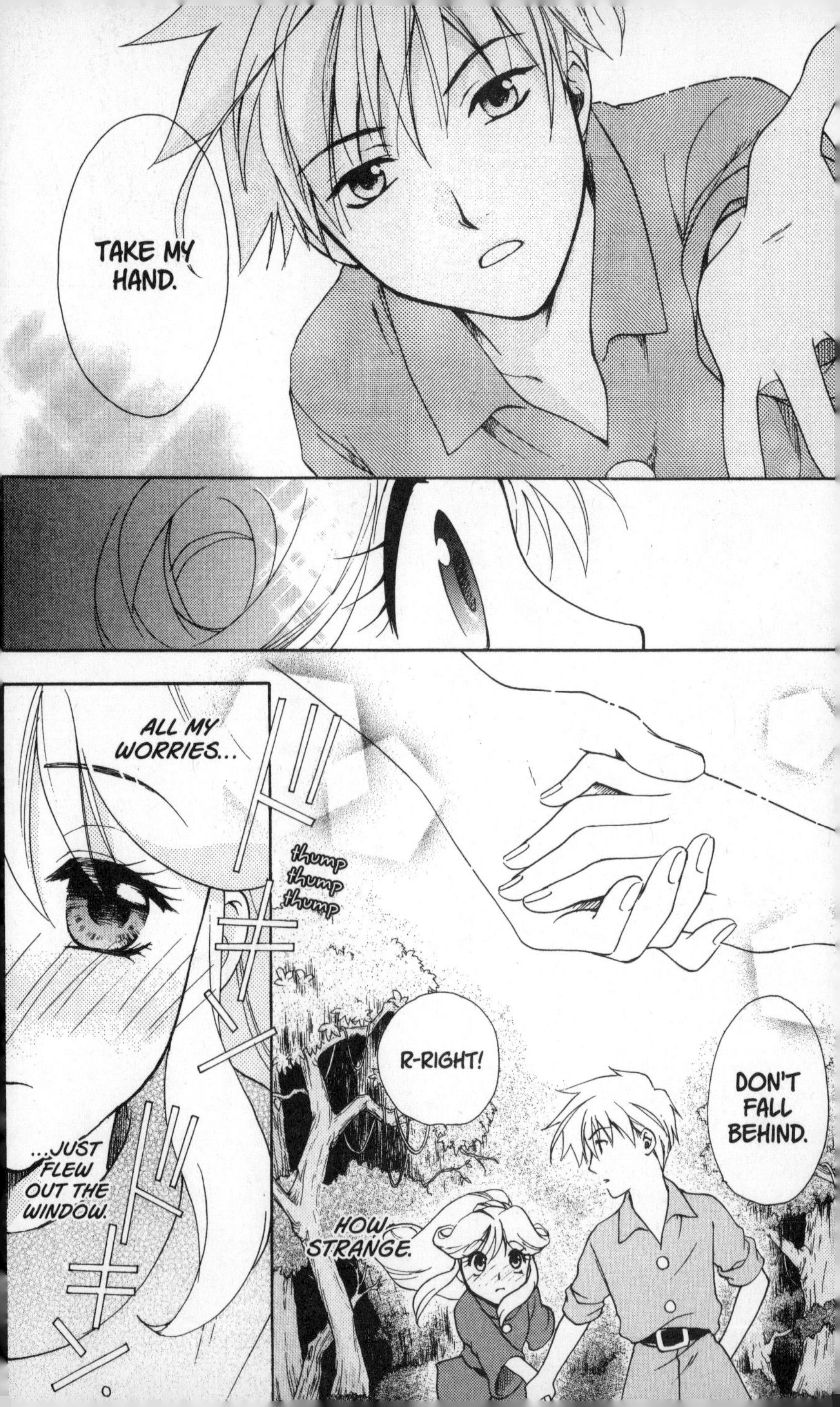
TAKE MY HAND.
DON'T FALL BEHIND.
R-RIGHT!
thump thump thump
HOW STRANGE.
ALL MY WORRIES...
...JUST FLEW OUT THE WINDOW.

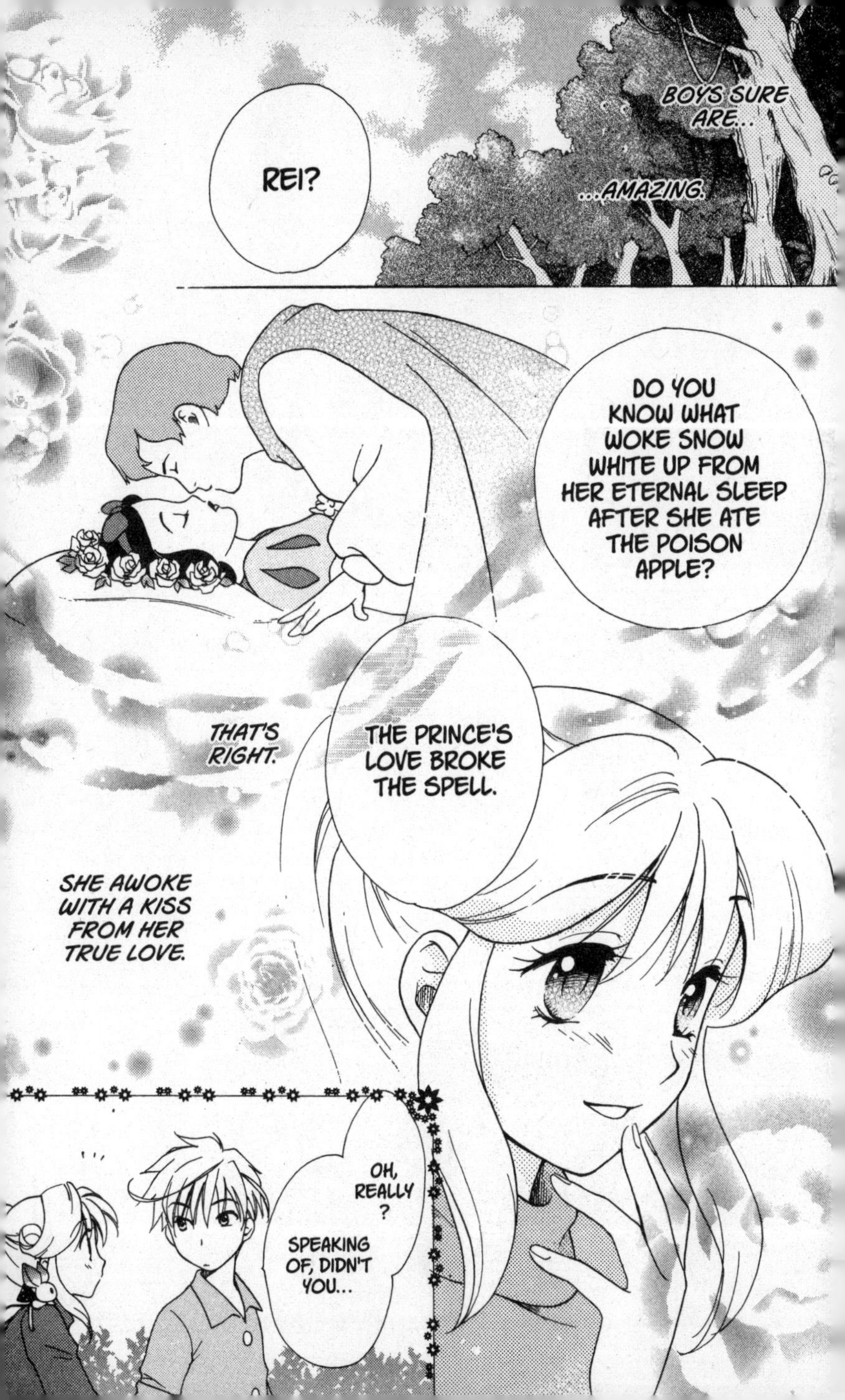
BOYS SURE ARE...
...AMAZING.
REI?
DO YOU KNOW WHAT WOKE SNOW WHITE UP FROM HER ETERNAL SLEEP AFTER SHE ATE THE POISON APPLE?
THE PRINCE'S LOVE BROKE THE SPELL.
THAT'S RIGHT.
SHE AWOKE WITH A KISS FROM HER TRUE LOVE.
OH, REALLY?
SPEAKING OF, DIDN'T YOU...

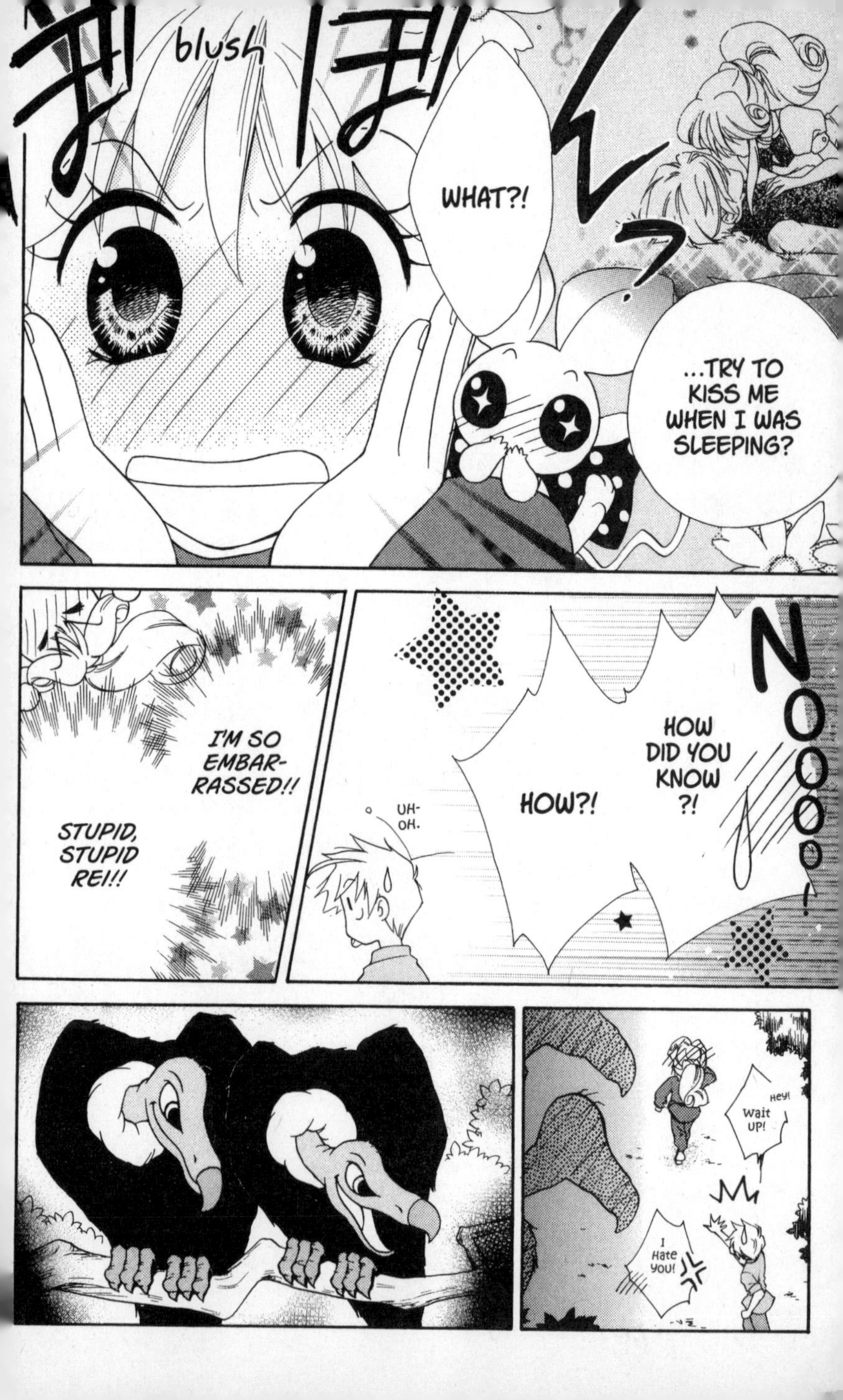

...TRY TO KISS ME WHEN I WAS SLEEPING?
WHAT?!
blush
NOOOO!
HOW DID YOU KNOW ?!
HOW?!
UH-OH.
I'M SO EMBARRASSED!!
STUPID, STUPID REI!!
Hey! Wait UP!
I Hate YOU!

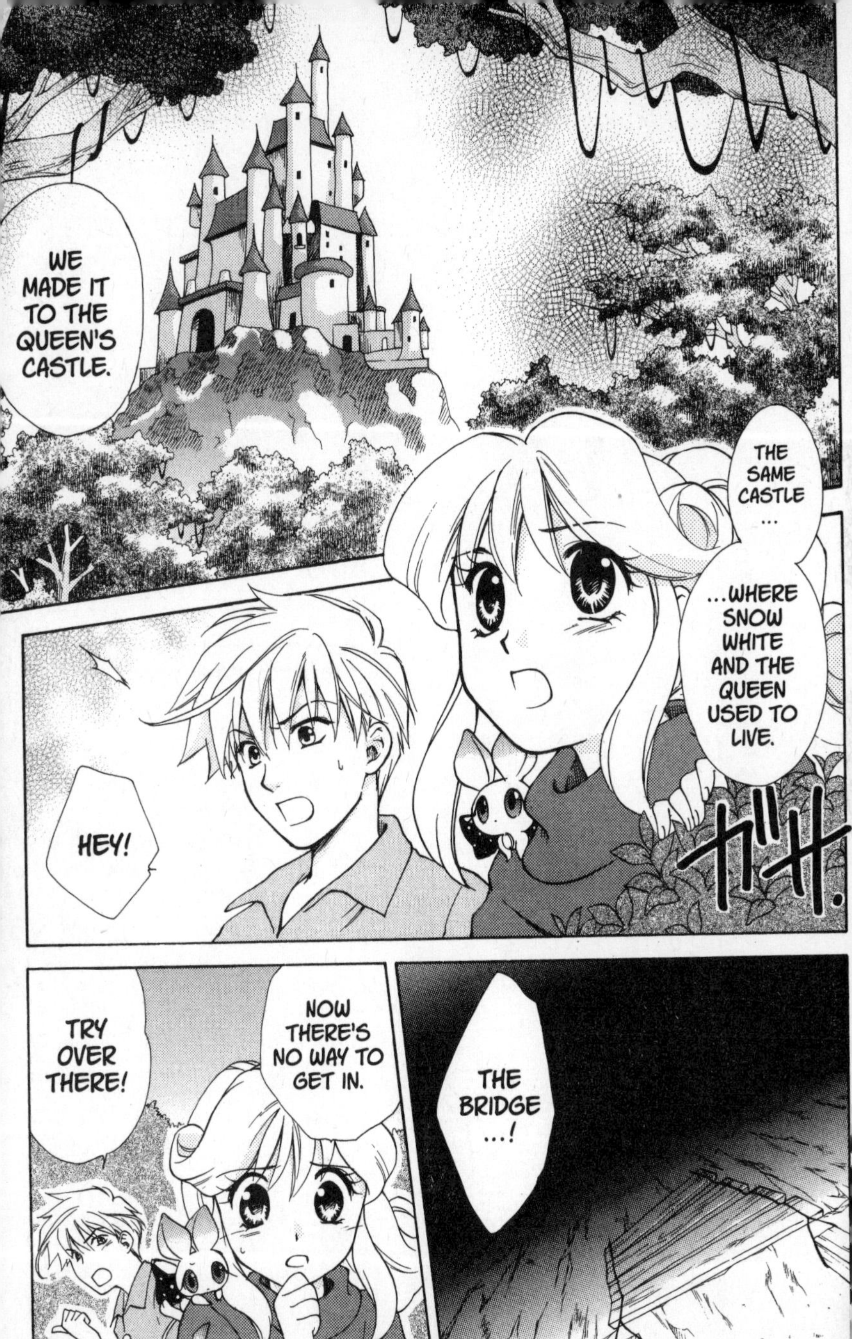
WE MADE IT TO THE QUEEN'S CASTLE.
THE SAME CASTLE...
...WHERE SNOW WHITE AND THE QUEEN USED TO LIVE.
ガサ.
HEY!
THE BRIDGE...!
NOW THERE'S NO WAY TO GET IN.
TRY OVER THERE!

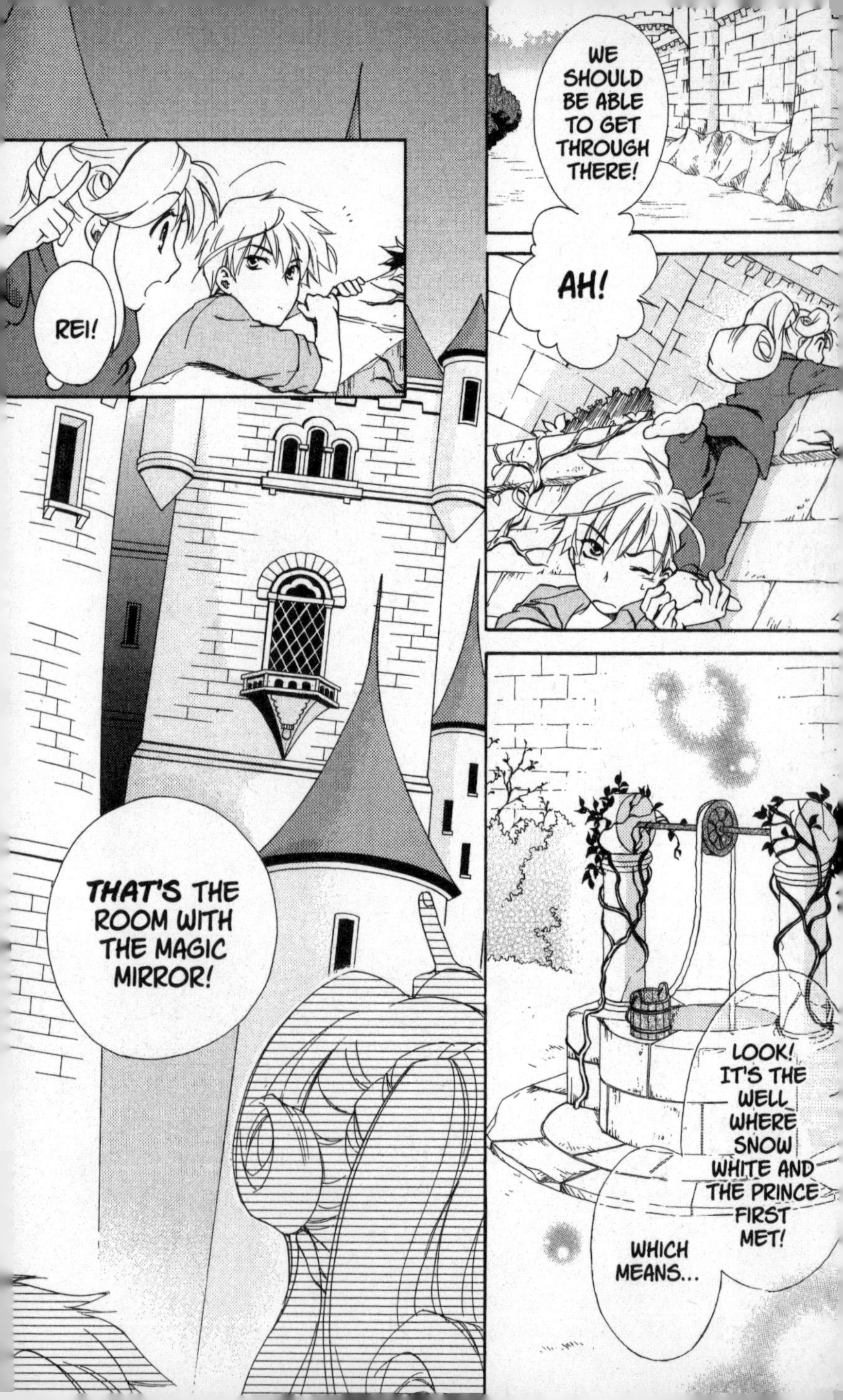
WE SHOULD BE ABLE TO GET THROUGH THERE!
AH!
LOOK! IT'S THE WELL WHERE SNOW WHITE AND THE PRINCE FIRST MET!
WHICH MEANS...
REI!
THAT'S THE ROOM WITH THE MAGIC MIRROR!

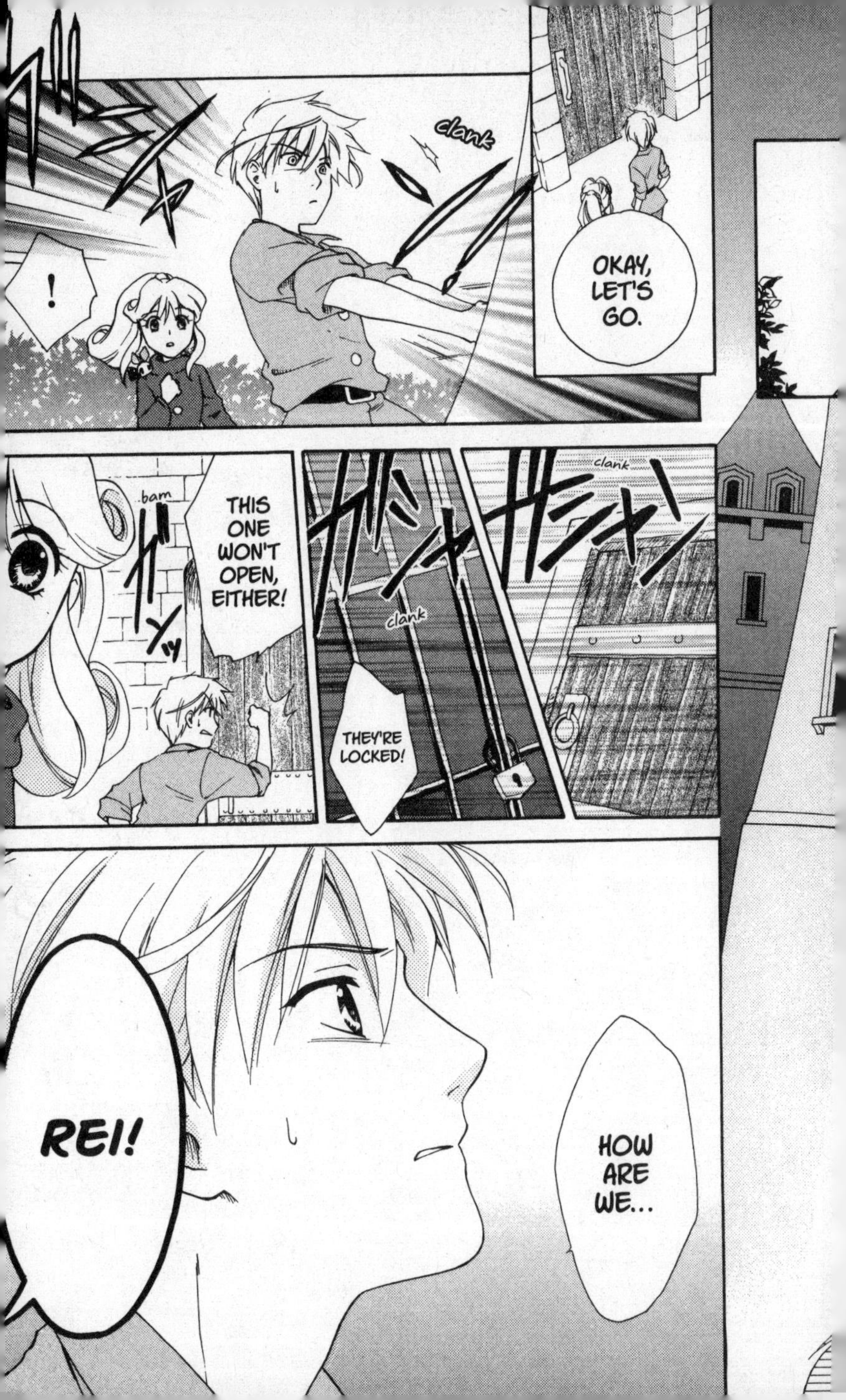
OKAY, LET'S GO.
clank
!
clank
clank
THEY'RE LOCKED!
bam
THIS ONE WON'T OPEN, EITHER!
HOW ARE WE...
REI!

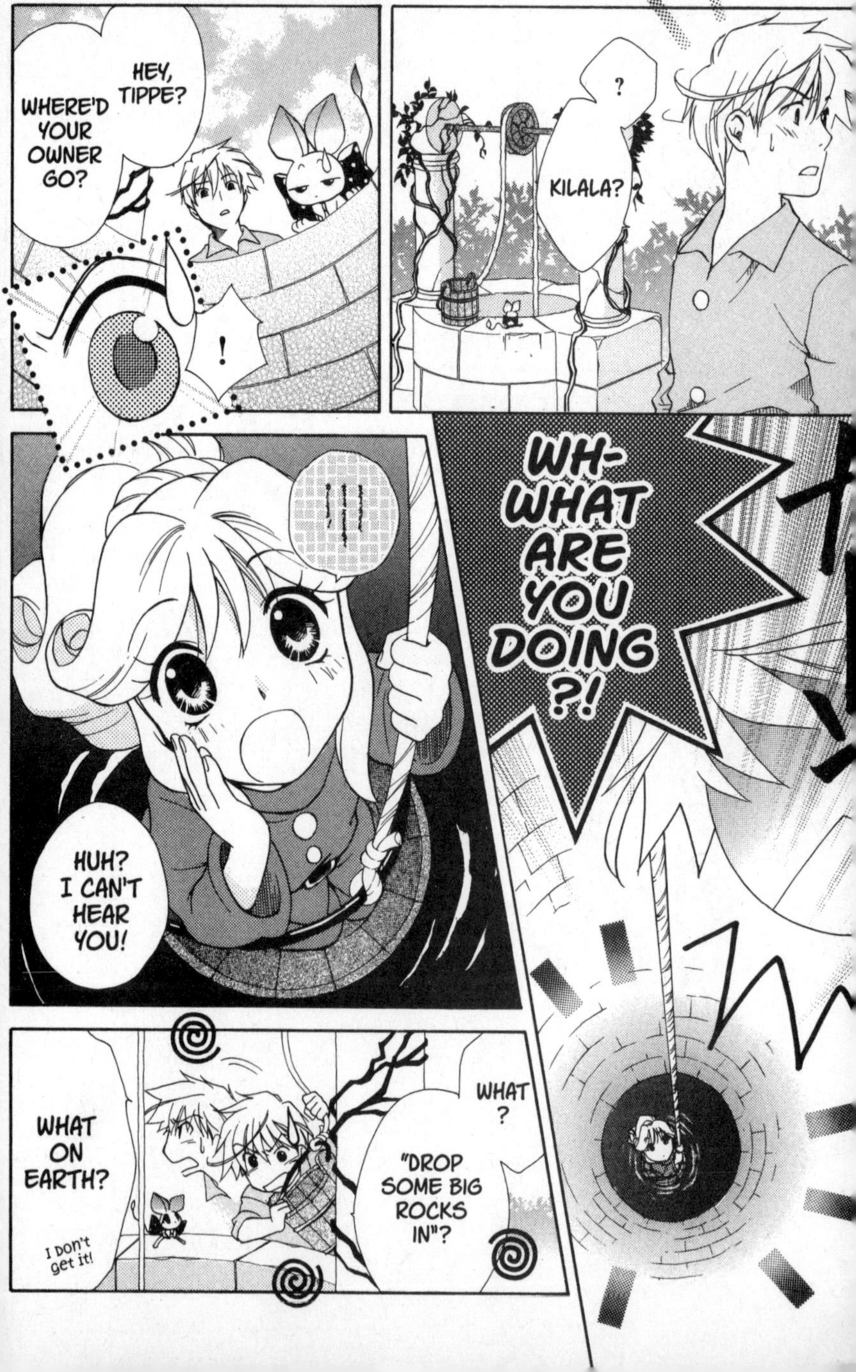
?
KILALA?
HEY, TIPPE?
WHERE'D YOUR OWNER GO?
!
WH-WHAT ARE YOU DOING ?!
HUH? I CAN'T HEAR YOU!
WHAT?
"DROP SOME BIG ROCKS IN"?
WHAT ON EARTH?
I Don't get it!

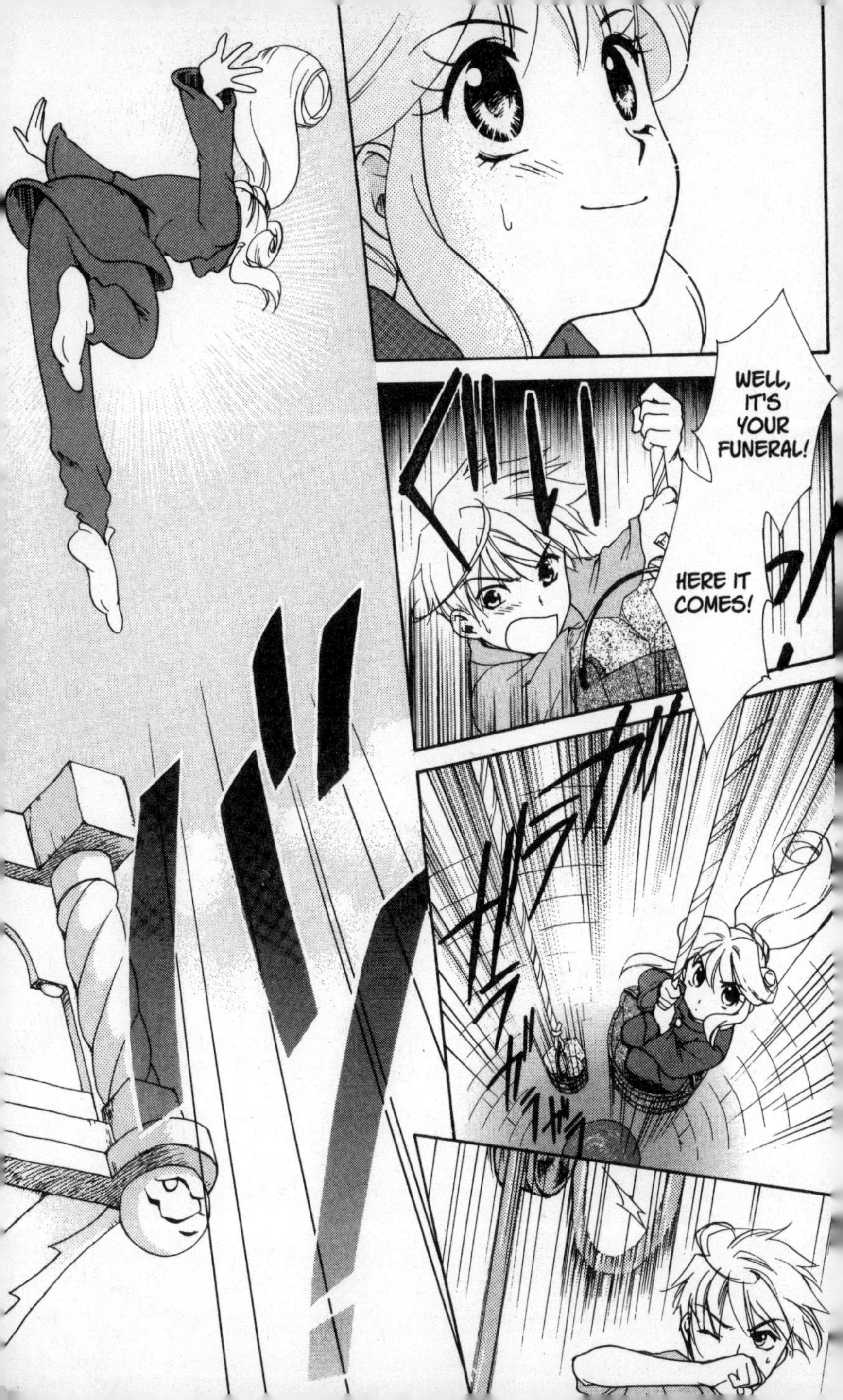
WELL, IT'S YOUR FUNERAL!
HERE IT COMES!

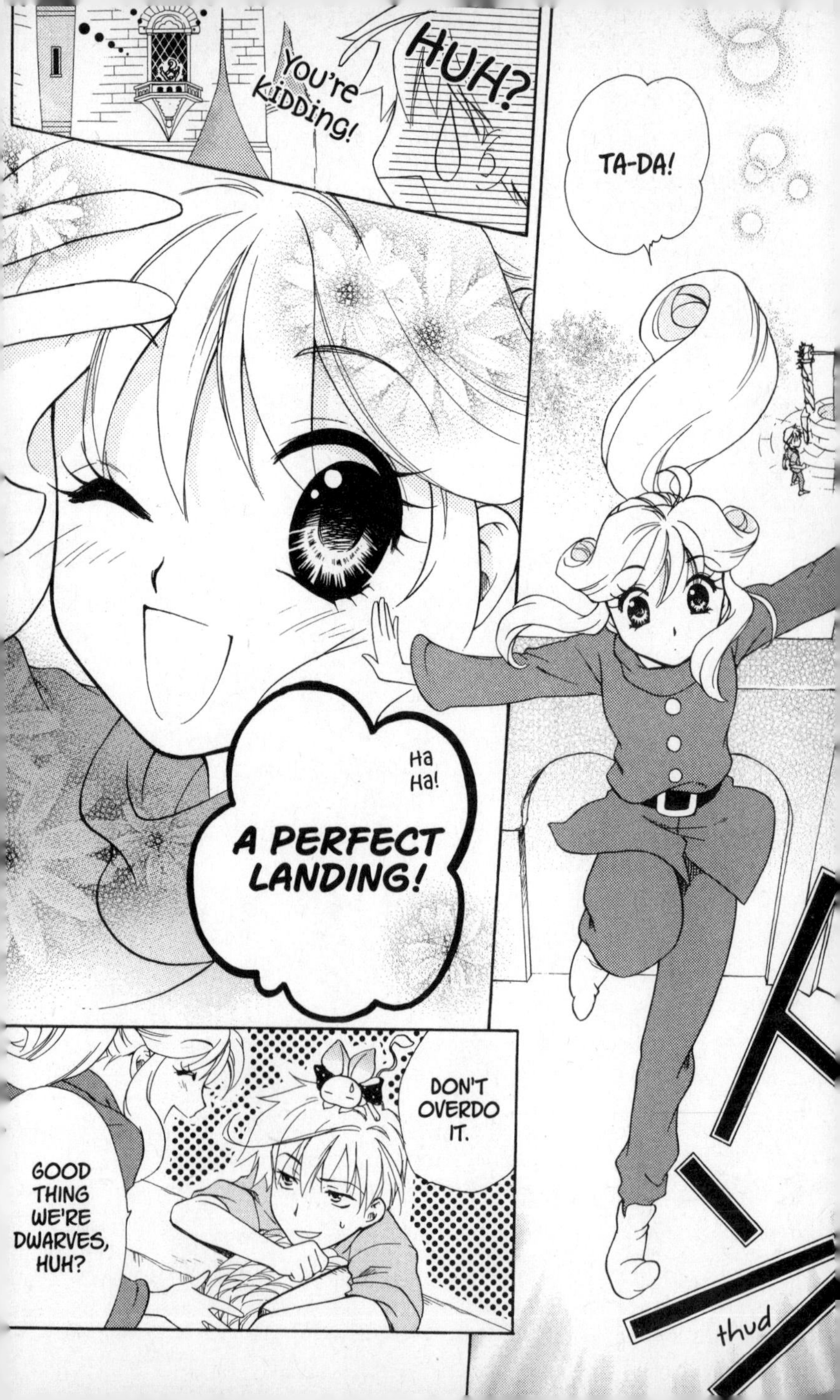
TA-DA!
thud
HUH?
You're kidding!
Ha Ha!
A PERFECT LANDING!
DON'T OVERDO IT.
GOOD THING WE'RE DWARVES, HUH?

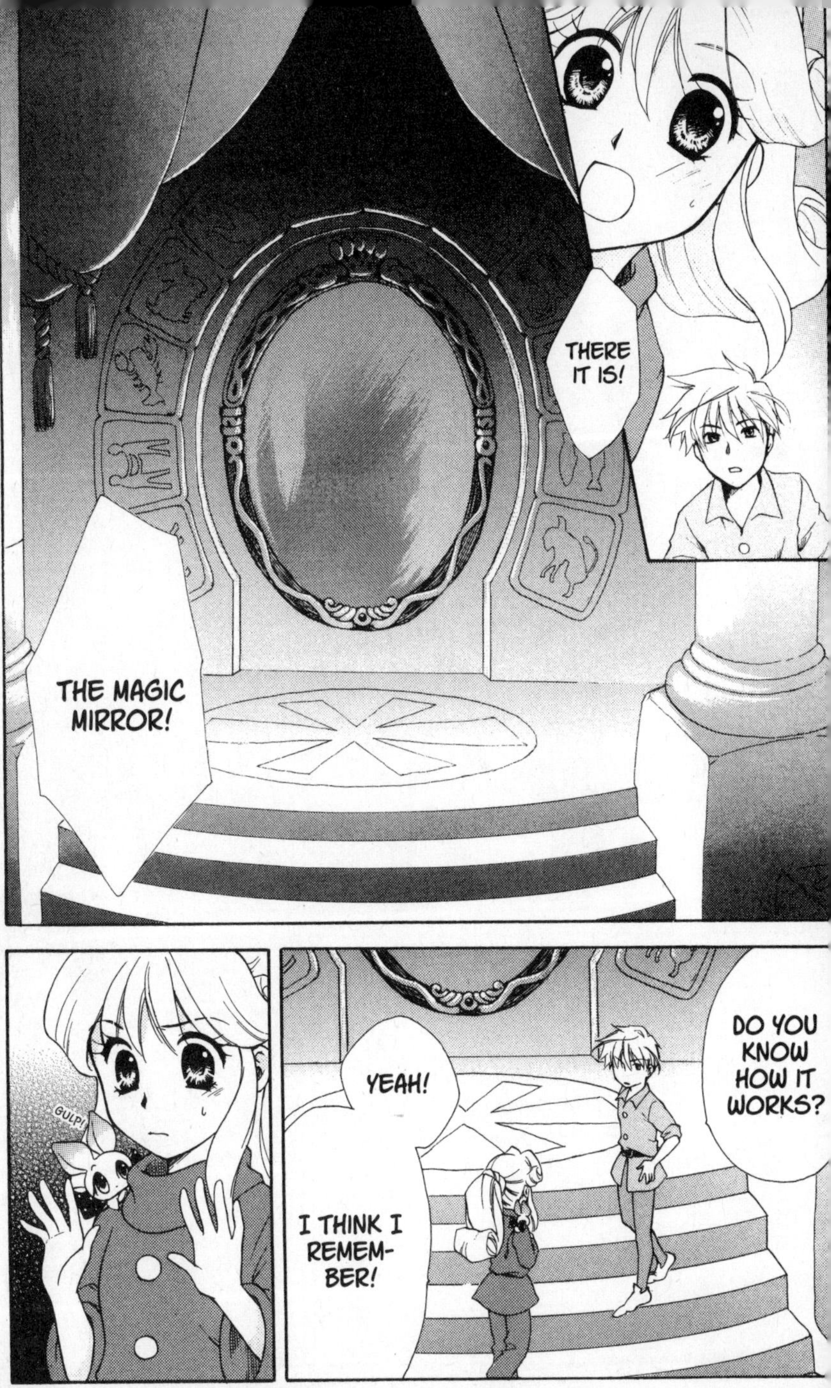
THERE IT IS!
THE MAGIC MIRROR!
DO YOU KNOW HOW IT WORKS?
YEAH!
I THINK I REMEMBER!
GULP!

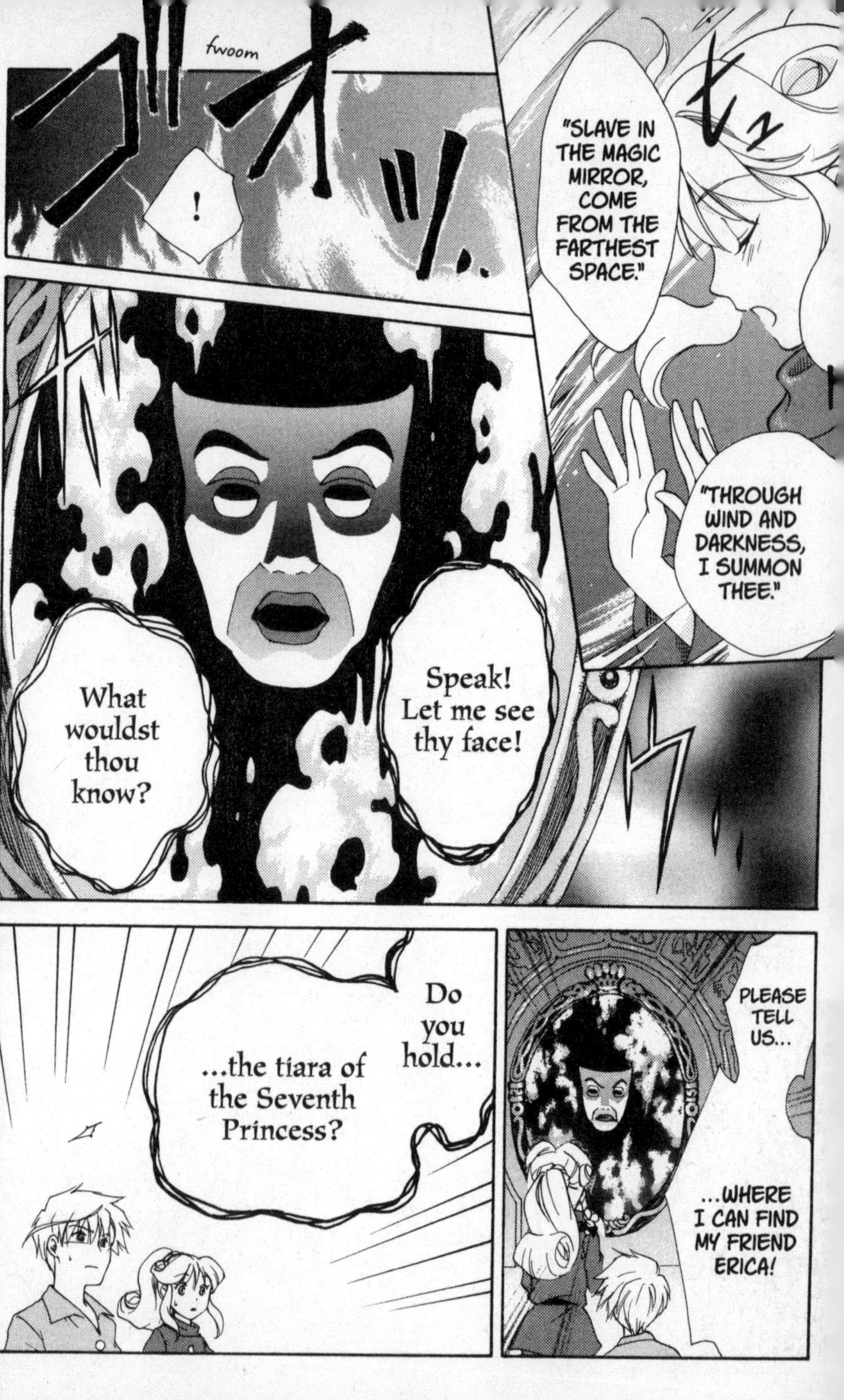
"SLAVE IN THE MAGIC MIRROR, COME FROM THE FARTHEST SPACE."
"THROUGH WIND AND DARKNESS, I SUMMON THEE."
fwoom
!
Speak! Let me see thy face!
What wouldst thou know?
PLEASE TELL US...
...WHERE I CAN FIND MY FRIEND ERICA!
Do you hold...
...the tiara of the Seventh Princess?

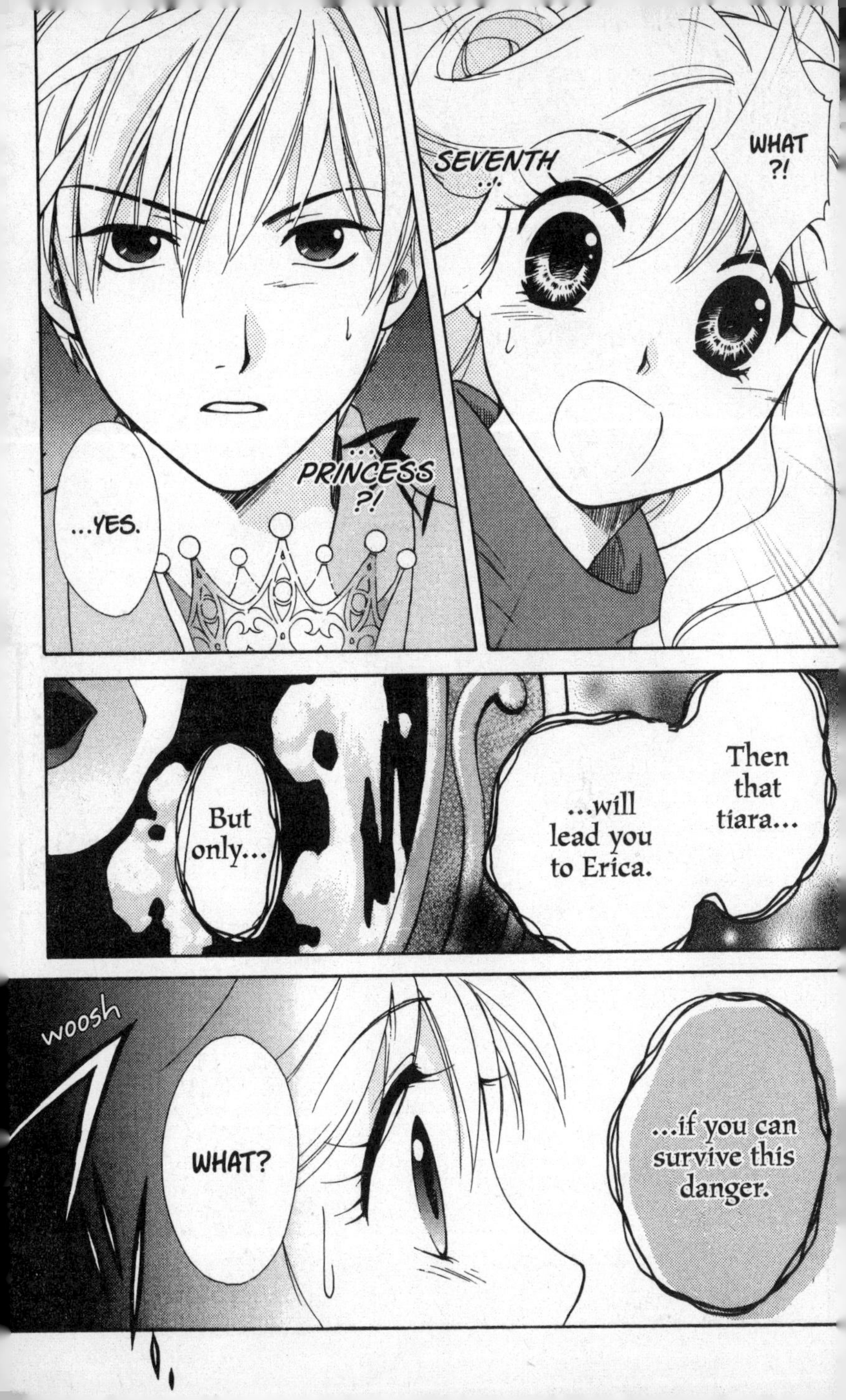
WHAT ?!
SEVENTH ...
...PRINCESS ?!
...YES.
Then that tiara...
...will lead you to Erica.
But only...
...if you can survive this danger.
WHAT?
woosh

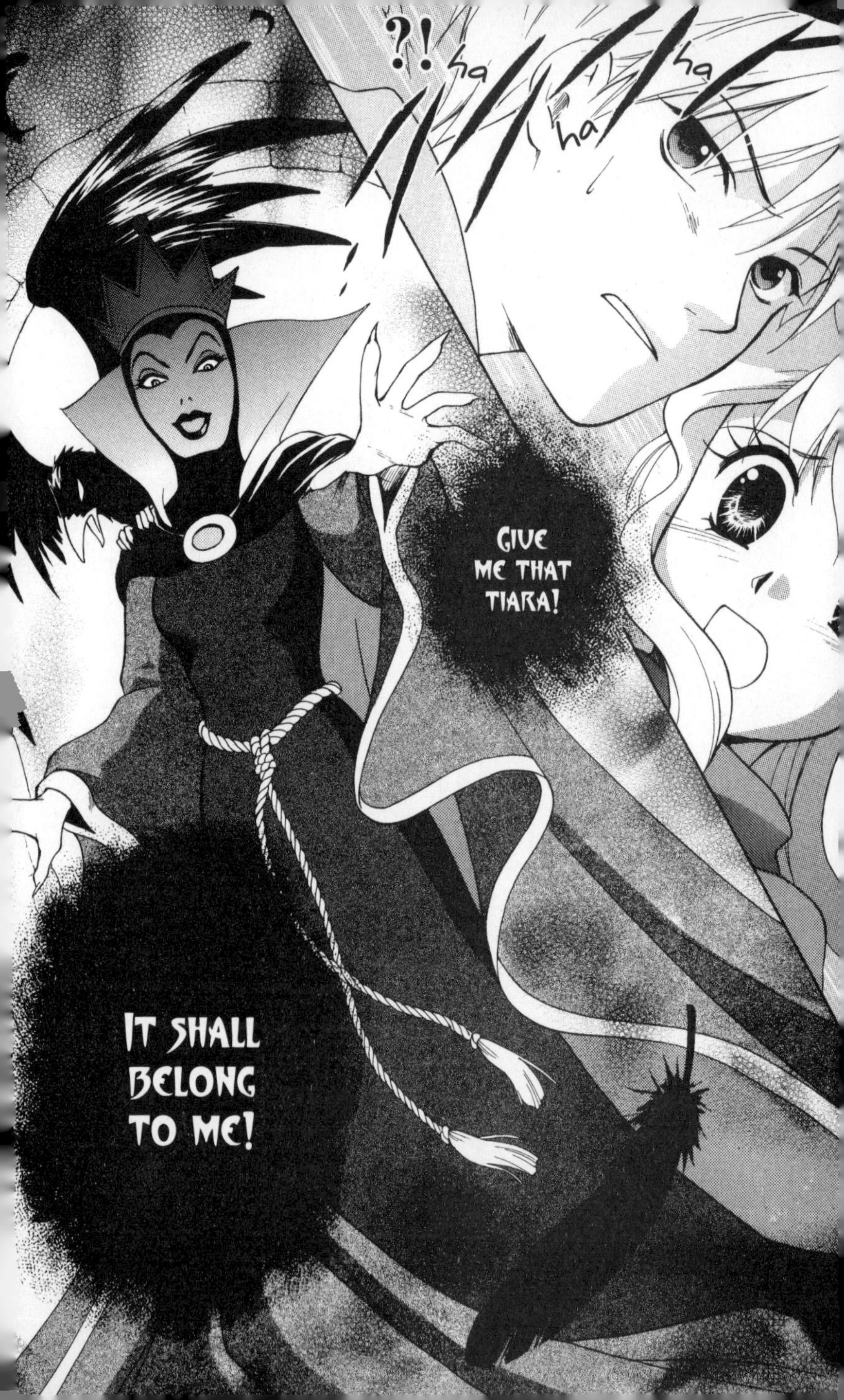
?!
ha
ha
ha
GIVE ME THAT TIARA!
IT SHALL BELONG TO ME!

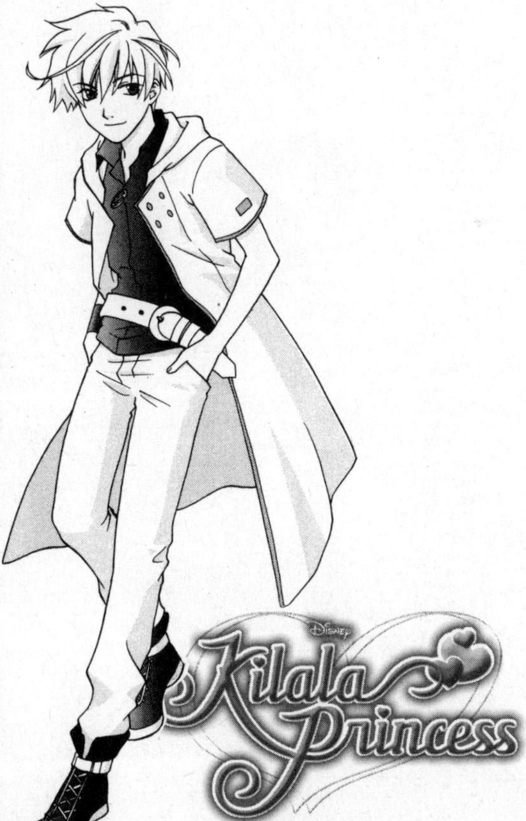
Disney
Kilala Princess

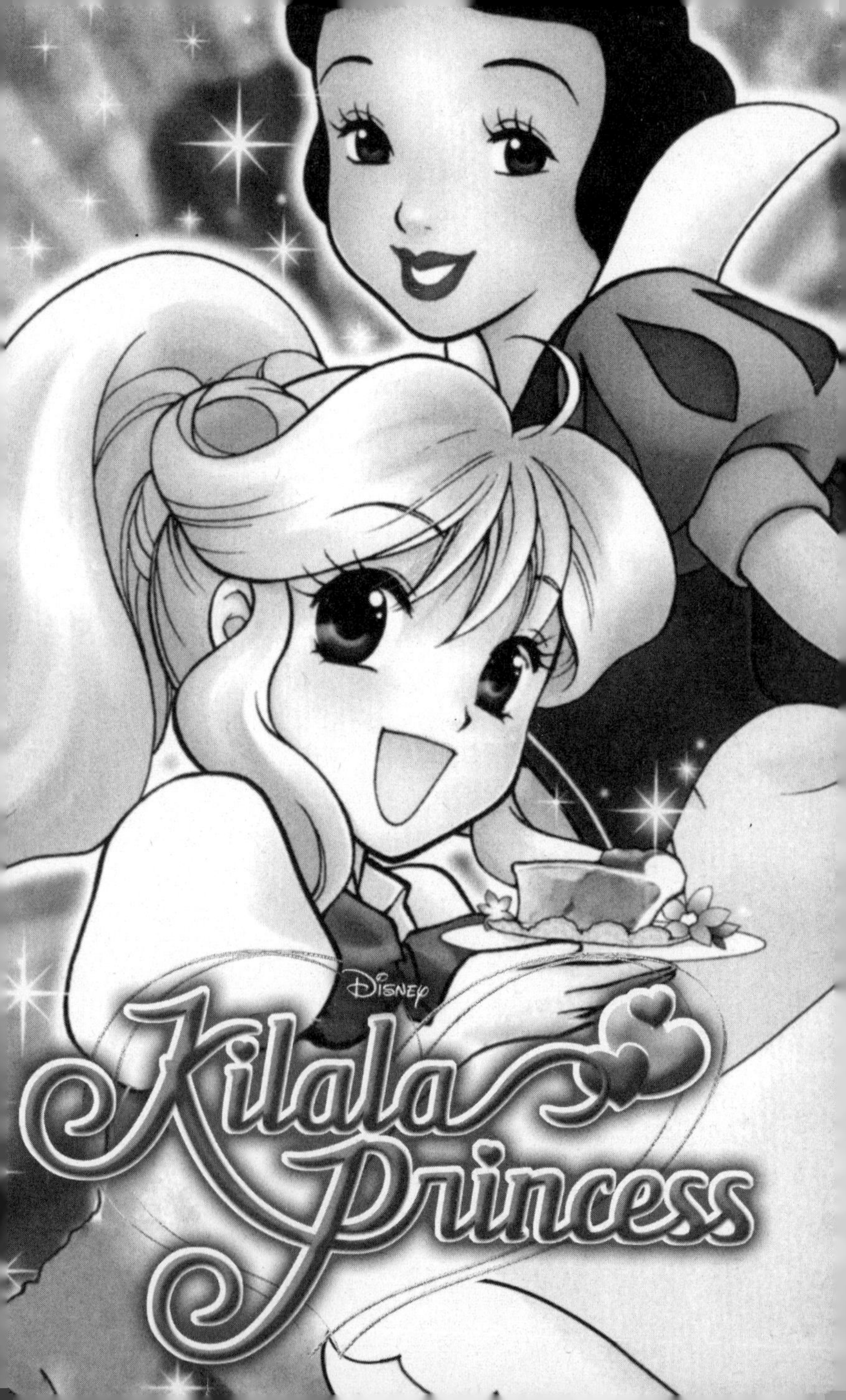
Disney
Kilala Princess

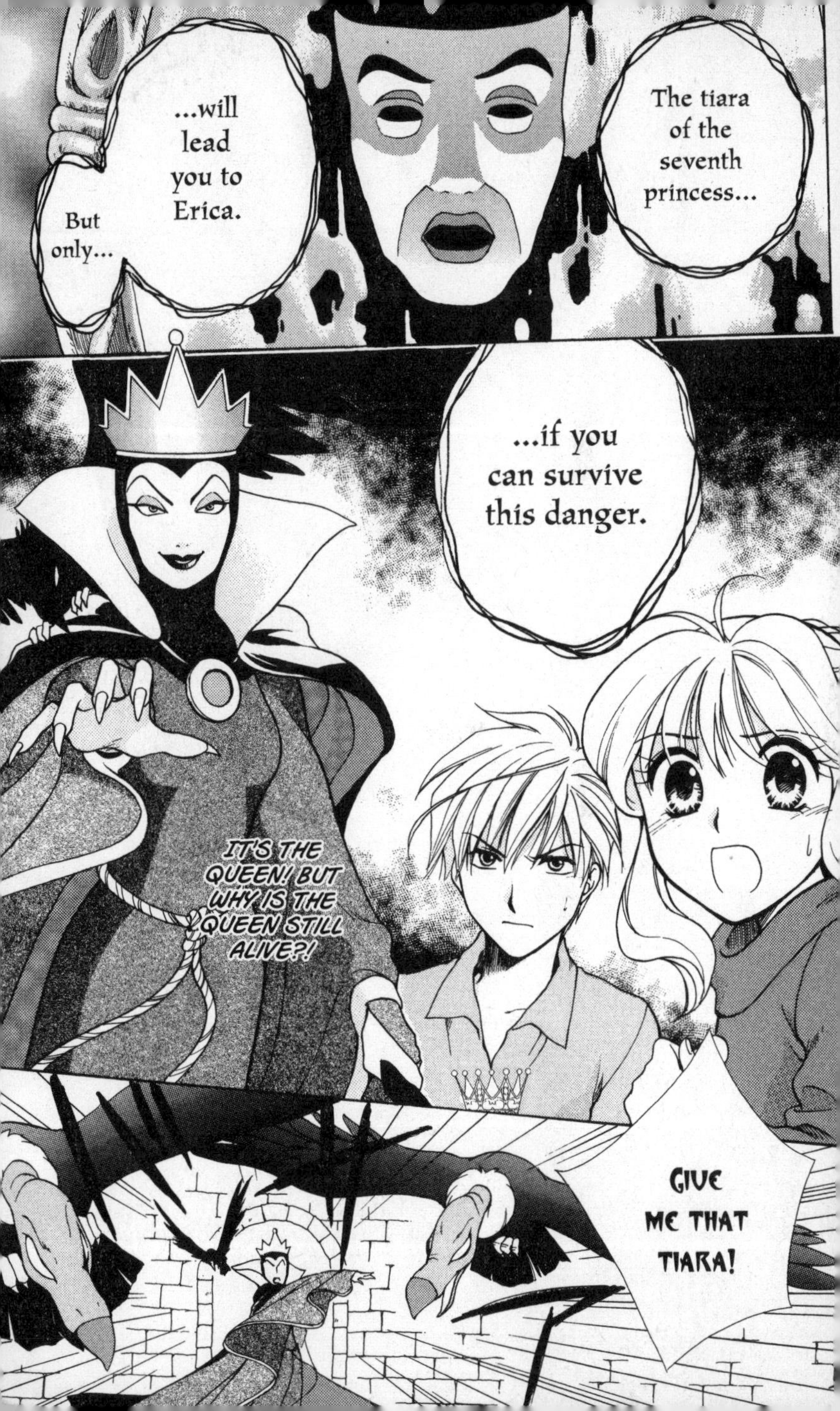
The tiara of the seventh princess...
...will lead you to Erica.
But only...
...if you can survive this danger.
IT'S THE QUEEN! BUT WHY IS THE QUEEN STILL ALIVE?!
GIVE ME THAT TIARA!

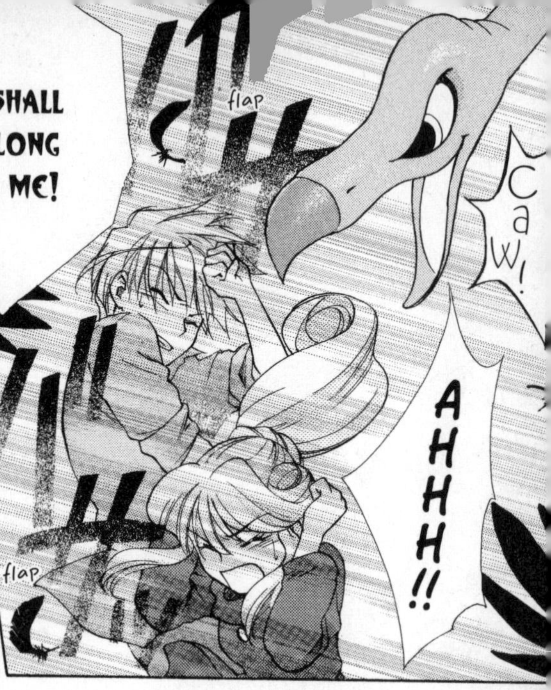
flap
CAW!
AHHHH!!
flap
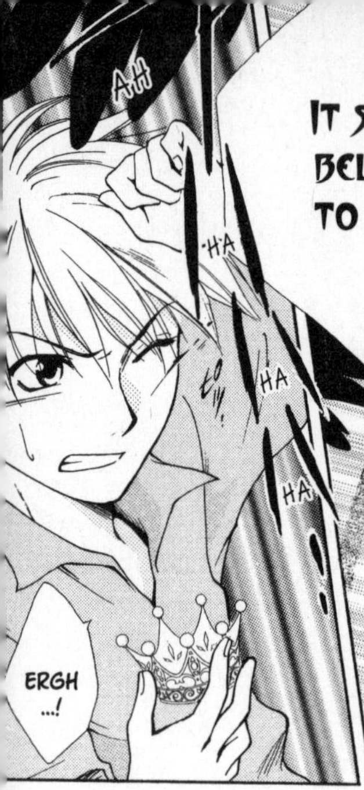
AH
IT SHALL BELONG TO ME!
HA
HA
HA
ERGH ...!
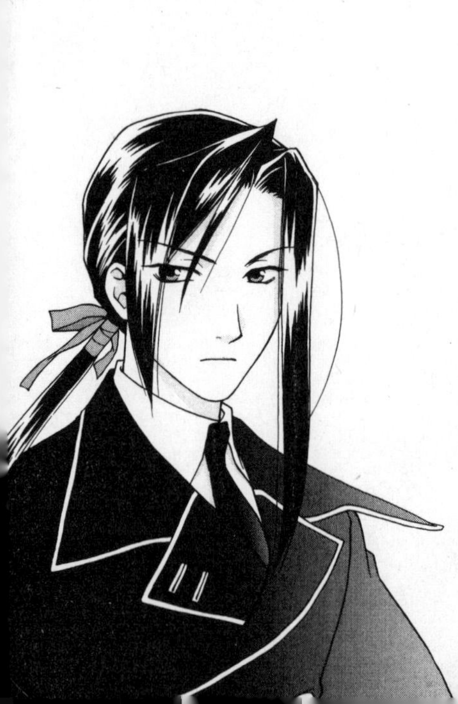
Valdou

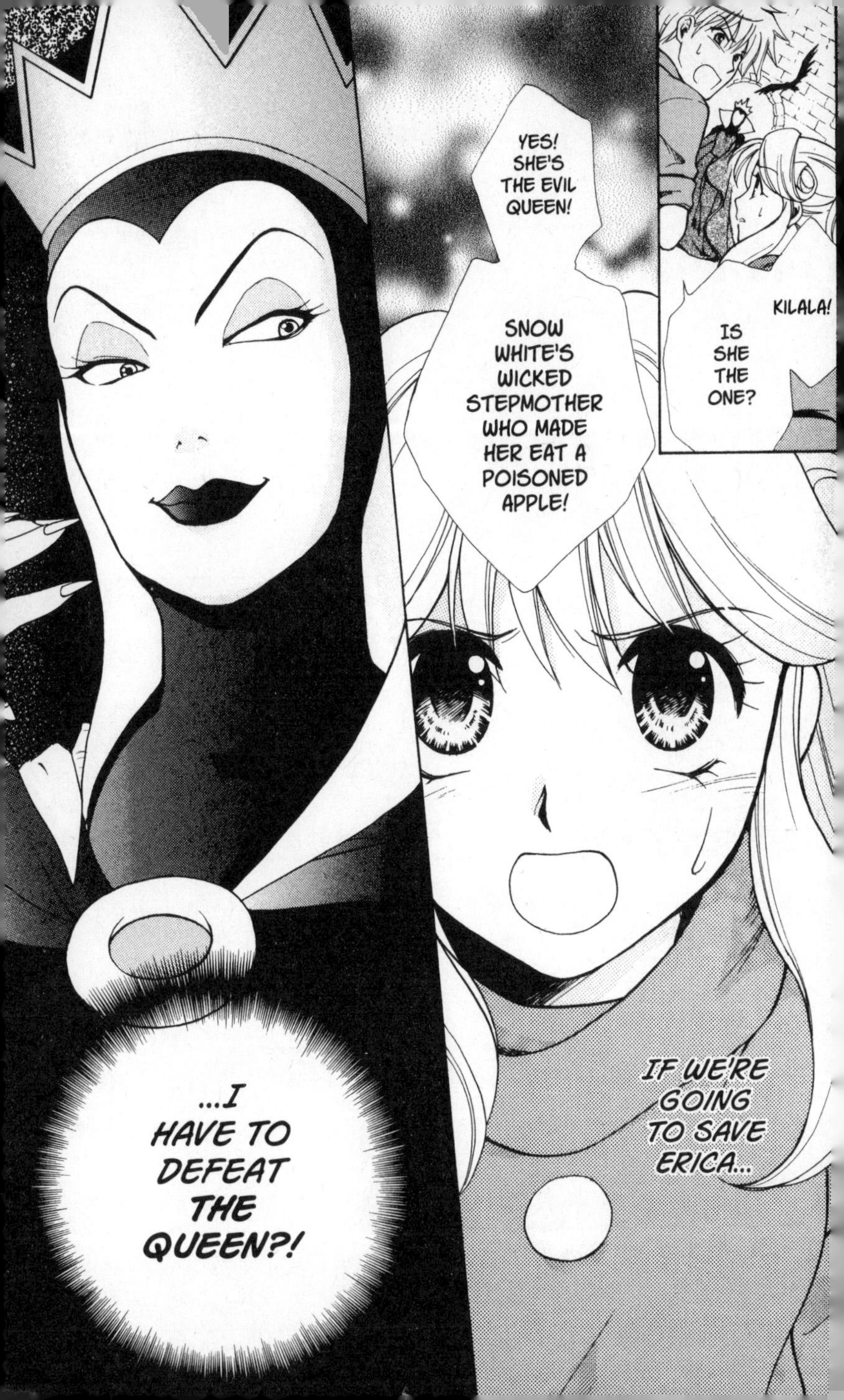
KILALA!
IS SHE THE ONE?
YES! SHE'S THE EVIL QUEEN!
SNOW WHITE'S WICKED STEPMOTHER WHO MADE HER EAT A POISONED APPLE!
IF WE'RE GOING TO SAVE ERICA...
...I HAVE TO DEFEAT THE QUEEN?!

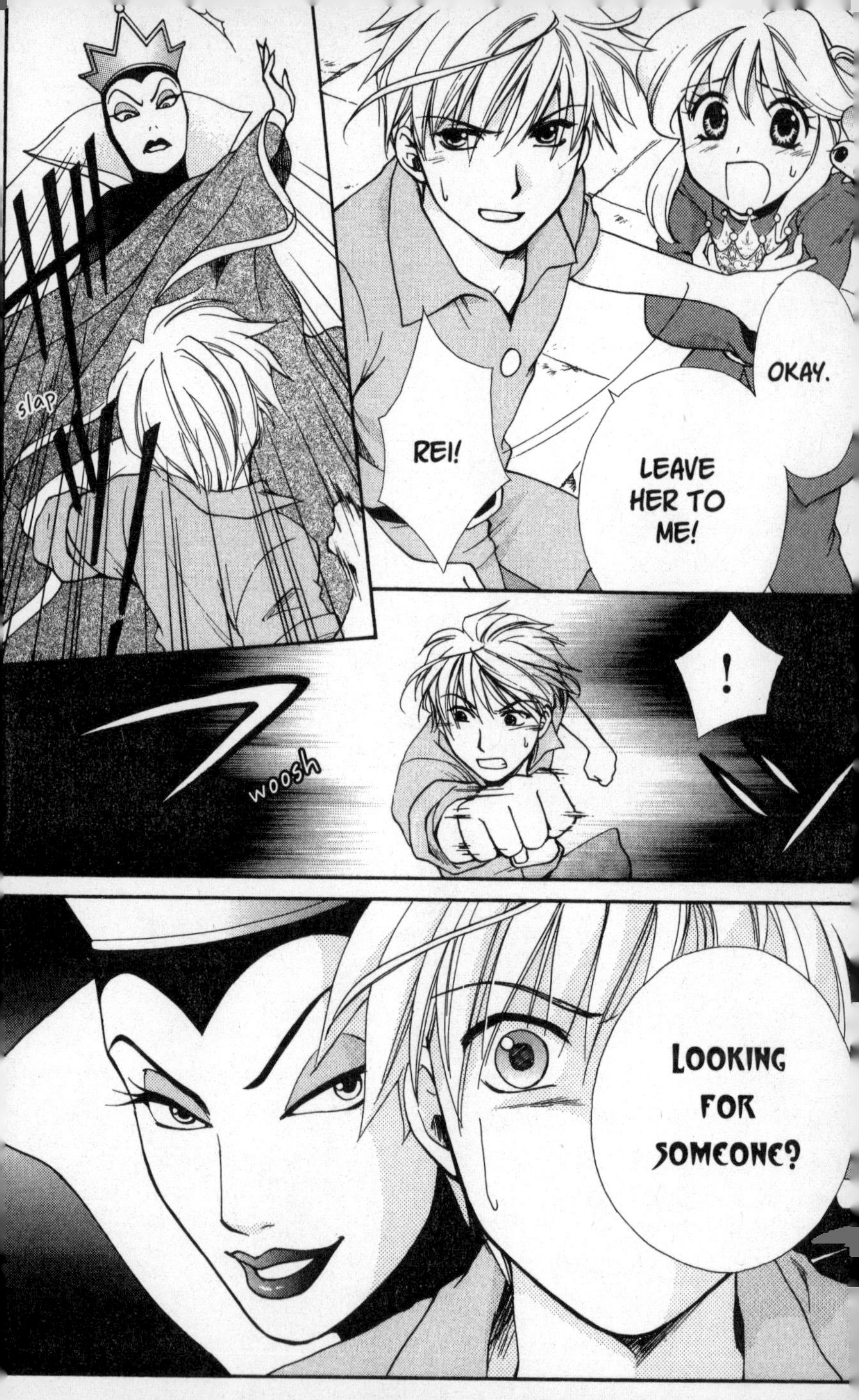
REI!
LEAVE HER TO ME!
OKAY.
slap
!
woosh
LOOKING FOR SOMEONE?

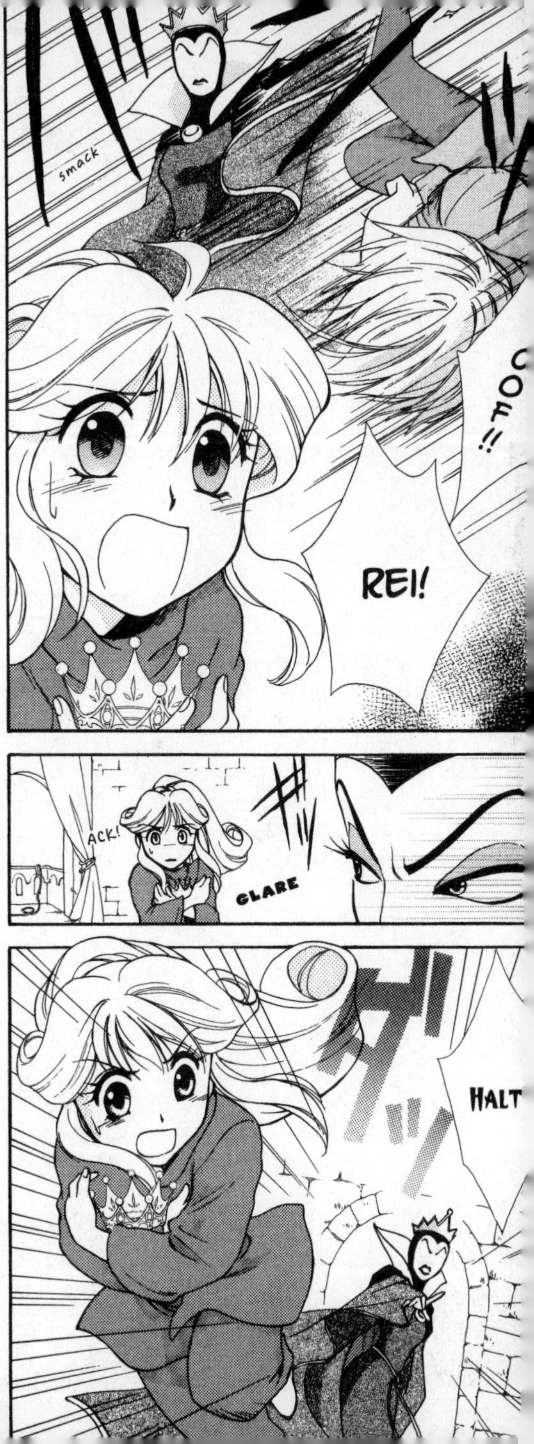
OOF!!
smack
REI!
GLARE
ACK!
HALT

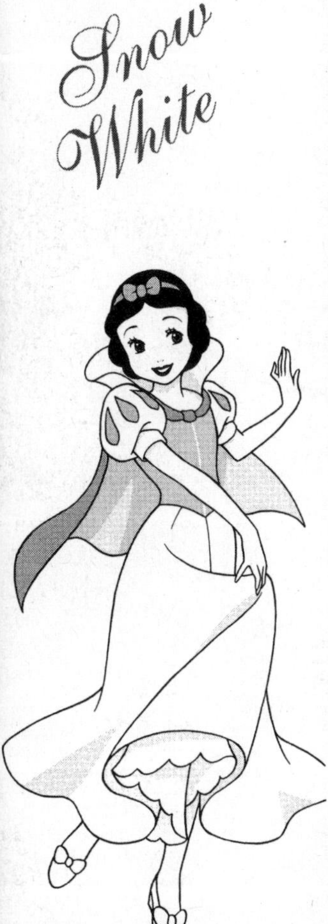
Snow White

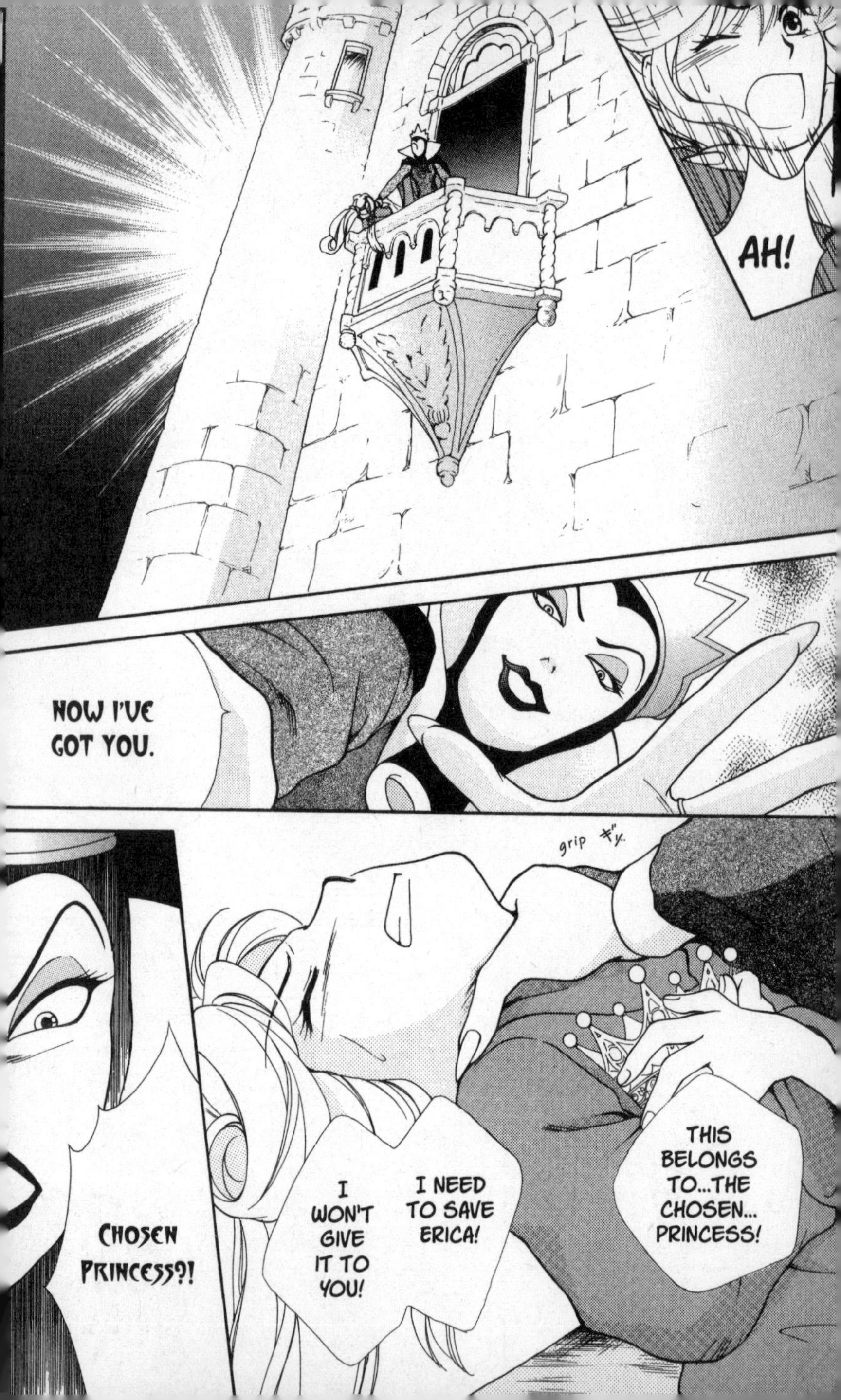
AH!
NOW I'VE GOT YOU.
grip
THIS BELONGS TO...THE CHOSEN... PRINCESS!
I NEED TO SAVE ERICA!
I WON'T GIVE IT TO YOU!
CHOSEN PRINCESS?!

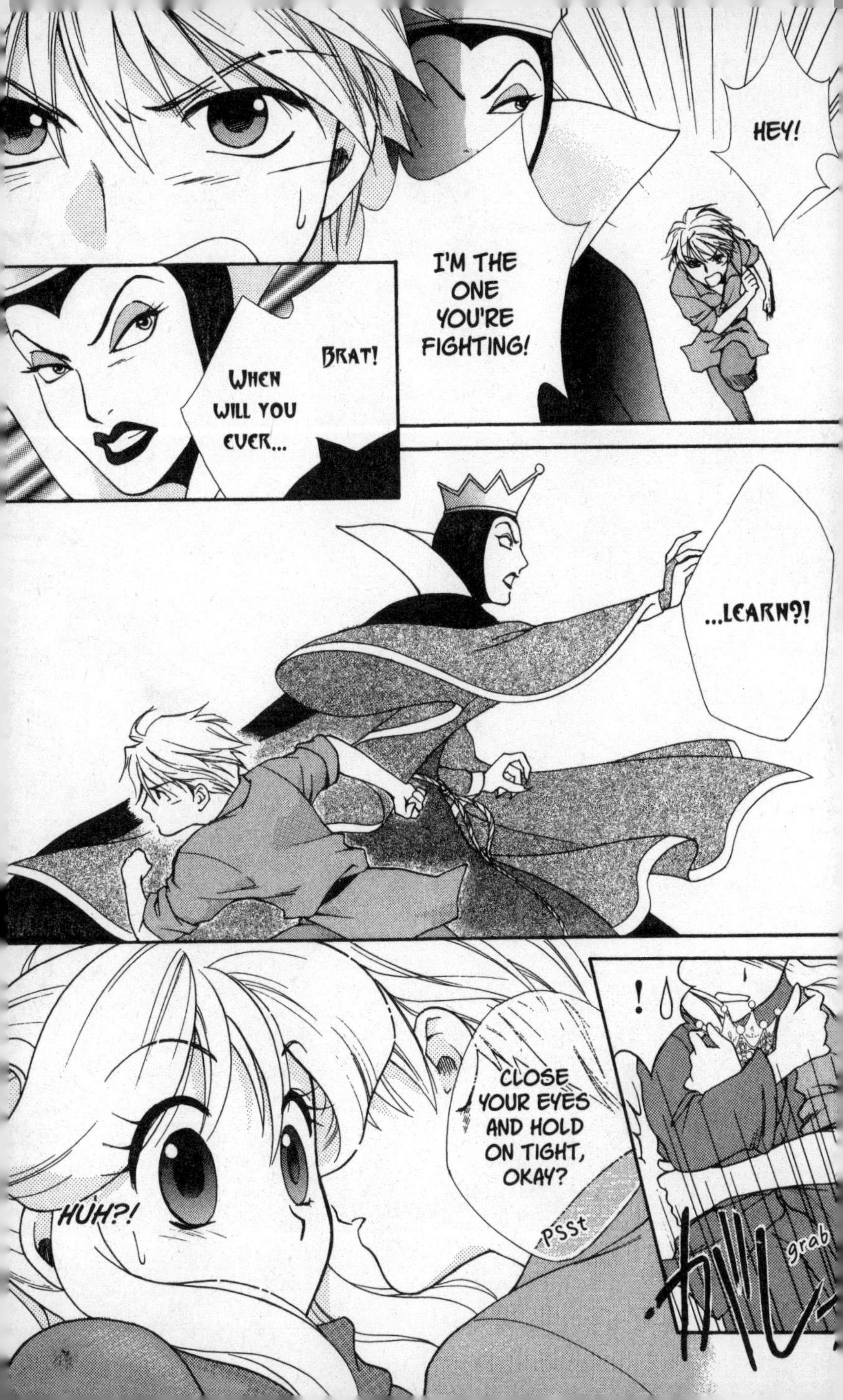
HEY!
I'M THE ONE YOU'RE FIGHTING!
BRAT!
WHEN WILL YOU EVER...
...LEARN?!
!
grab
CLOSE YOUR EYES AND HOLD ON TIGHT, OKAY?
PSSt
HUH?!

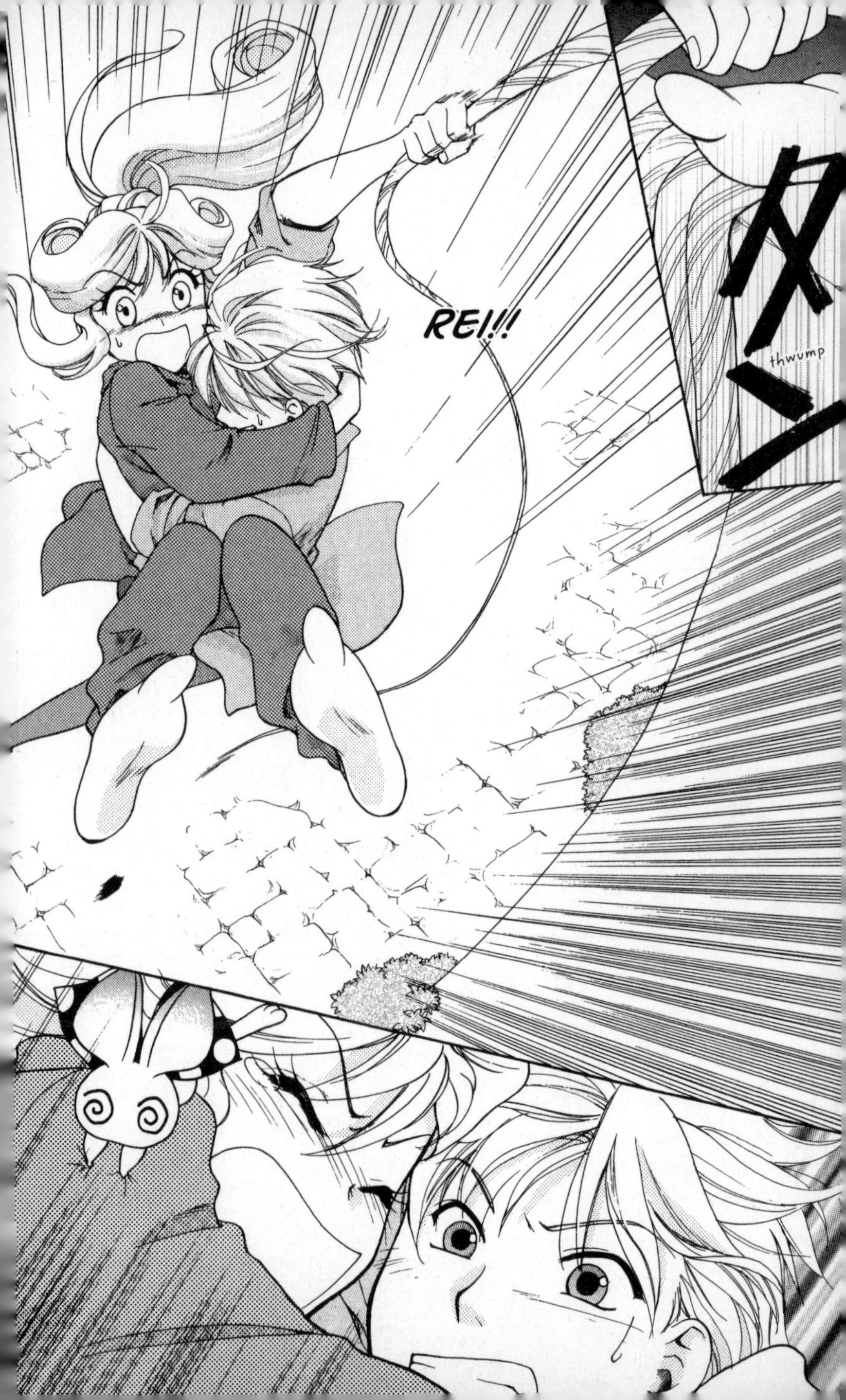
thwump
REI!!

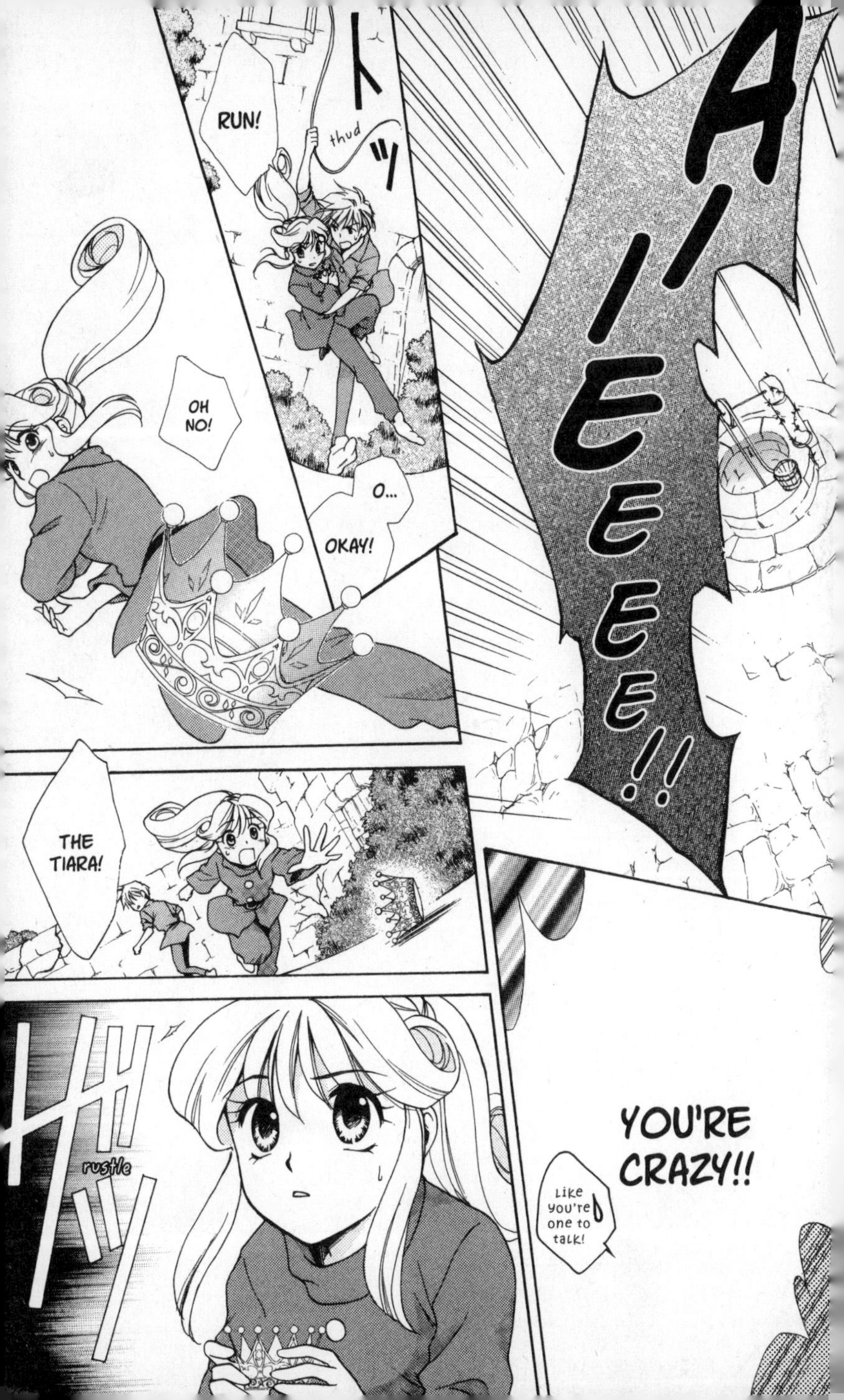
AIIEEEEE!!
RUN!
thud
O...
OKAY!
OH NO!
THE TIARA!
YOU'RE CRAZY!!
Like you're one to talk!
rustle

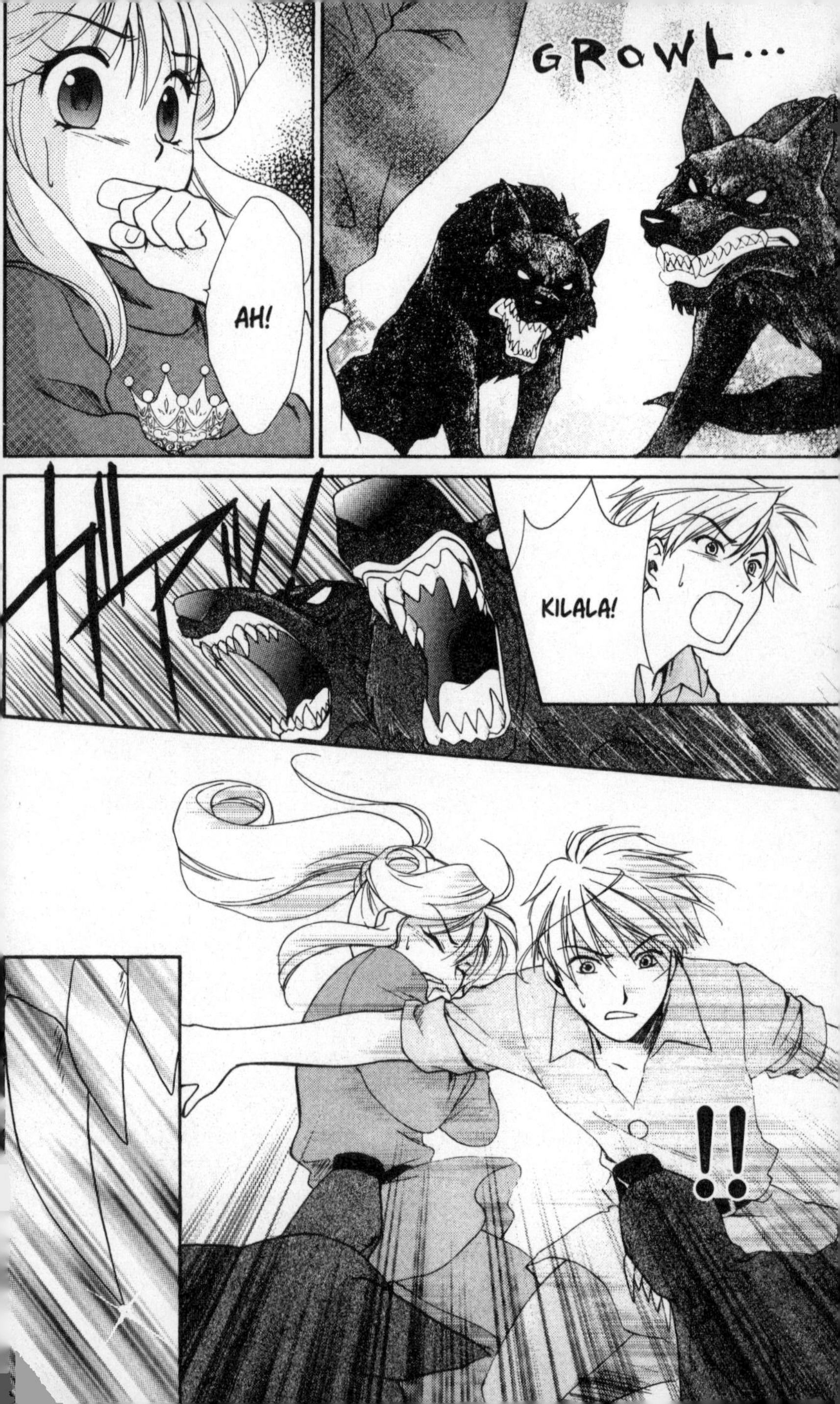
GROWL...
AH!
KILALA!
!!

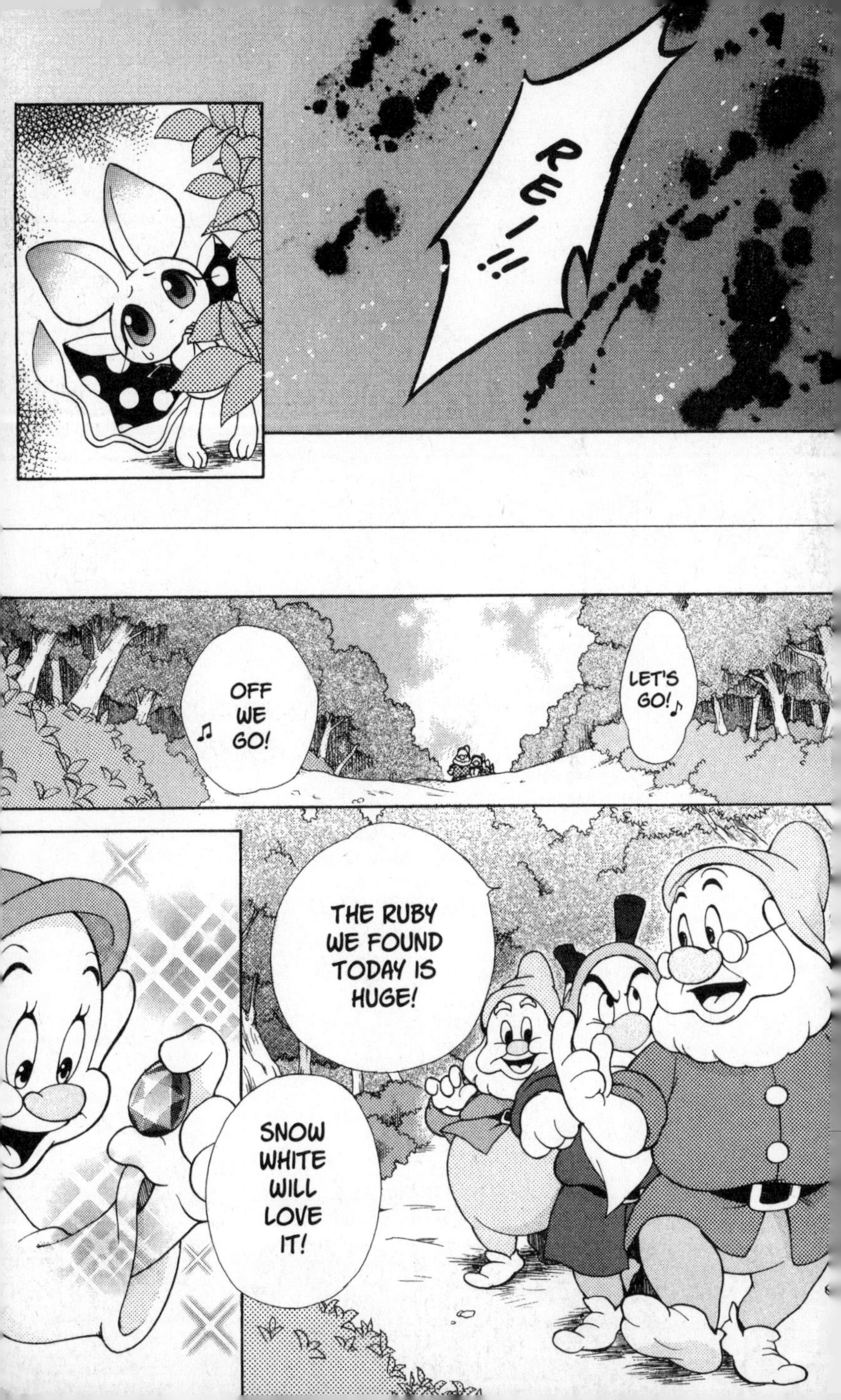
RE-!!
LET'S GO!♪
♫ OFF WE GO!
THE RUBY WE FOUND TODAY IS HUGE!
SNOW WHITE WILL LOVE IT!

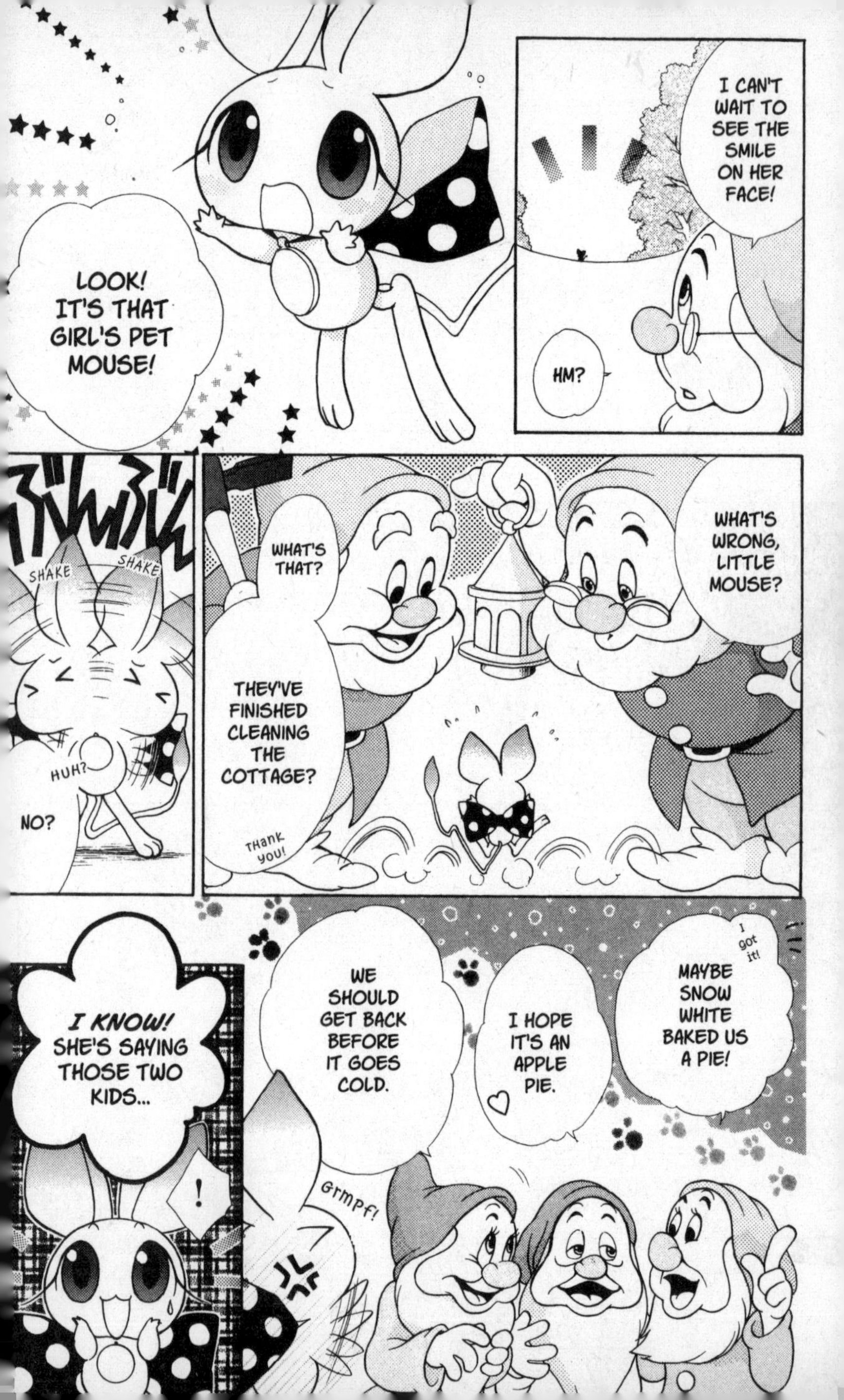
I CAN'T WAIT TO SEE THE SMILE ON HER FACE!
HM?
LOOK! IT'S THAT GIRL'S PET MOUSE!
WHAT'S WRONG, LITTLE MOUSE?
WHAT'S THAT?
THEY'VE FINISHED CLEANING THE COTTAGE?
THANK YOU!
SHAKE
SHAKE
HUH?
NO?
I got it!
MAYBE SNOW WHITE BAKED US A PIE!
I HOPE IT'S AN APPLE PIE.
WE SHOULD GET BACK BEFORE IT GOES COLD.
Grmpf!
I KNOW! SHE'S SAYING THOSE TWO KIDS...
!

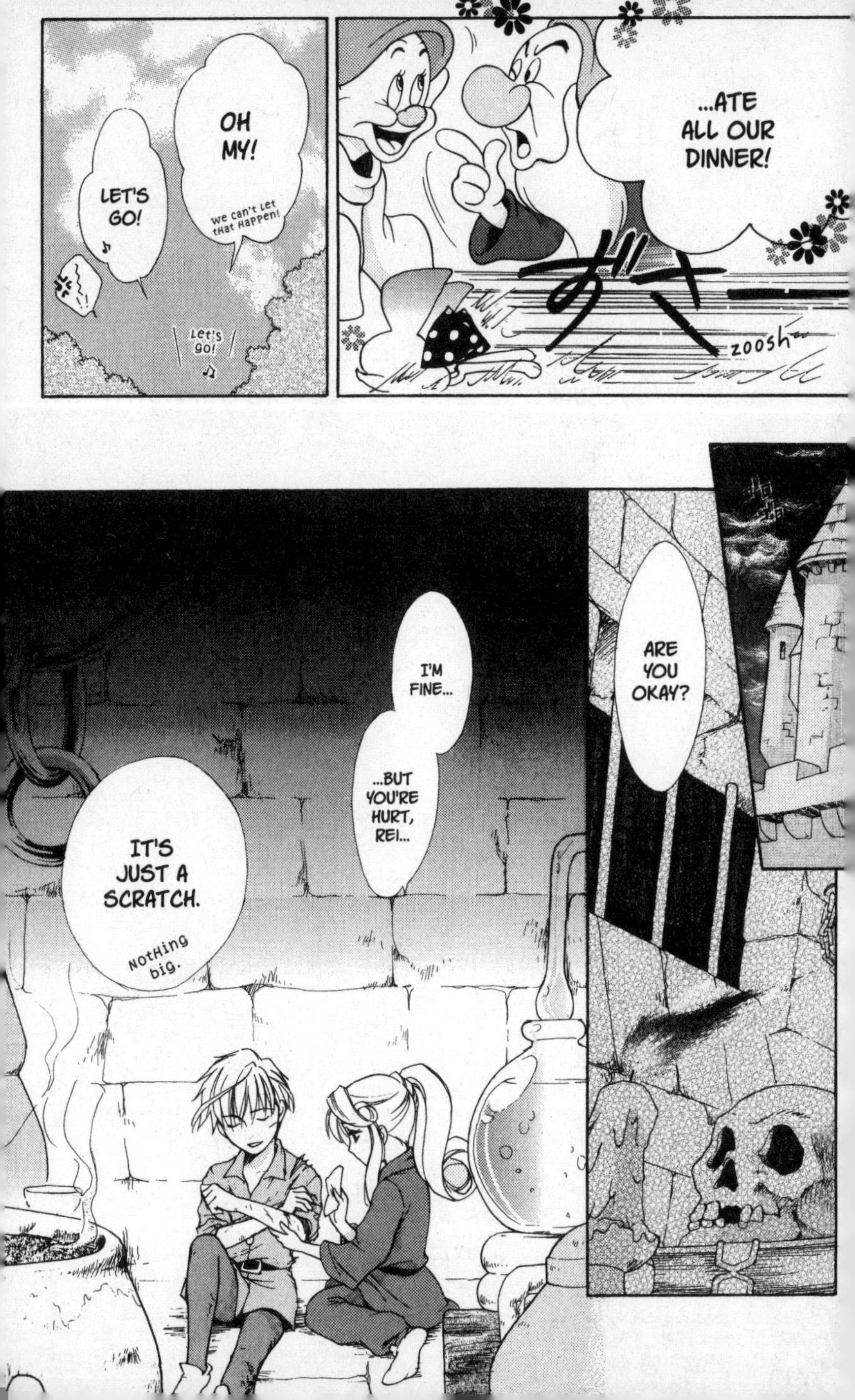
...ATE ALL OUR DINNER!
zoosh
OH MY!
We can't let that happen!
LET'S GO!
Let's go!
ARE YOU OKAY?
I'M FINE...
...BUT YOU'RE HURT, REI...
IT'S JUST A SCRATCH.
Nothing big.

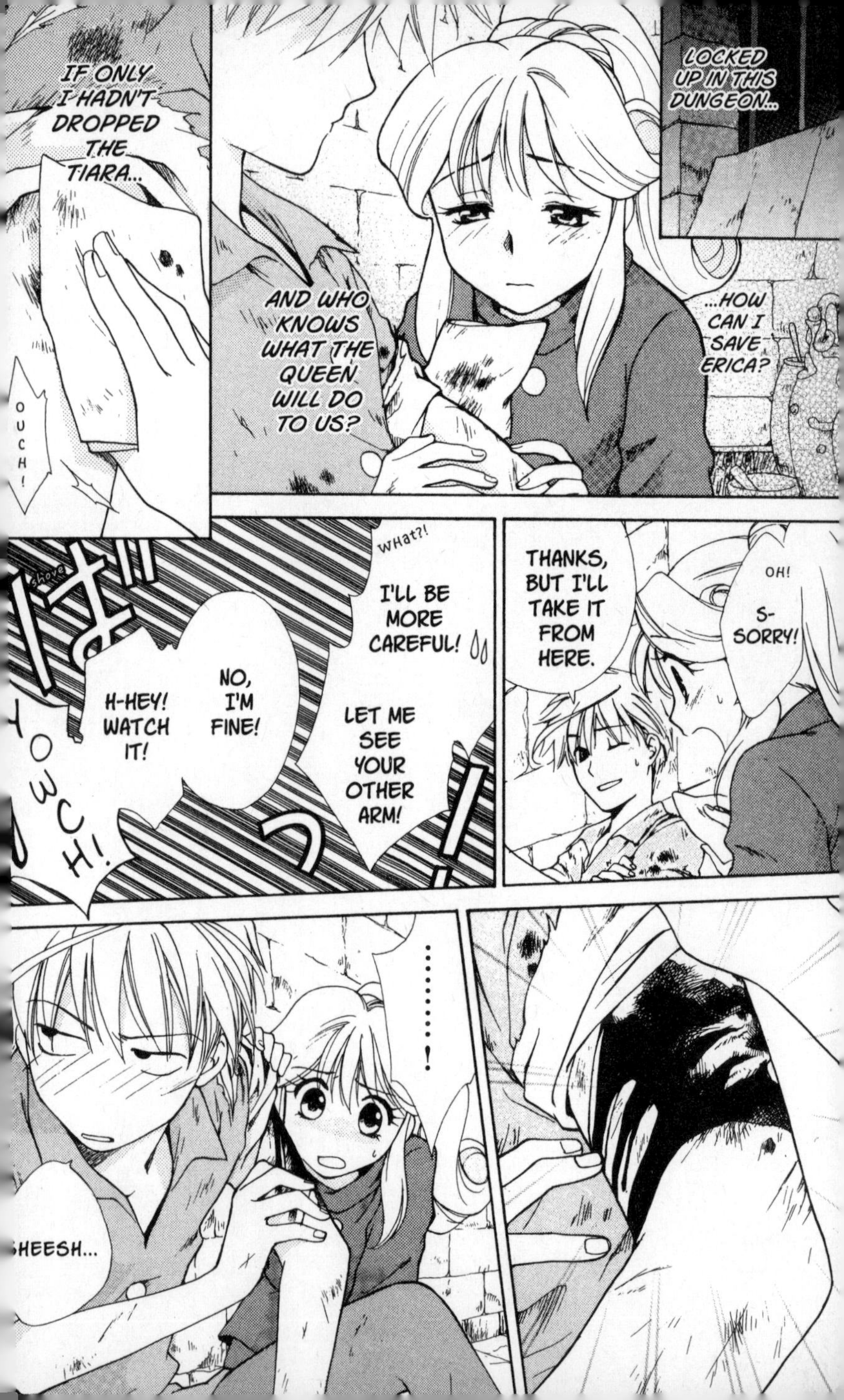
LOCKED UP IN THIS DUNGEON...
...HOW CAN I SAVE ERICA?
AND WHO KNOWS WHAT THE QUEEN WILL DO TO US?
IF ONLY I HADN'T DROPPED THE TIARA...
OUCH!
OH! S-SORRY!
THANKS, BUT I'LL TAKE IT FROM HERE.
WHAT?!
I'LL BE MORE CAREFUL!
LET ME SEE YOUR OTHER ARM!
NO, I'M FINE!
H-HEY! WATCH IT!
OWCH!
shove
......!
SHEESH...

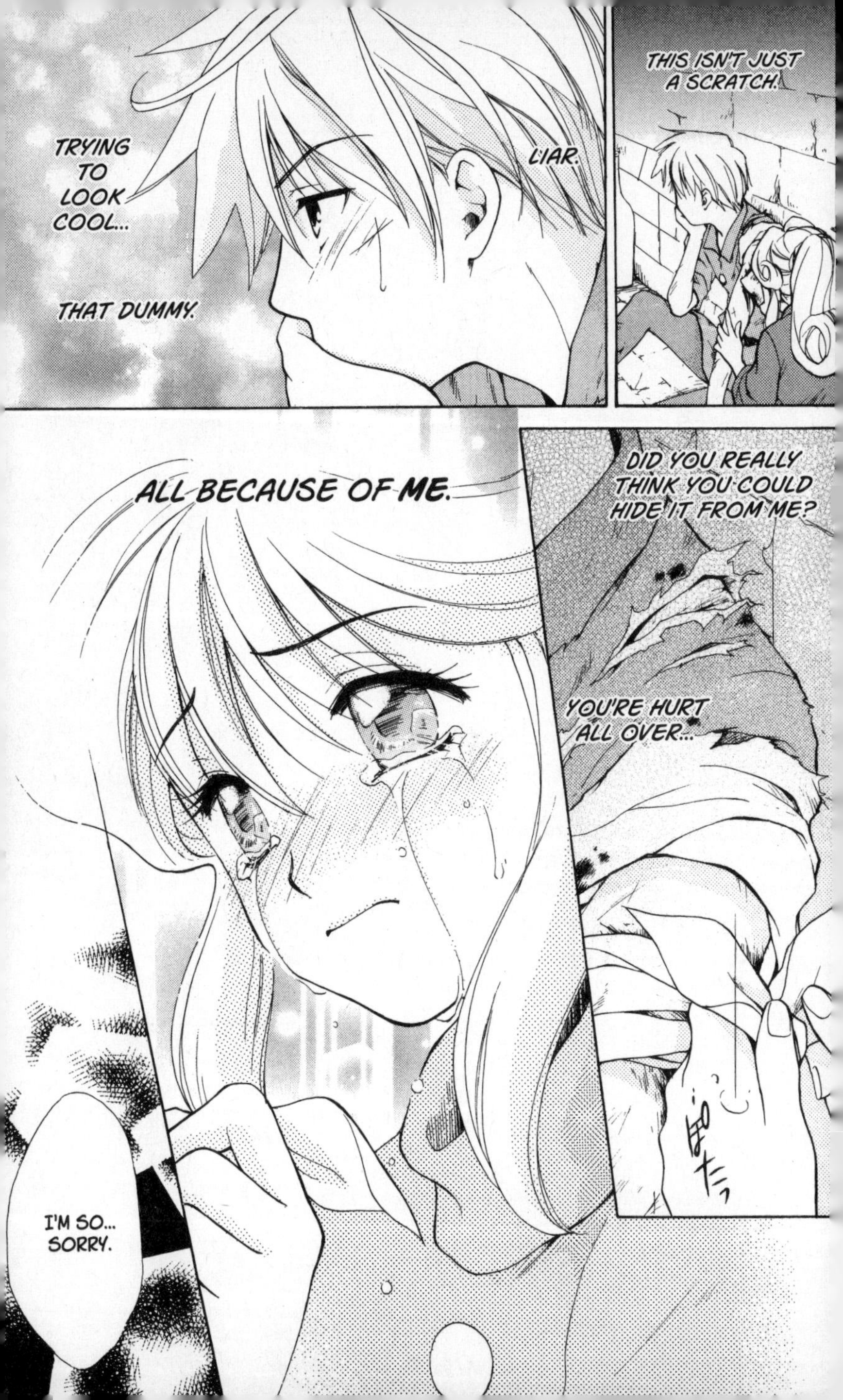
THIS ISN'T JUST A SCRATCH.
LIAR.
TRYING TO LOOK COOL...
THAT DUMMY.
DID YOU REALLY THINK YOU COULD HIDE IT FROM ME?
YOU'RE HURT ALL OVER...
ぽたっ
ALL BECAUSE OF ME.
I'M SO... SORRY.

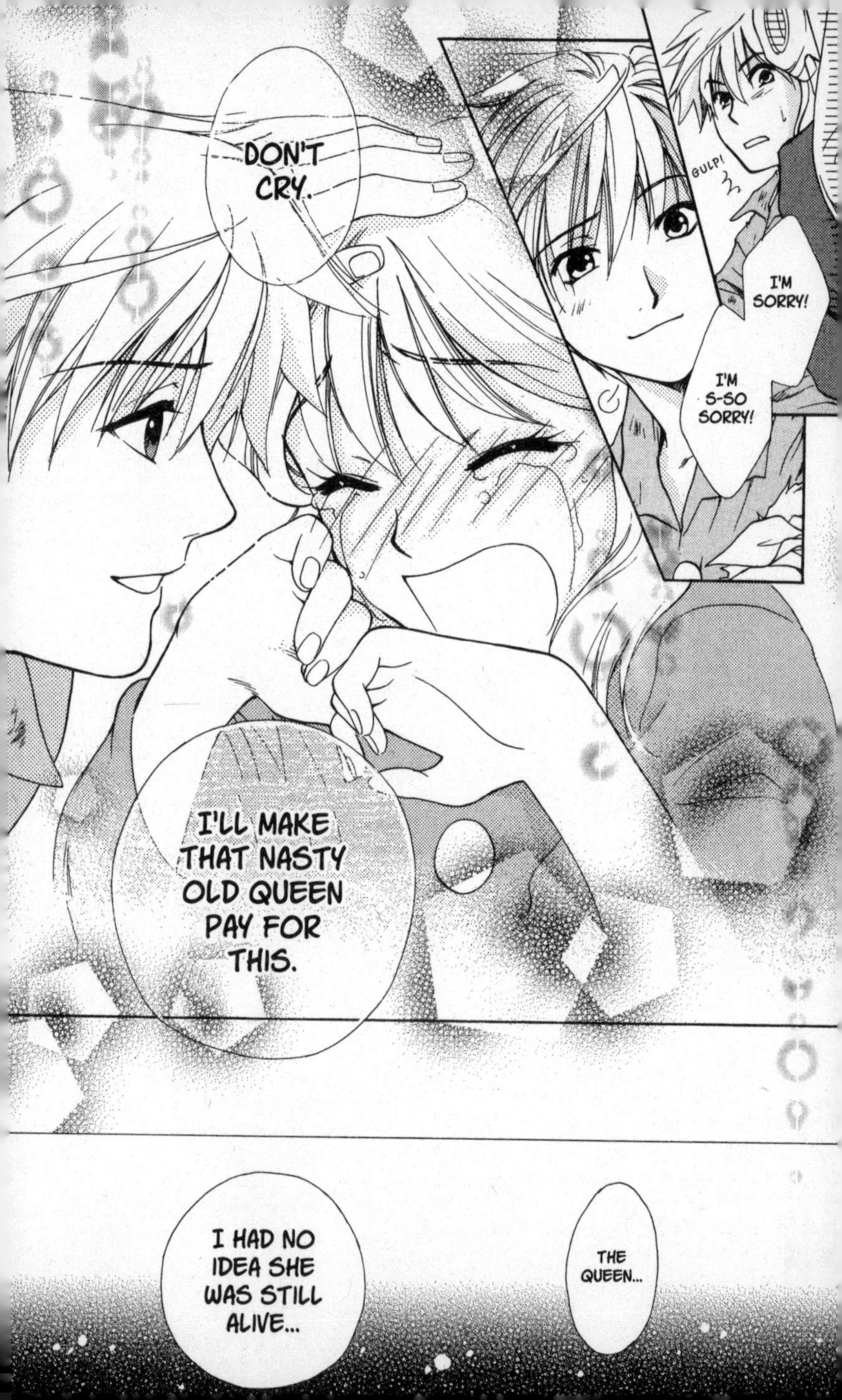
GULP!
I'M SORRY!
I'M S-SO SORRY!
DON'T CRY.
I'LL MAKE THAT NASTY OLD QUEEN PAY FOR THIS.
THE QUEEN...
I HAD NO IDEA SHE WAS STILL ALIVE...

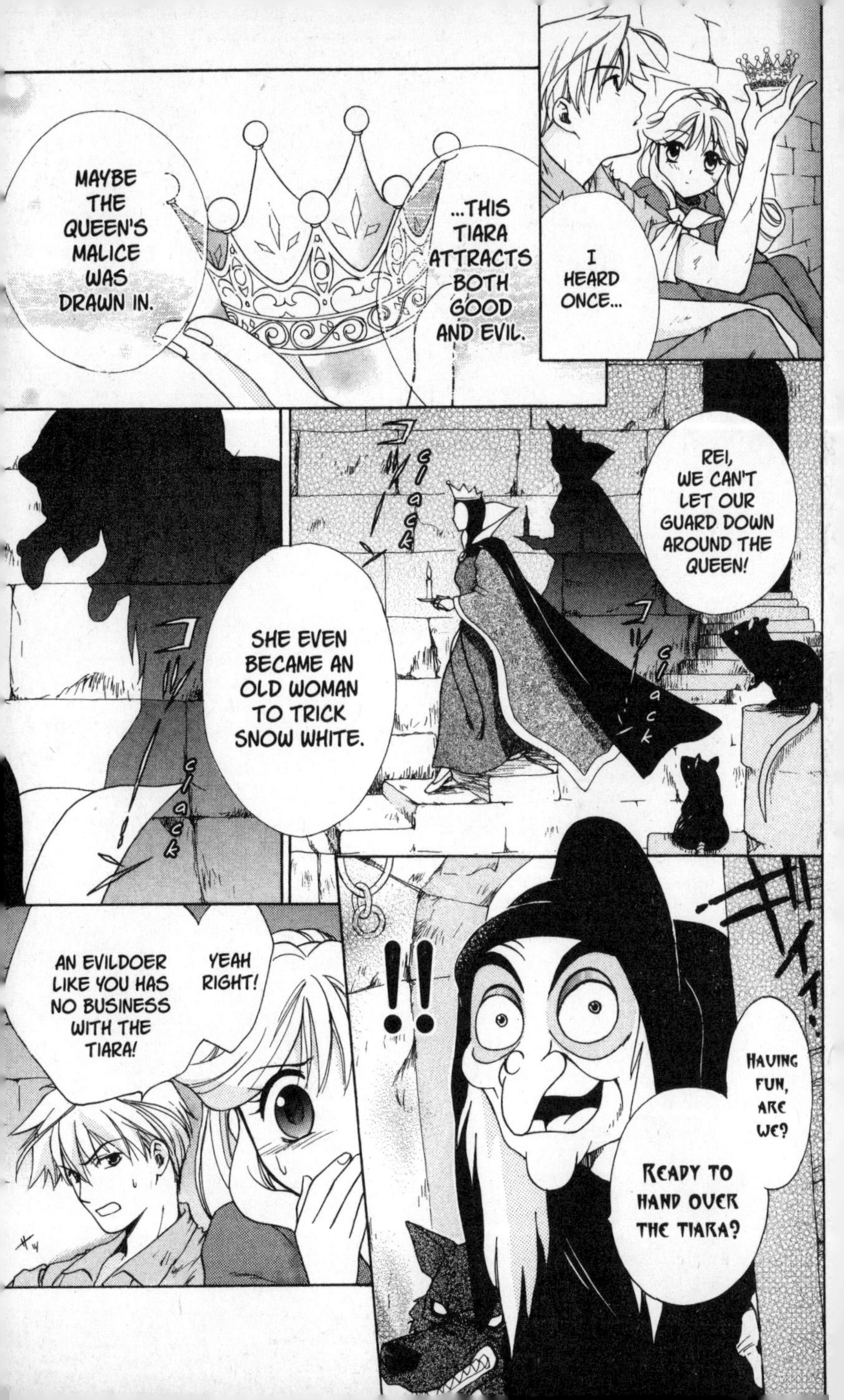
I HEARD ONCE...
...THIS TIARA ATTRACTS BOTH GOOD AND EVIL.
MAYBE THE QUEEN'S MALICE WAS DRAWN IN.
clack
REI, WE CAN'T LET OUR GUARD DOWN AROUND THE QUEEN!
clack
SHE EVEN BECAME AN OLD WOMAN TO TRICK SNOW WHITE.
clack
!!
HAVING FUN, ARE WE?
READY TO HAND OVER THE TIARA?
YEAH RIGHT!
AN EVILDOER LIKE YOU HAS NO BUSINESS WITH THE TIARA!

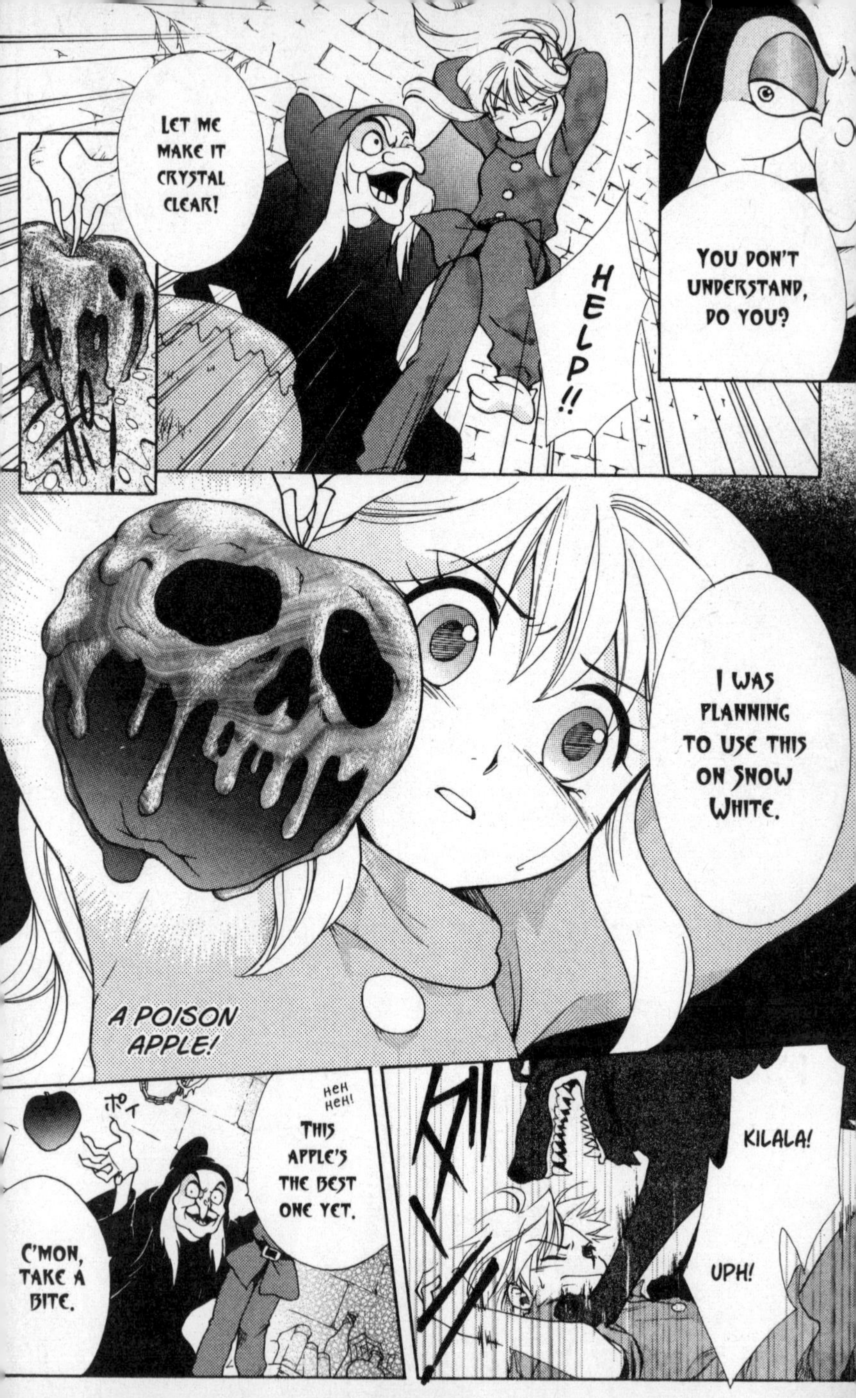

You don't understand, do you?
Let me make it crystal clear!
HELP!!
I was planning to use this on Snow White.
A POISON APPLE!
Kilala!
Uph!
Heh heh!
This apple's the best one yet.
C'mon, take a bite.

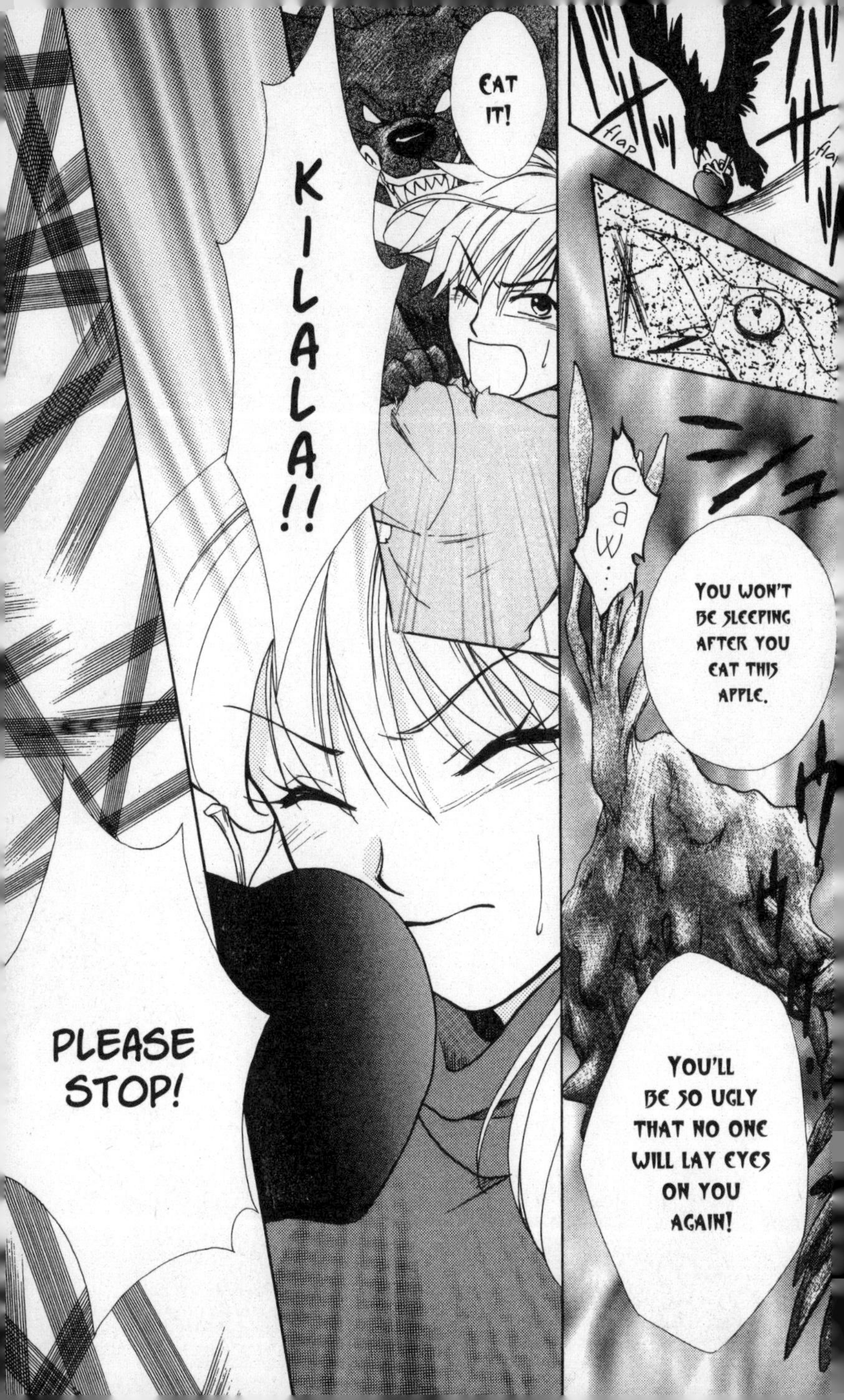

flap
flap
Caw...
YOU WON'T BE SLEEPING AFTER YOU EAT THIS APPLE.
YOU'LL BE SO UGLY THAT NO ONE WILL LAY EYES ON YOU AGAIN!
EAT IT!
KILLALA!!
PLEASE STOP!

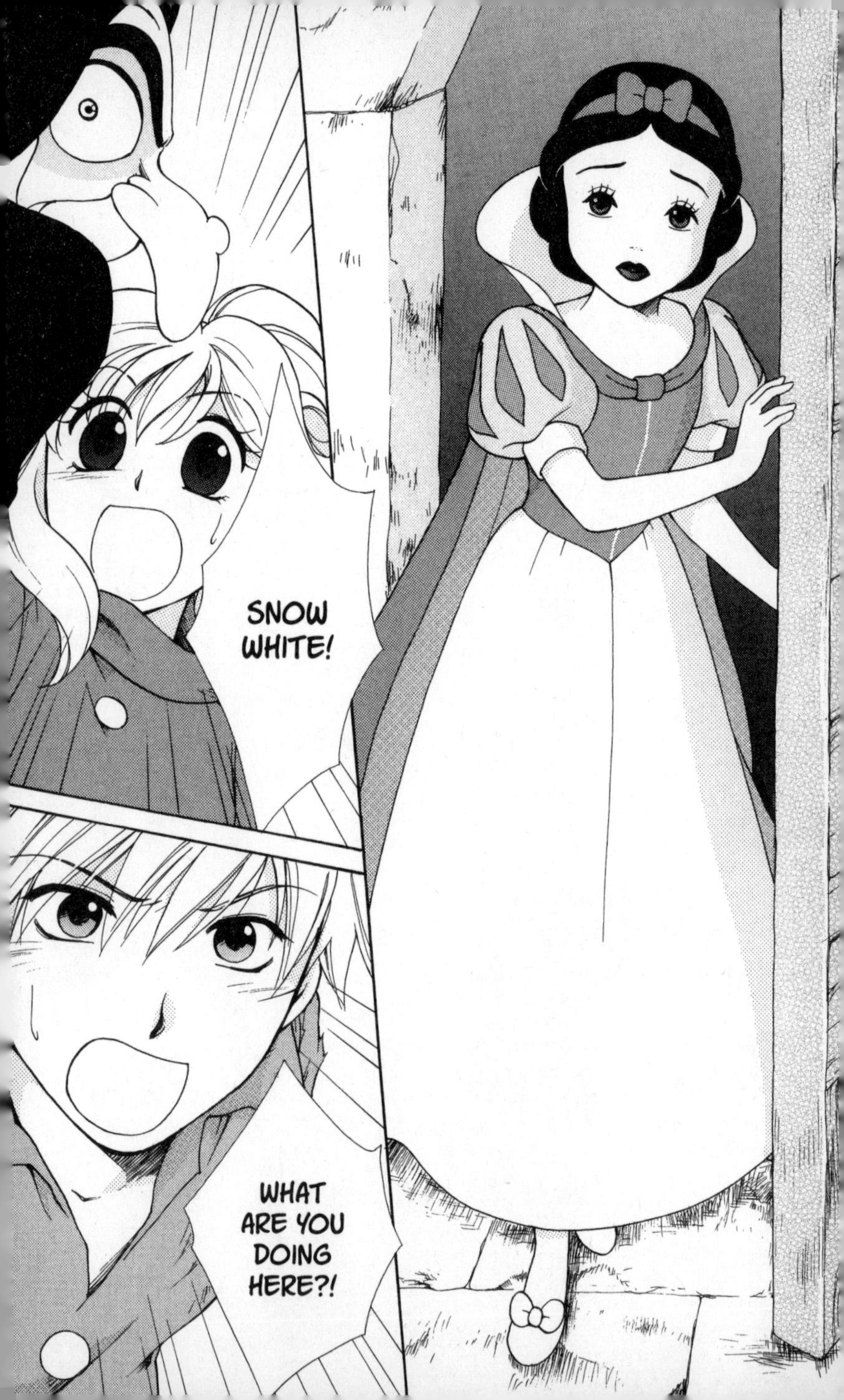
SNOW WHITE!
WHAT ARE YOU DOING HERE?!

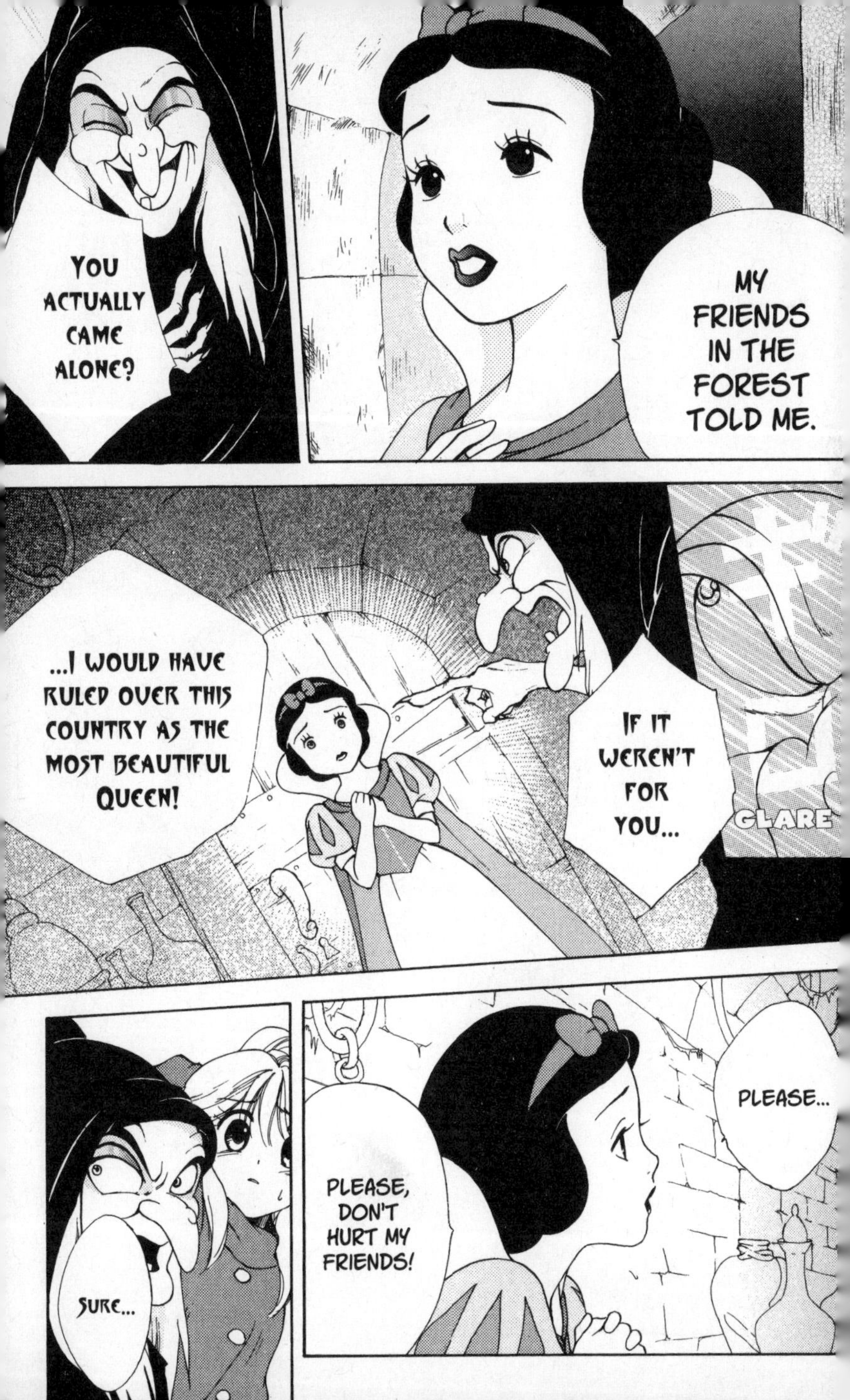
MY FRIENDS IN THE FOREST TOLD ME.
YOU ACTUALLY CAME ALONE?
GLARE
IF IT WEREN'T FOR YOU...
...I WOULD HAVE RULED OVER THIS COUNTRY AS THE MOST BEAUTIFUL QUEEN!
PLEASE...
PLEASE, DON'T HURT MY FRIENDS!
SURE...

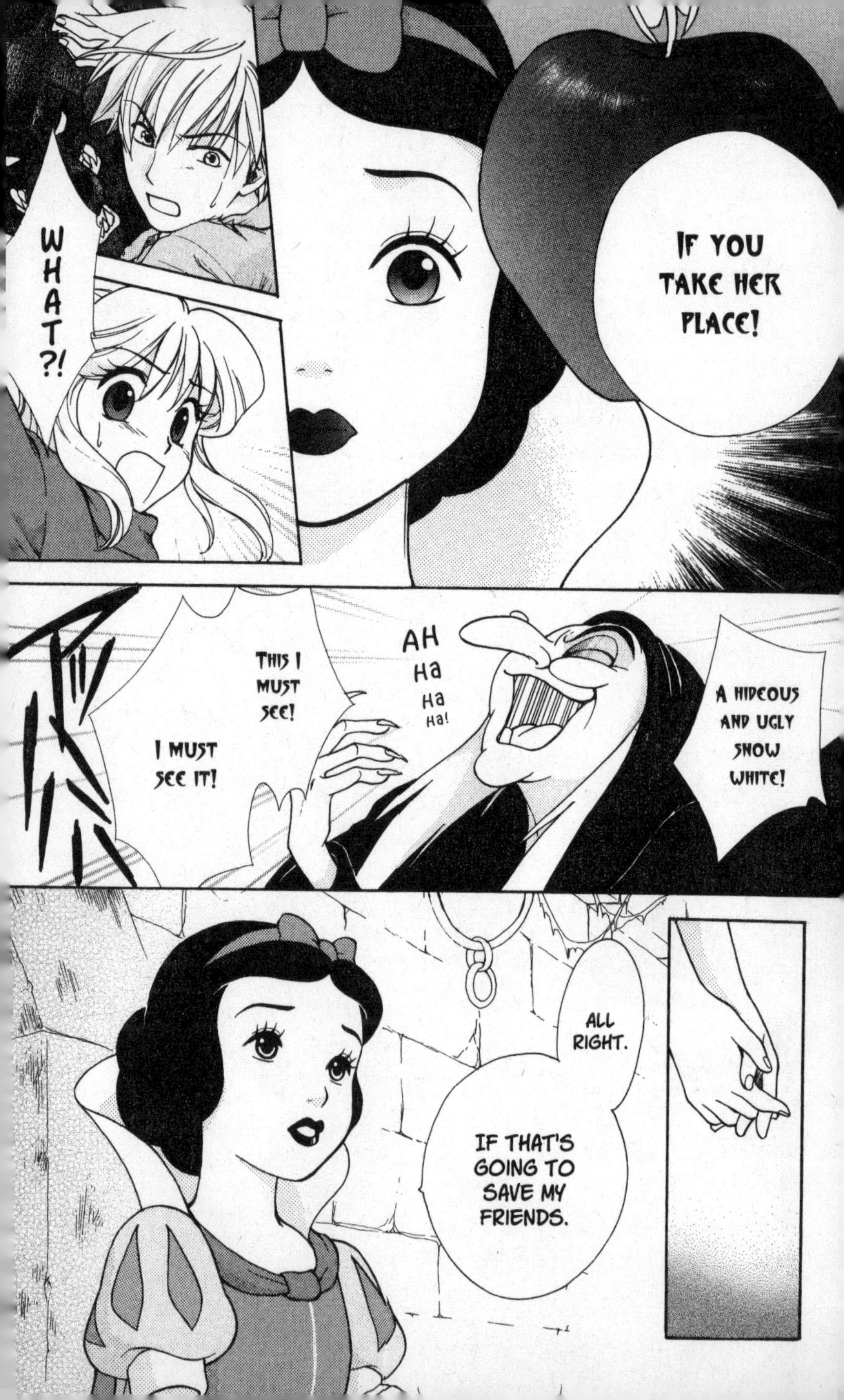
IF YOU TAKE HER PLACE!
WHAT?!
A HIDEOUS AND UGLY SNOW WHITE!
AH HA HA HA!
THIS I MUST SEE!
I MUST SEE IT!
ALL RIGHT.
IF THAT'S GOING TO SAVE MY FRIENDS.

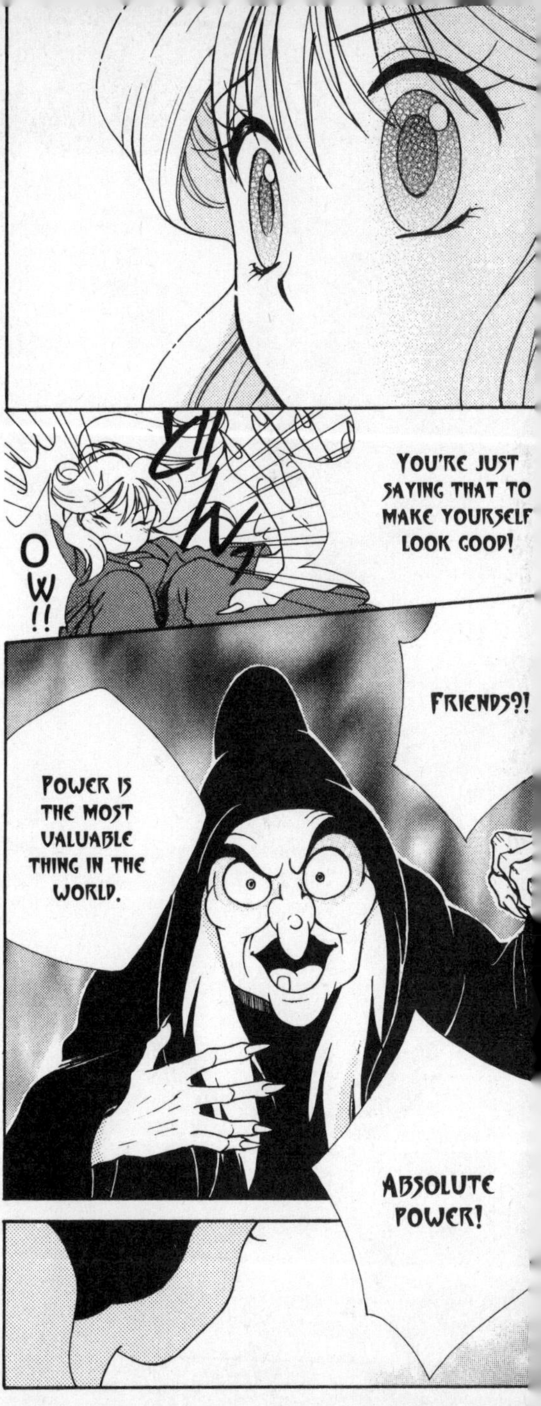
YOU'RE JUST SAYING THAT TO MAKE YOURSELF LOOK GOOD!
OW!!
FRIENDS?!
POWER IS THE MOST VALUABLE THING IN THE WORLD.
ABSOLUTE POWER!

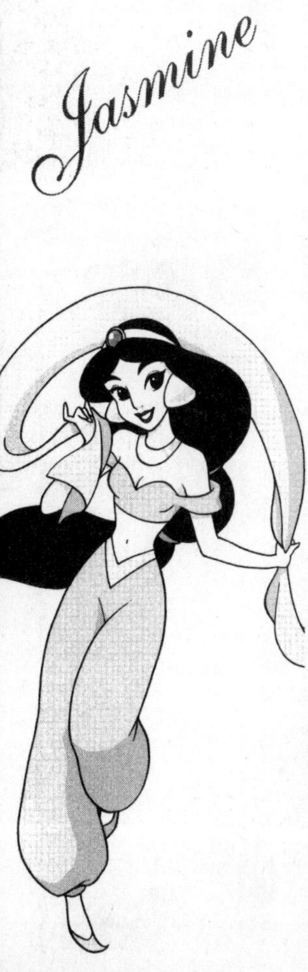
Jasmine

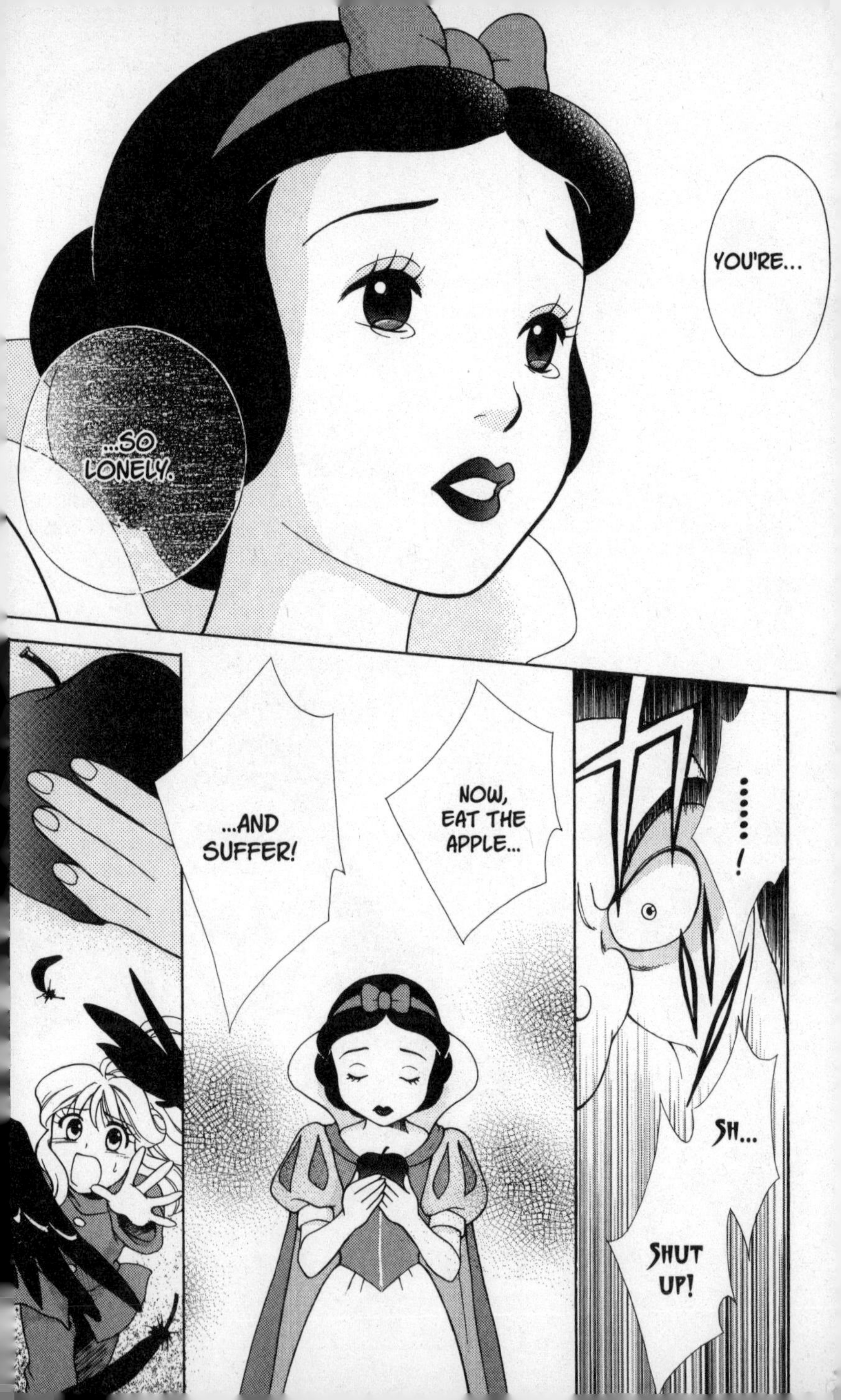
YOU'RE...
...SO LONELY.
......!
SH...
SHUT UP!
NOW, EAT THE APPLE...
...AND SUFFER!

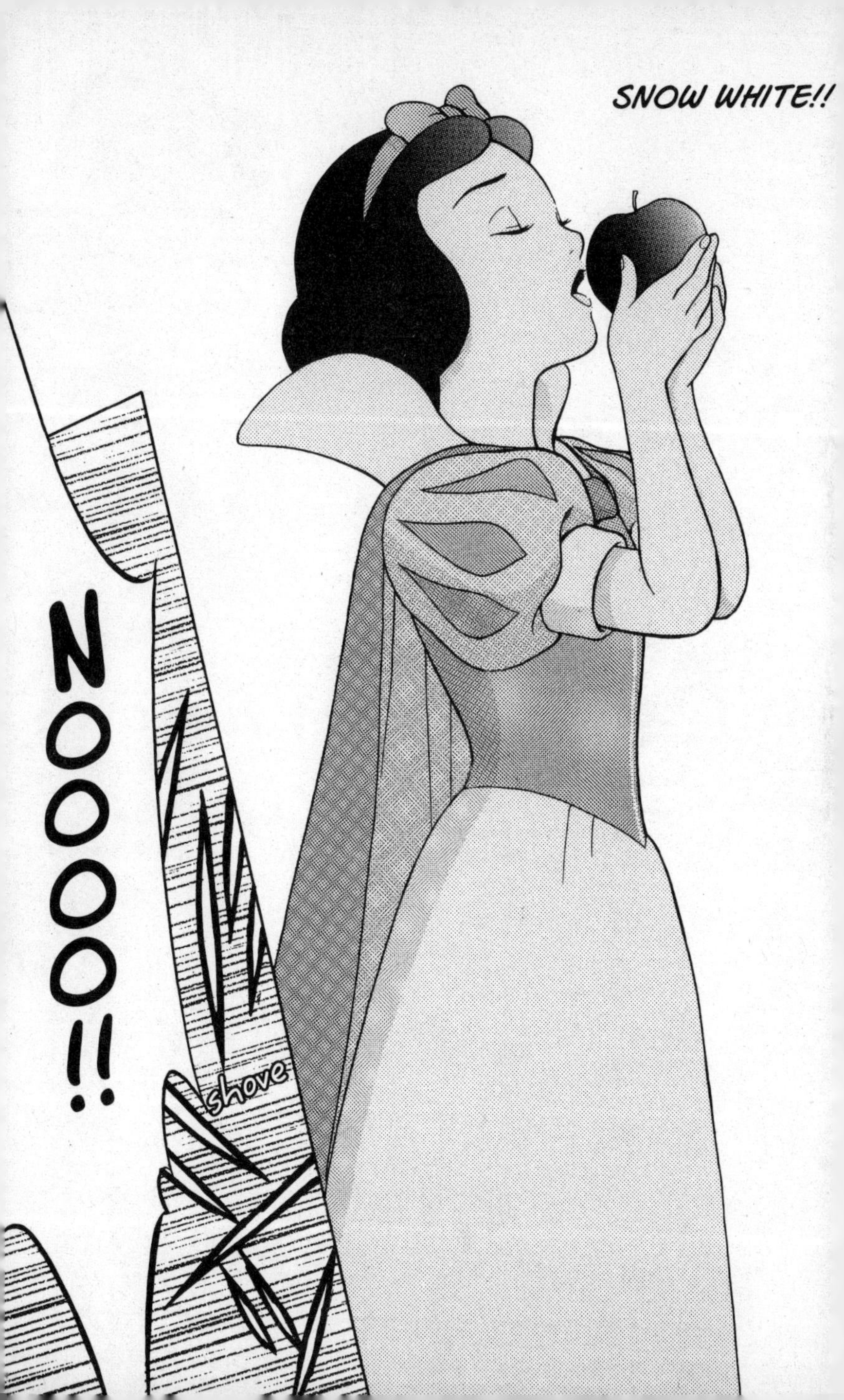
SNOW WHITE!!
NOOOO!!
shove

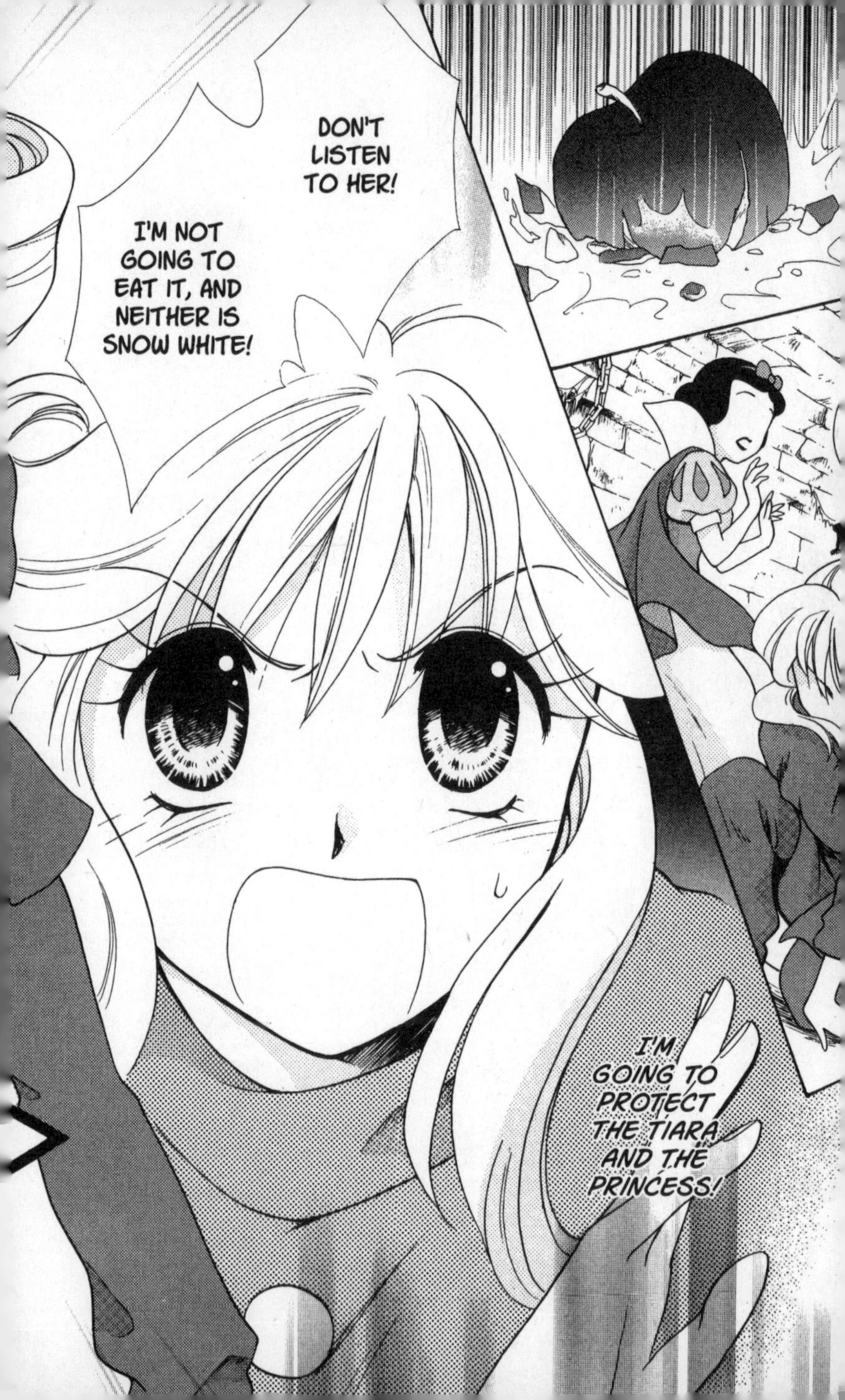
DON'T LISTEN TO HER!
I'M NOT GOING TO EAT IT, AND NEITHER IS SNOW WHITE!
I'M GOING TO PROTECT THE TIARA AND THE PRINCESS!

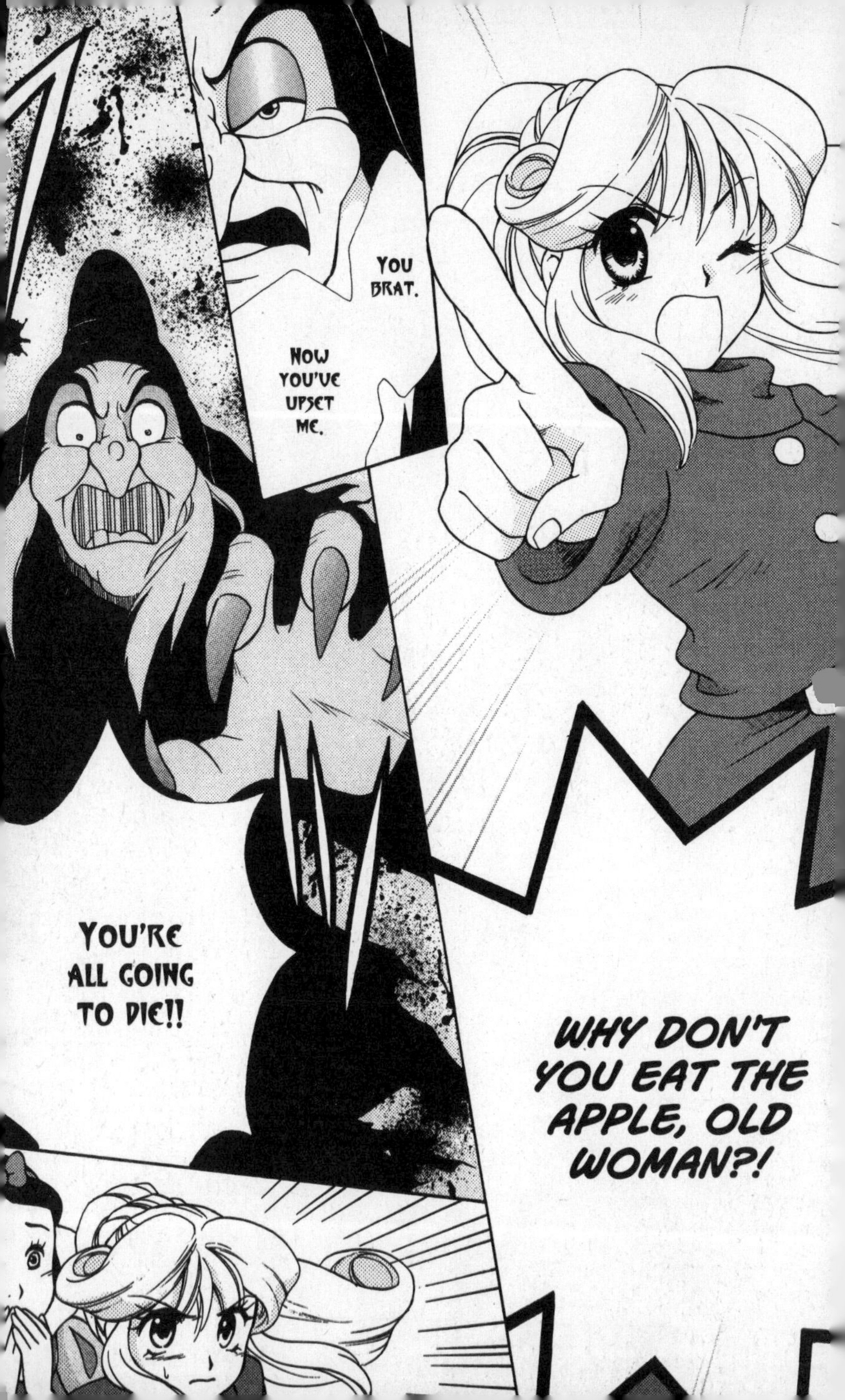
WHY DON'T YOU EAT THE APPLE, OLD WOMAN?!
YOU BRAT.
NOW YOU'VE UPSET ME.
YOU'RE ALL GOING TO DIE!!

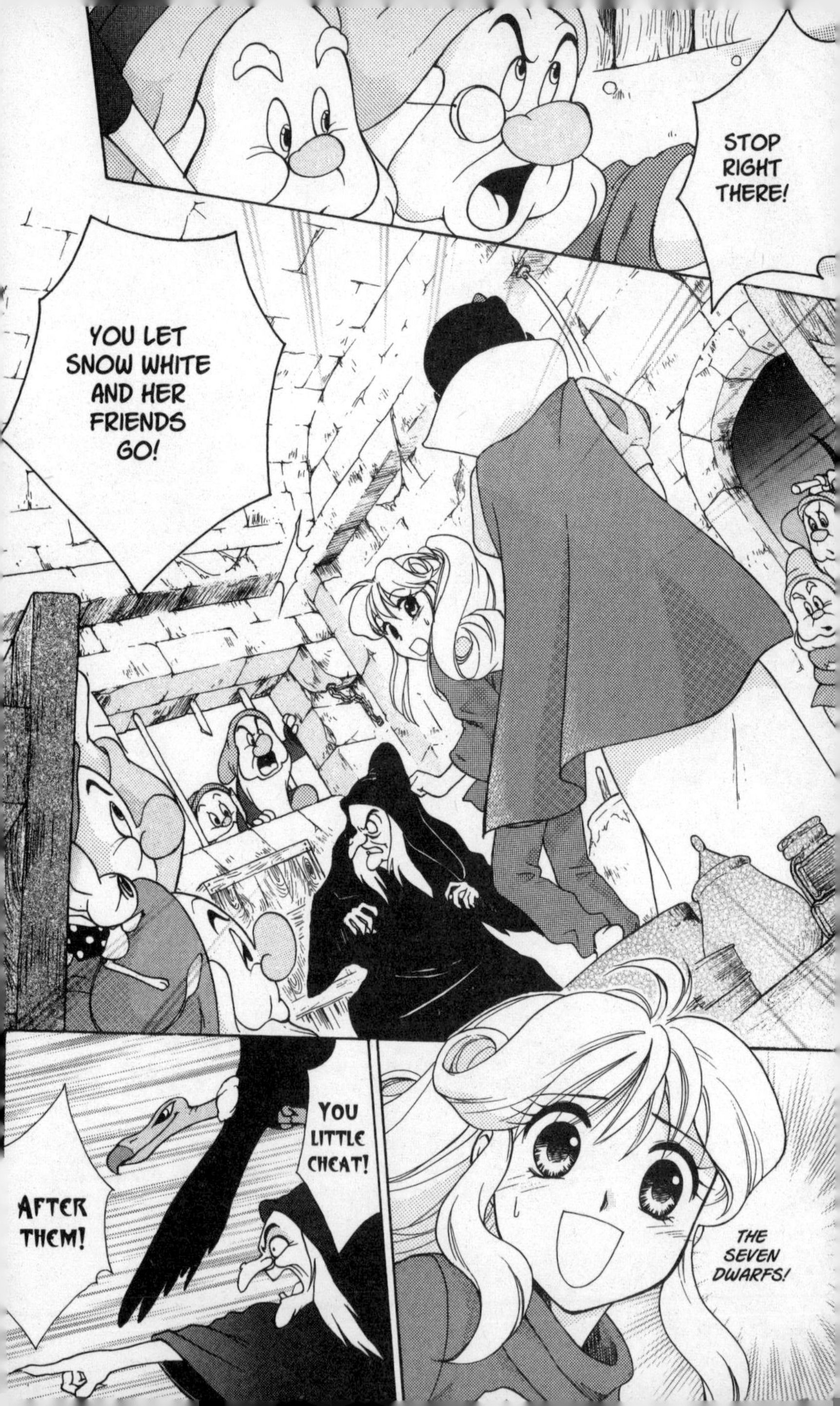
STOP RIGHT THERE!
YOU LET SNOW WHITE AND HER FRIENDS GO!
THE SEVEN DWARFS!
YOU LITTLE CHEAT!
AFTER THEM!

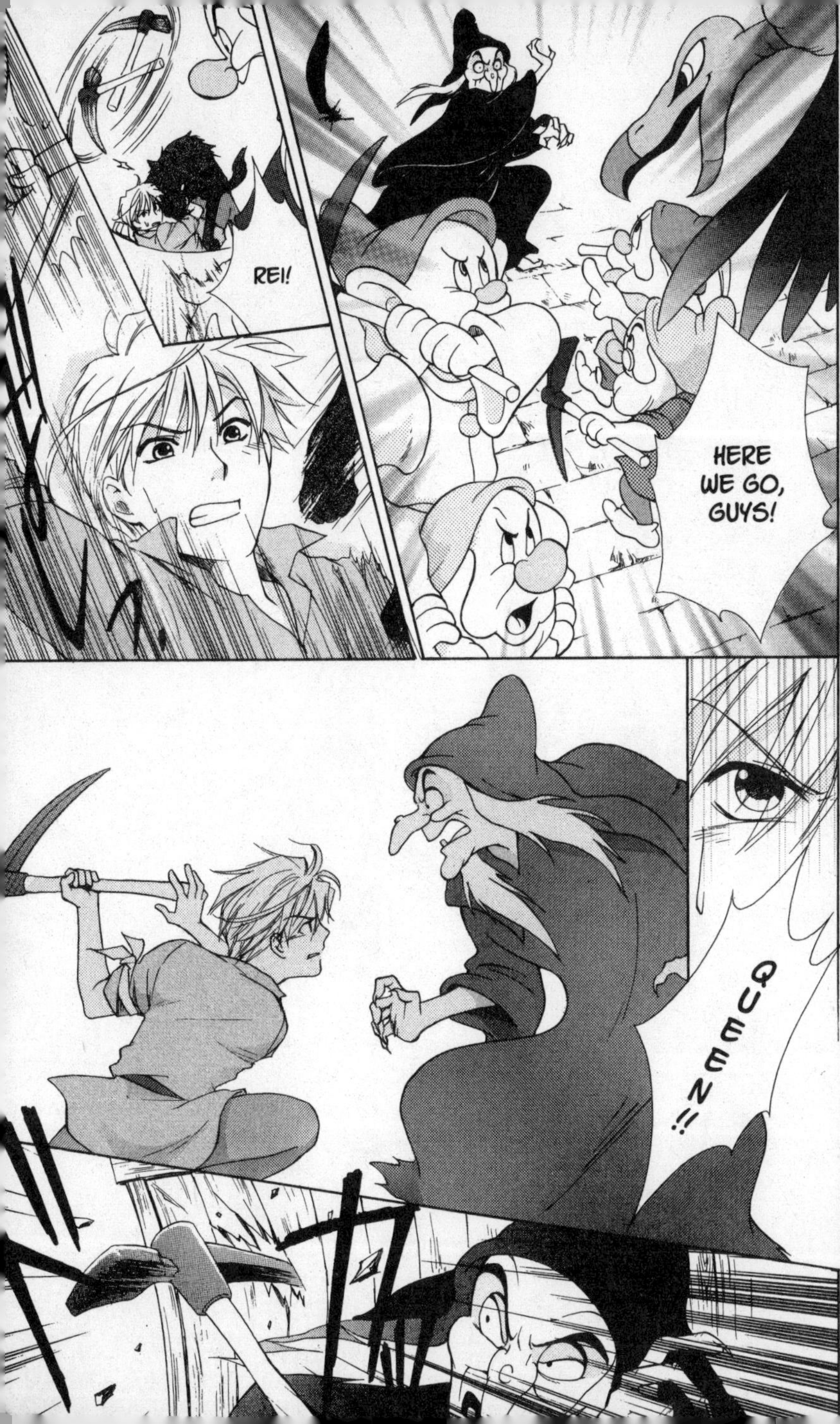
HERE WE GO, GUYS!
REI!
QUEEN!!

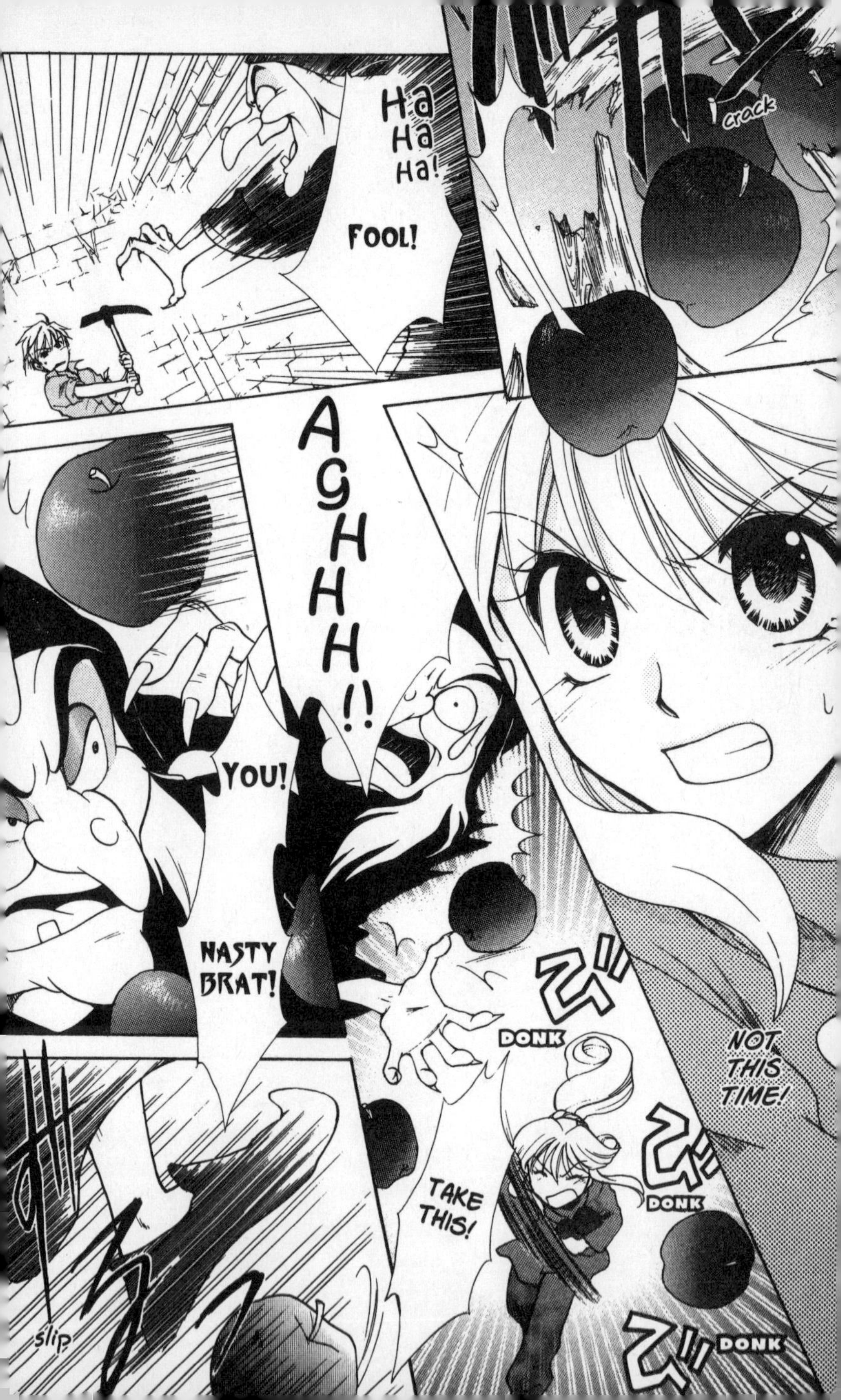
crack
Ha Ha Ha!
FOOL!
NOT THIS TIME!
AGHHH!!
YOU!
NASTY BRAT!
DONK
TAKE THIS!
DONK
DONK
slip

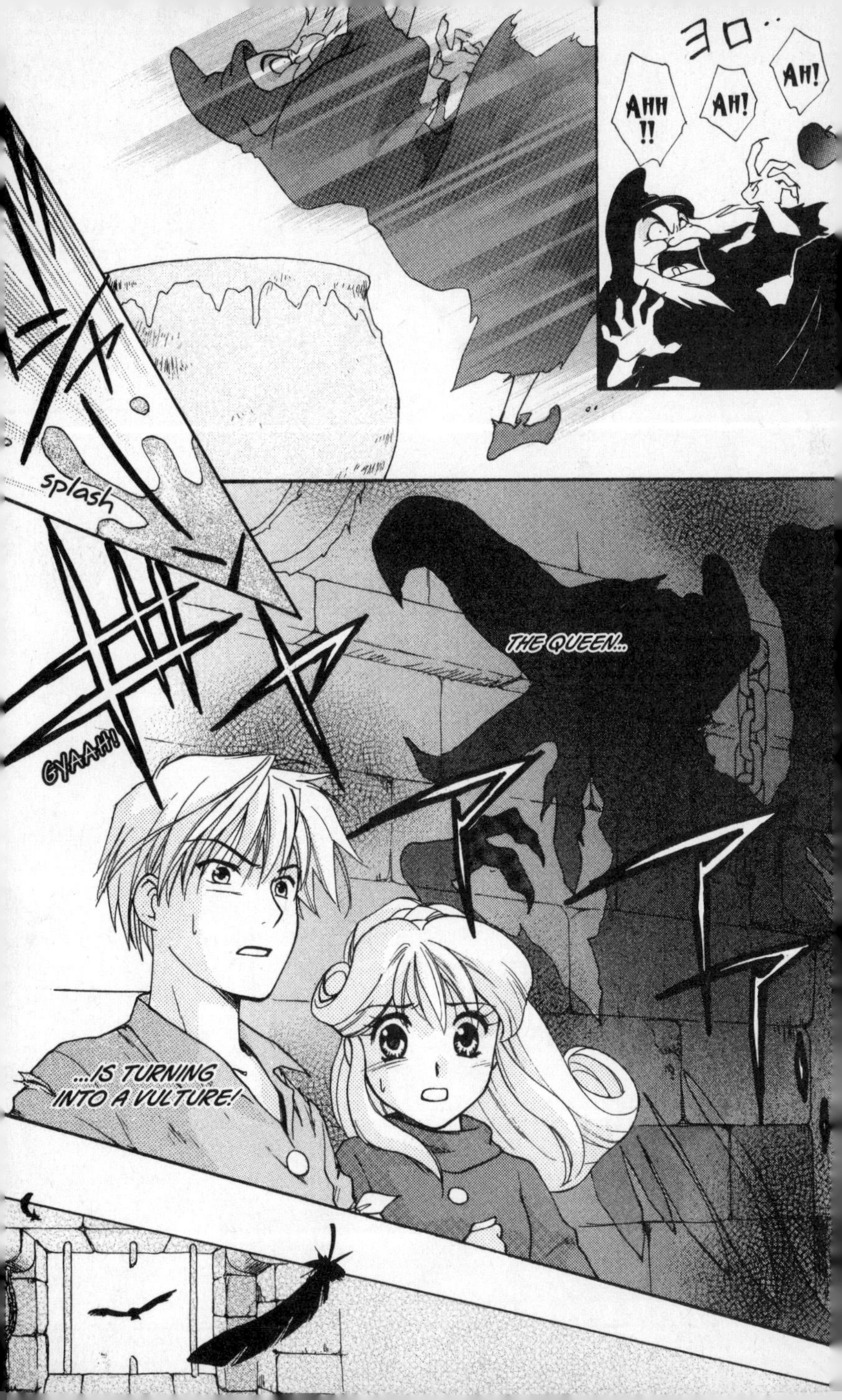
ヨロ..
AH!
AH!
AHH !!
splash
GYAAHH!
THE QUEEN...
...IS TURNING INTO A VULTURE!

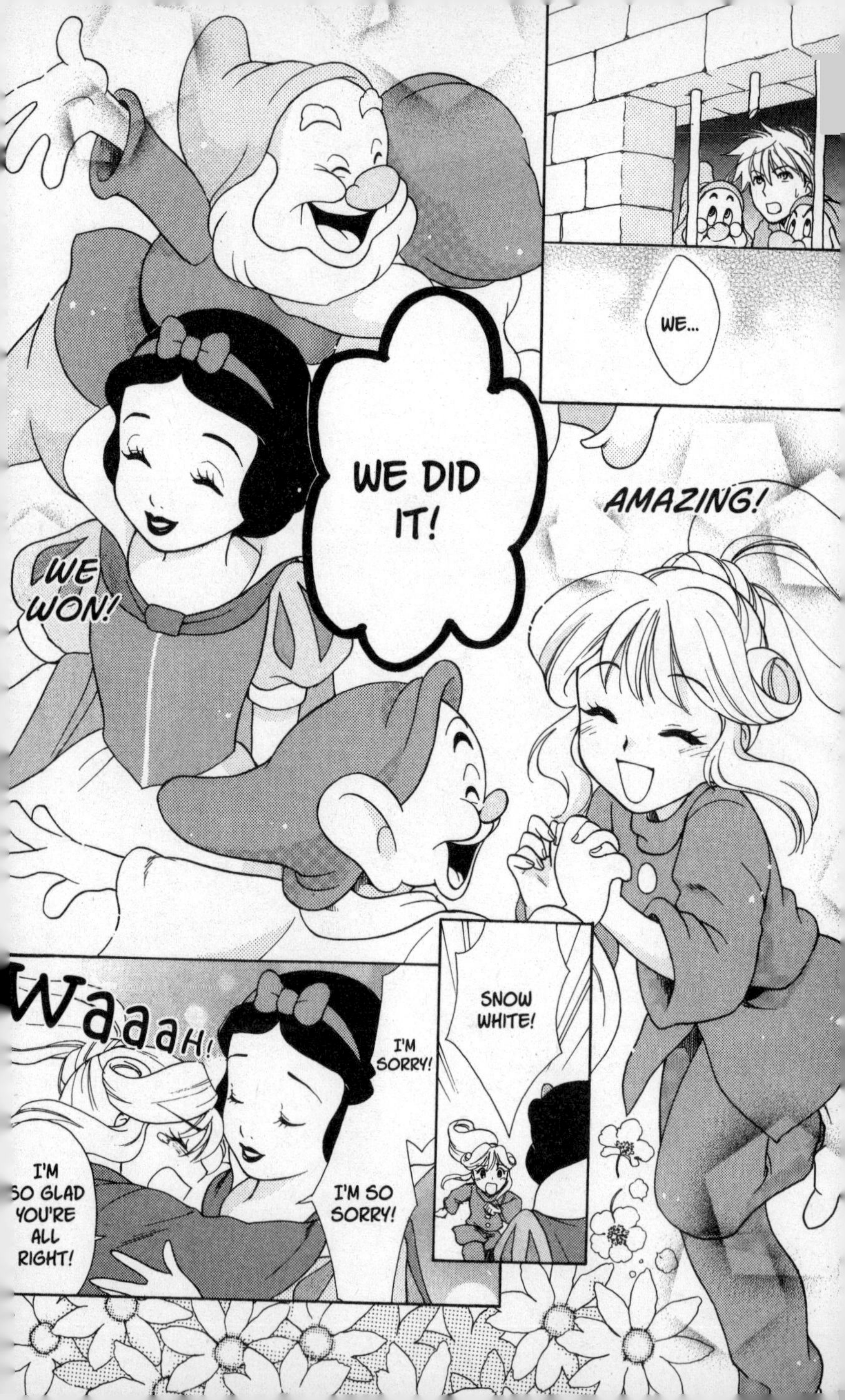
WE...
WE DID IT!
AMAZING!
WE WON!
SNOW WHITE!
I'M SORRY!
I'M SO SORRY!
Waaaah!
I'M SO GLAD YOU'RE ALL RIGHT!

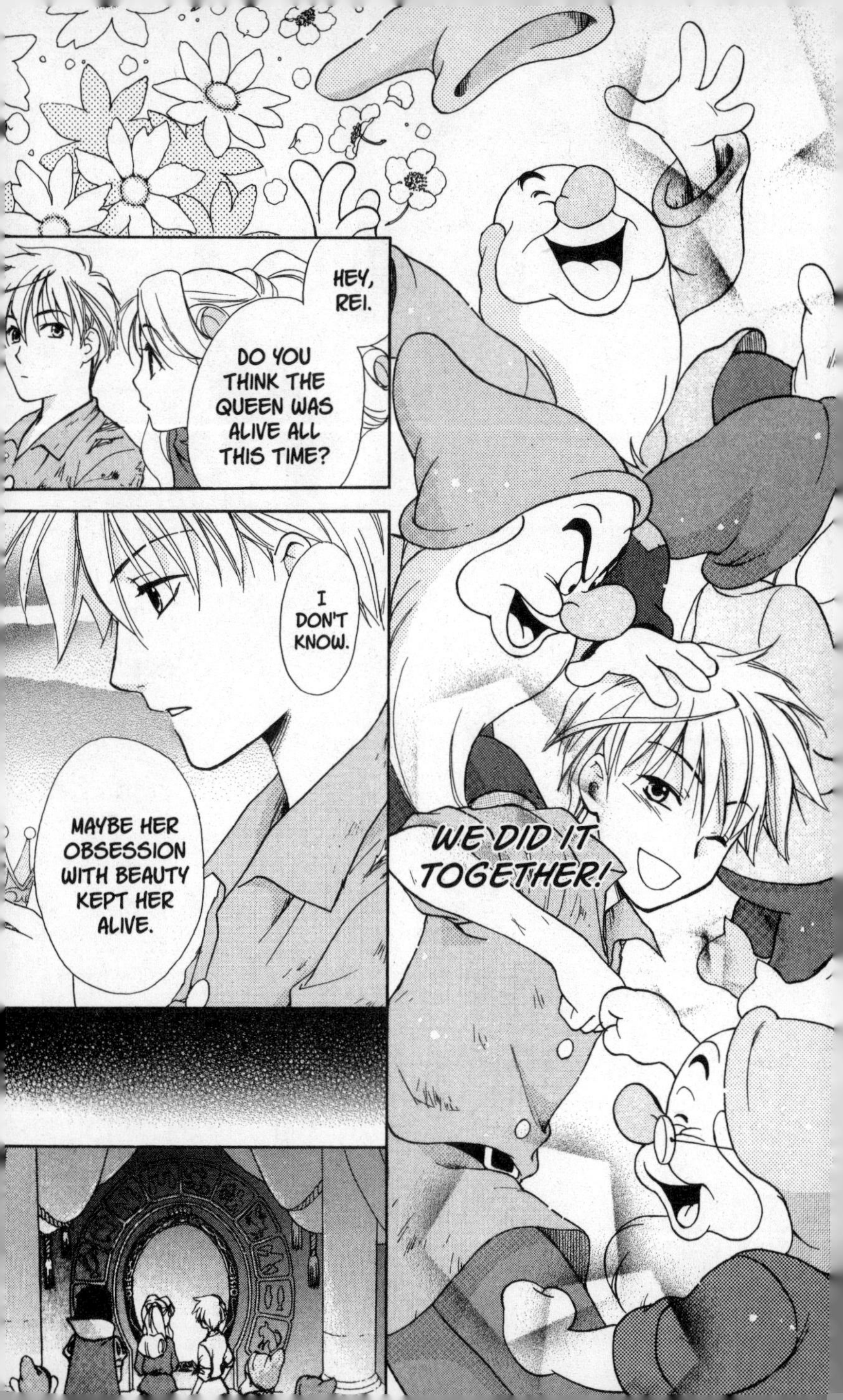
WE DID IT TOGETHER!
HEY, REI.
DO YOU THINK THE QUEEN WAS ALIVE ALL THIS TIME?
I DON'T KNOW.
MAYBE HER OBSESSION WITH BEAUTY KEPT HER ALIVE.

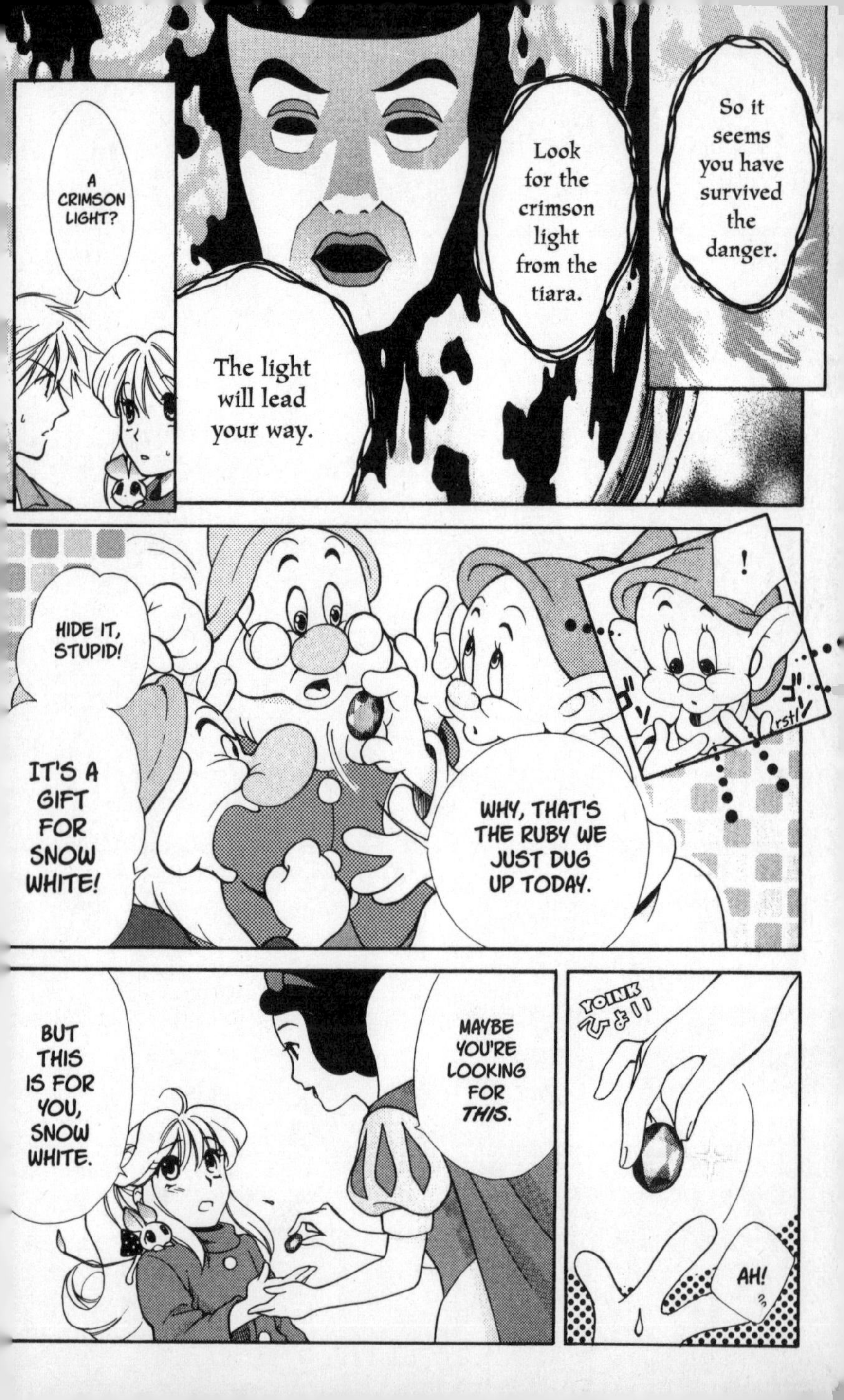
So it seems you have survived the danger.
Look for the crimson light from the tiara.
The light will lead your way.
A CRIMSON LIGHT?
!
rstl
WHY, THAT'S THE RUBY WE JUST DUG UP TODAY.
HIDE IT, STUPID!
IT'S A GIFT FOR SNOW WHITE!
YOINK
AH!
MAYBE YOU'RE LOOKING FOR *THIS*.
BUT THIS IS FOR YOU, SNOW WHITE.

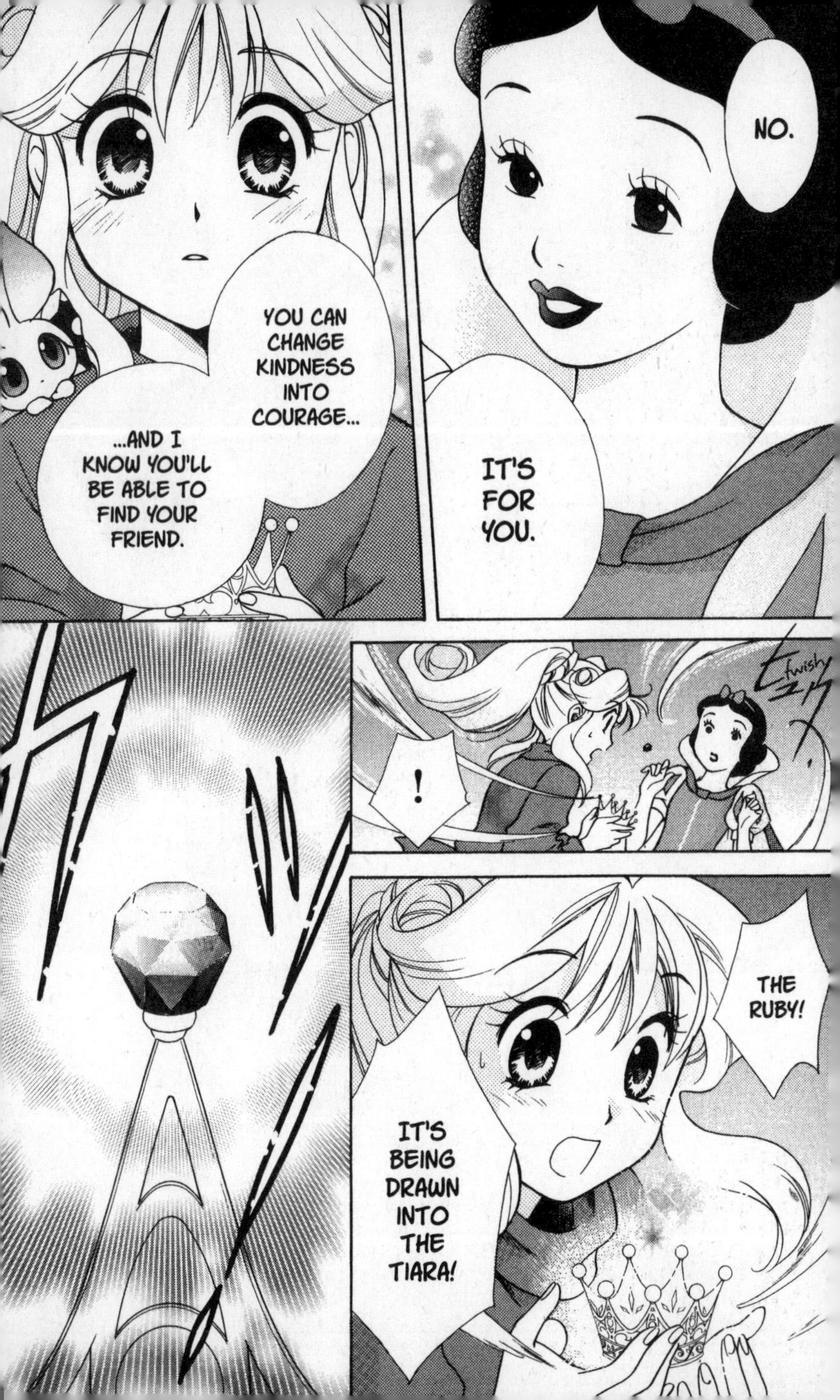
NO.
IT'S FOR YOU.
YOU CAN CHANGE KINDNESS INTO COURAGE...
...AND I KNOW YOU'LL BE ABLE TO FIND YOUR FRIEND.
fwish
!
THE RUBY!
IT'S BEING DRAWN INTO THE TIARA!

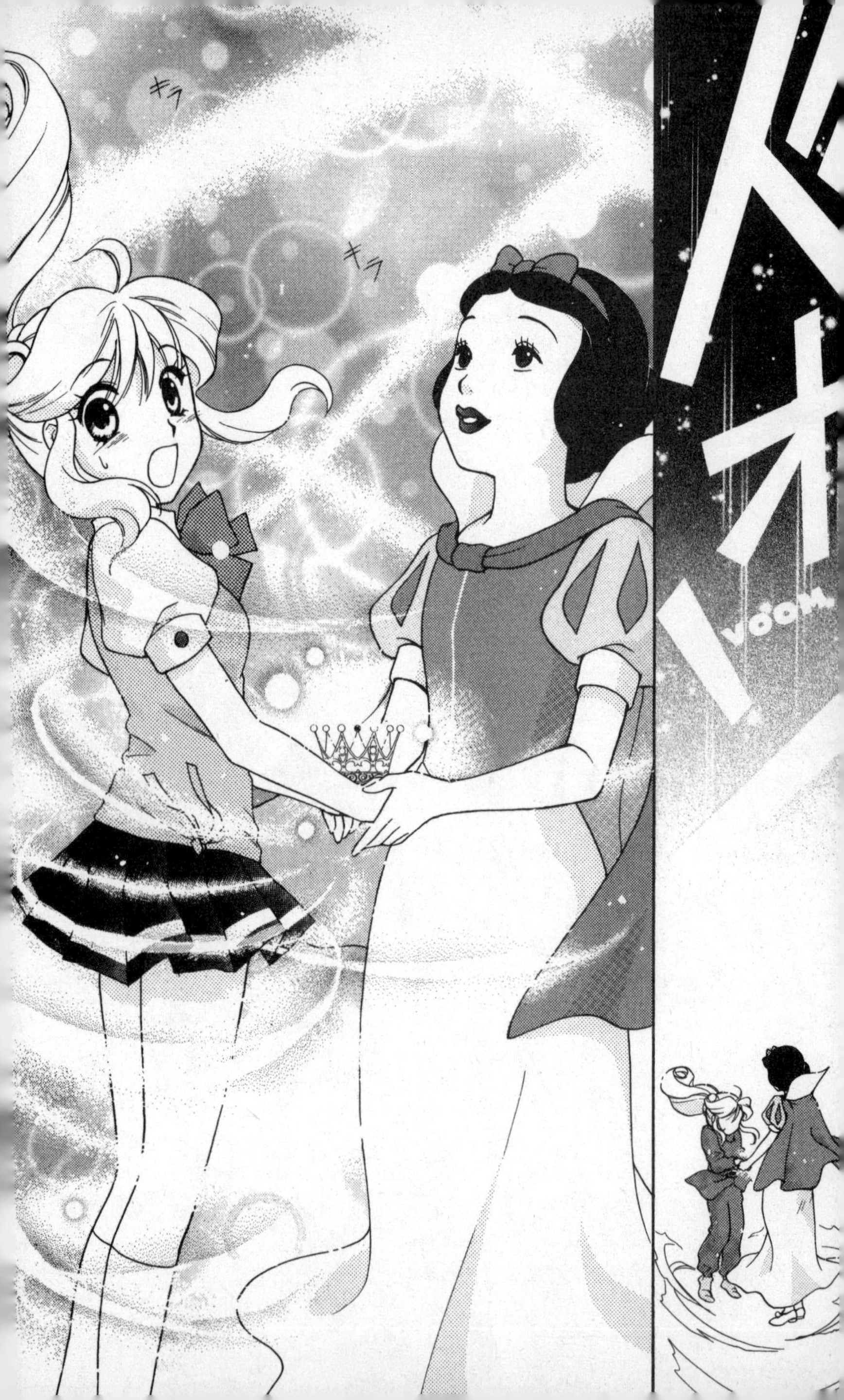
ドオン
VOOM
キラ
キラ

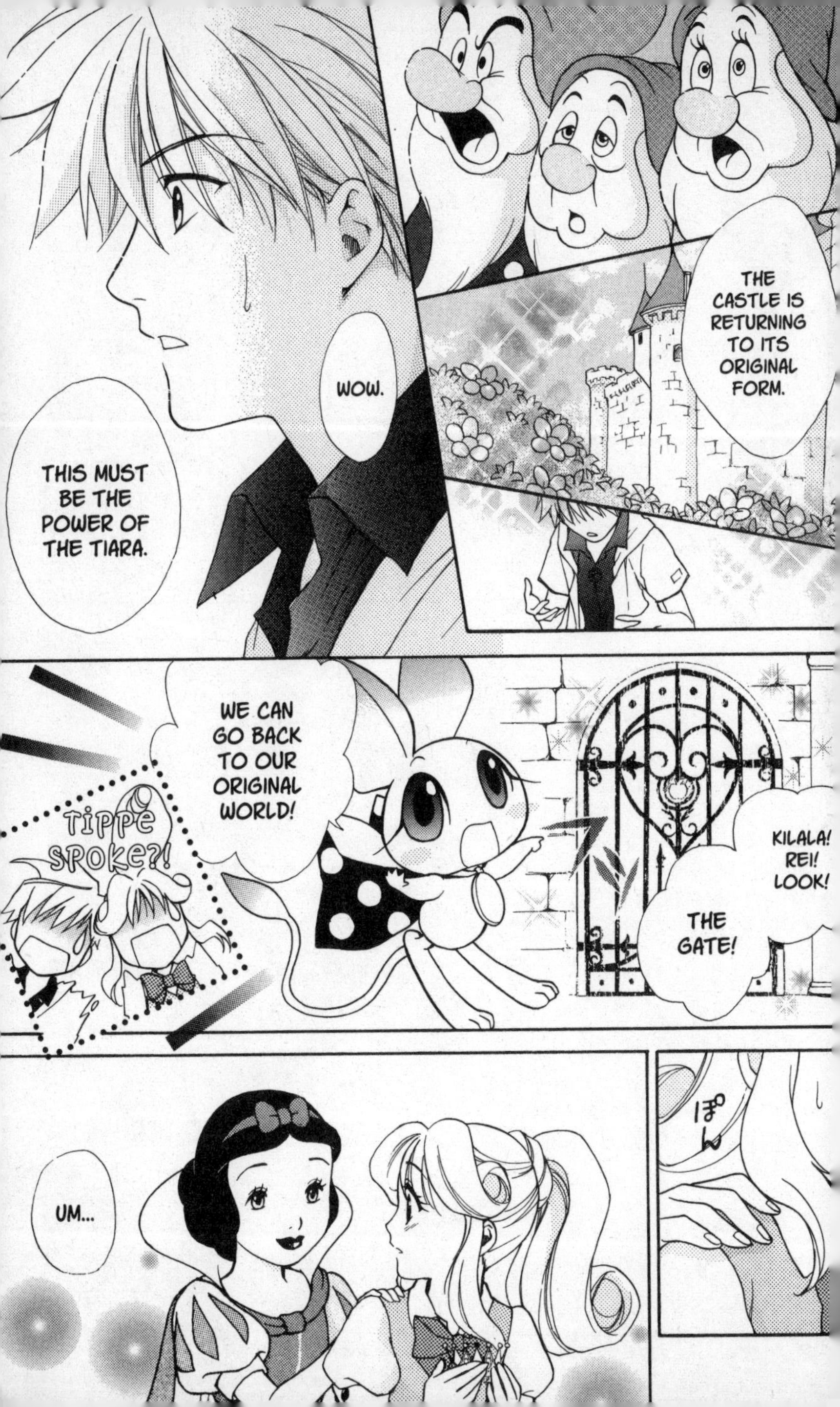
THE CASTLE IS RETURNING TO ITS ORIGINAL FORM.
WOW.
THIS MUST BE THE POWER OF THE TIARA.
KILALA! REI! LOOK!
THE GATE!
WE CAN GO BACK TO OUR ORIGINAL WORLD!
Tippe spoke?!
ぽん
UM...

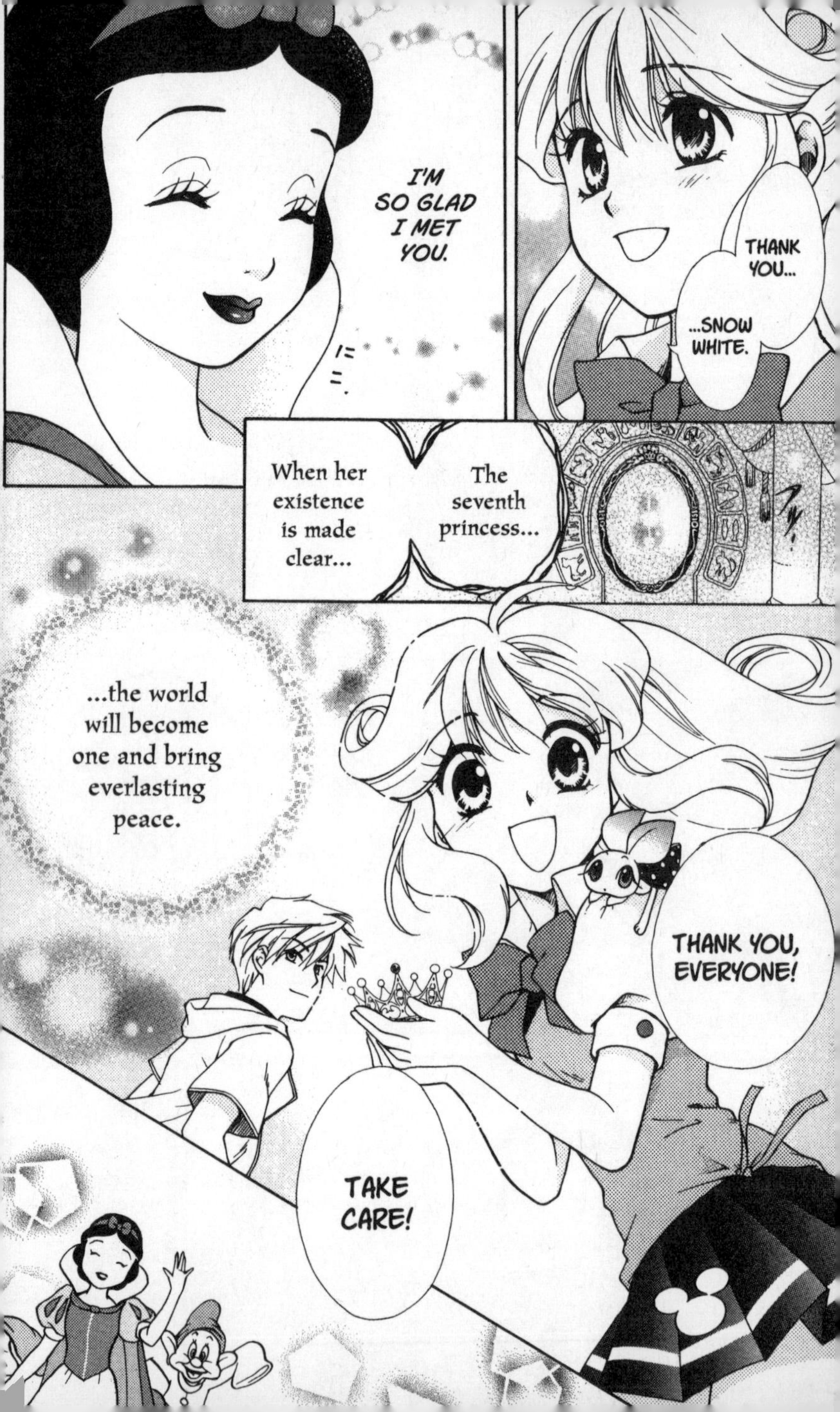
THANK YOU...
...SNOW WHITE.
I'M SO GLAD I MET YOU.
The seventh princess...
When her existence is made clear...
...the world will become one and bring everlasting peace.
THANK YOU, EVERYONE!
TAKE CARE!

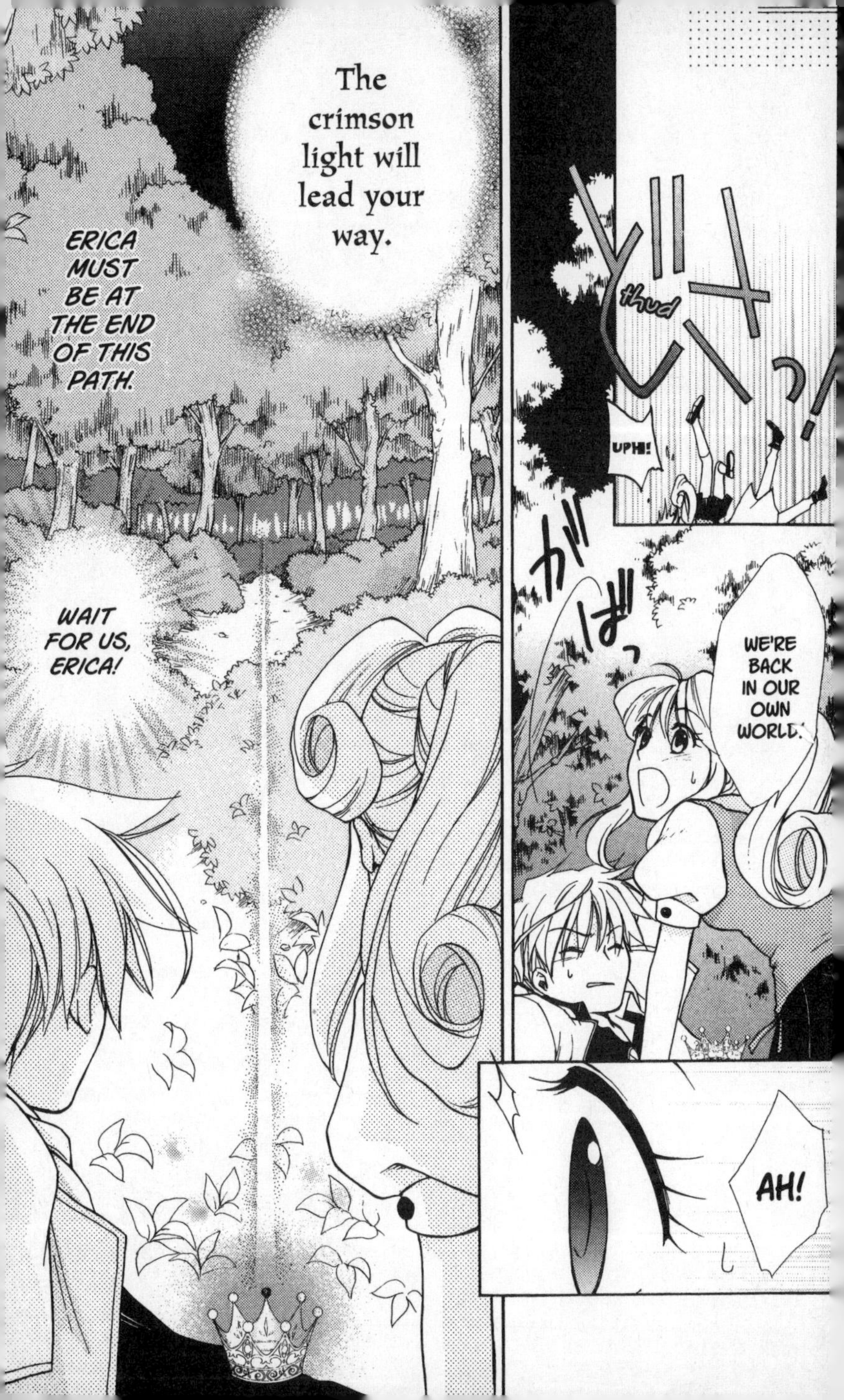
thud
UPH!
WE'RE BACK IN OUR OWN WORLD.
AH!
The crimson light will lead your way.
ERICA MUST BE AT THE END OF THIS PATH.
WAIT FOR US, ERICA!

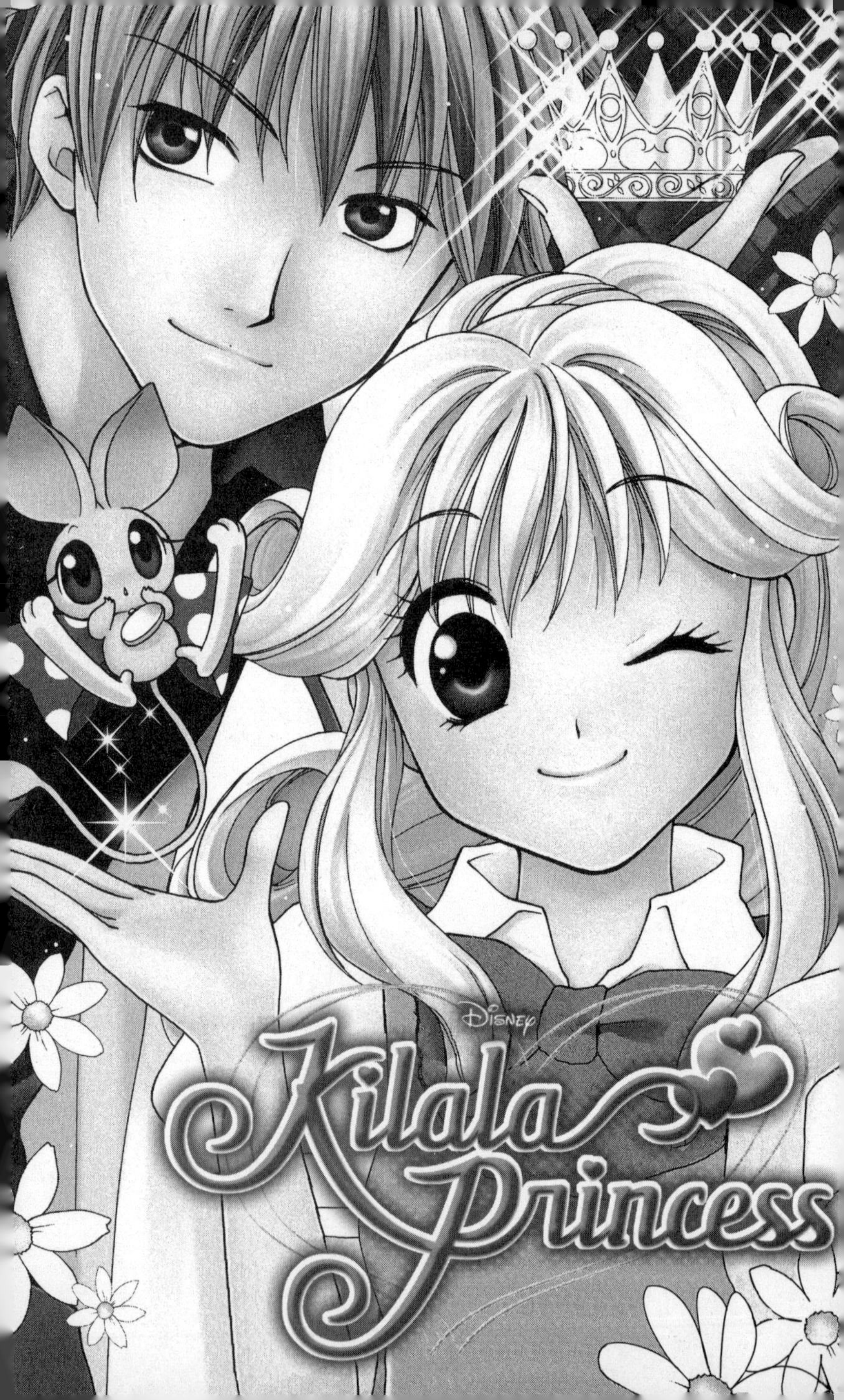
Disney
Kilala Princess

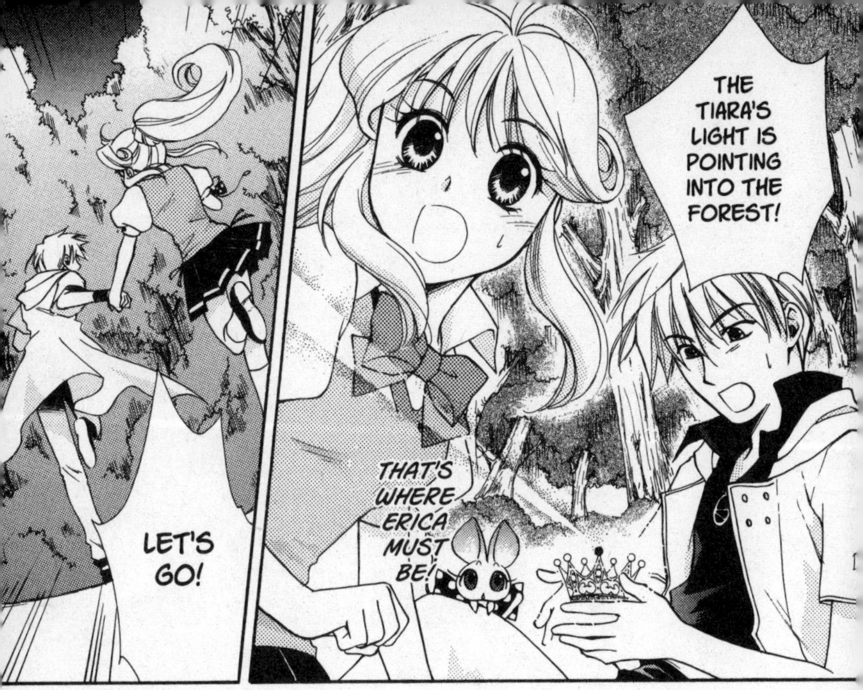
THE TIARA'S LIGHT IS POINTING INTO THE FOREST!
THAT'S WHERE ERICA MUST BE!
LET'S GO!

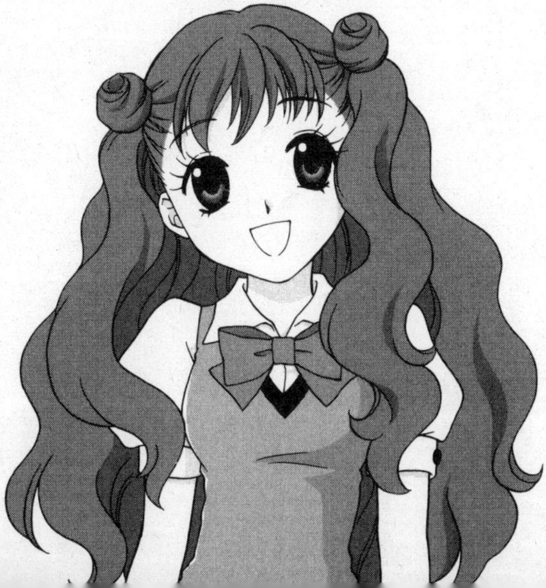

Erica

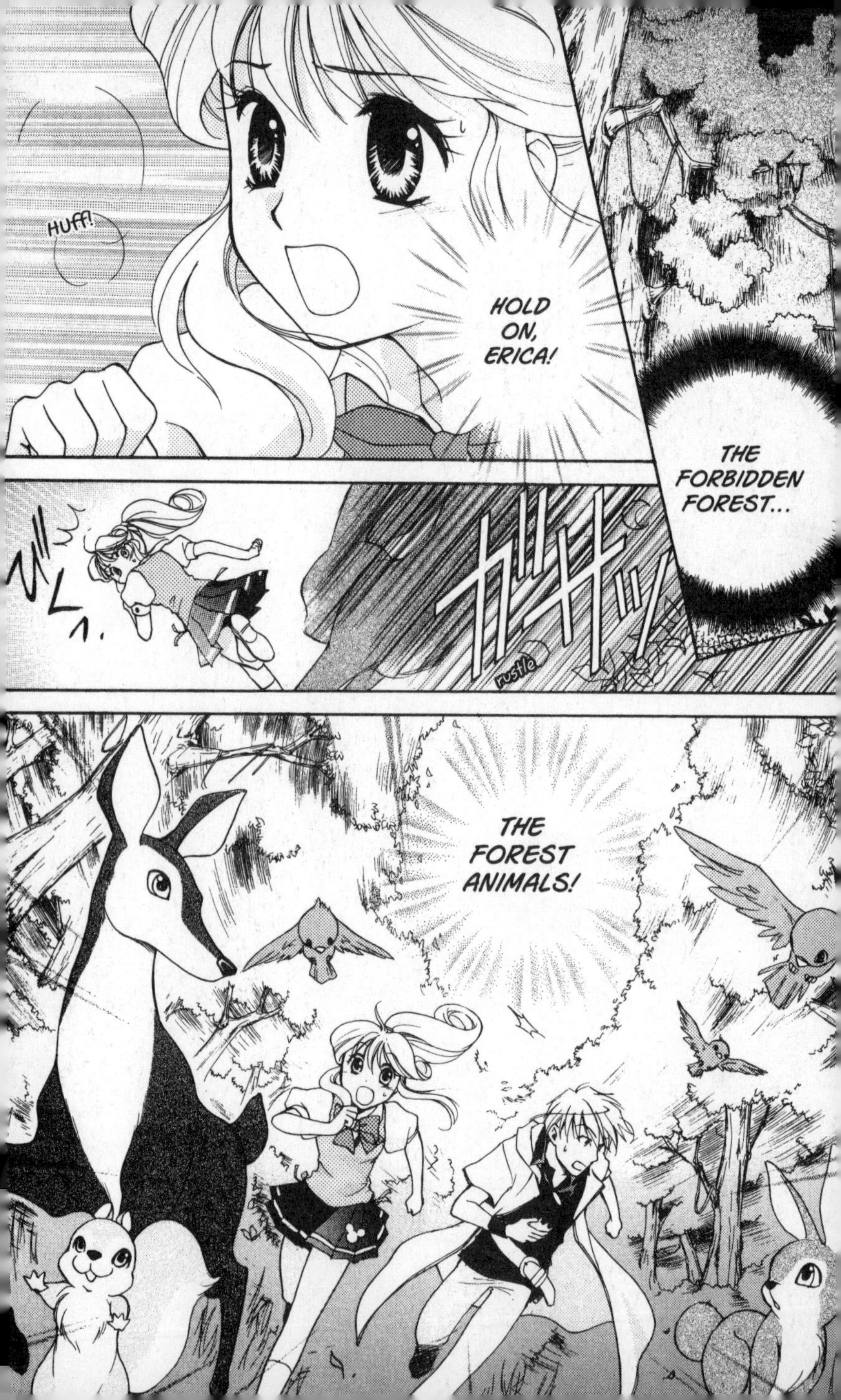
THE FORBIDDEN FOREST...
HOLD ON, ERICA!
HUFF!
カサッ
rustle
THE FOREST ANIMALS!

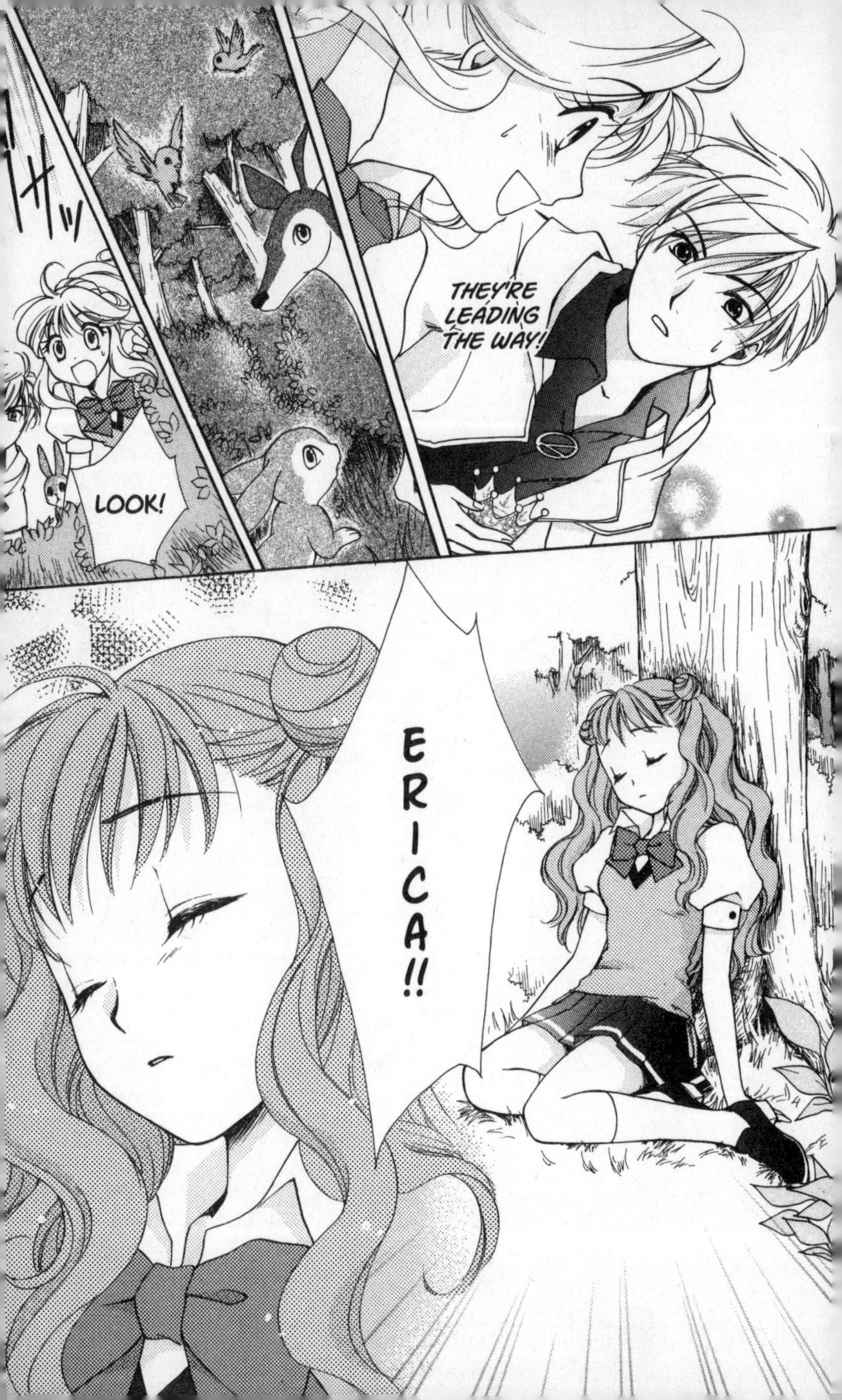
THEY'RE LEADING THE WAY!
ザッ
LOOK!
ERICA!!

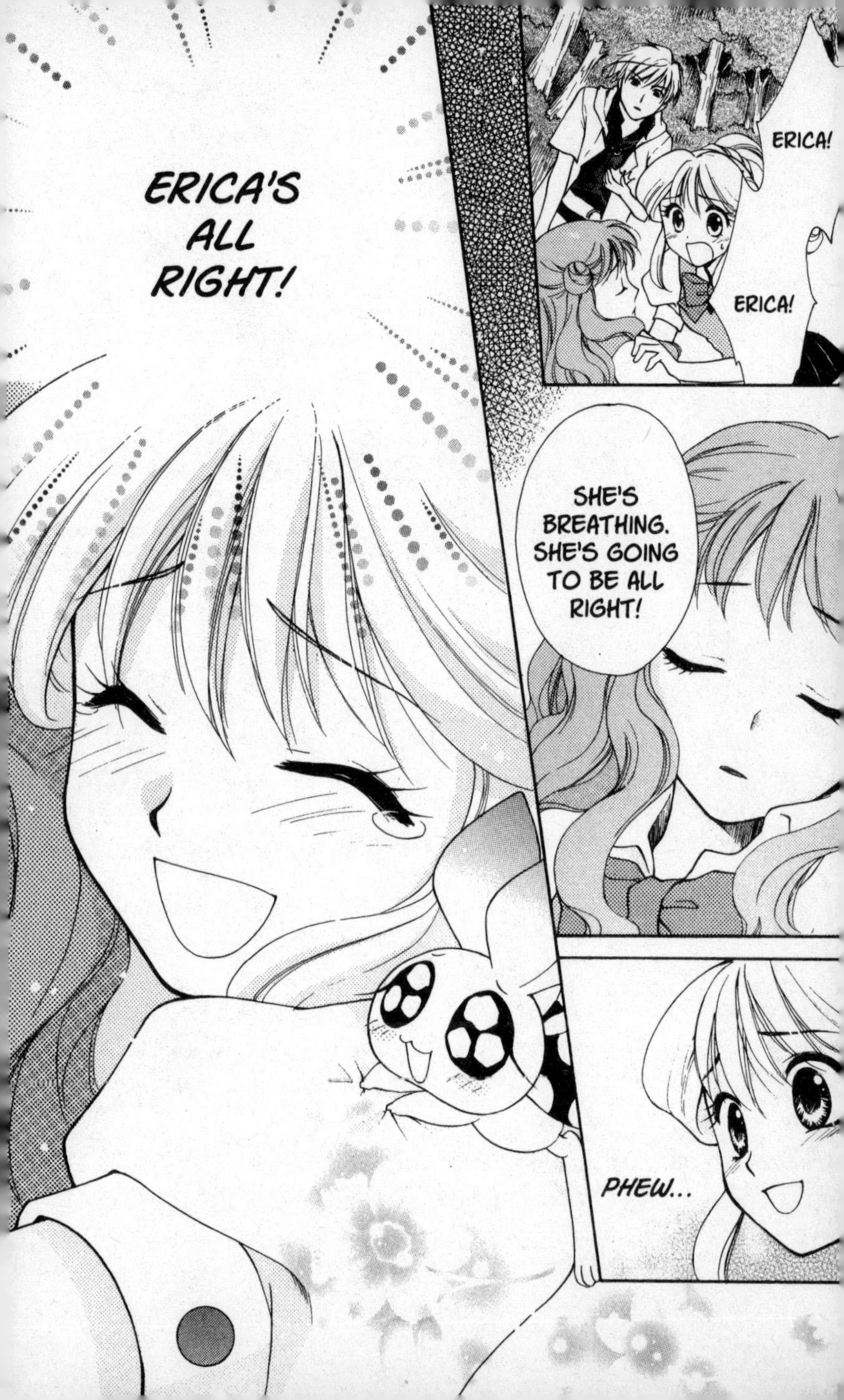
ERICA!
ERICA!
SHE'S BREATHING. SHE'S GOING TO BE ALL RIGHT!
PHEW...
ERICA'S ALL RIGHT!

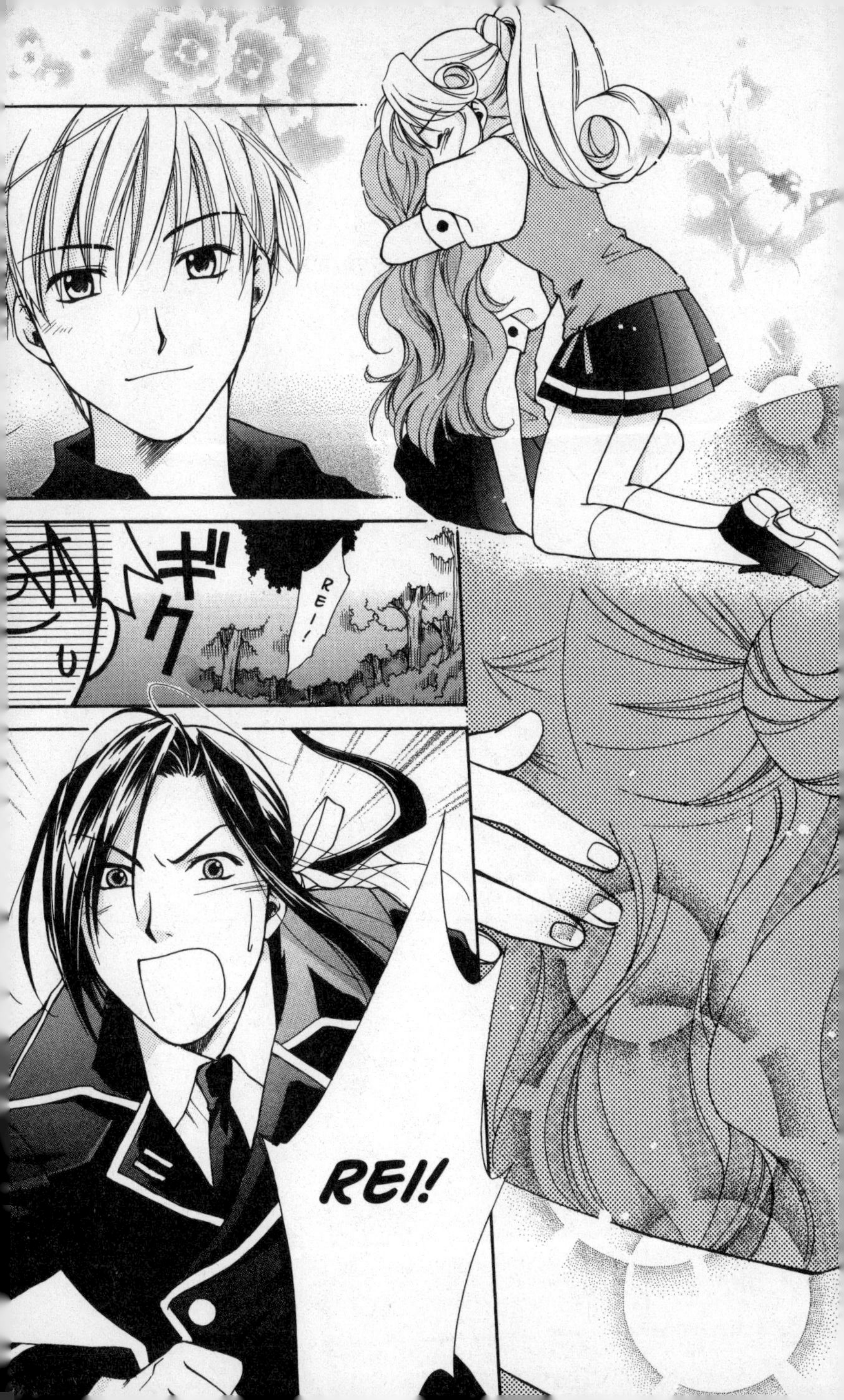
ギク
REI!
REI!

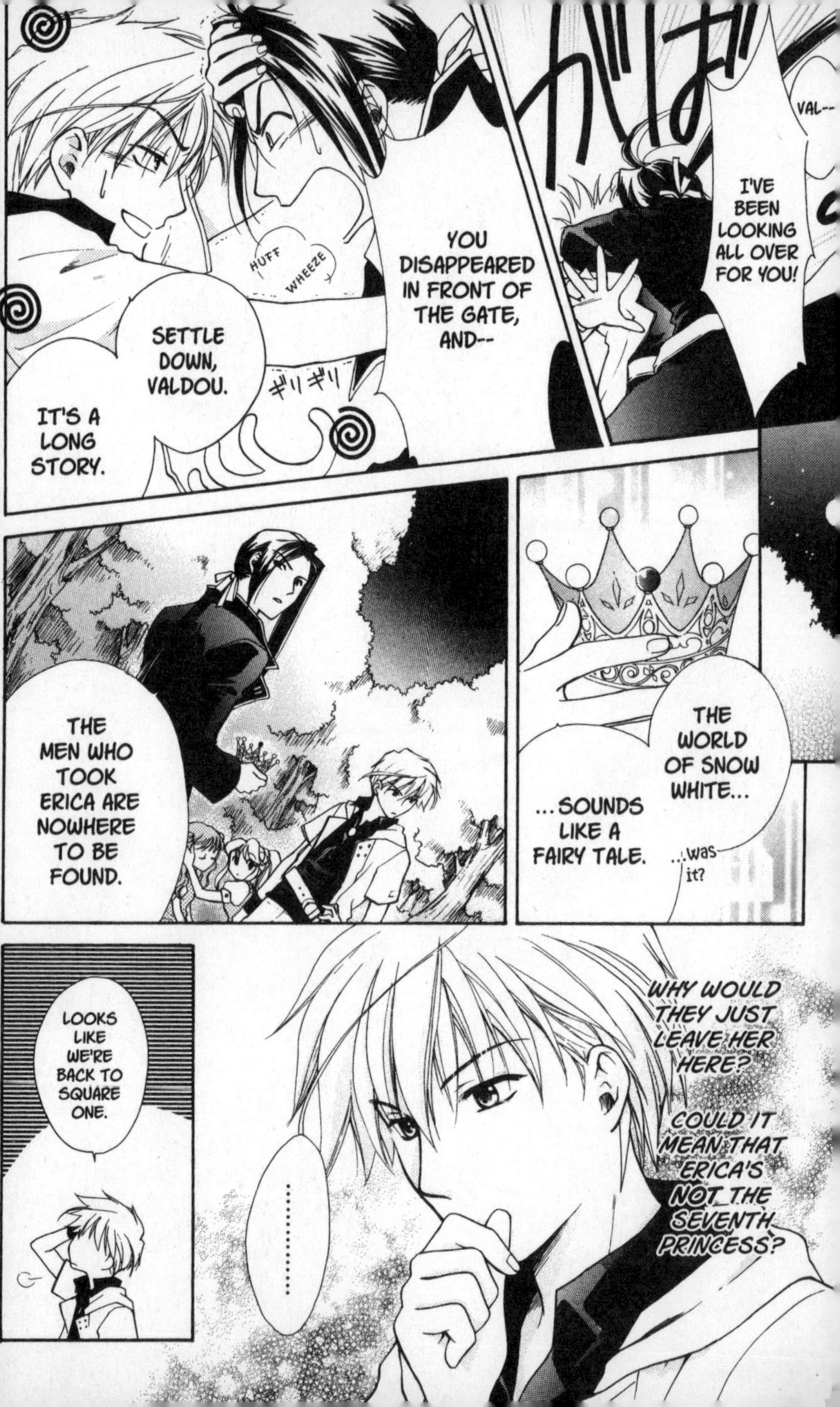
VAL--
I'VE BEEN LOOKING ALL OVER FOR YOU!
YOU DISAPPEARED IN FRONT OF THE GATE, AND--
HUFF
WHEEZE
SETTLE DOWN, VALDOU.
ギリギリ
IT'S A LONG STORY.
THE WORLD OF SNOW WHITE...
...SOUNDS LIKE A FAIRY TALE.
...was it?
THE MEN WHO TOOK ERICA ARE NOWHERE TO BE FOUND.
WHY WOULD THEY JUST LEAVE HER HERE?
COULD IT MEAN THAT ERICA'S NOT THE SEVENTH PRINCESS?
....
LOOKS LIKE WE'RE BACK TO SQUARE ONE.

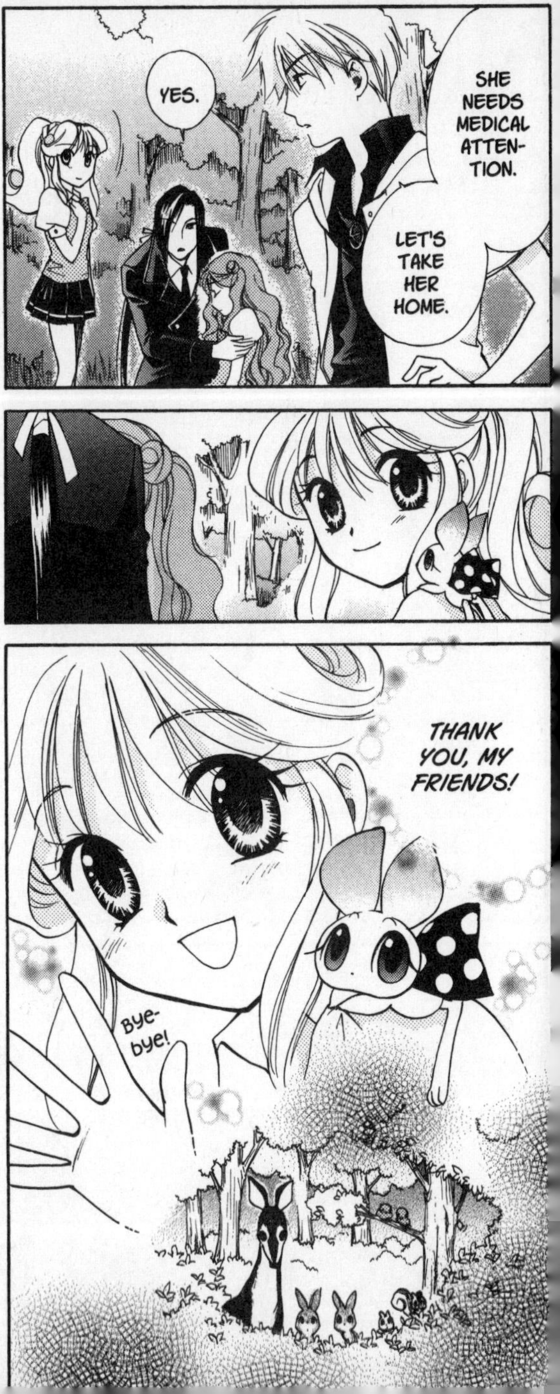
SHE NEEDS MEDICAL ATTEN-TION.
LET'S TAKE HER HOME.
YES.
THANK YOU, MY FRIENDS!
Bye-bye!

Belle

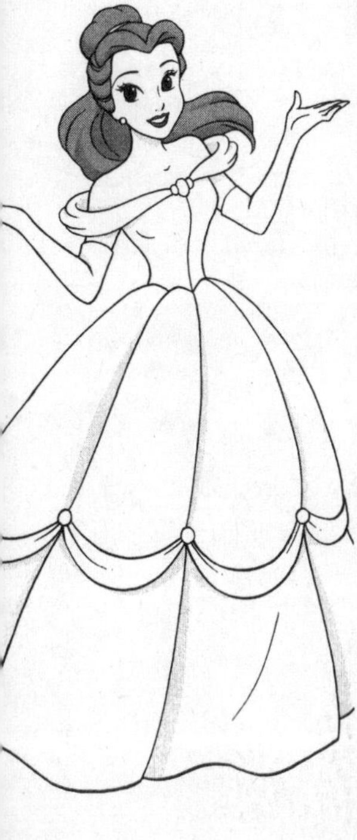

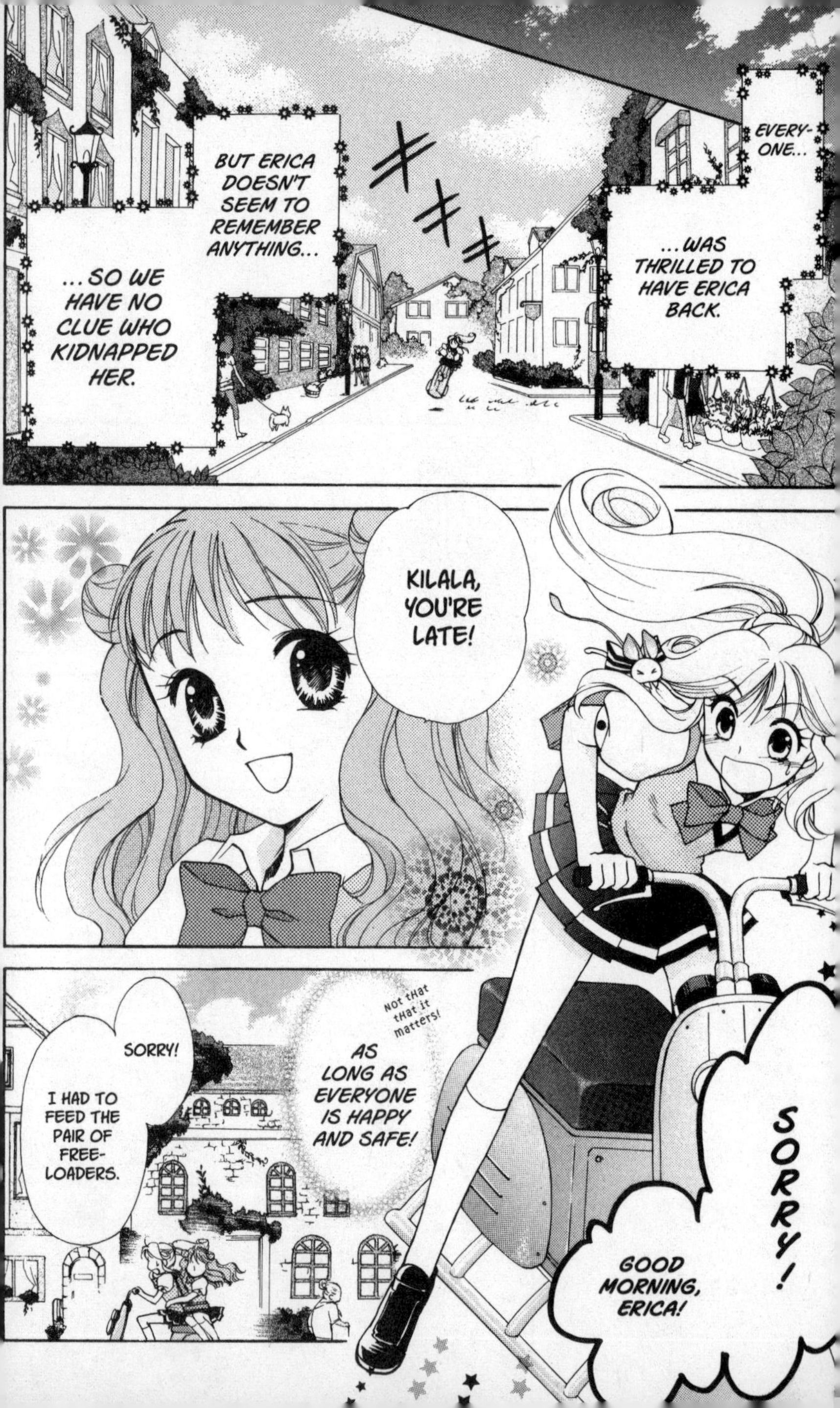
EVERY-ONE...
...WAS THRILLED TO HAVE ERICA BACK.
BUT ERICA DOESN'T SEEM TO REMEMBER ANYTHING...
...SO WE HAVE NO CLUE WHO KIDNAPPED HER.
KILALA, YOU'RE LATE!
SORRY!
GOOD MORNING, ERICA!
AS LONG AS EVERYONE IS HAPPY AND SAFE!
Not that it matters!
SORRY!
I HAD TO FEED THE PAIR OF FREE-LOADERS.

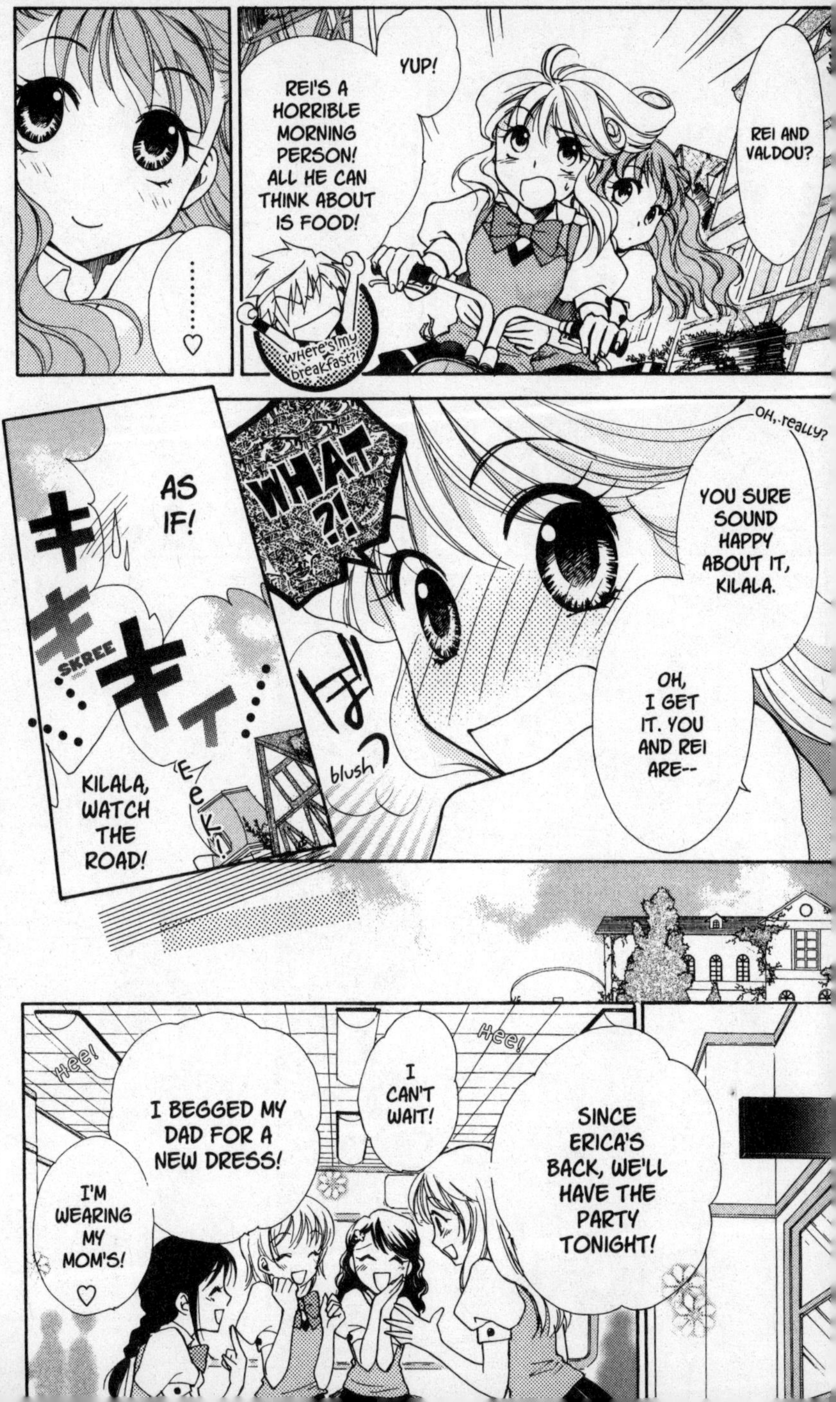
REI AND VALDOU?
YUP!
REI'S A HORRIBLE MORNING PERSON! ALL HE CAN THINK ABOUT IS FOOD!
Where's my breakfast?!
......♡
Oh,-really?
YOU SURE SOUND HAPPY ABOUT IT, KILALA.
OH, I GET IT. YOU AND REI ARE--
WHAT?!
ぽっ
blush
AS IF!
キキキィ
SKREE
KILALA, WATCH THE ROAD!
Eeek!
Hee!
SINCE ERICA'S BACK, WE'LL HAVE THE PARTY TONIGHT!
I CAN'T WAIT!
I BEGGED MY DAD FOR A NEW DRESS!
Hee!
I'M WEARING MY MOM'S! ♡

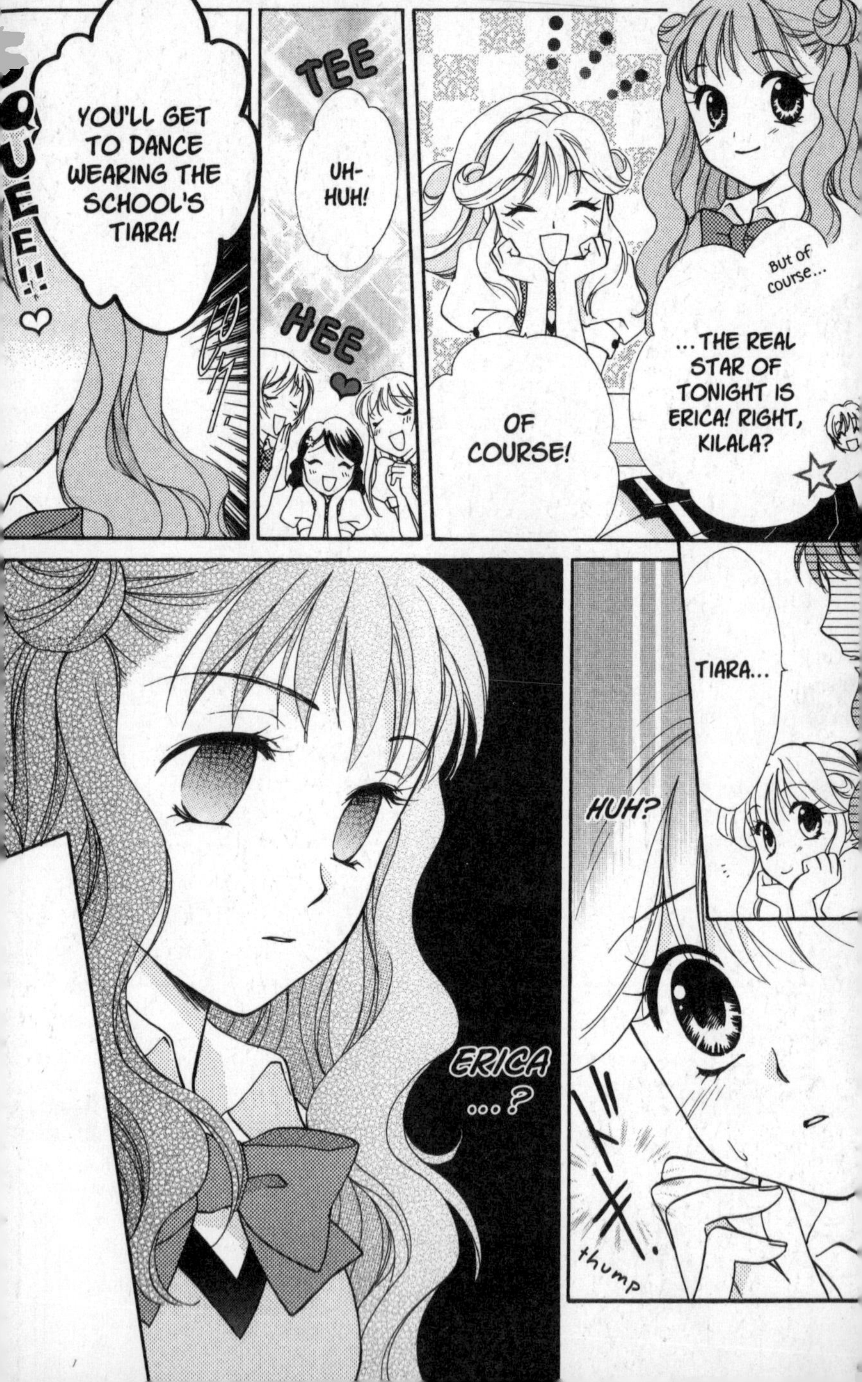
But of course...
...THE REAL STAR OF TONIGHT IS ERICA! RIGHT, KILALA?
OF COURSE!
TEE
UH-HUH!
HEE
YOU'LL GET TO DANCE WEARING THE SCHOOL'S TIARA!
QUEE!!
TIARA...
HUH?
thump
ERICA...?

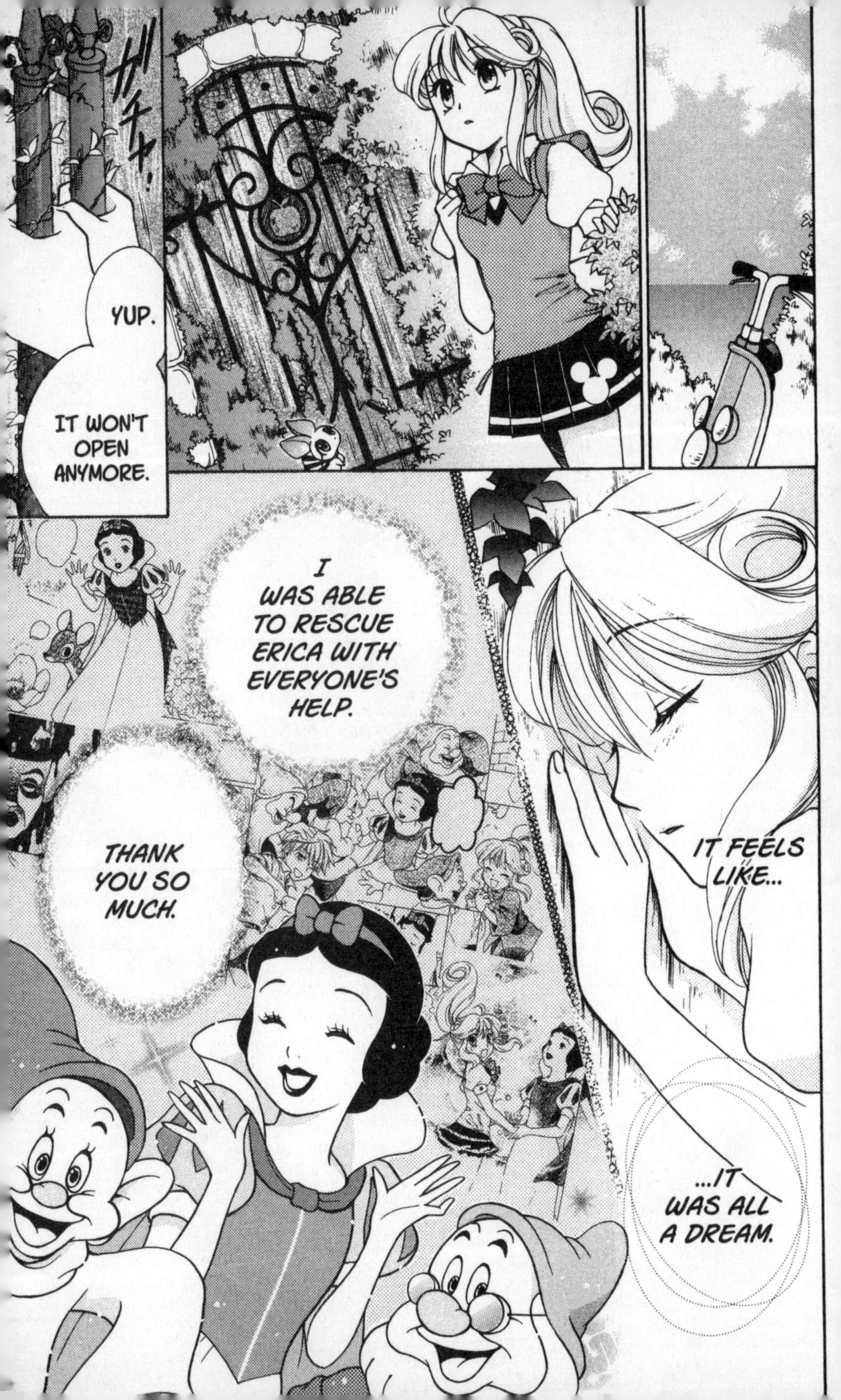
ガチャ!
YUP.
IT WON'T OPEN ANYMORE.
IT FEELS LIKE...
...IT WAS ALL A DREAM.
I WAS ABLE TO RESCUE ERICA WITH EVERYONE'S HELP.
THANK YOU SO MUCH.

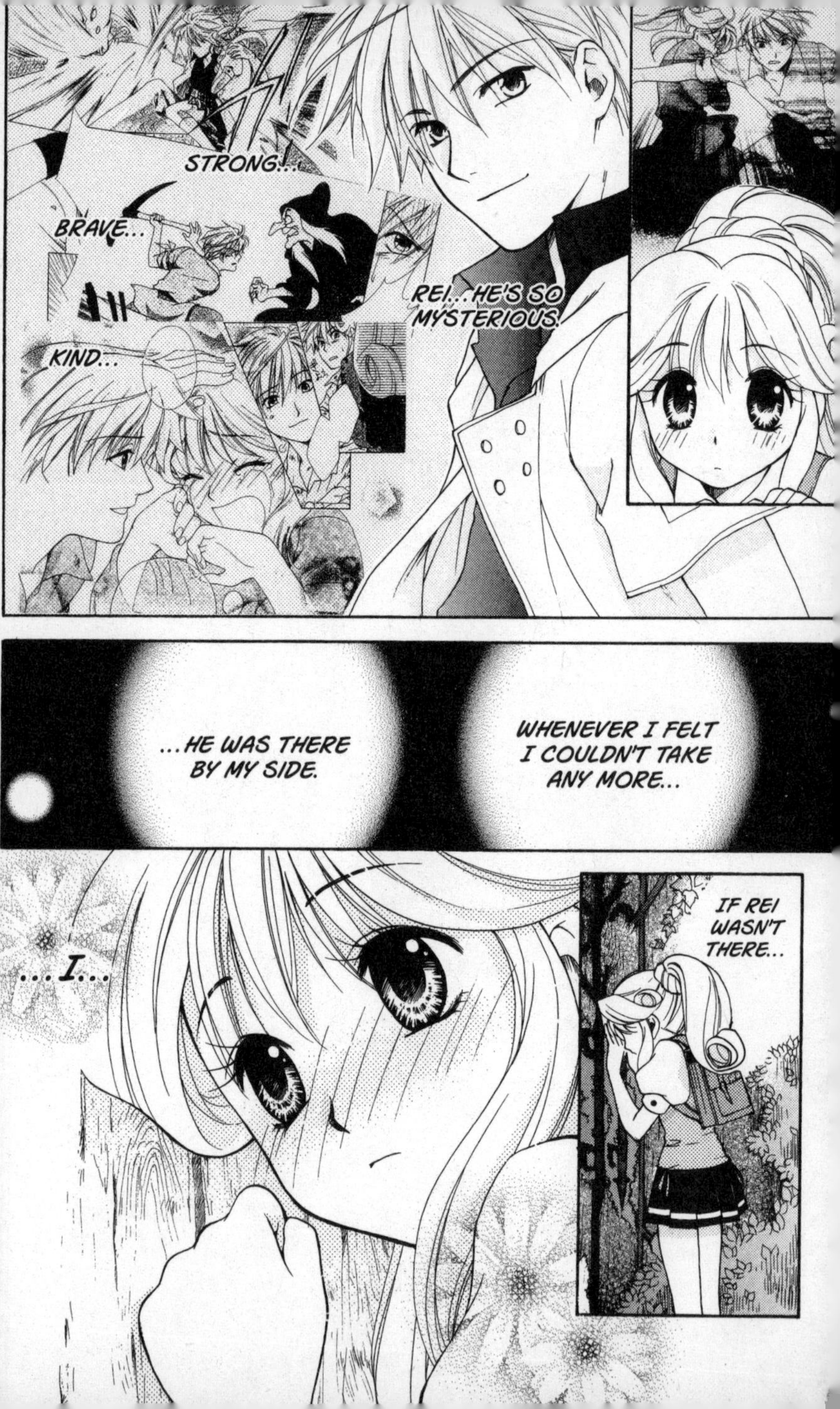
STRONG...
BRAVE...
KIND...
REI... HE'S SO MYSTERIOUS.
WHENEVER I FELT I COULDN'T TAKE ANY MORE...
...HE WAS THERE BY MY SIDE.
IF REI WASN'T THERE...
...I...

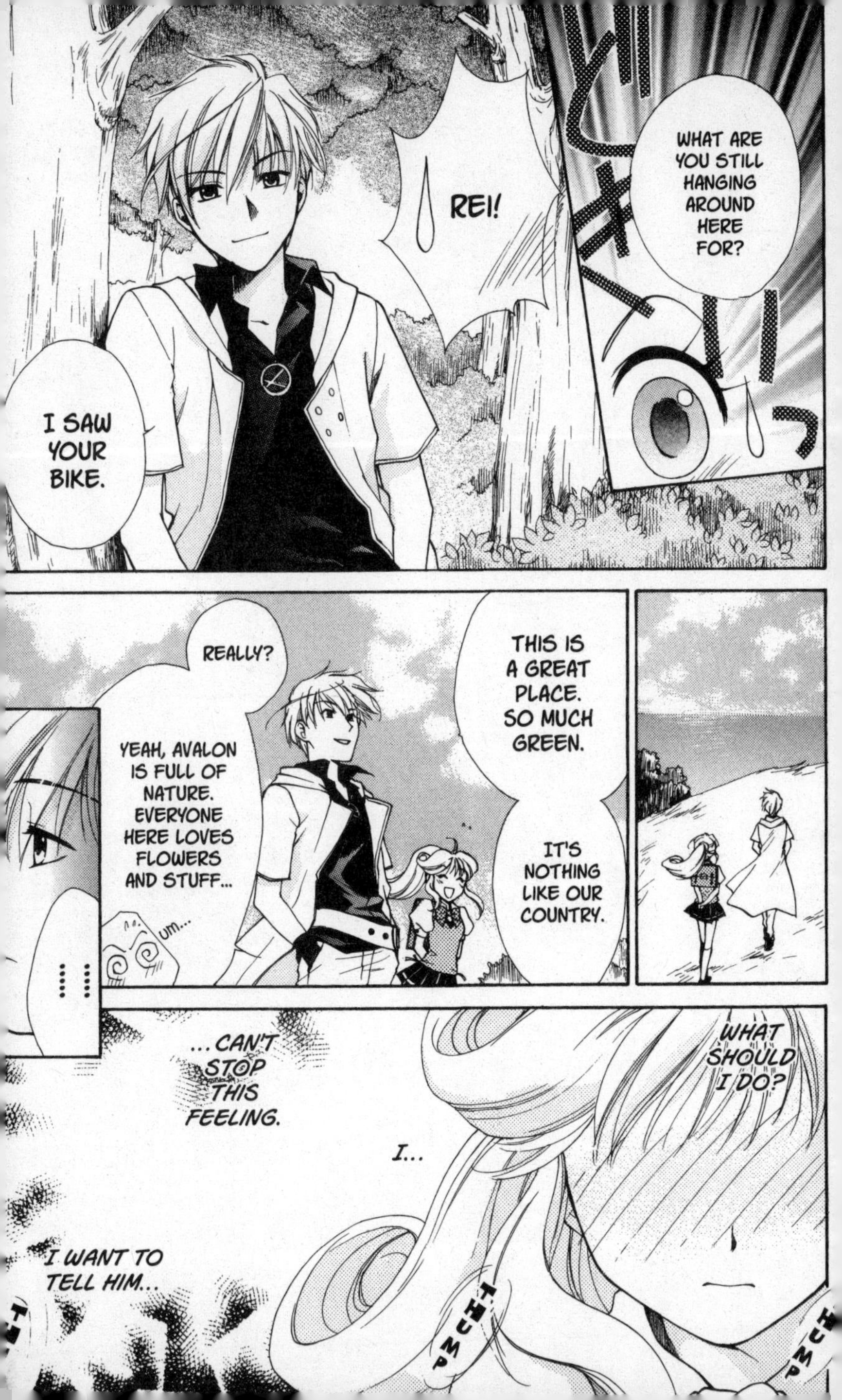
REI!
WHAT ARE YOU STILL HANGING AROUND HERE FOR?
I SAW YOUR BIKE.
THIS IS A GREAT PLACE. SO MUCH GREEN.
IT'S NOTHING LIKE OUR COUNTRY.
REALLY?
YEAH, AVALON IS FULL OF NATURE. EVERYONE HERE LOVES FLOWERS AND STUFF...
UM...
......
WHAT SHOULD I DO?
...CAN'T STOP THIS FEELING.
I...
I WANT TO TELL HIM...
THUMP
THUMP

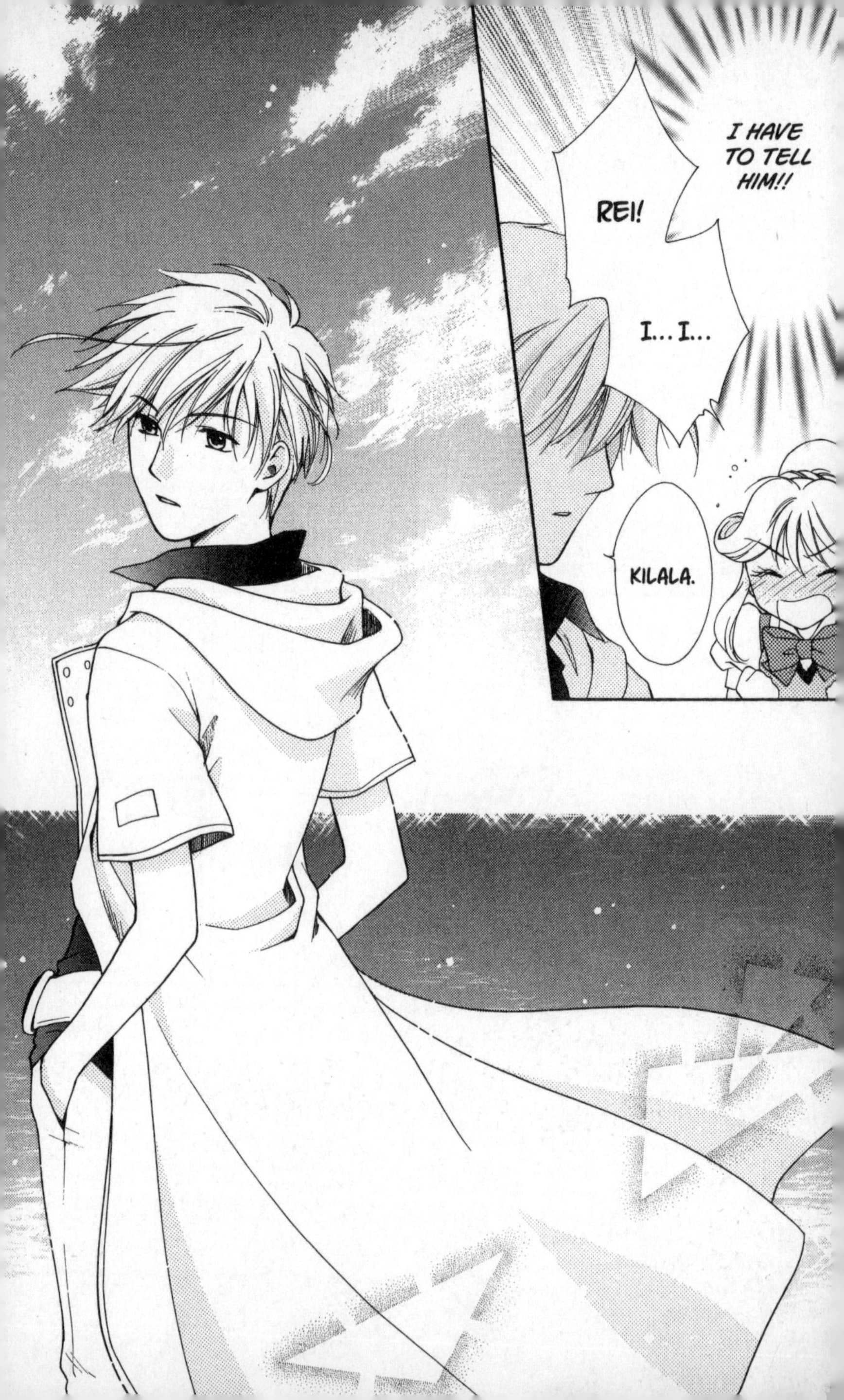
I HAVE TO TELL HIM!!
REI!
I... I...
KILALA.

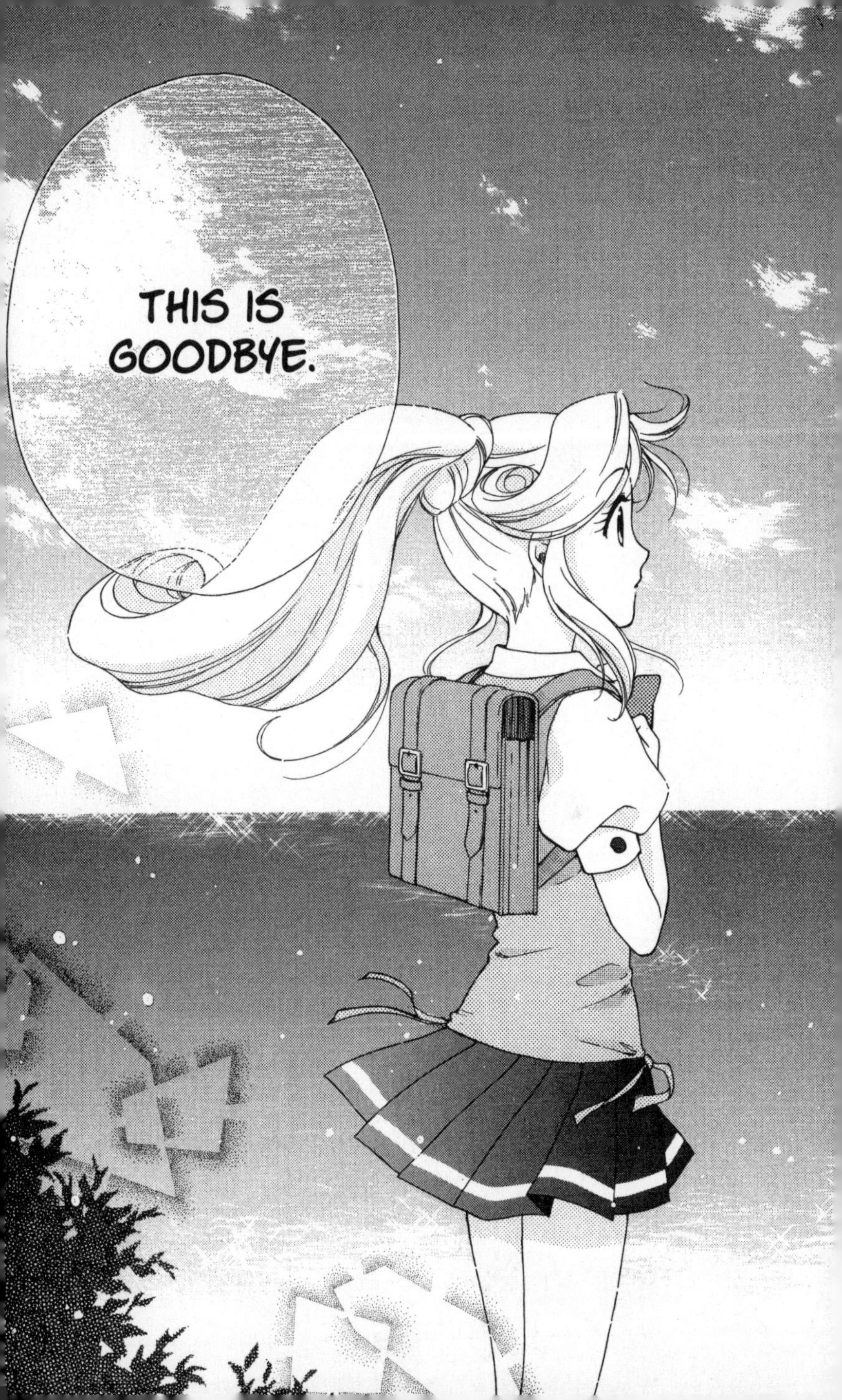
THIS IS GOODBYE.

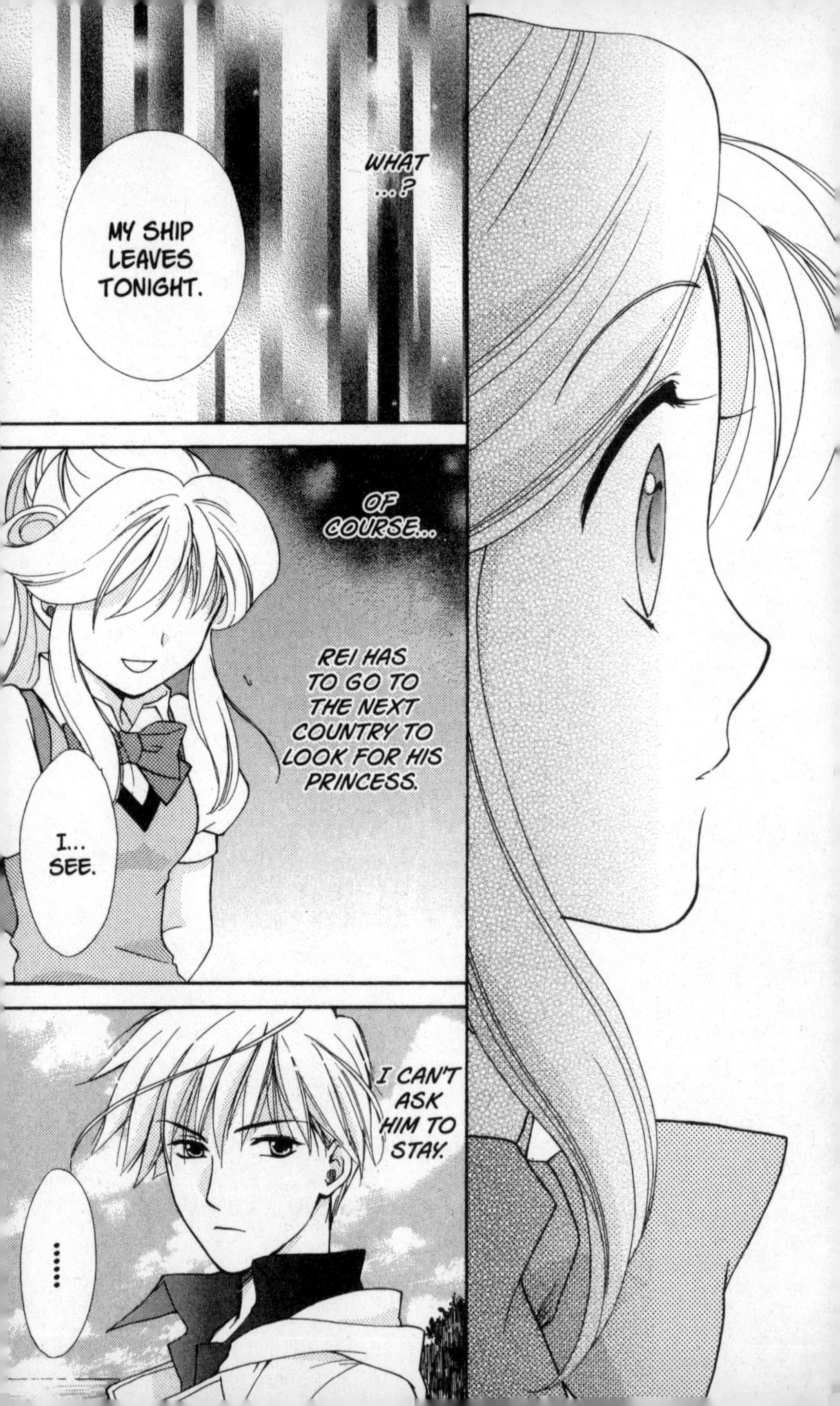
WHAT ...?
MY SHIP LEAVES TONIGHT.
OF COURSE...
REI HAS TO GO TO THE NEXT COUNTRY TO LOOK FOR HIS PRINCESS.
I... SEE.
I CAN'T ASK HIM TO STAY.
......

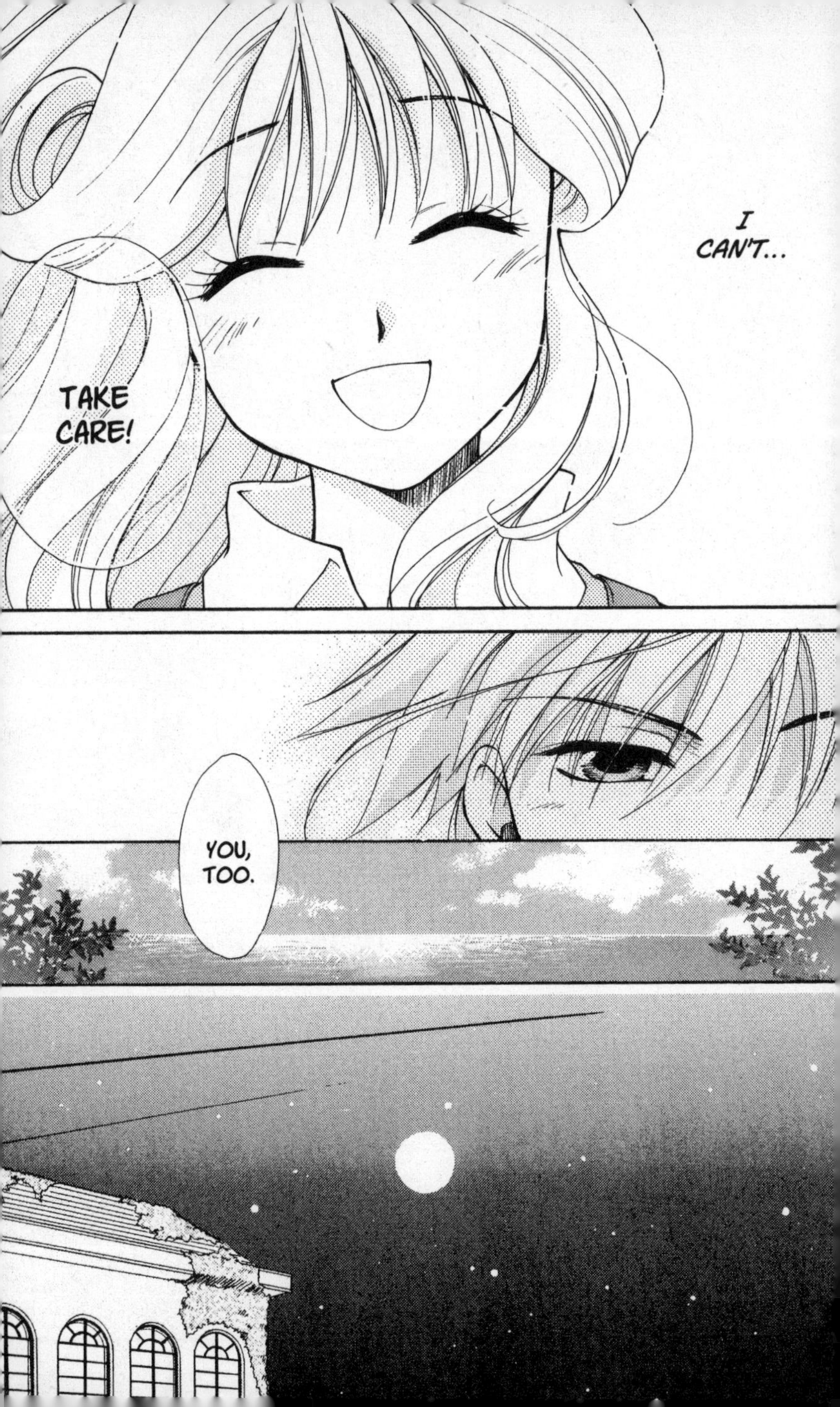
I CAN'T...
TAKE CARE!
YOU, TOO.

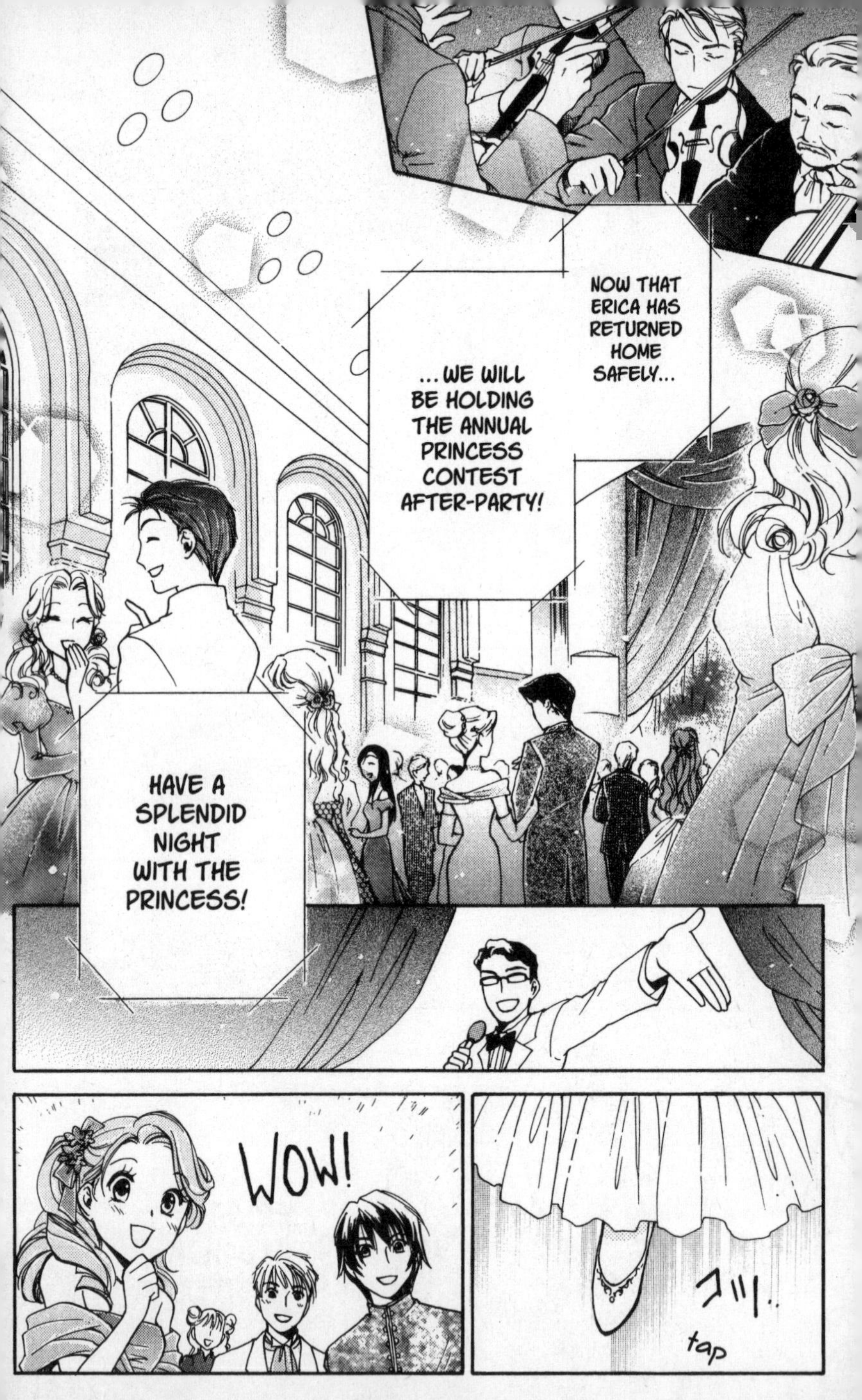
NOW THAT ERICA HAS RETURNED HOME SAFELY...
...WE WILL BE HOLDING THE ANNUAL PRINCESS CONTEST AFTER-PARTY!
HAVE A SPLENDID NIGHT WITH THE PRINCESS!
コツ..
tap
WOW!

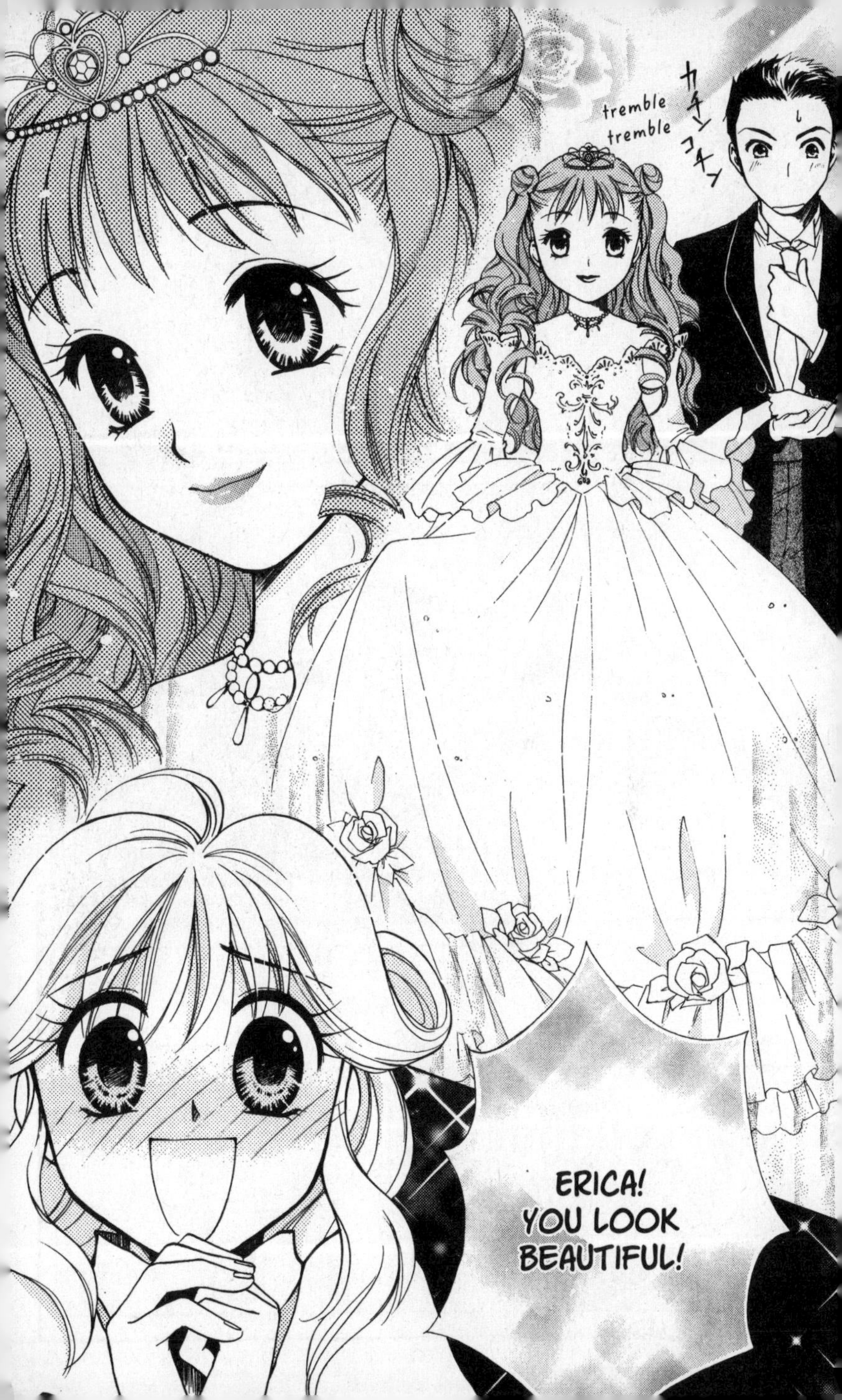
tremble tremble
カチンコチン
ERICA! YOU LOOK BEAUTIFUL!

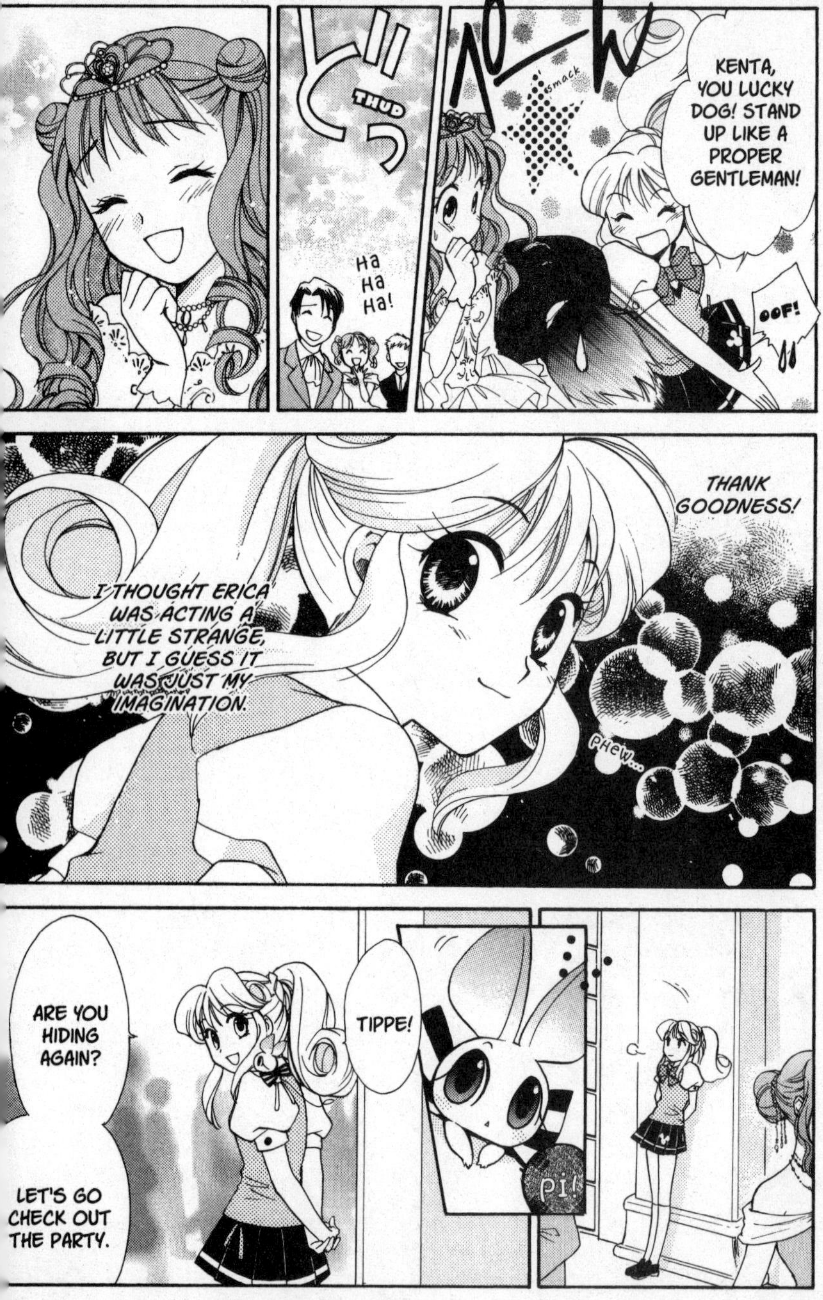
KENTA, YOU LUCKY DOG! STAND UP LIKE A PROPER GENTLEMAN!
smack
OOF!
THUD
Ha Ha Ha!
THANK GOODNESS!
I THOUGHT ERICA WAS ACTING A LITTLE STRANGE, BUT I GUESS IT WAS JUST MY IMAGINATION.
Phew...
TIPPE!
pi!
ARE YOU HIDING AGAIN?
LET'S GO CHECK OUT THE PARTY.

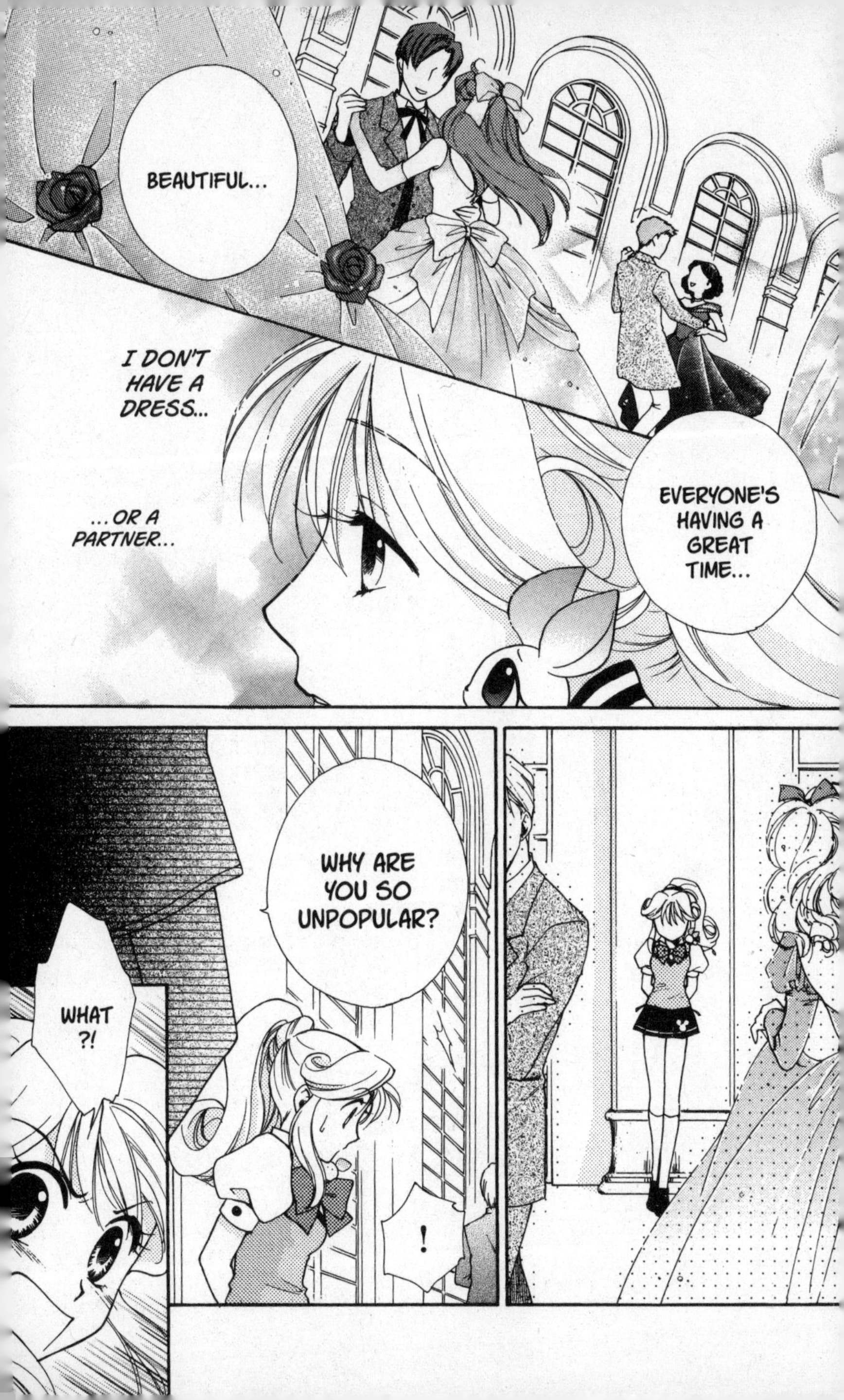

BEAUTIFUL...
EVERYONE'S HAVING A GREAT TIME...
I DON'T HAVE A DRESS...
...OR A PARTNER...
WHY ARE YOU SO UNPOPULAR?
!
WHAT ?!

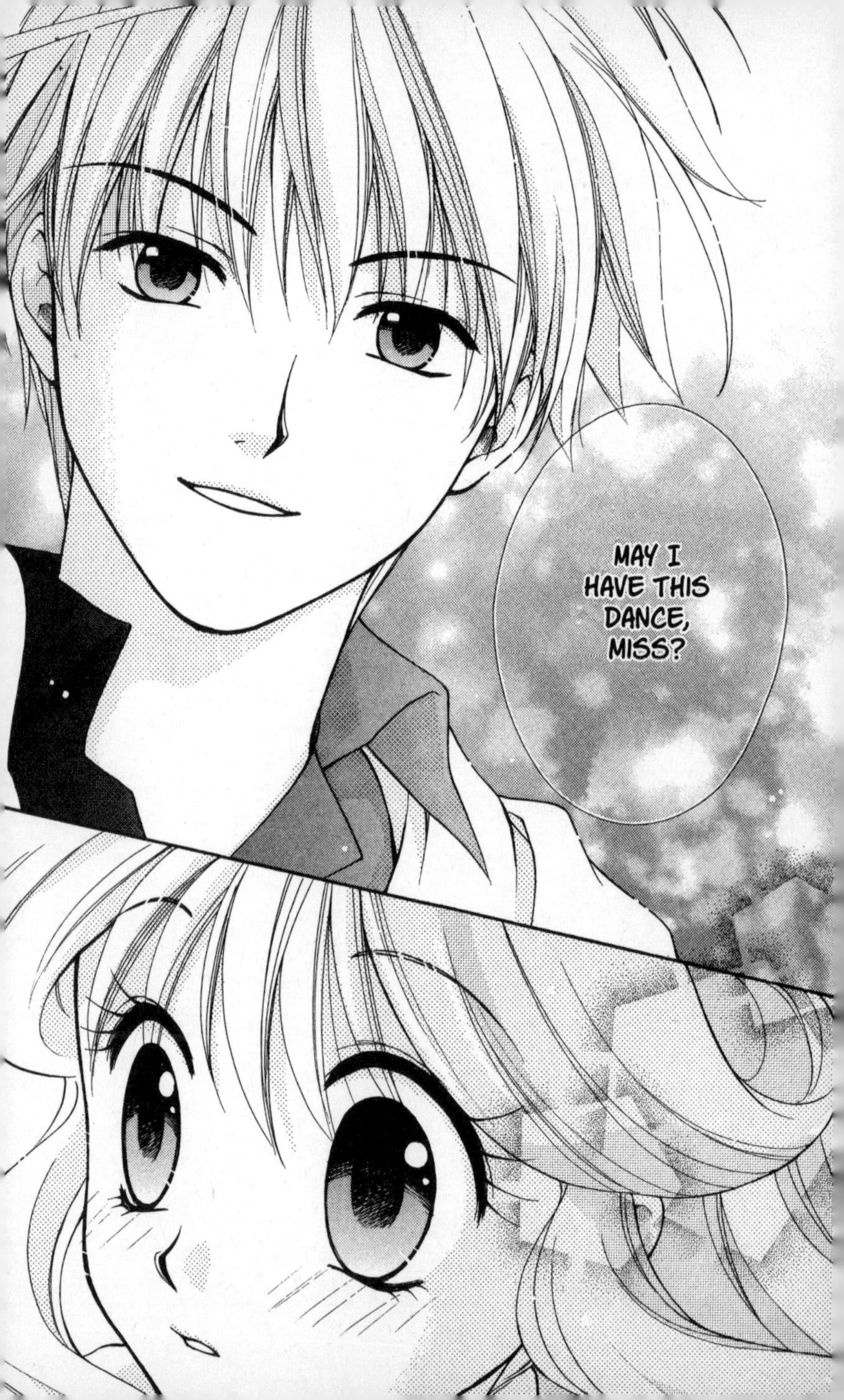
MAY I HAVE THIS DANCE, MISS?

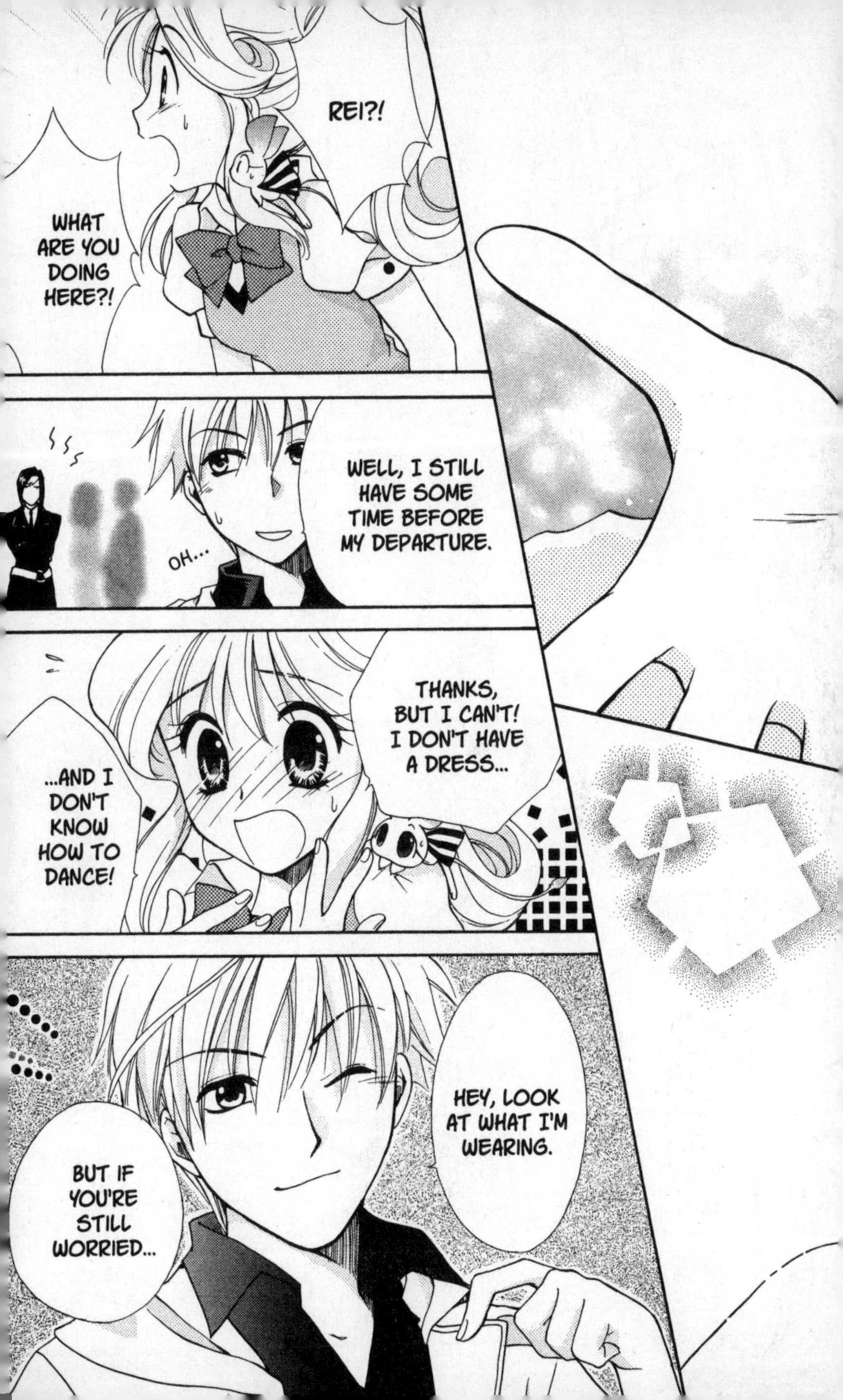
REI?!
WHAT ARE YOU DOING HERE?!
WELL, I STILL HAVE SOME TIME BEFORE MY DEPARTURE.
OH...
THANKS, BUT I CAN'T! I DON'T HAVE A DRESS...
...AND I DON'T KNOW HOW TO DANCE!
HEY, LOOK AT WHAT I'M WEARING.
BUT IF YOU'RE STILL WORRIED...

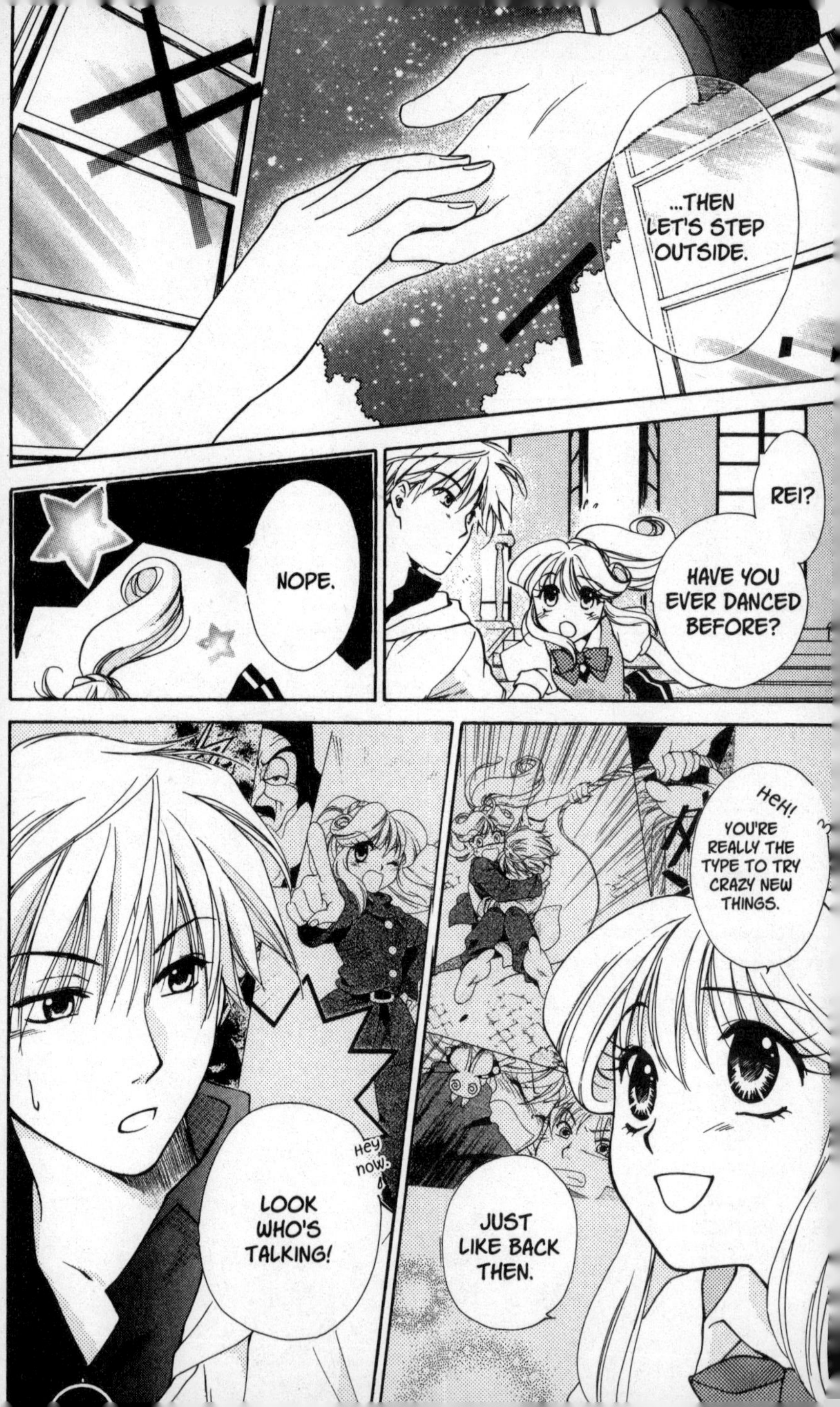
...THEN LET'S STEP OUTSIDE.
REI?
HAVE YOU EVER DANCED BEFORE?
NOPE.
HEH!
YOU'RE REALLY THE TYPE TO TRY CRAZY NEW THINGS.
JUST LIKE BACK THEN.
Hey now.
LOOK WHO'S TALKING!

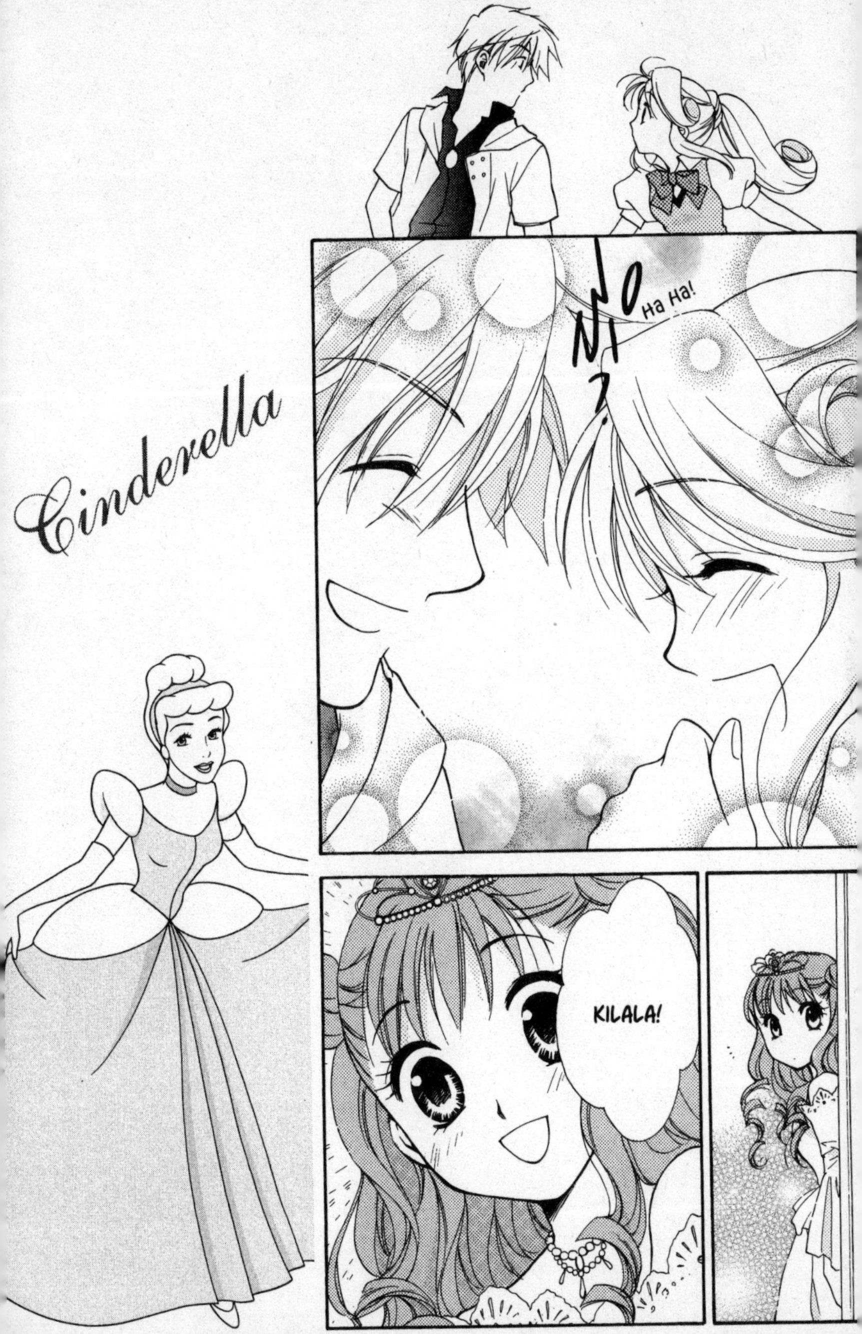
Ha Ha!
KILALA!
Cinderella

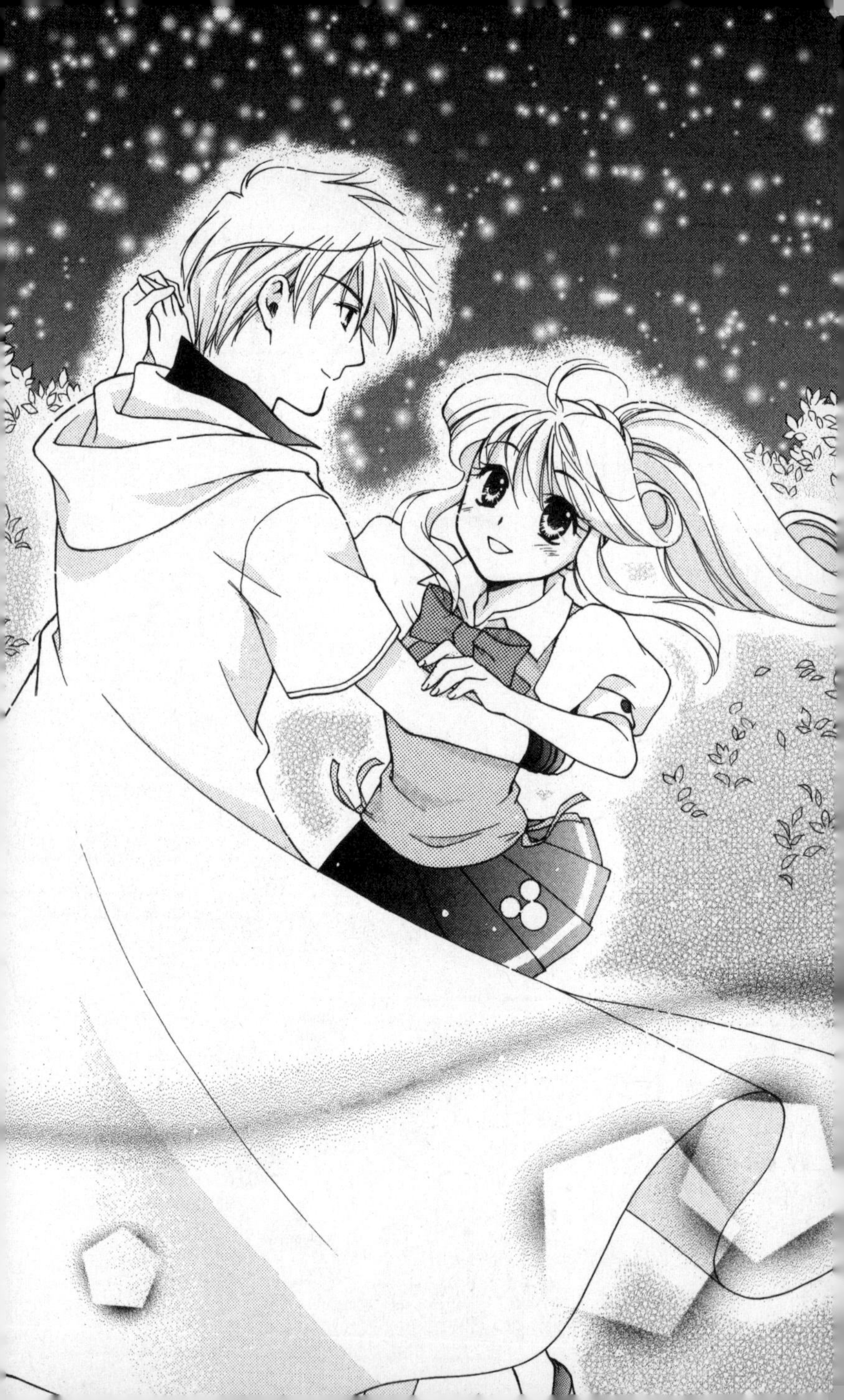

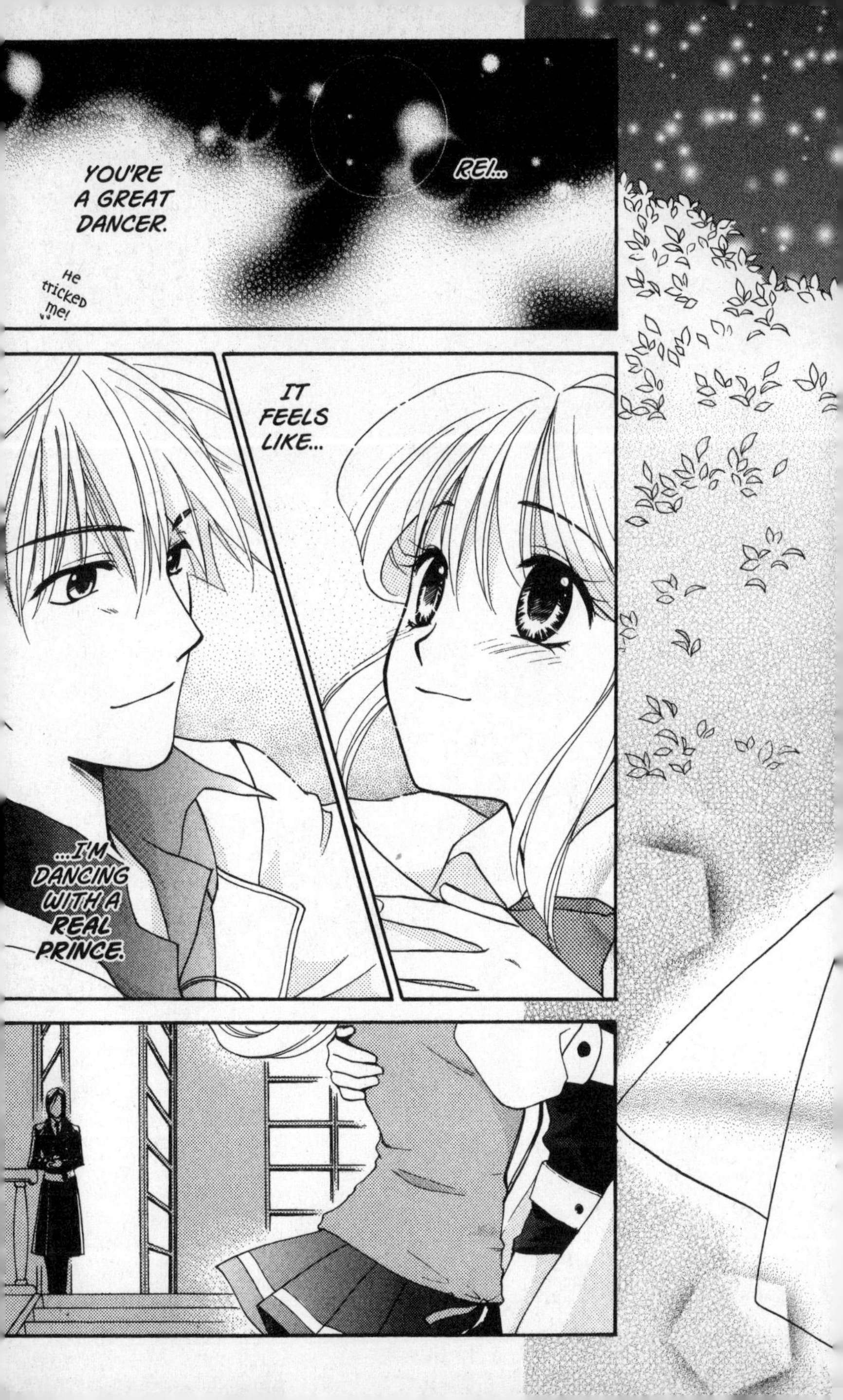
REI...
YOU'RE A GREAT DANCER.
He tricked me!
IT FEELS LIKE...
...I'M DANCING WITH A REAL PRINCE.

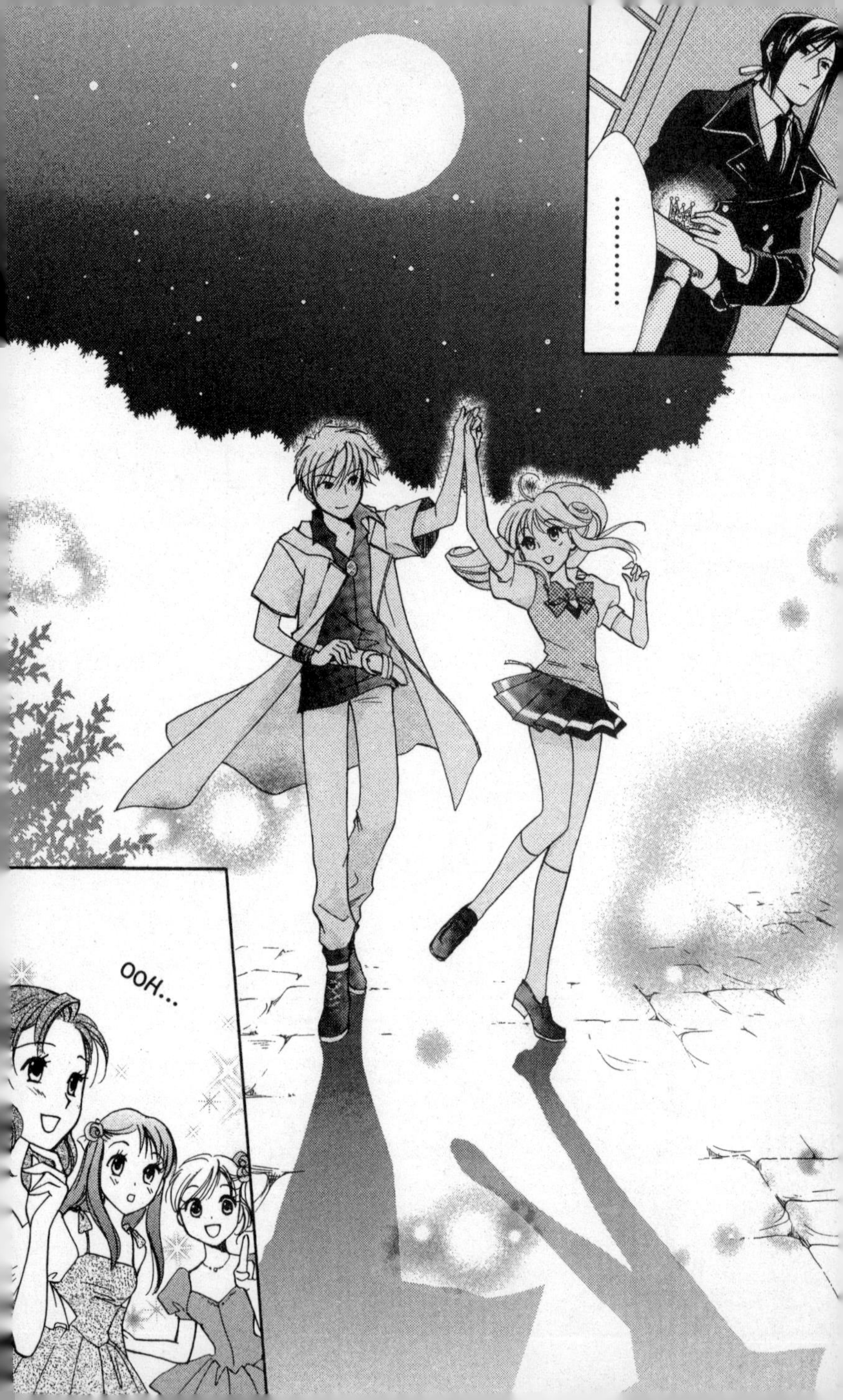
......
OOH...

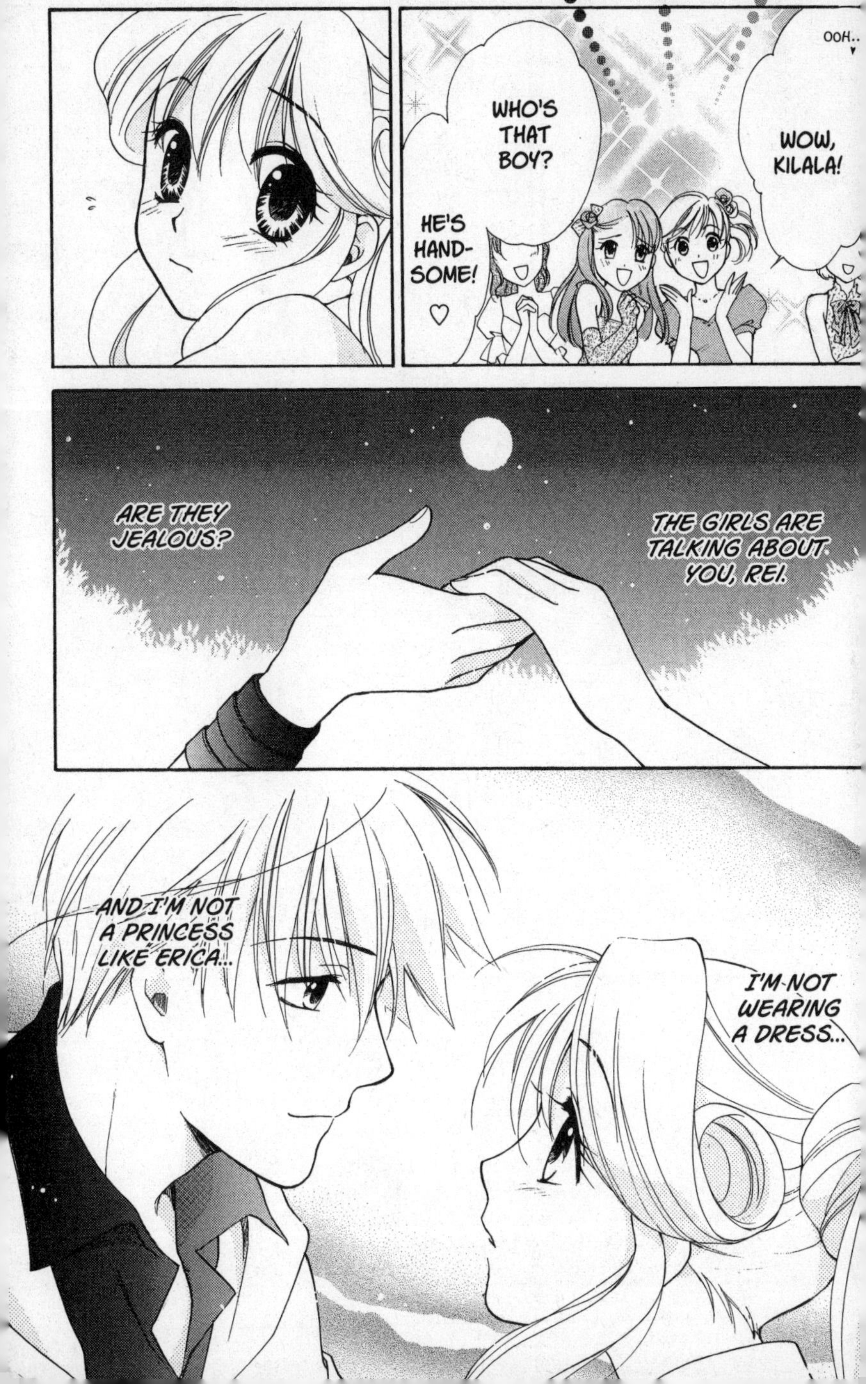
OOH..
WOW, KILALA!
WHO'S THAT BOY?
HE'S HAND-SOME!
THE GIRLS ARE TALKING ABOUT YOU, REI.
ARE THEY JEALOUS?
I'M NOT WEARING A DRESS...
AND I'M NOT A PRINCESS LIKE ERICA...

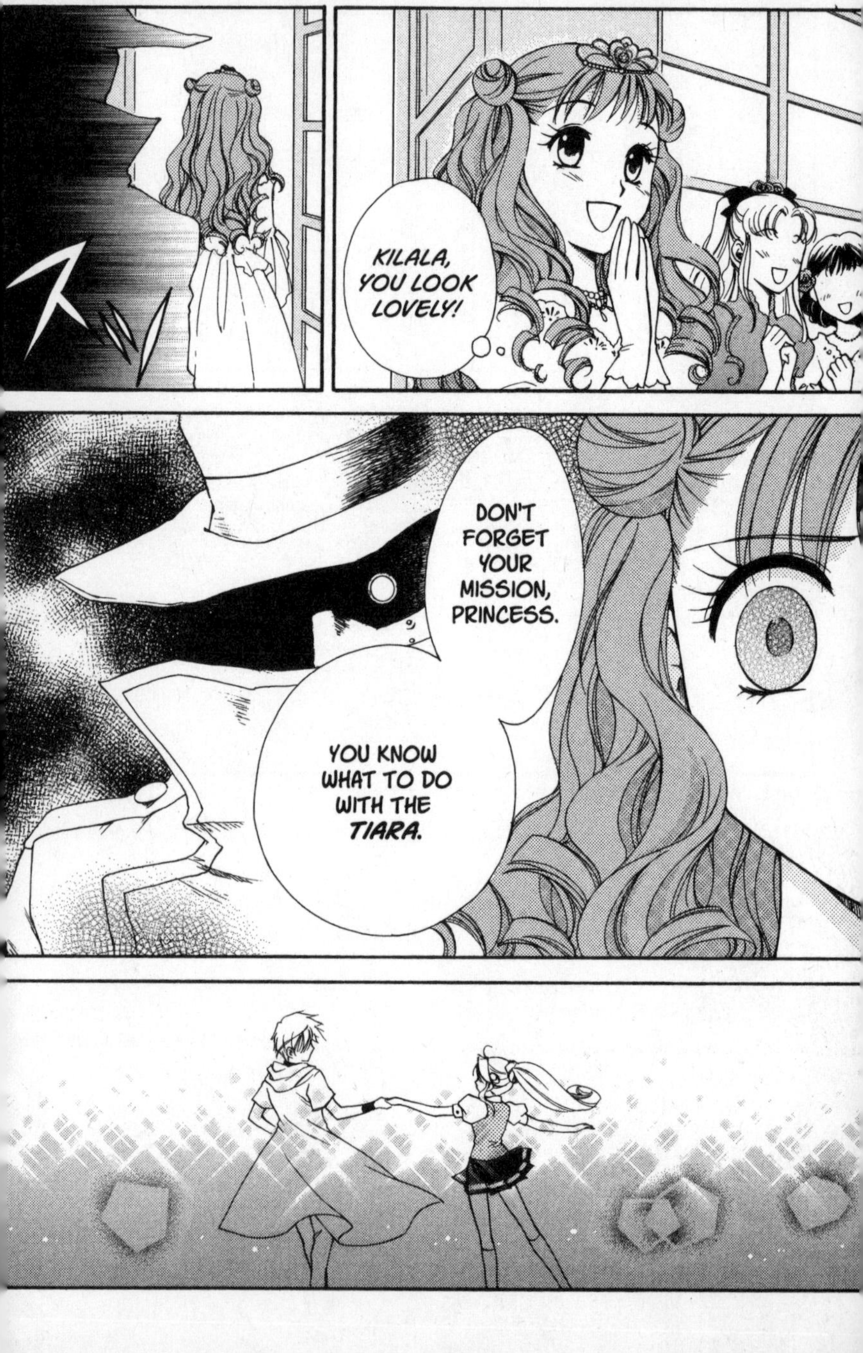
KILALA, YOU LOOK LOVELY!
DON'T FORGET YOUR MISSION, PRINCESS.
YOU KNOW WHAT TO DO WITH THE *TIARA.*

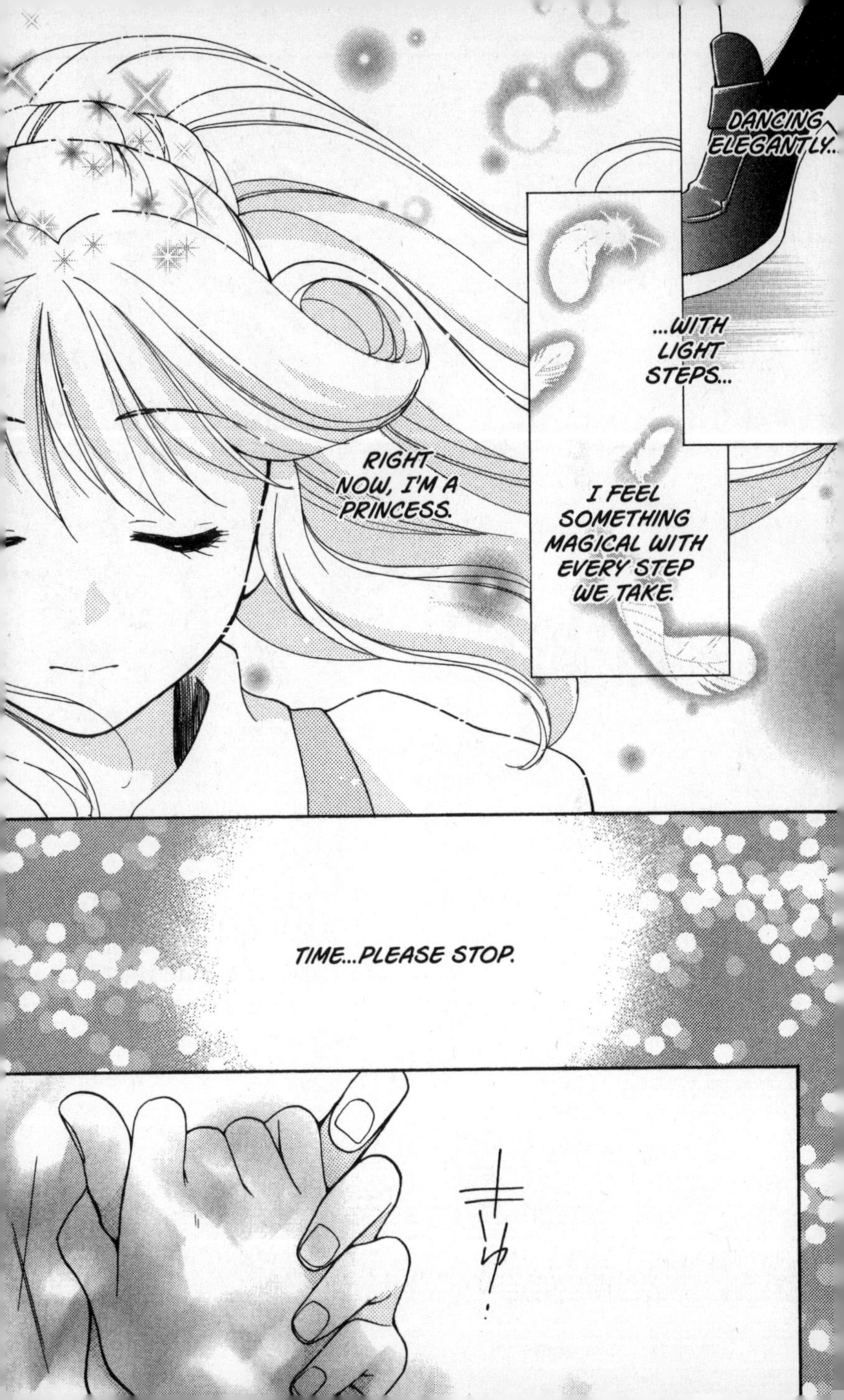
DANCING ELEGANTLY...
...WITH LIGHT STEPS...
I FEEL SOMETHING MAGICAL WITH EVERY STEP WE TAKE.
RIGHT NOW, I'M A PRINCESS.
TIME...PLEASE STOP.
キゅ!

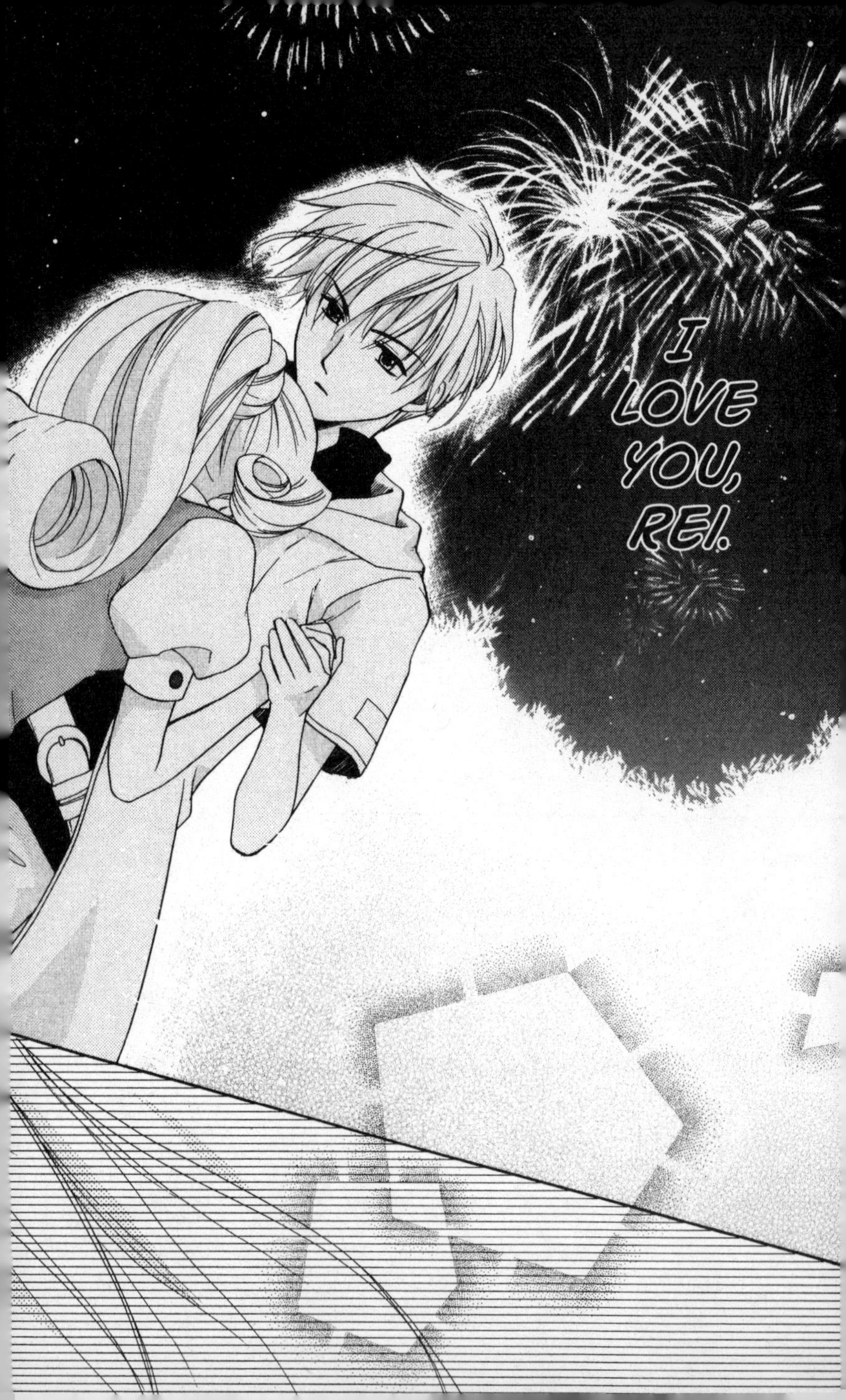
I LOVE YOU, REI.

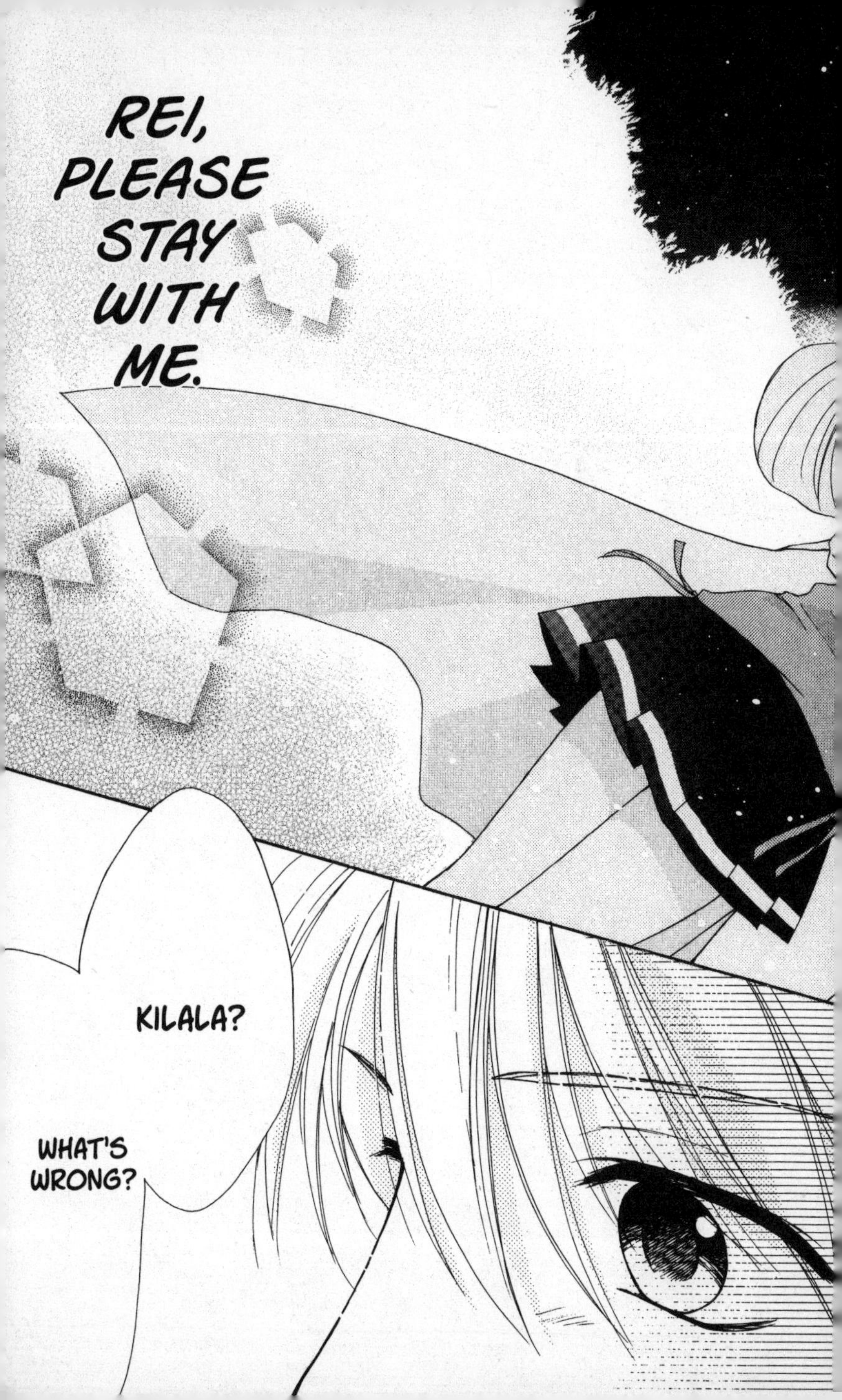
REI, PLEASE STAY WITH ME.
KILALA?
WHAT'S WRONG?

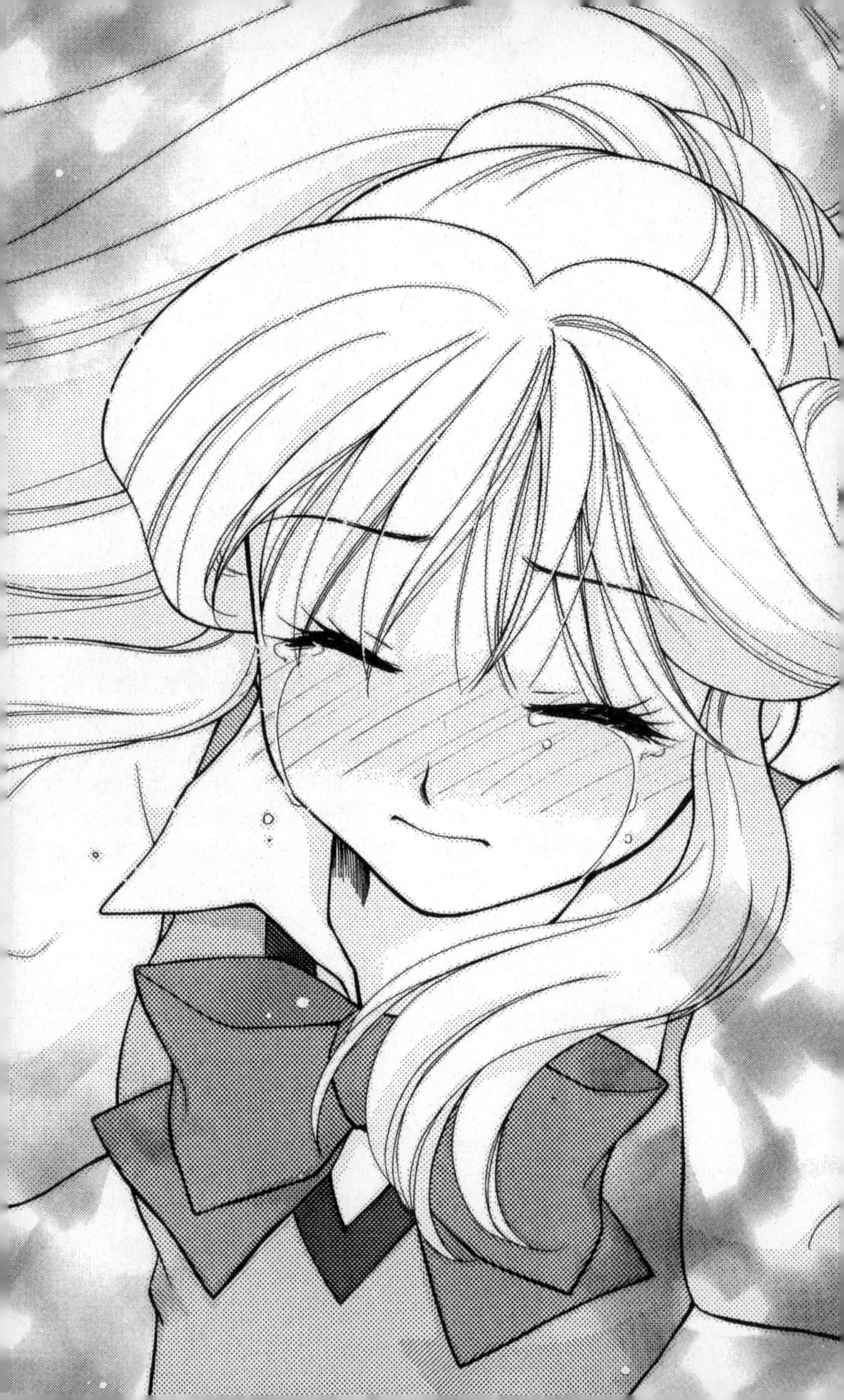

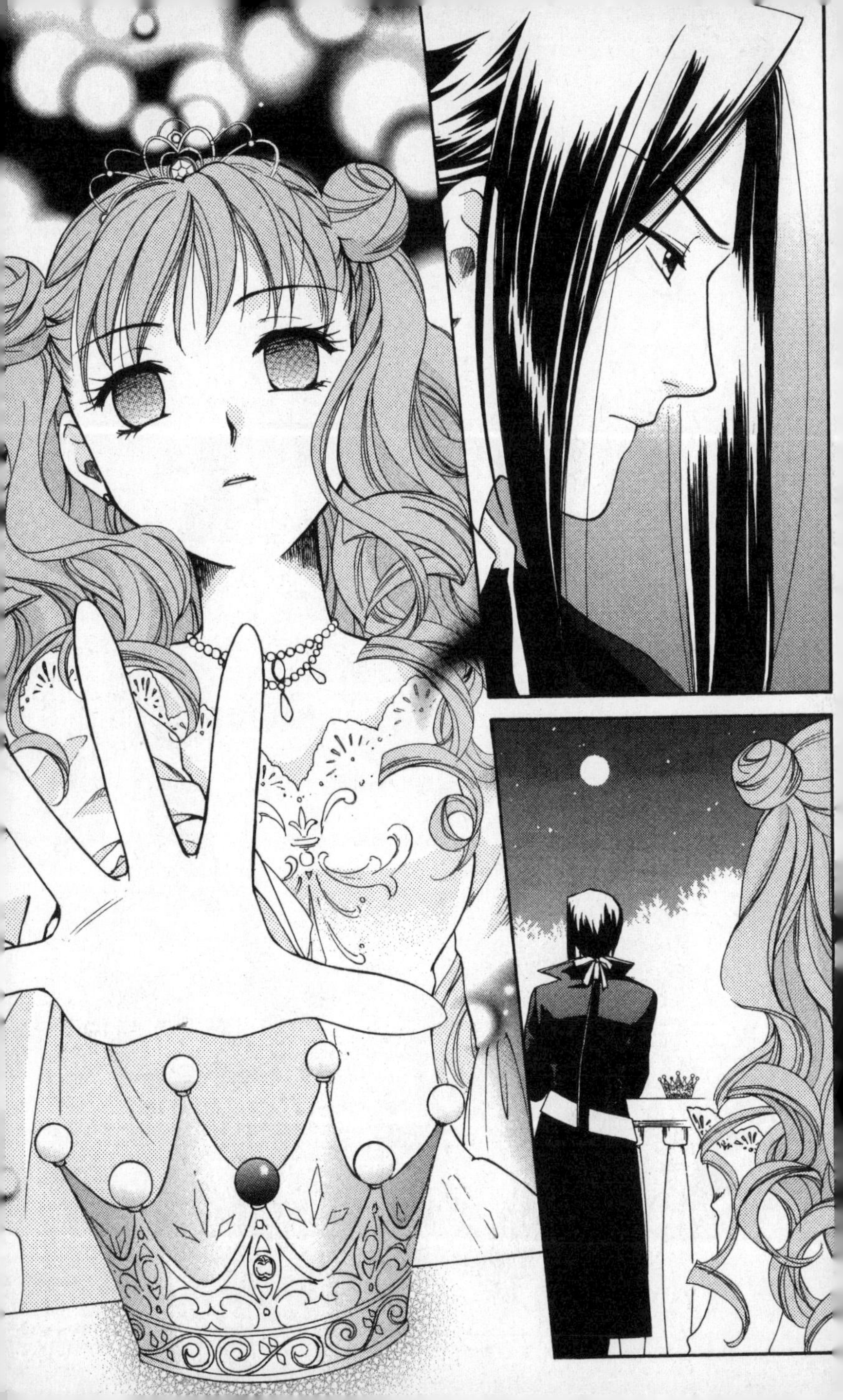

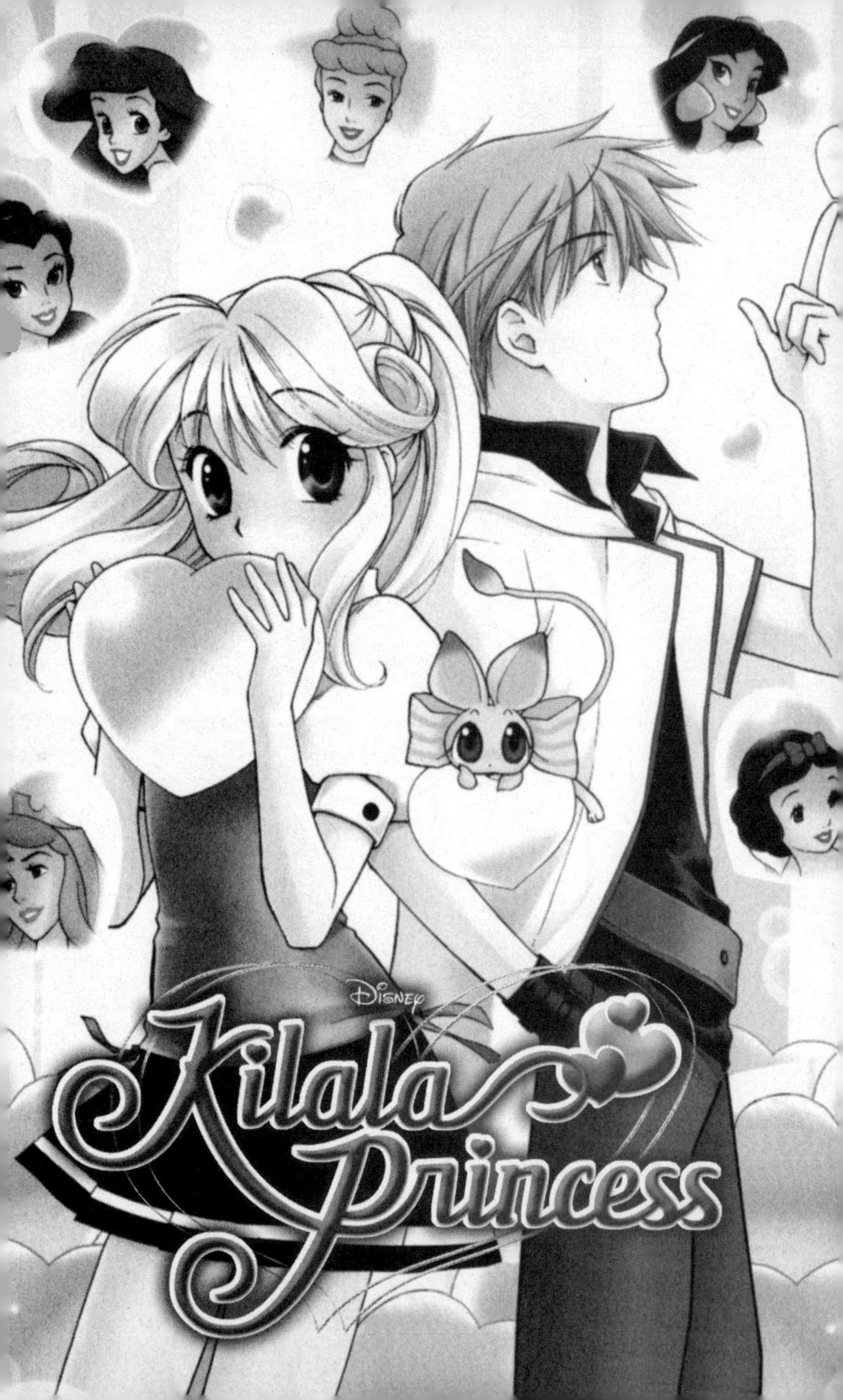
Disney
Kilala Princess

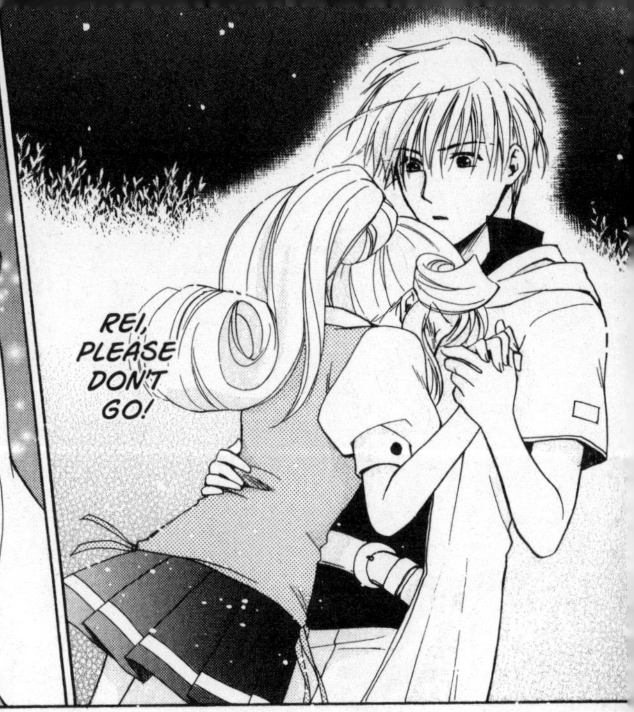
REI, PLEASE DON'T GO!

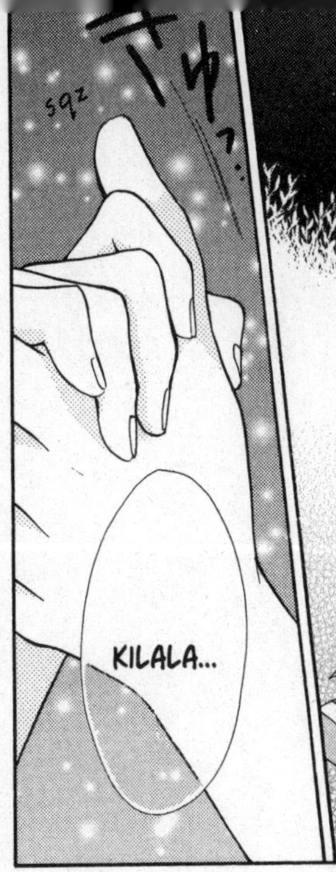
キュッ
sqz
KILALA...

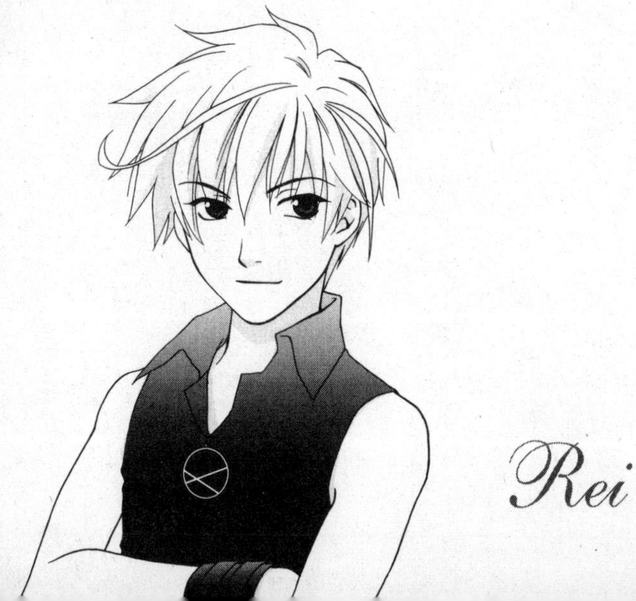
Rei

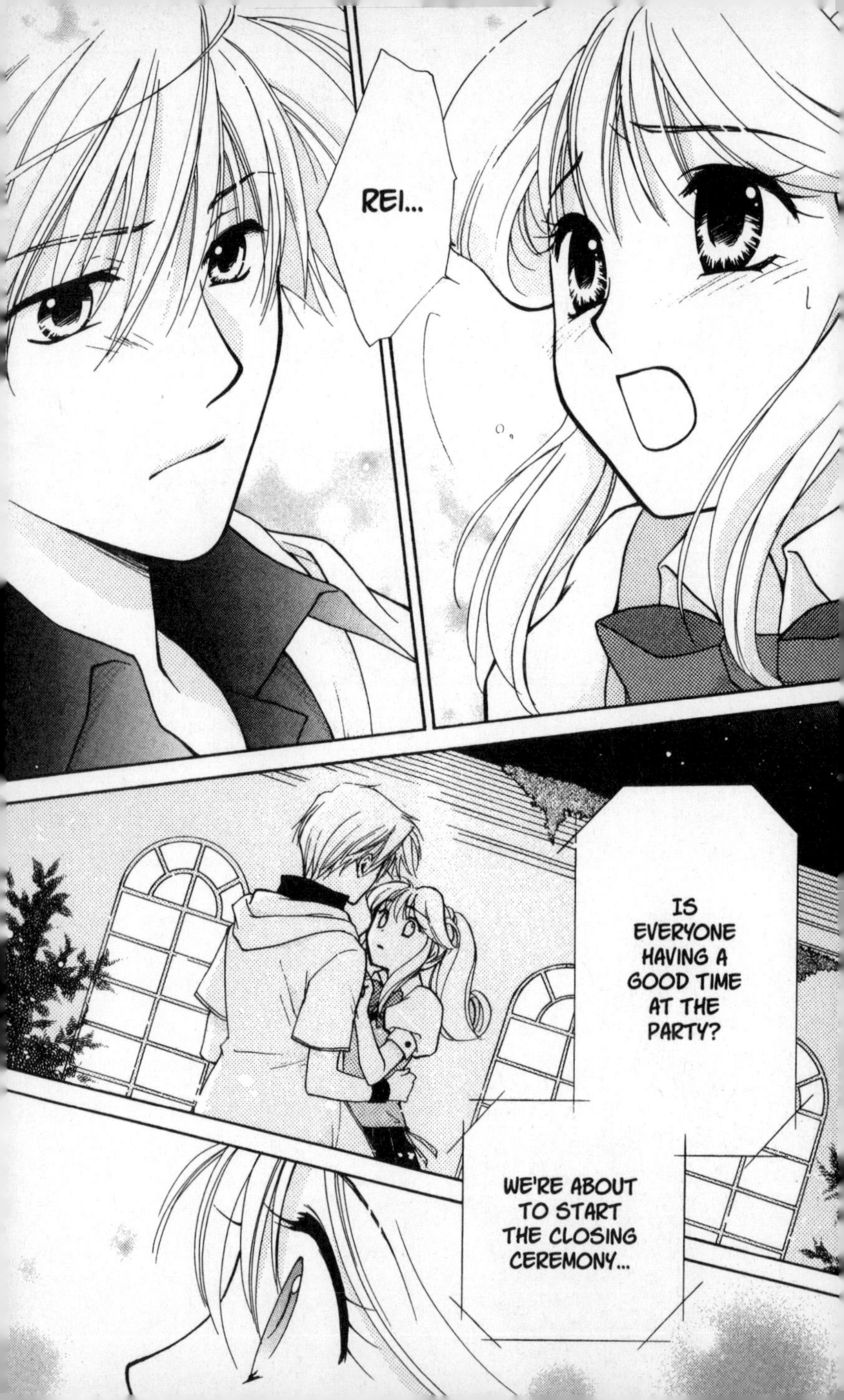
REI...
IS EVERYONE HAVING A GOOD TIME AT THE PARTY?
WE'RE ABOUT TO START THE CLOSING CEREMONY...

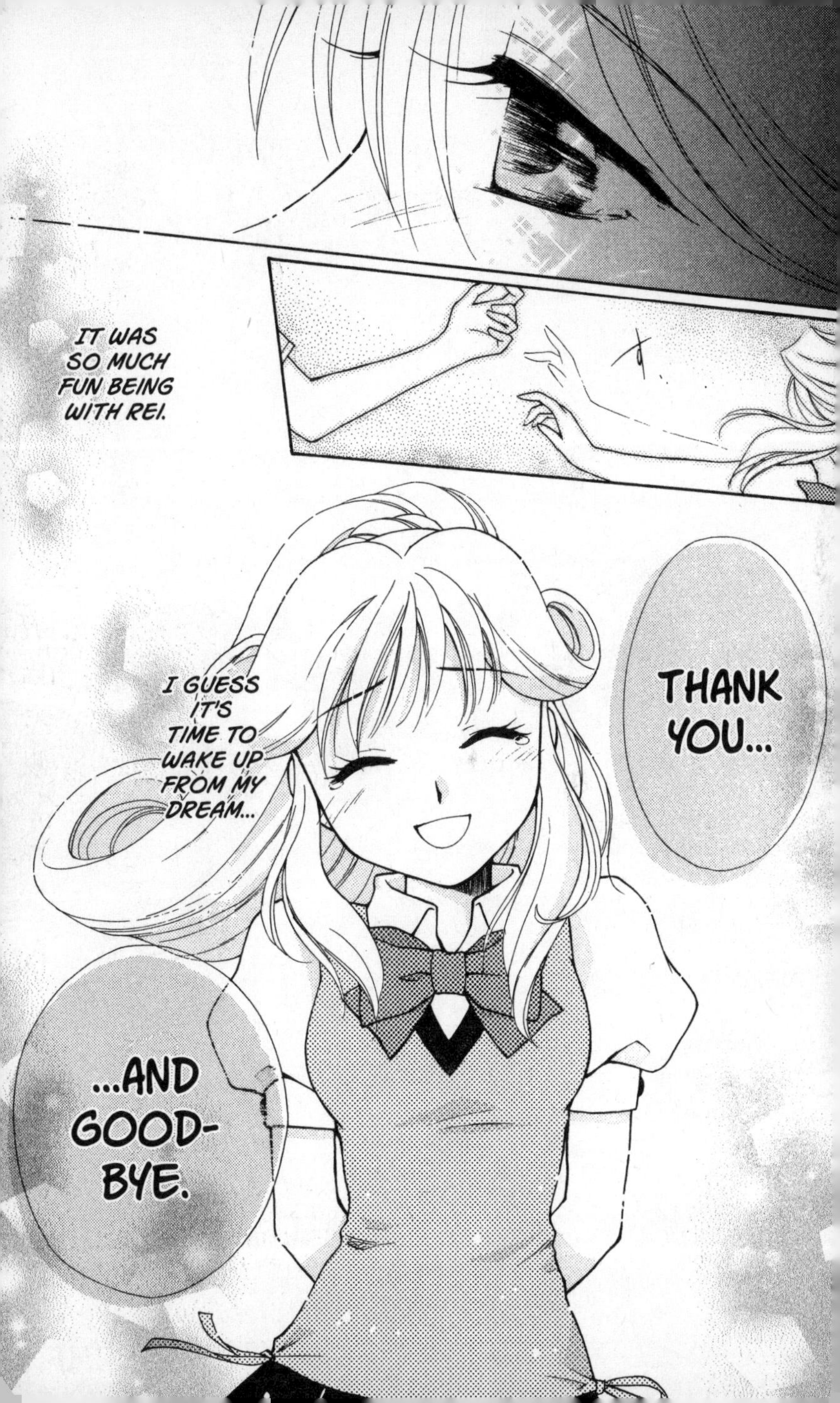
IT WAS SO MUCH FUN BEING WITH REI.
THANK YOU...
I GUESS IT'S TIME TO WAKE UP FROM MY DREAM...
...AND GOOD-BYE.

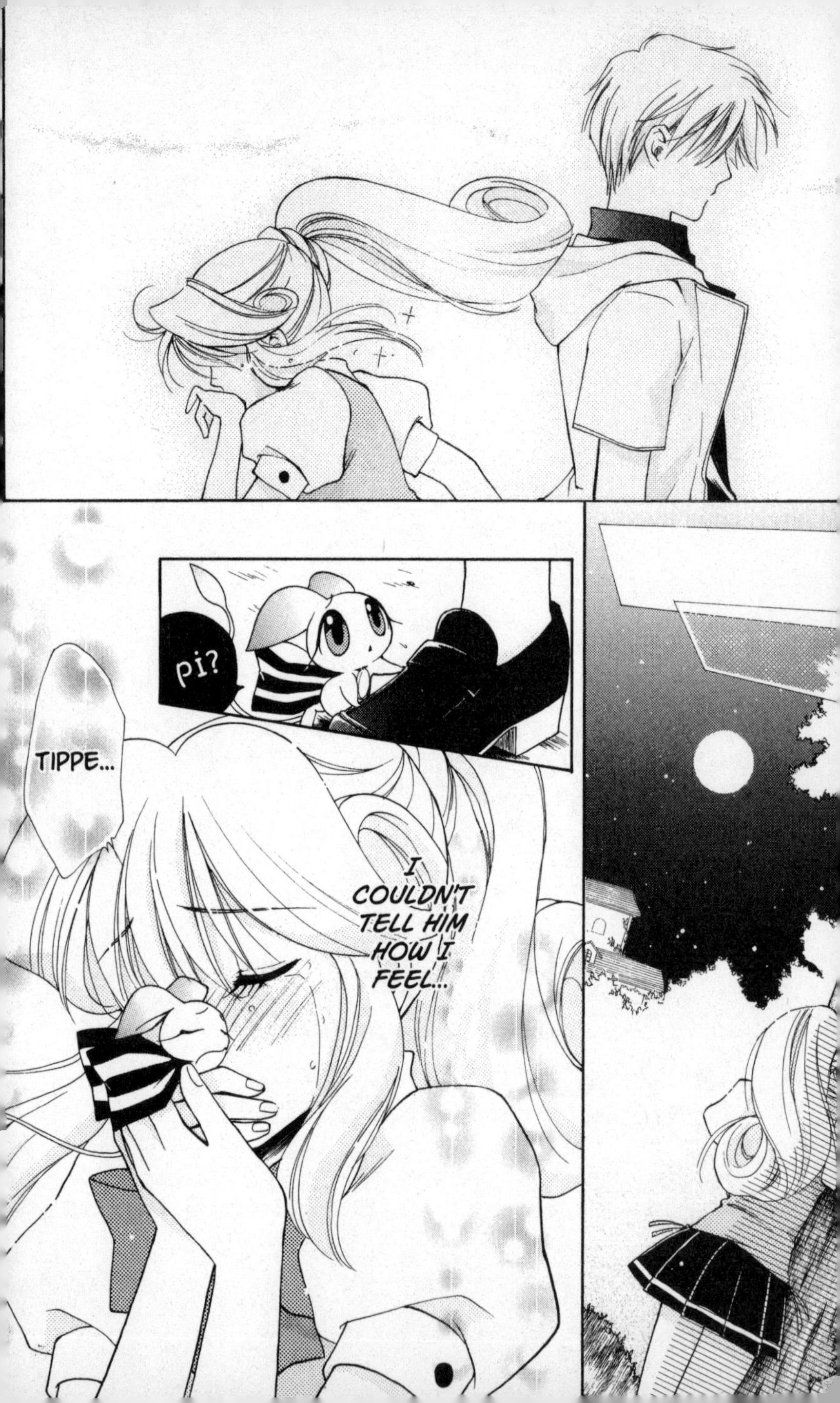
pi?
TIPPE...
I COULDN'T TELL HIM HOW I FEEL...

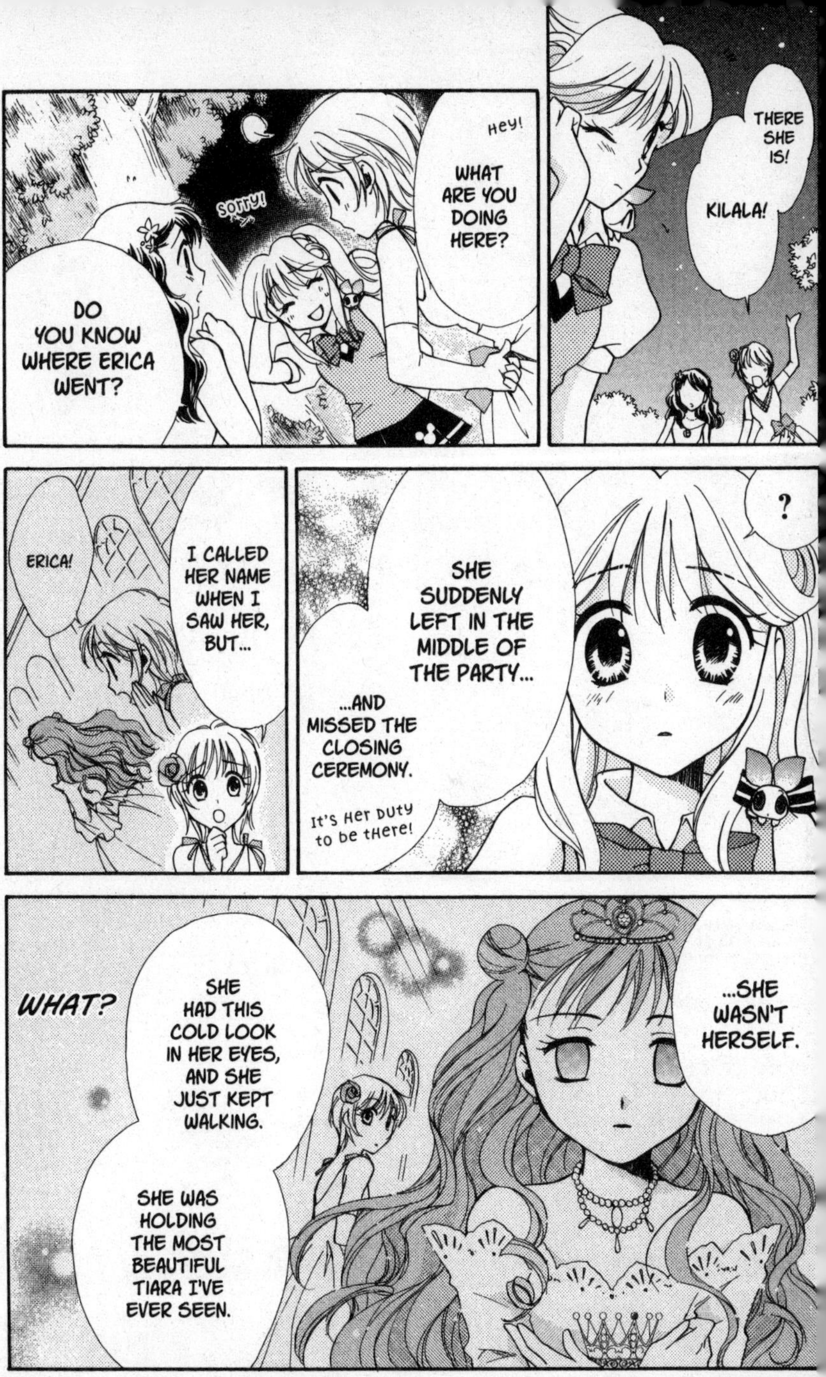
THERE SHE IS!
KILALA!
Hey!
WHAT ARE YOU DOING HERE?
Sorry!
DO YOU KNOW WHERE ERICA WENT?
?
SHE SUDDENLY LEFT IN THE MIDDLE OF THE PARTY...
...AND MISSED THE CLOSING CEREMONY.
It's Her Duty to be tHere!
I CALLED HER NAME WHEN I SAW HER, BUT...
ERICA!
...SHE WASN'T HERSELF.
SHE HAD THIS COLD LOOK IN HER EYES, AND SHE JUST KEPT WALKING.
SHE WAS HOLDING THE MOST BEAUTIFUL TIARA I'VE EVER SEEN.
WHAT?

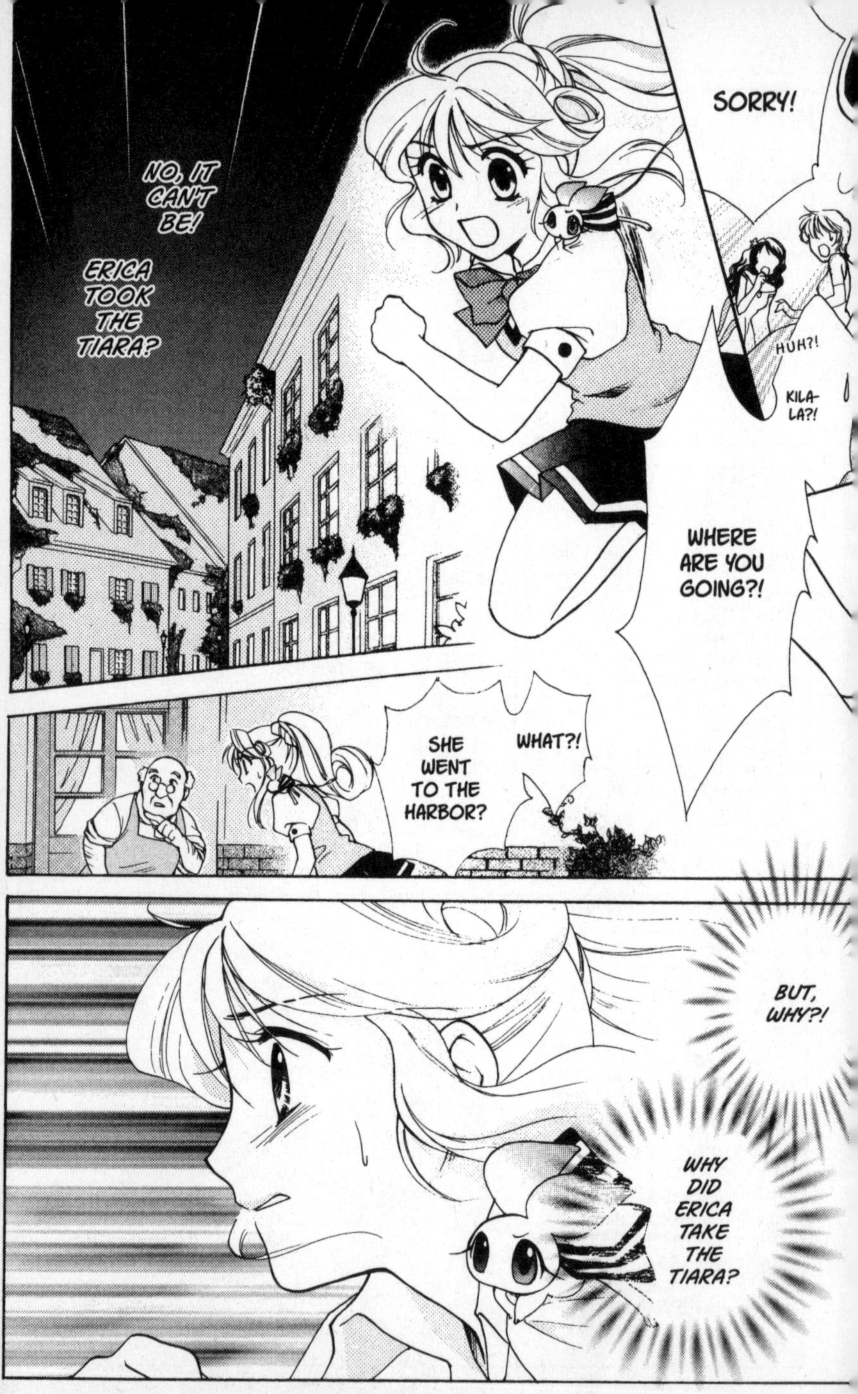
SORRY!
HUH?!
KILA-LA?!
WHERE ARE YOU GOING?!
NO, IT CAN'T BE!
ERICA TOOK THE TIARA?
WHAT?!
SHE WENT TO THE HARBOR?
BUT, WHY?!
WHY DID ERICA TAKE THE TIARA?

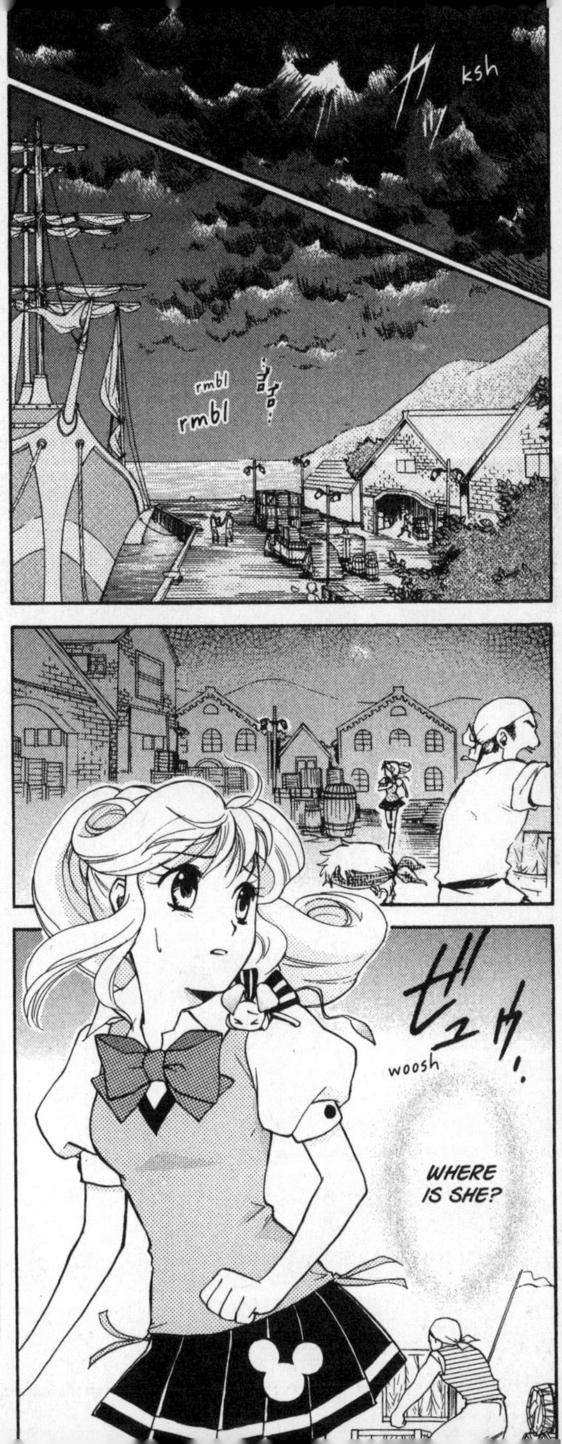
ksh
rmbl
rmbl
woosh
WHERE IS SHE?

Rika Tanaka

HELLO! MY NAME IS RIKA TANAKA, AND I'M WRITING THE STORY FOR *KILALA PRINCESS*. I'VE LOVED DISNEY ANIMATION EVER SINCE I WAS A CHILD, AND I'M EXCITED TO WRITE THIS STORY.

ENTERING THE LOVELY WORLDS OF THE DISNEY PRINCESSES, BECOMING FRIENDS AND GOING ON ADVENTURES TOGETHER... IT'S A DREAM COME TRUE FOR ME! WHEN I'M WRITING THIS STORY, I FEEL LIKE I'M KILALA, AND I CRY WITH HER, LAUGH WITH HER, AND FALL IN LOVE WITH REI. MY DESK IS ALWAYS A MESS. HA HA!

BY THE WAY, YOU'RE PROBABLY WONDERING WHAT'S GOING TO HAPPEN TO KILALA. WHAT ABOUT KILALA AND REI? ACTUALLY, I DON'T EVEN KNOW YET. HA HA! I HOPE TO WRITE THE REST OF THE STORY AND REACH A WONDERFUL ENDING--LEAVING BUTTERFLIES IN YOUR STOMACH DURING THE JOURNEY!

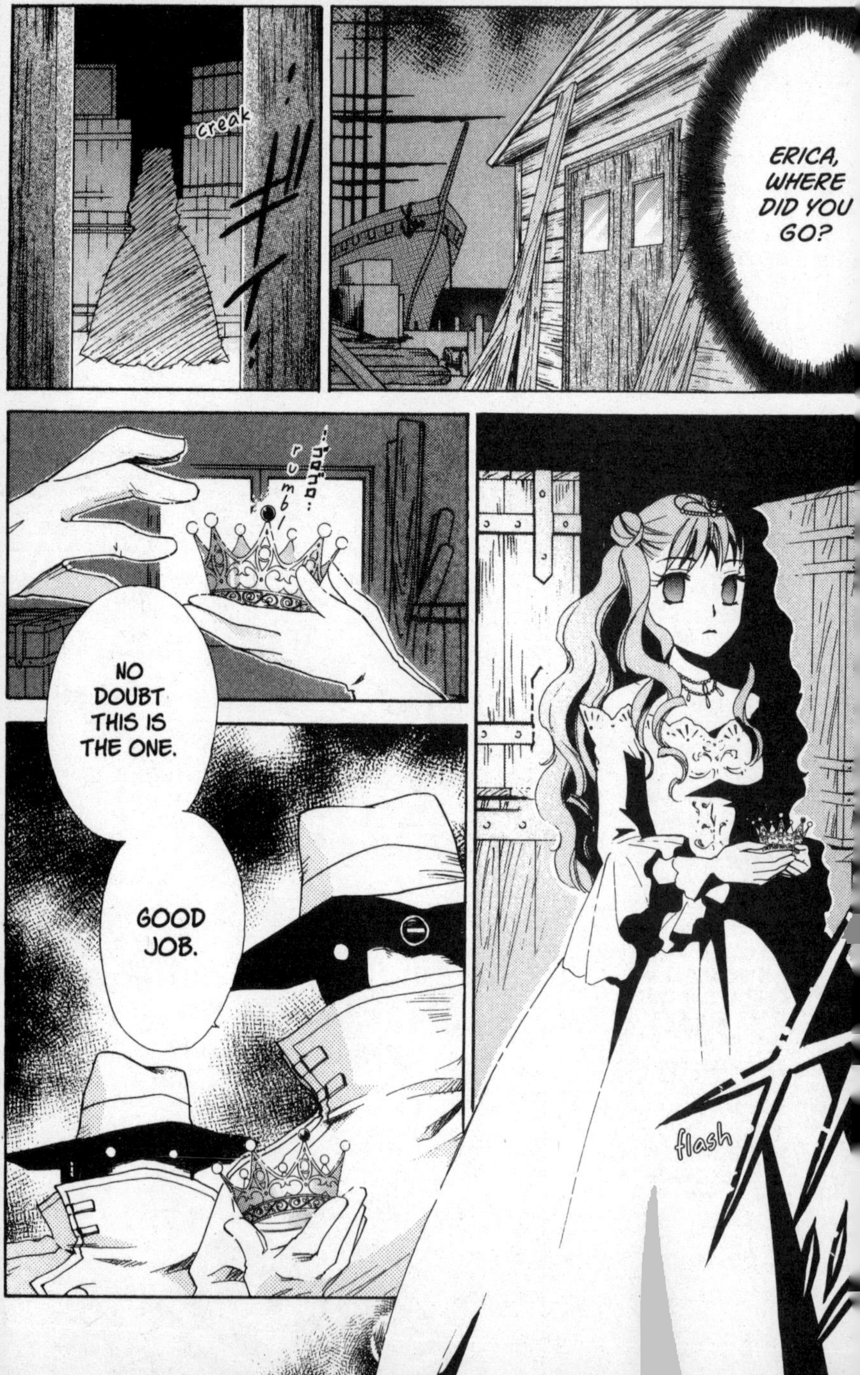
ERICA, WHERE DID YOU GO?
creak
flash
rumble
NO DOUBT THIS IS THE ONE.
GOOD JOB.

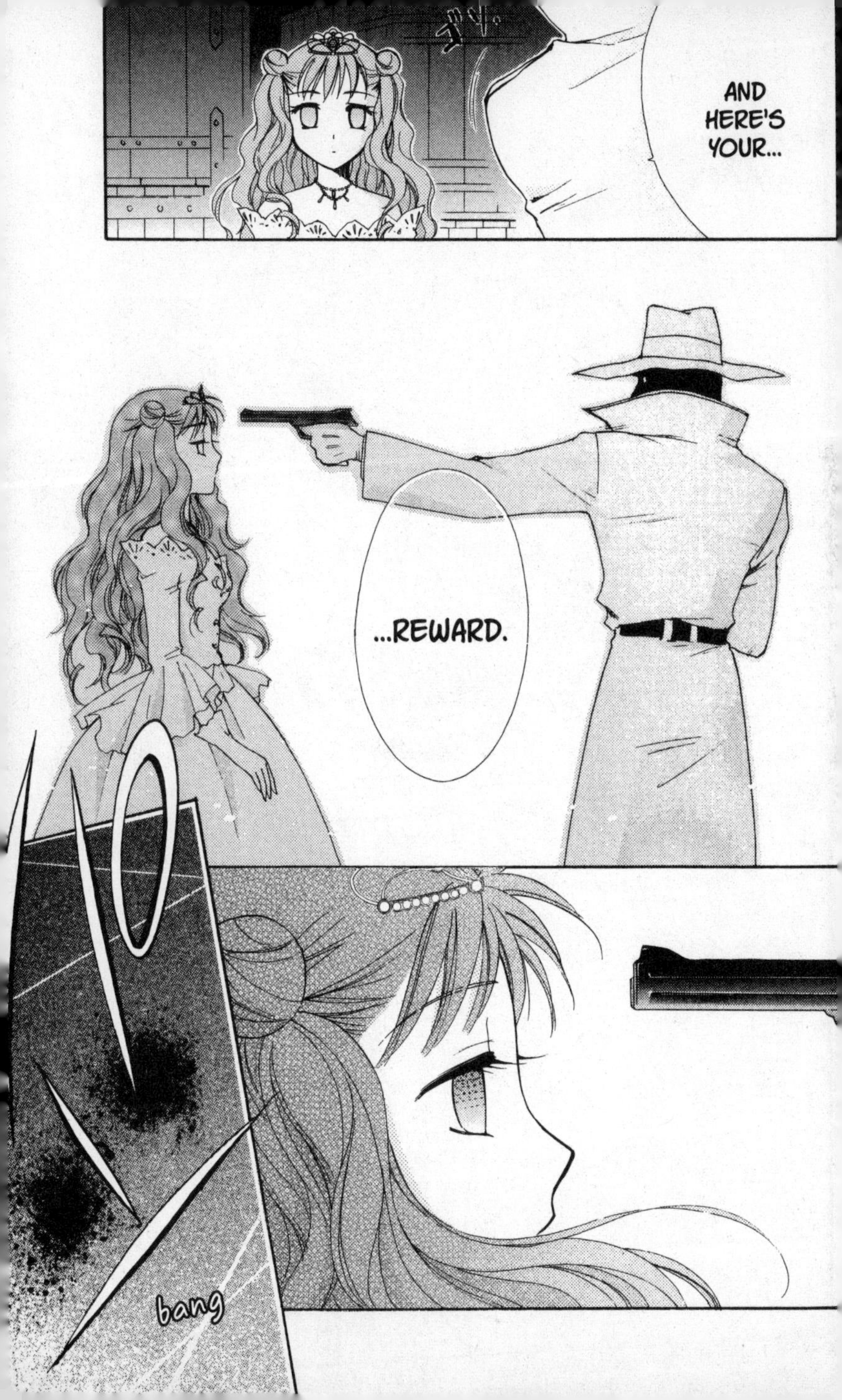
AND HERE'S YOUR...
...REWARD.
bang

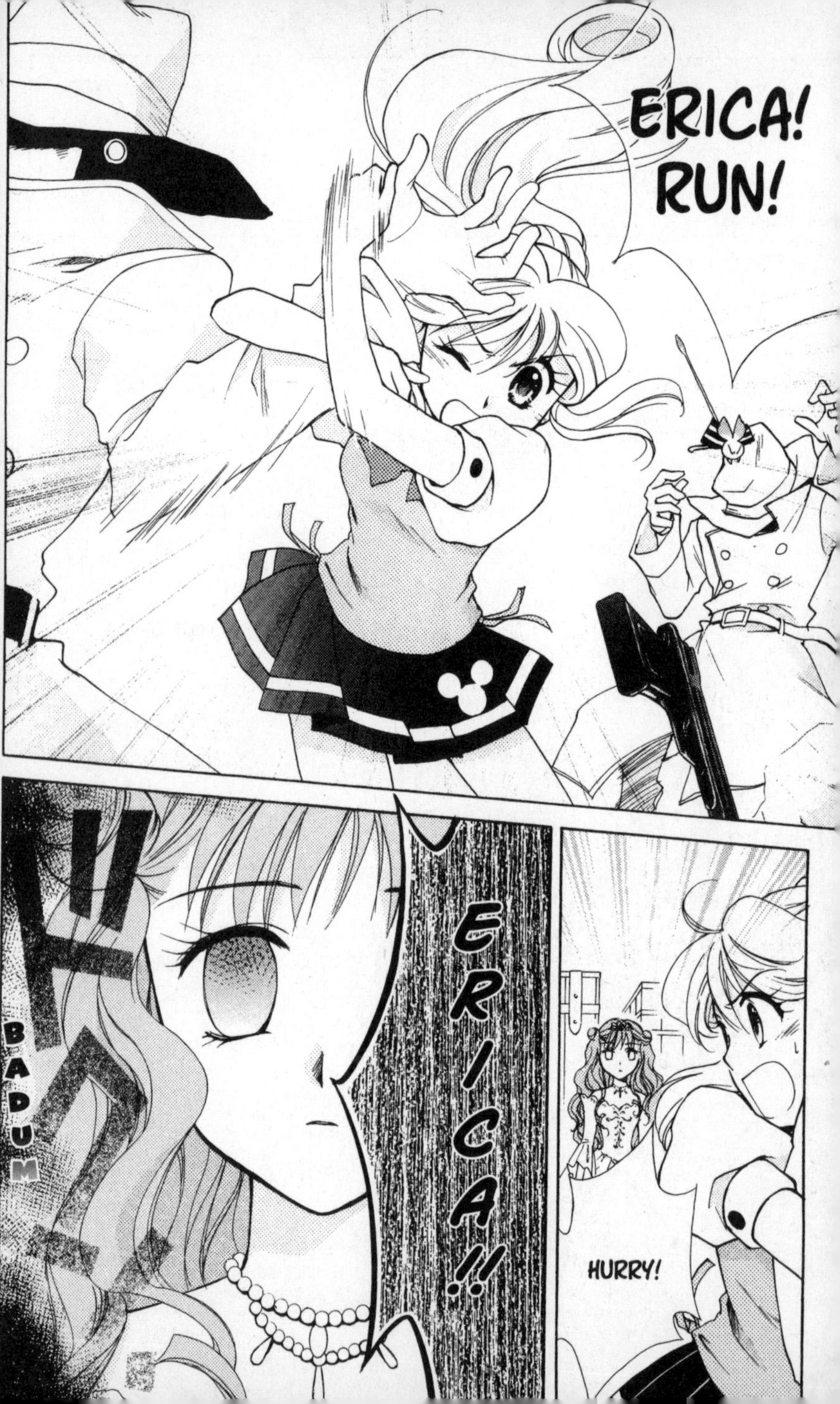
ERICA! RUN!
HURRY!
ERICA!!
BADUM

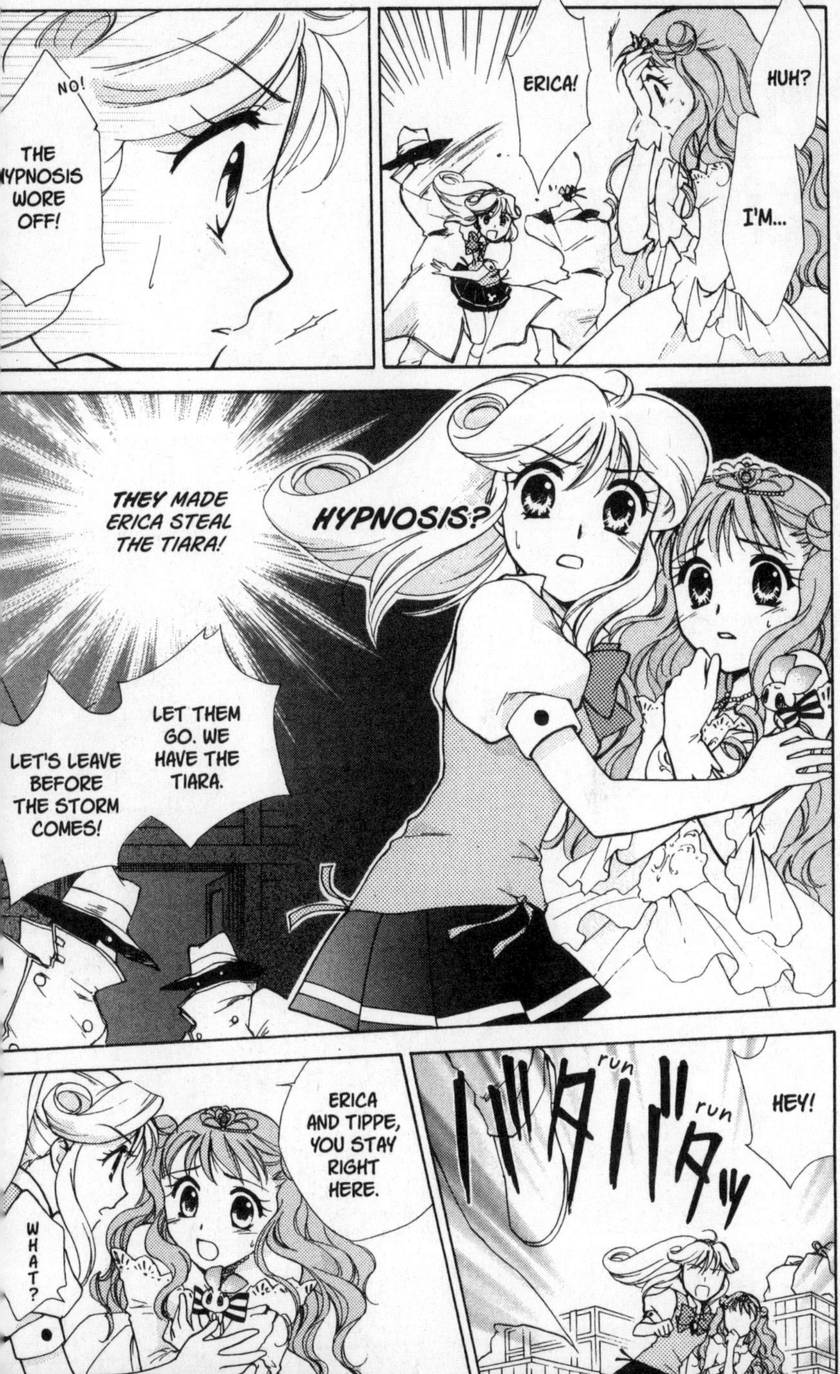
ERICA!
HUH?
I'M...
NO!
THE HYPNOSIS WORE OFF!
HYPNOSIS?
THEY MADE ERICA STEAL THE TIARA!
LET THEM GO. WE HAVE THE TIARA.
LET'S LEAVE BEFORE THE STORM COMES!
HEY!
run run
バタバタッ
ERICA AND TIPPE, YOU STAY RIGHT HERE.
WHAT?

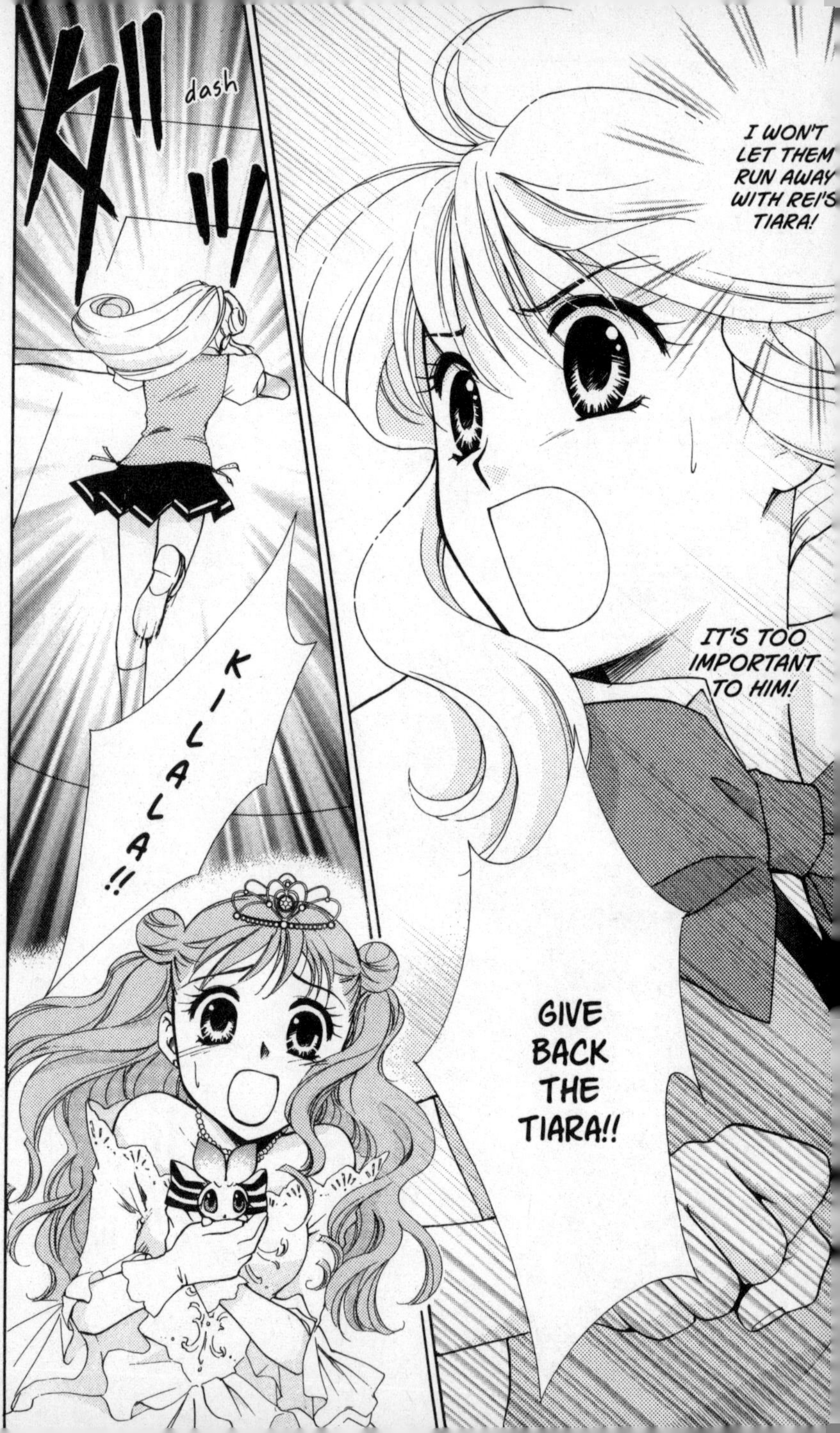
I WON'T LET THEM RUN AWAY WITH REI'S TIARA!
IT'S TOO IMPORTANT TO HIM!
GIVE BACK THE TIARA!!
ダッ
dash
KILALA!!

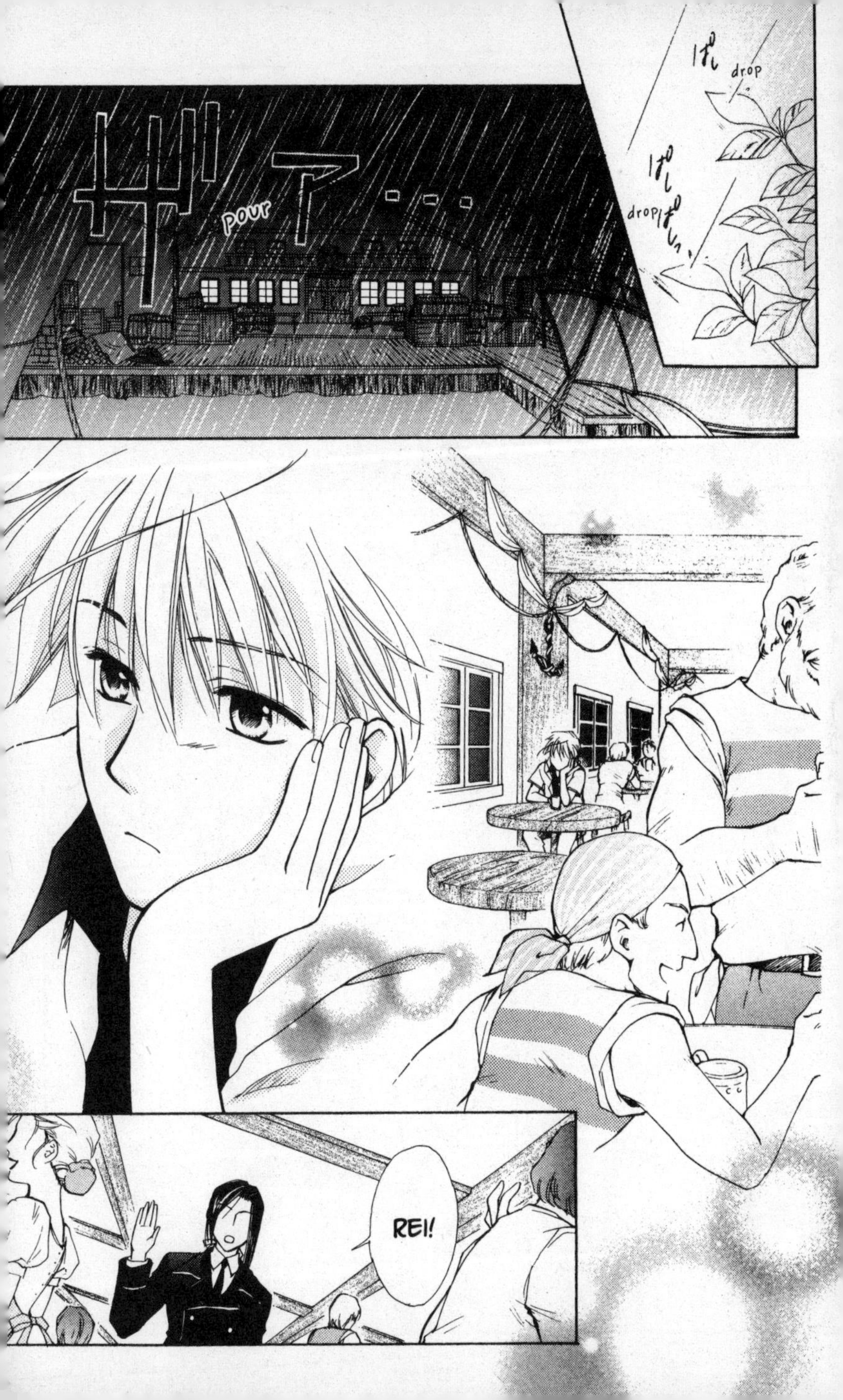
drop
drop
pour
REI!

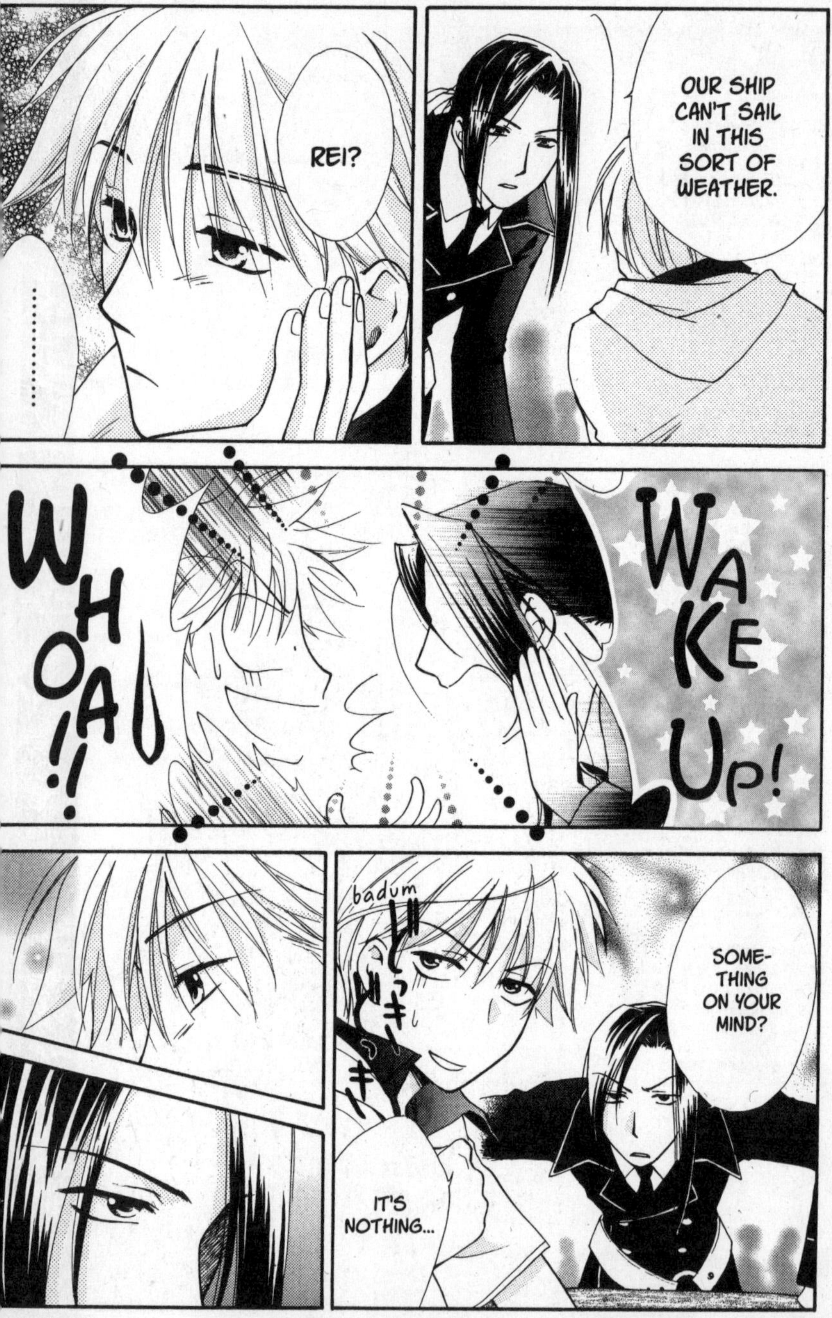
OUR SHIP CAN'T SAIL IN THIS SORT OF WEATHER.
REI?
......
WAKE UP!
WHOA!!
badum
SOME-THING ON YOUR MIND?
IT'S NOTHING...

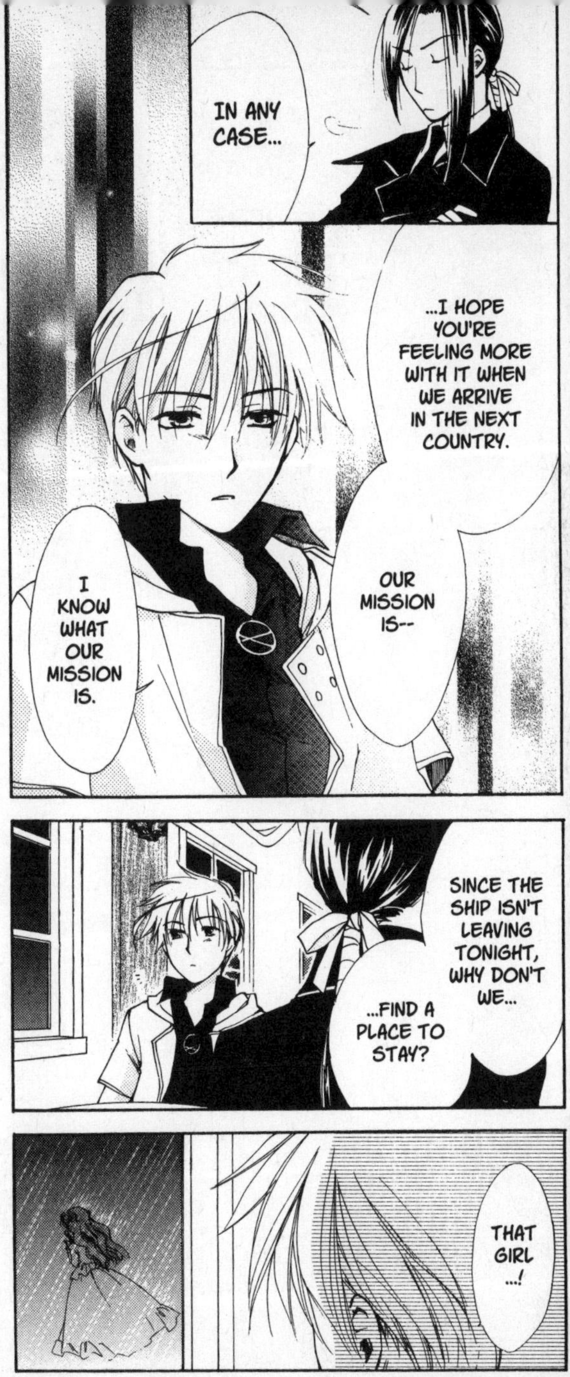
IN ANY CASE...
...I HOPE YOU'RE FEELING MORE WITH IT WHEN WE ARRIVE IN THE NEXT COUNTRY.
OUR MISSION IS--
I KNOW WHAT OUR MISSION IS.
SINCE THE SHIP ISN'T LEAVING TONIGHT, WHY DON'T WE...
...FIND A PLACE TO STAY?
THAT GIRL ...!

Nao Kodaka

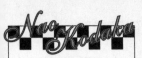

HELLO! MY NAME IS NAO KODAKA, AND THE FIRST VOLUME OF *KILALA PRINCESS* IS THE FIRST COMIC BOOK I'VE EVER DRAWN!

SINCE I WAS A CHILD, I'VE BEEN SURROUNDED BY DISNEY BOOKS. THE CINDERELLA ART BOOK WAS MY MOST PRIZED POSSESSION. AND I HAD NO IDEA THAT I'D BE DRAWING HER IN MY MANGA. LIFE CAN BE STRANGE SOMETIMES...

TO DRAW THE SIX PRINCESSES RIGHT, I PLAY THE DVDS ALL DAY IN MY ROOM. I CAN'T COUNT HOW MANY TIMES I'VE WATCHED THE MOVIES, BUT I CAN TELL YOU WHICH SCENE OF *SNOW WHITE* IS PLAYING JUST BY THE AUDIO ALONE (I'M NOT SURE THIS IS SOMETHING I SHOULD BRAG ABOUT...).

KILALA AND REI ARE MY ORIGINAL CHARACTERS, BUT IT WASN'T EASY ARRIVING AT THEIR CURRENT FORM. THERE'S A FINE LINE BETWEEN THE DETAILED STYLE USED FOR GIRLS' COMICS AND THE SIMPLIFIED DRAWING OF DISNEY COMICS!

THIS MANGA IS THE CROWNING ACHIEVEMENT OF EVERYONE'S HARD WORK AND EFFORTS, AND I WAS NEARLY IN TEARS WHEN I FIRST HELD THE FIRST COMIC BOOK.

AND LAST BUT NOT LEAST, I THANK YOU, THE READERS, FOR TAKING THE TIME TO READ *KILALA PRINCESS*!

★ ★ ★

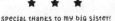

Special thanks to my big sister!

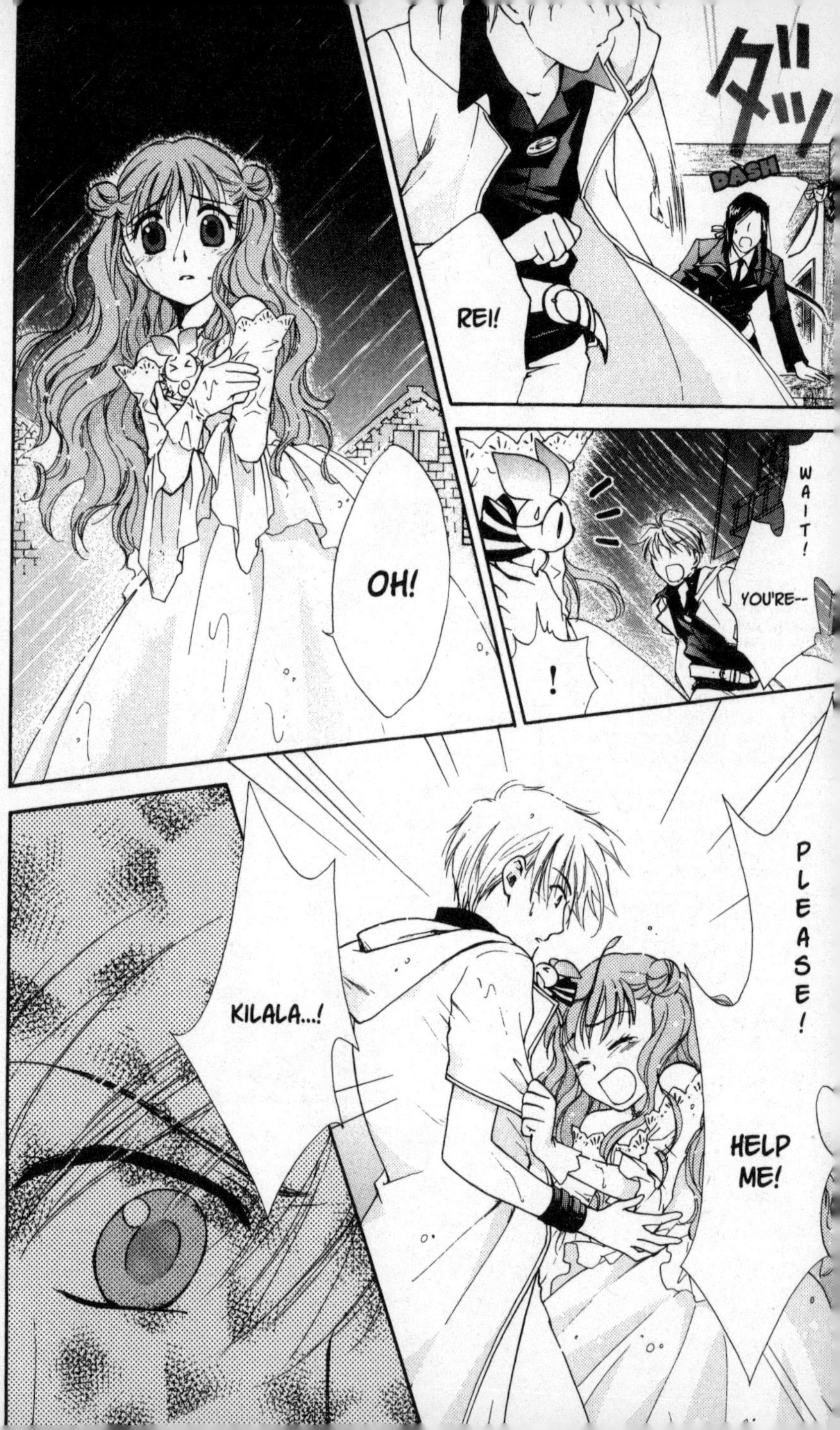
ダッ
DASH
REI!
WAIT! YOU'RE--
!
OH!
PLEASE! HELP ME!
KILALA...!

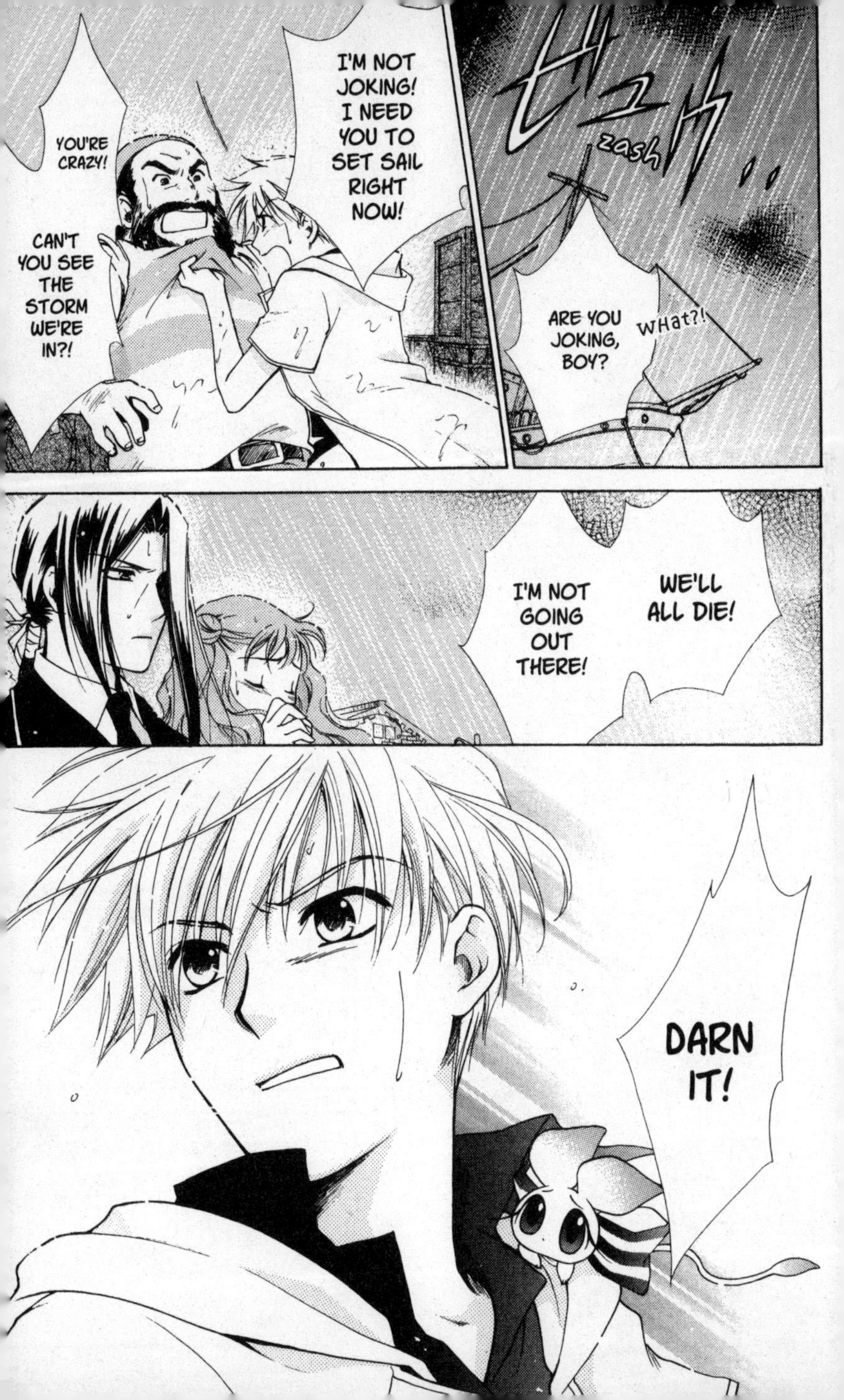
zash
ARE YOU JOKING, BOY?
WHAT?!
I'M NOT JOKING! I NEED YOU TO SET SAIL RIGHT NOW!
YOU'RE CRAZY!
CAN'T YOU SEE THE STORM WE'RE IN?!
WE'LL ALL DIE!
I'M NOT GOING OUT THERE!
DARN IT!

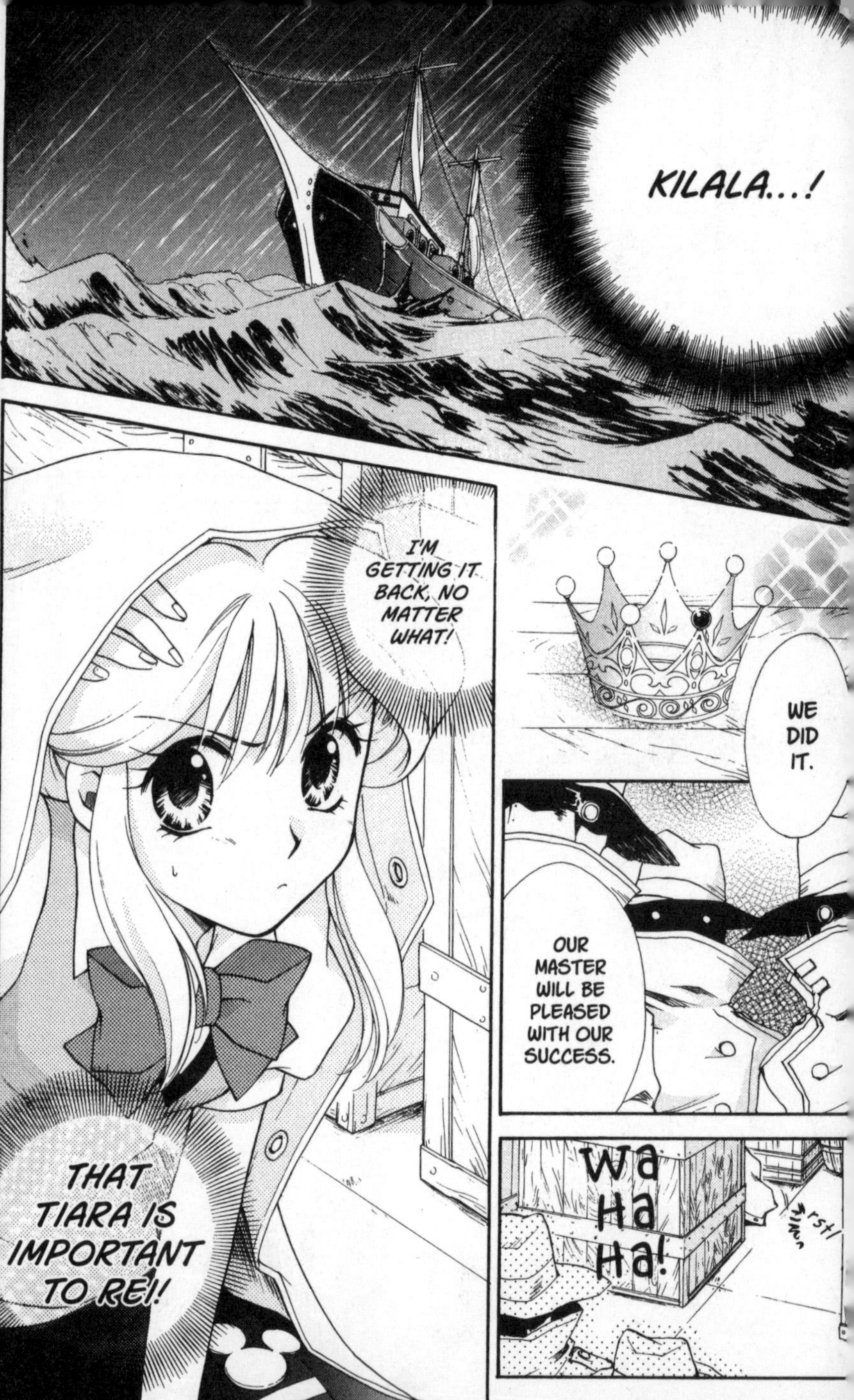
KILALA...!
WE DID IT.
OUR MASTER WILL BE PLEASED WITH OUR SUCCESS.
WA HA HA!
I'M GETTING IT BACK, NO MATTER WHAT!
THAT TIARA IS IMPORTANT TO REI!

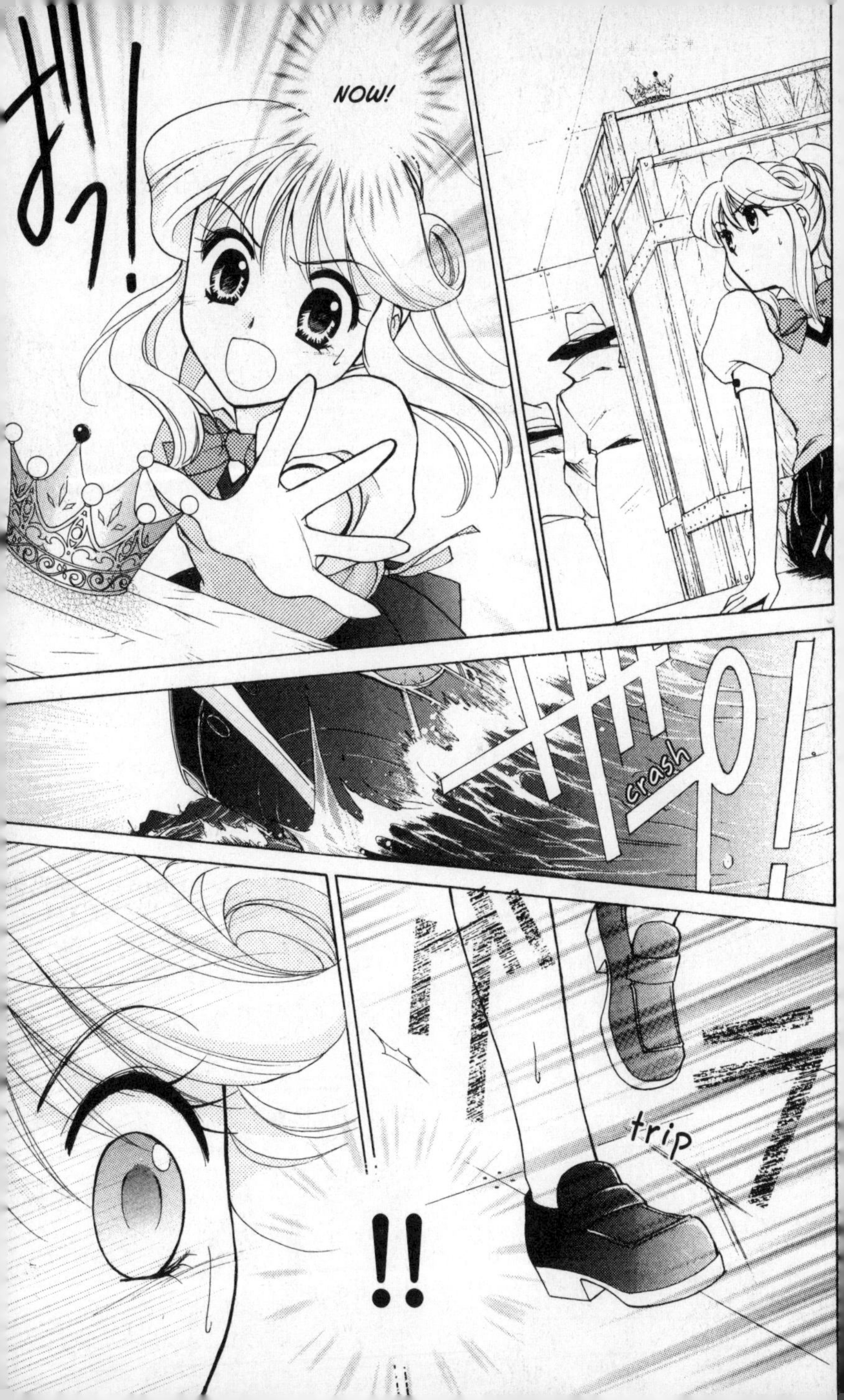
NOW!
crash
trip
!!

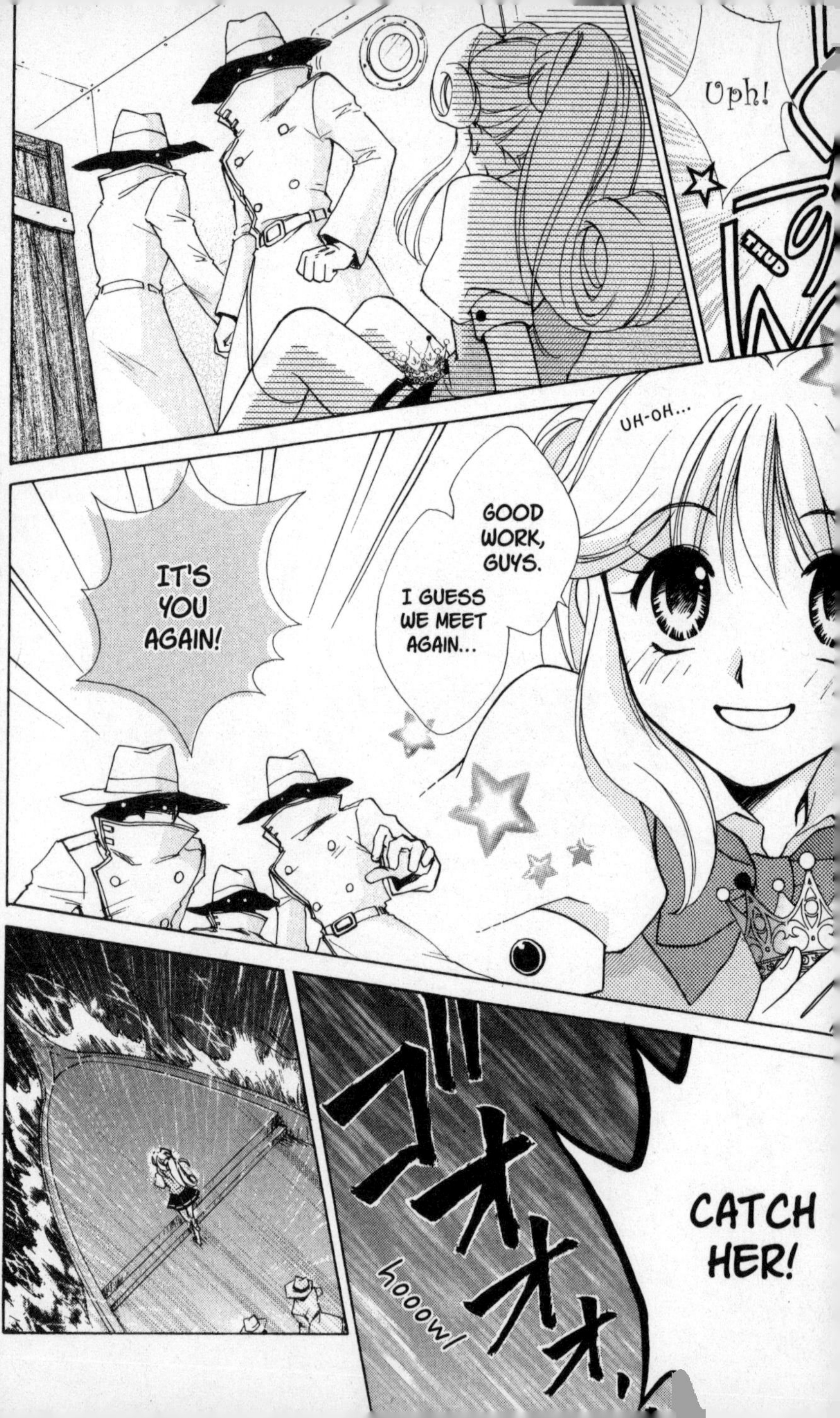
Uph!
THUD
UH-OH...
GOOD WORK, GUYS.
I GUESS WE MEET AGAIN...
IT'S YOU AGAIN!
CATCH HER!
hooow!

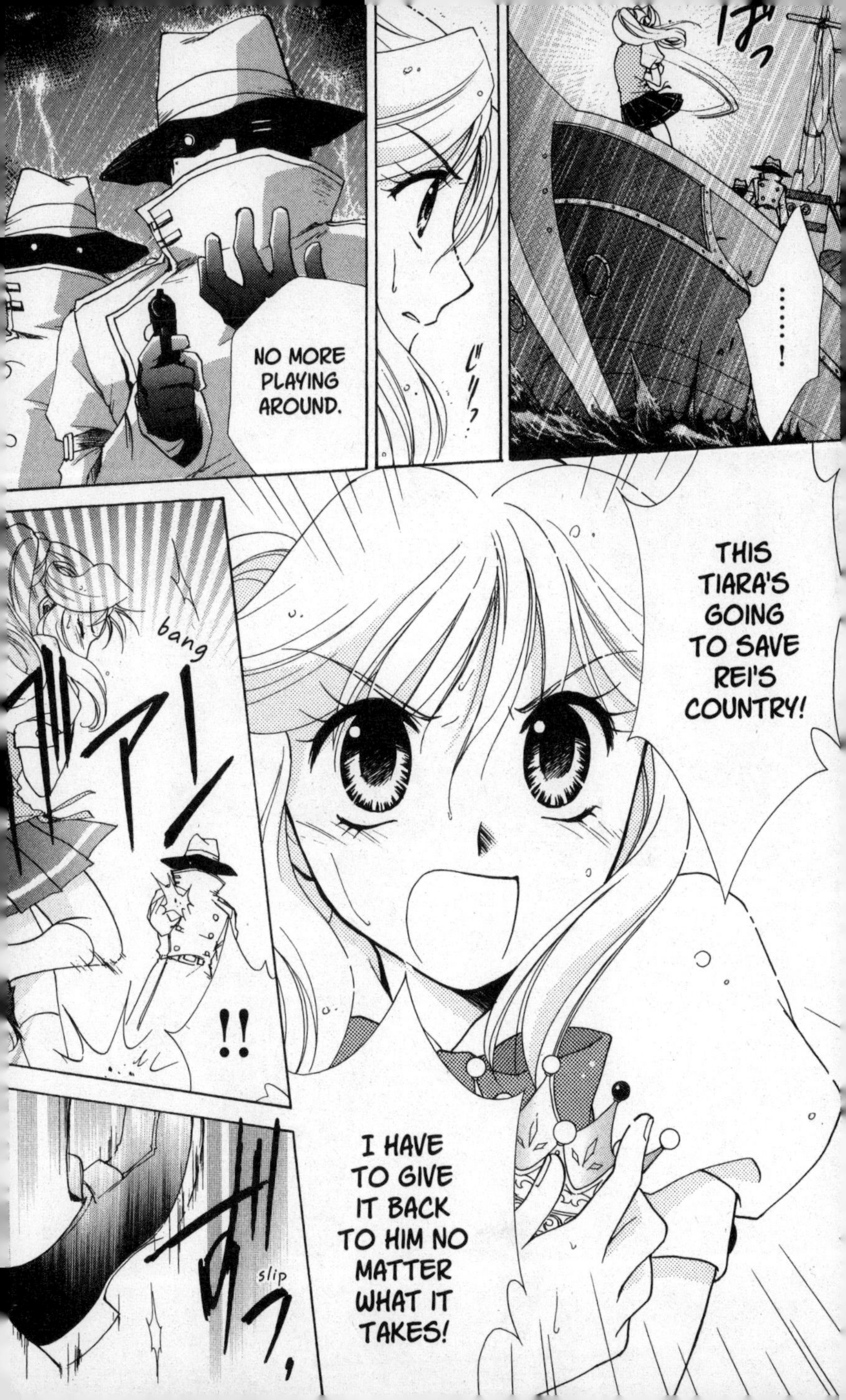
……!
NO MORE PLAYING AROUND.
THIS TIARA'S GOING TO SAVE REI'S COUNTRY!
bang
!!
I HAVE TO GIVE IT BACK TO HIM NO MATTER WHAT IT TAKES!
slip

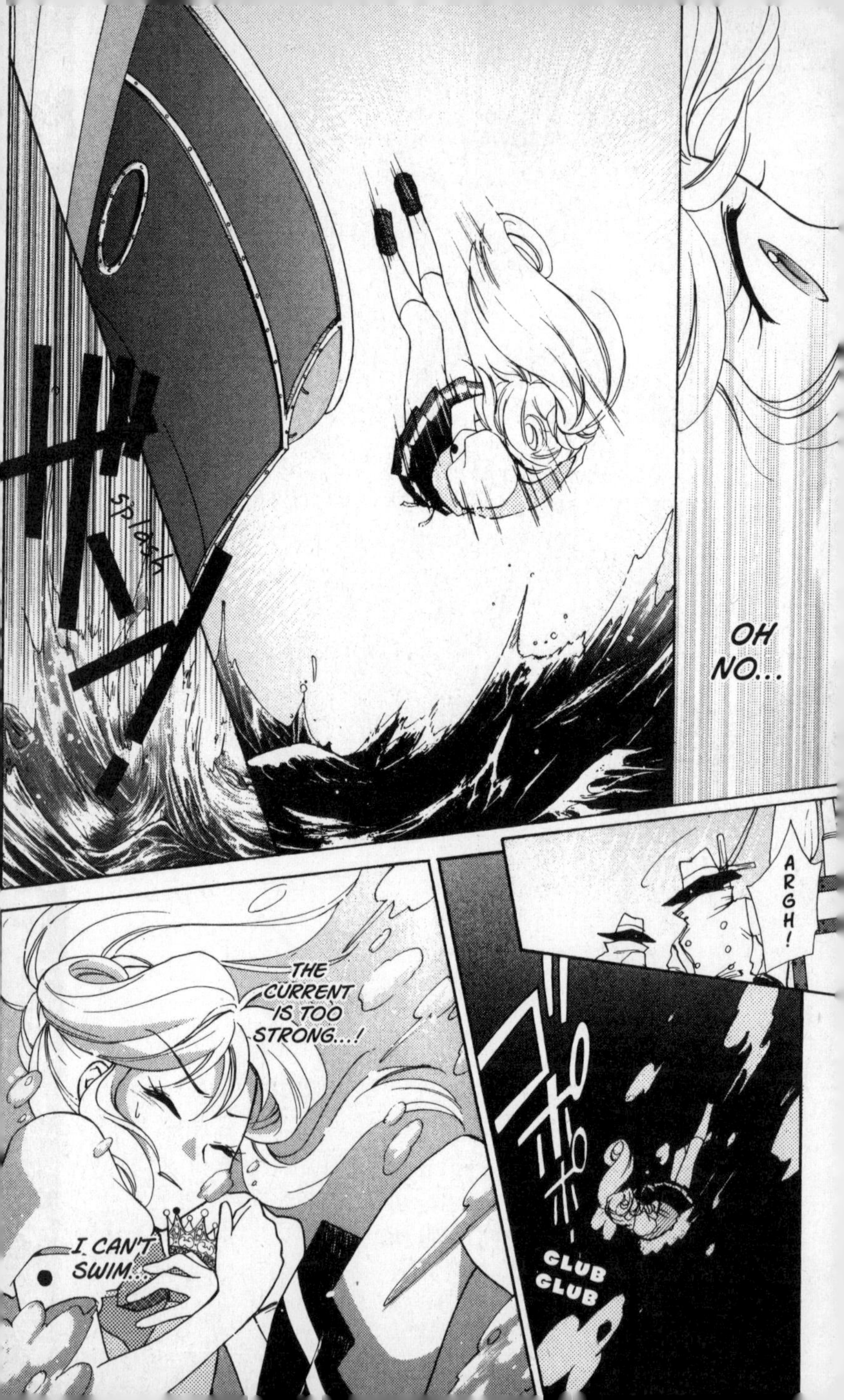
OH NO...
splash
ARGH!
GLUB GLUB
THE CURRENT IS TOO STRONG...!
I CAN'T SWIM...

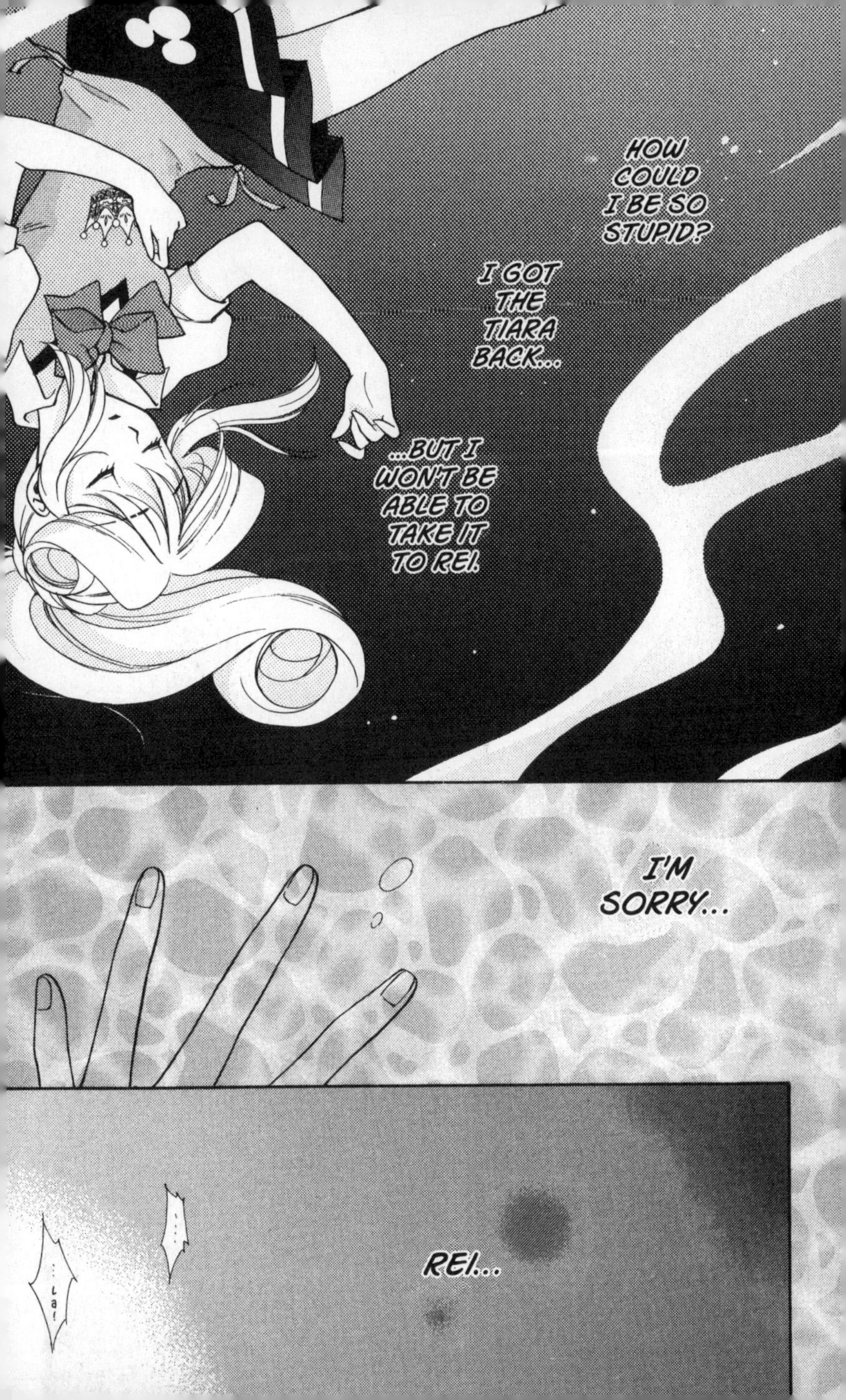
HOW COULD I BE SO STUPID?
I GOT THE TIARA BACK...
...BUT I WON'T BE ABLE TO TAKE IT TO REI.
I'M SORRY...
REI...

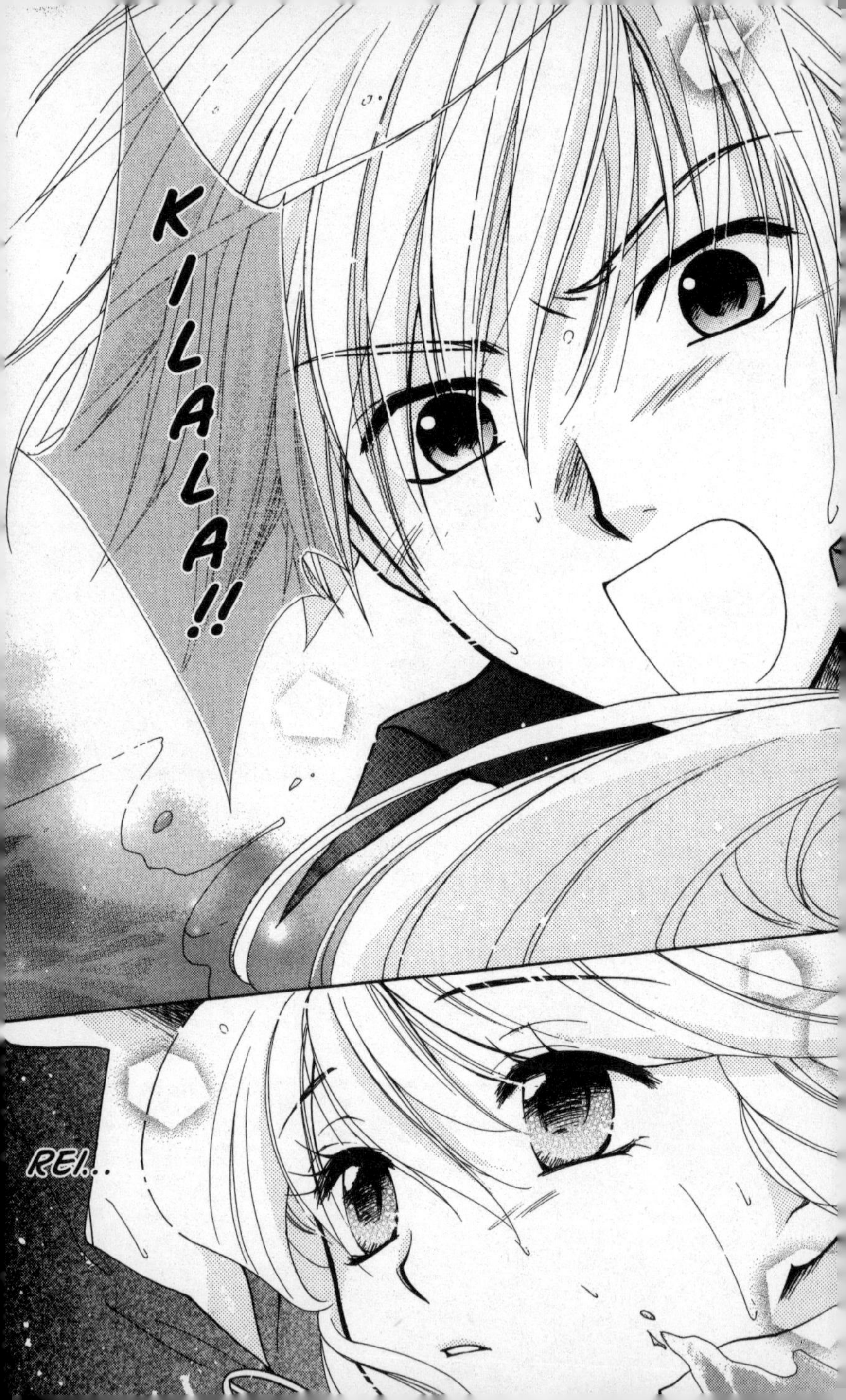
KILALA!!
REI...

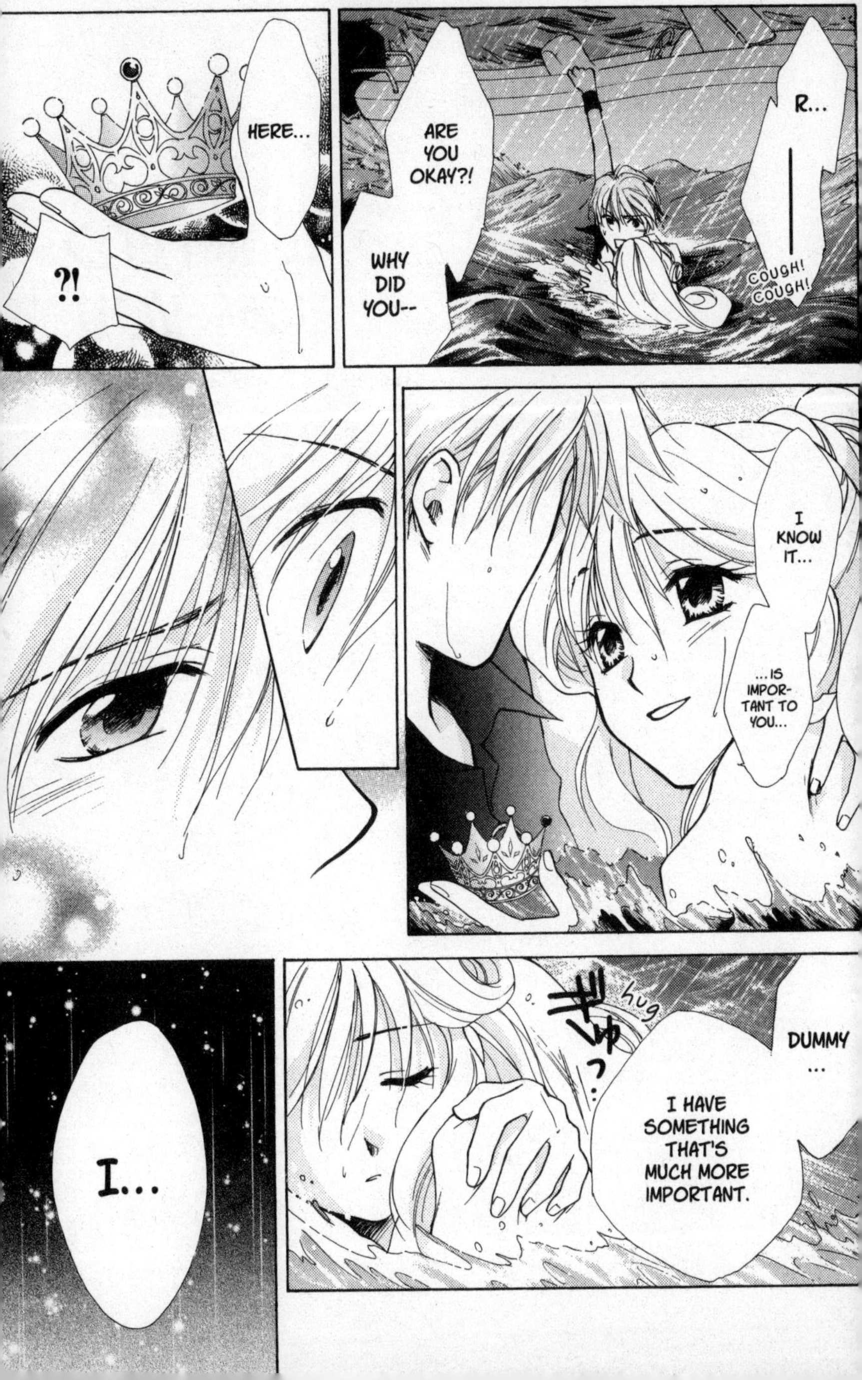
R... —
COUGH! COUGH!
ARE YOU OKAY?!
WHY DID YOU--
HERE...
?!
I KNOW IT...
...IS IMPORTANT TO YOU...
ぎゅっ
hug
DUMMY...
I HAVE SOMETHING THAT'S MUCH MORE IMPORTANT.
I...

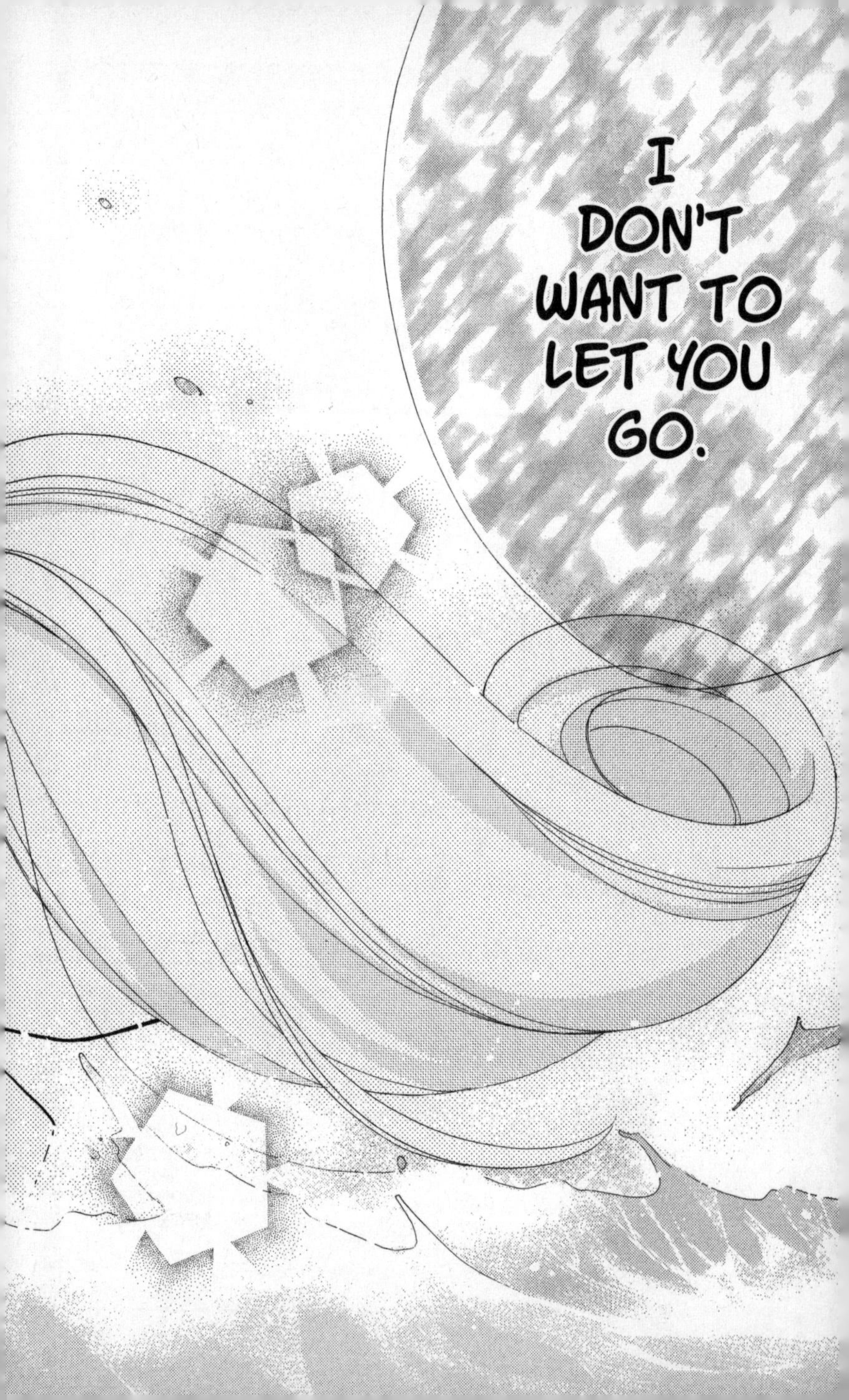
I DON'T WANT TO LET YOU GO.

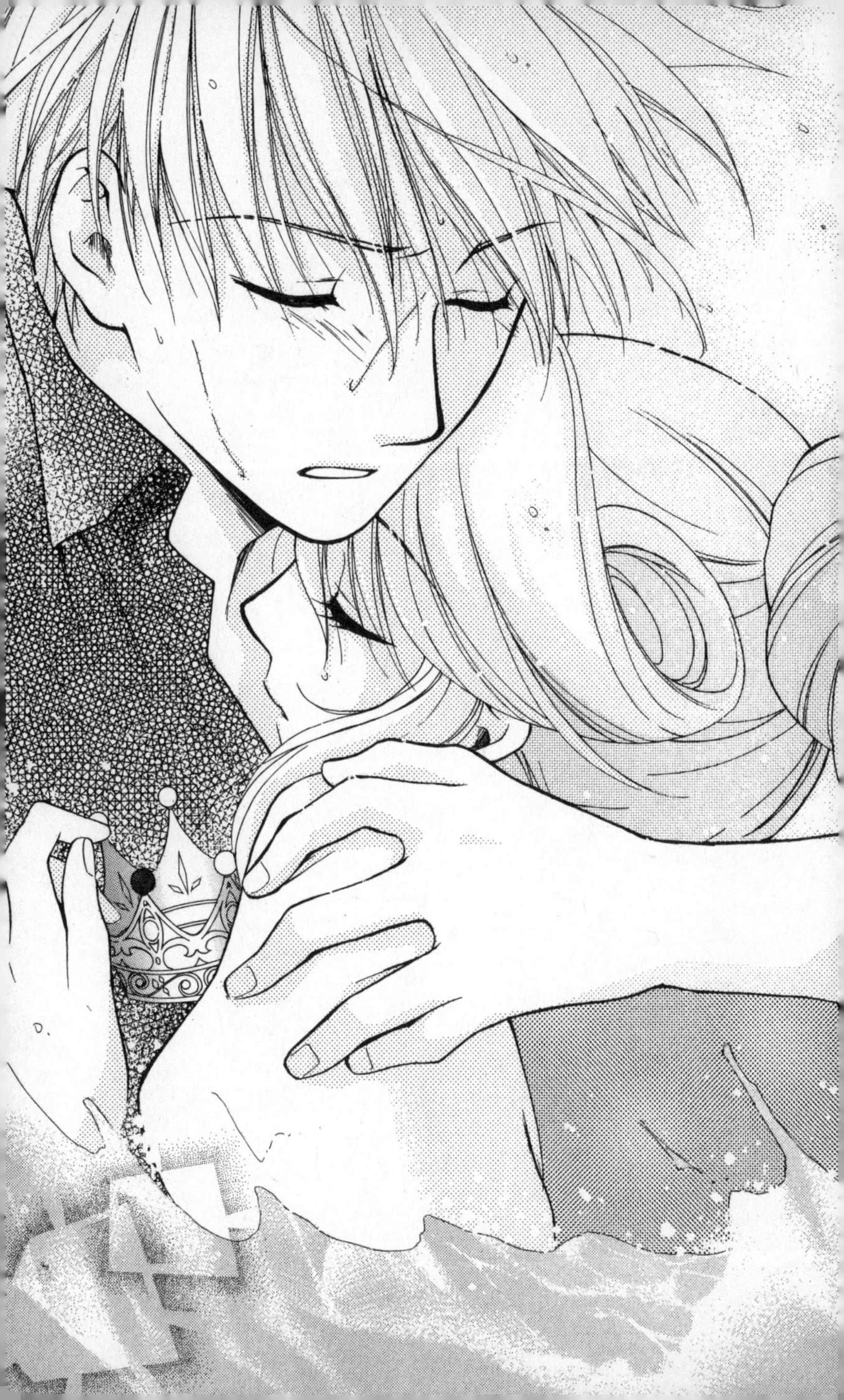

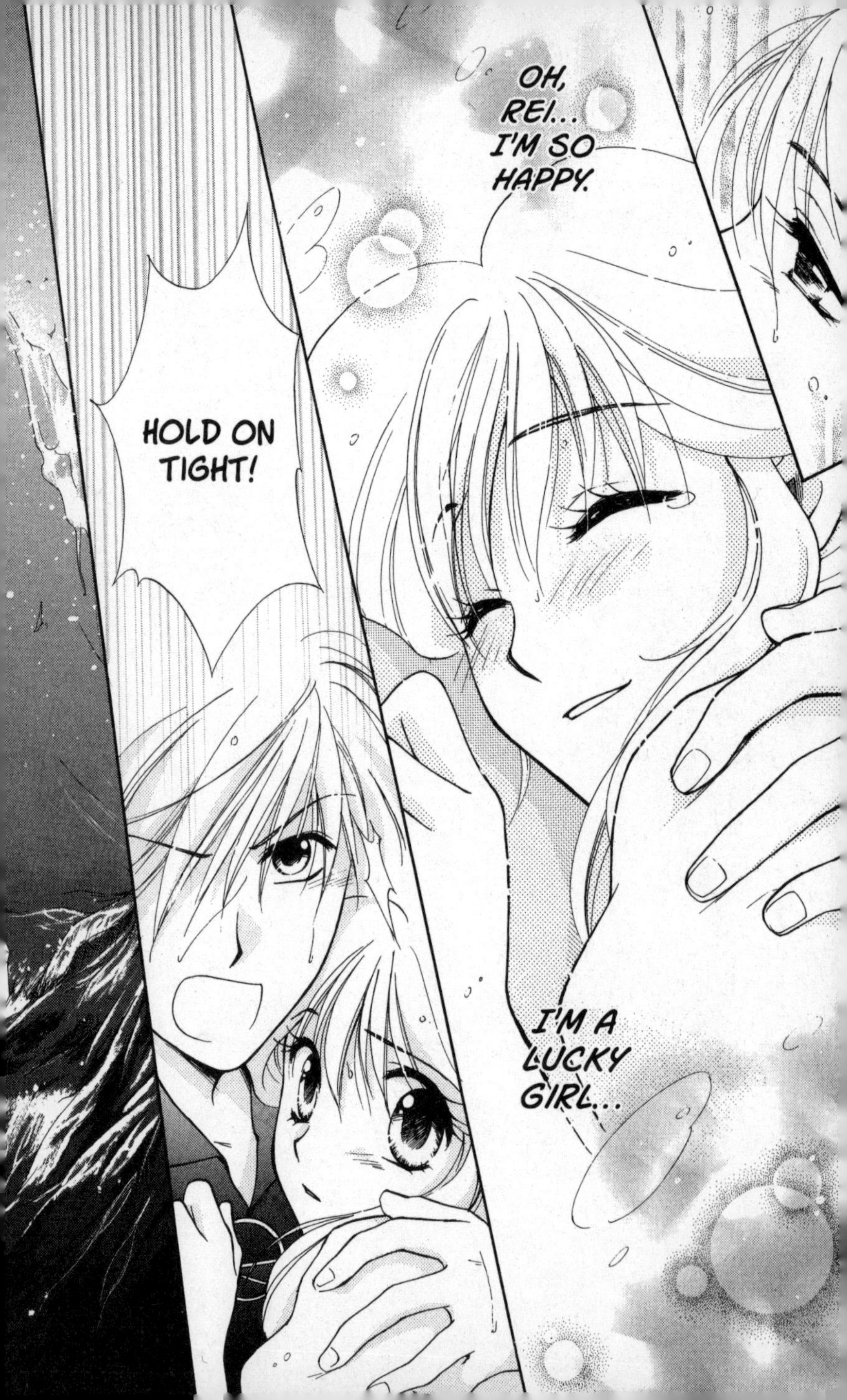
OH, REI... I'M SO HAPPY.
I'M A LUCKY GIRL...
HOLD ON TIGHT!

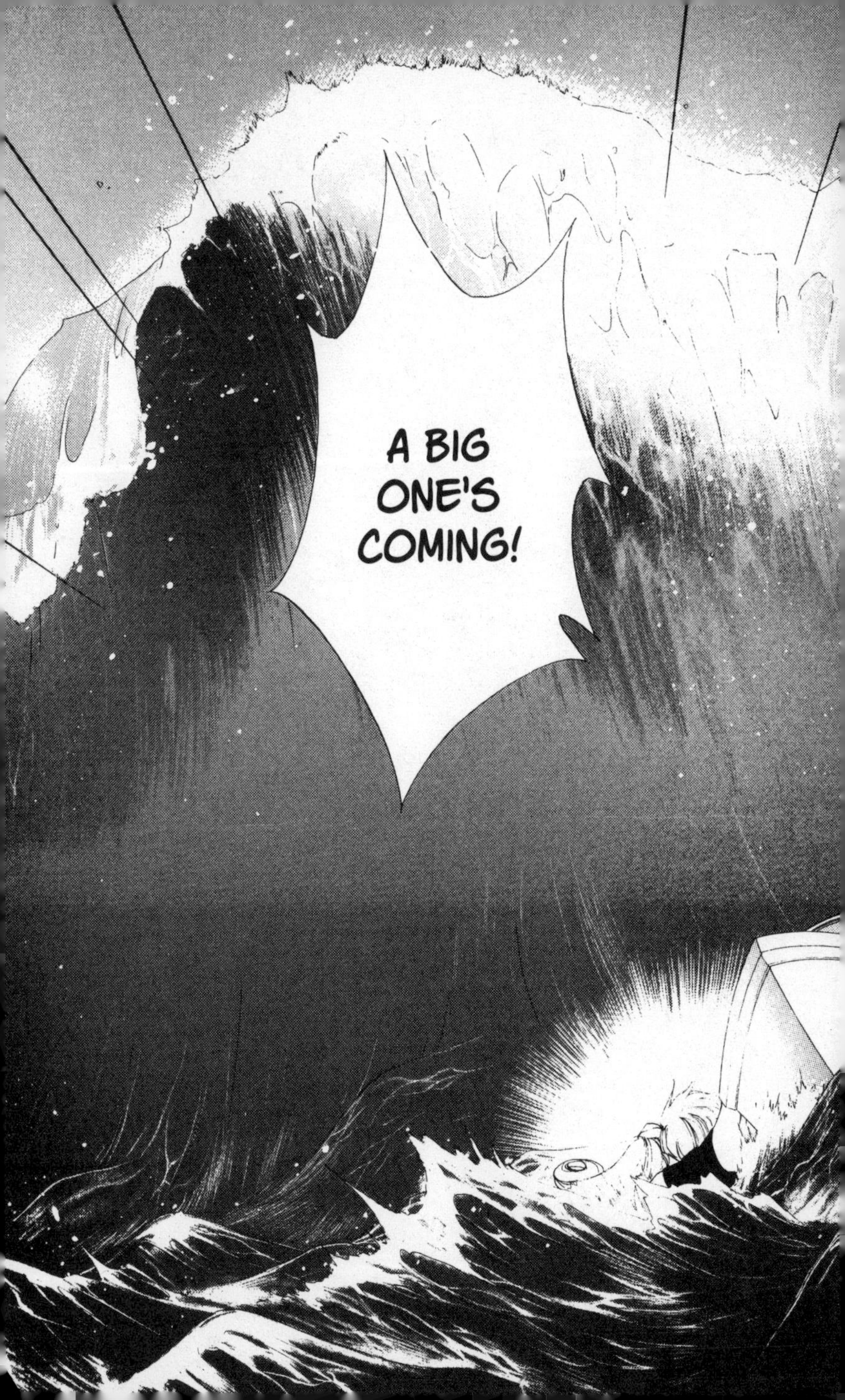
A BIG ONE'S COMING!

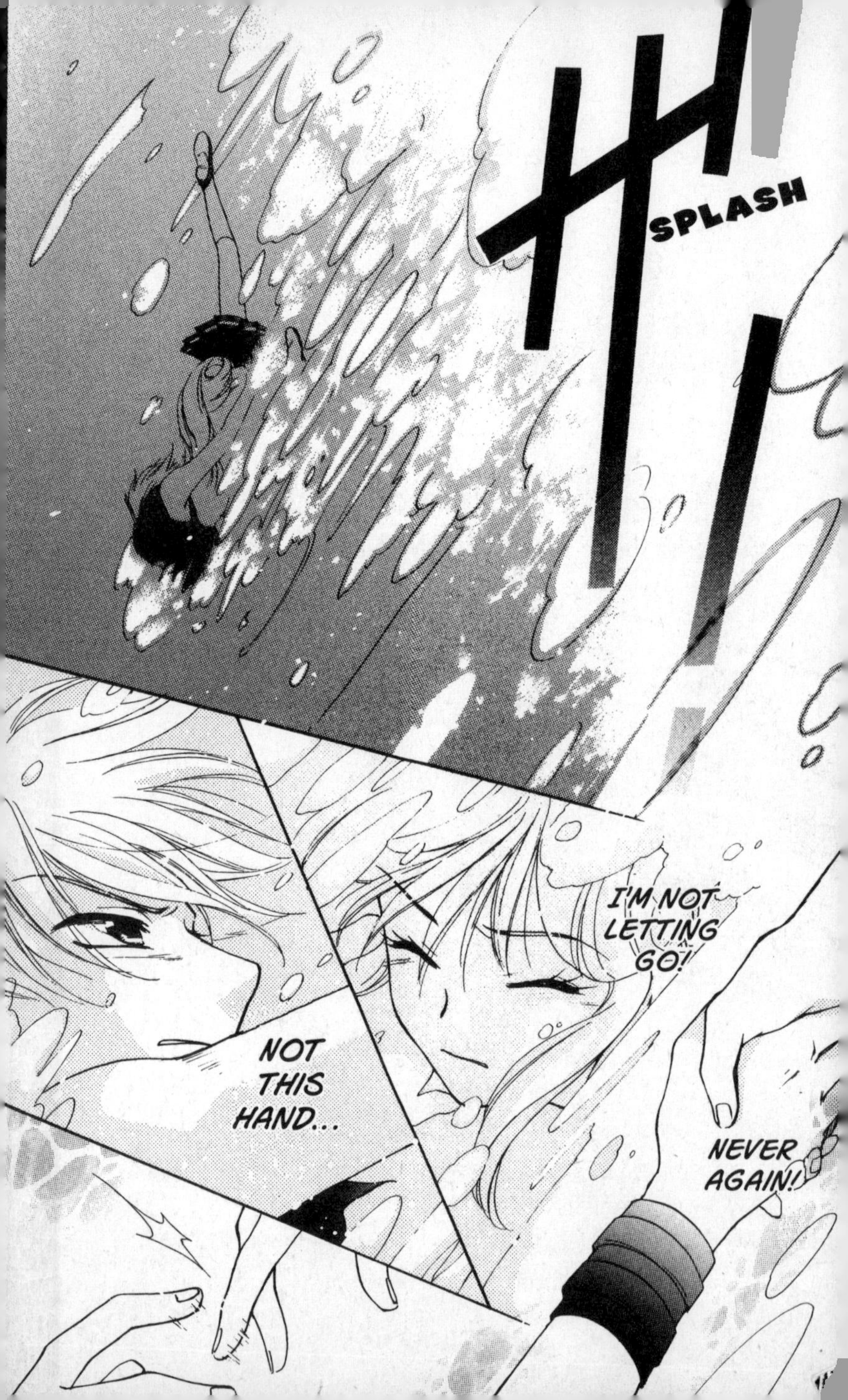
SPLASH
I'M NOT LETTING GO!
NOT THIS HAND...
NEVER AGAIN!

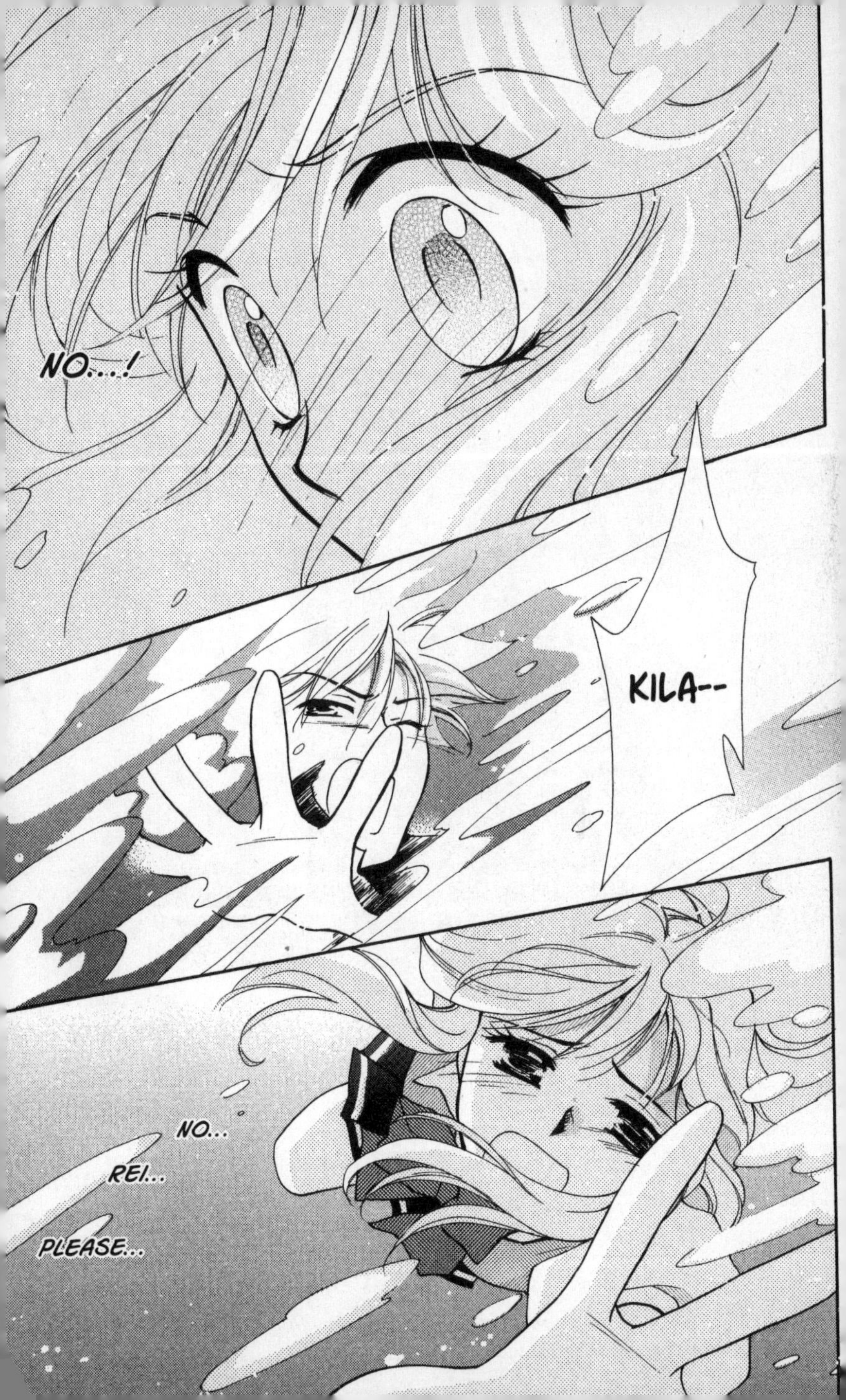
NO...!
KILA--
NO...
REI...
PLEASE...

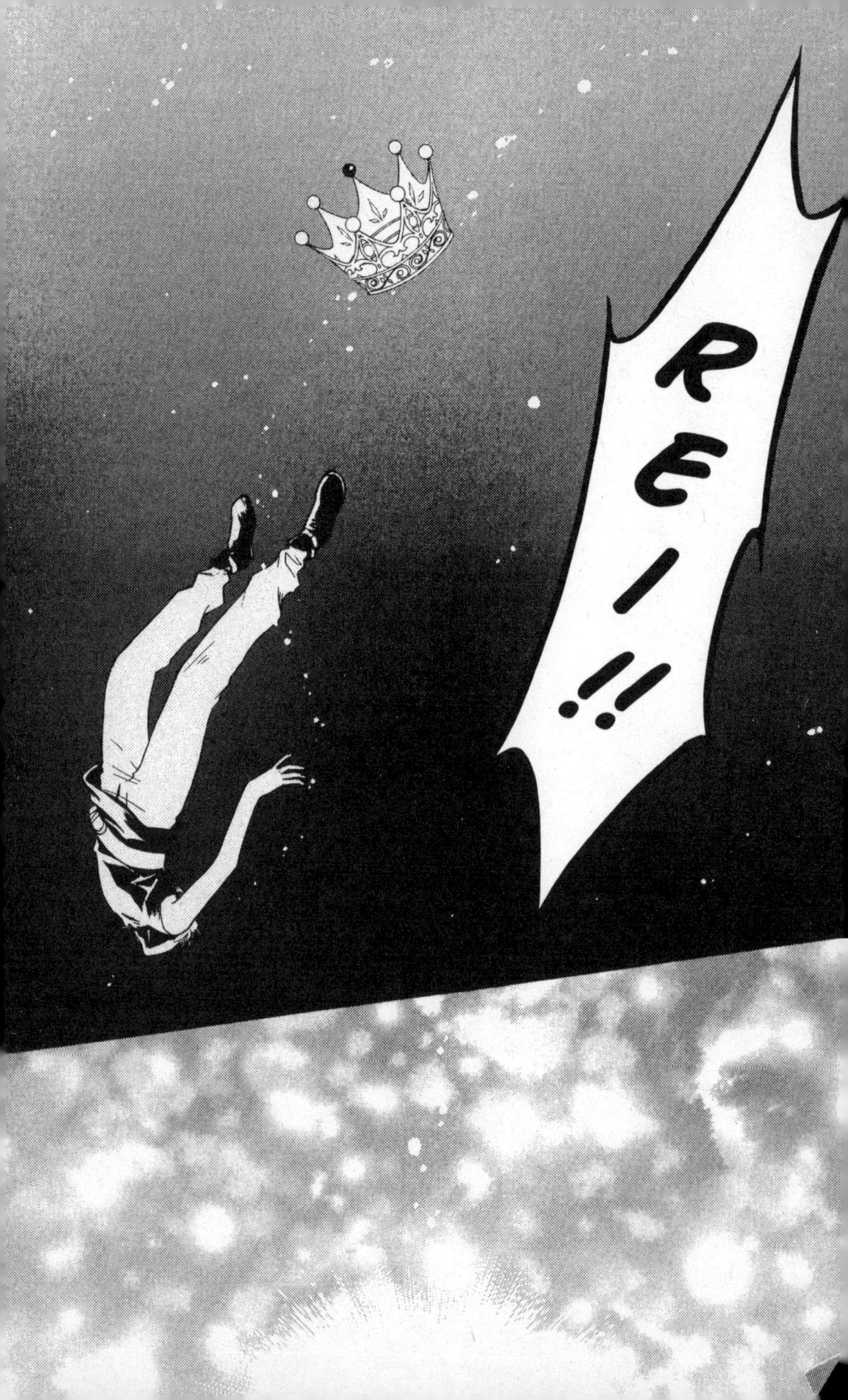
REI!!

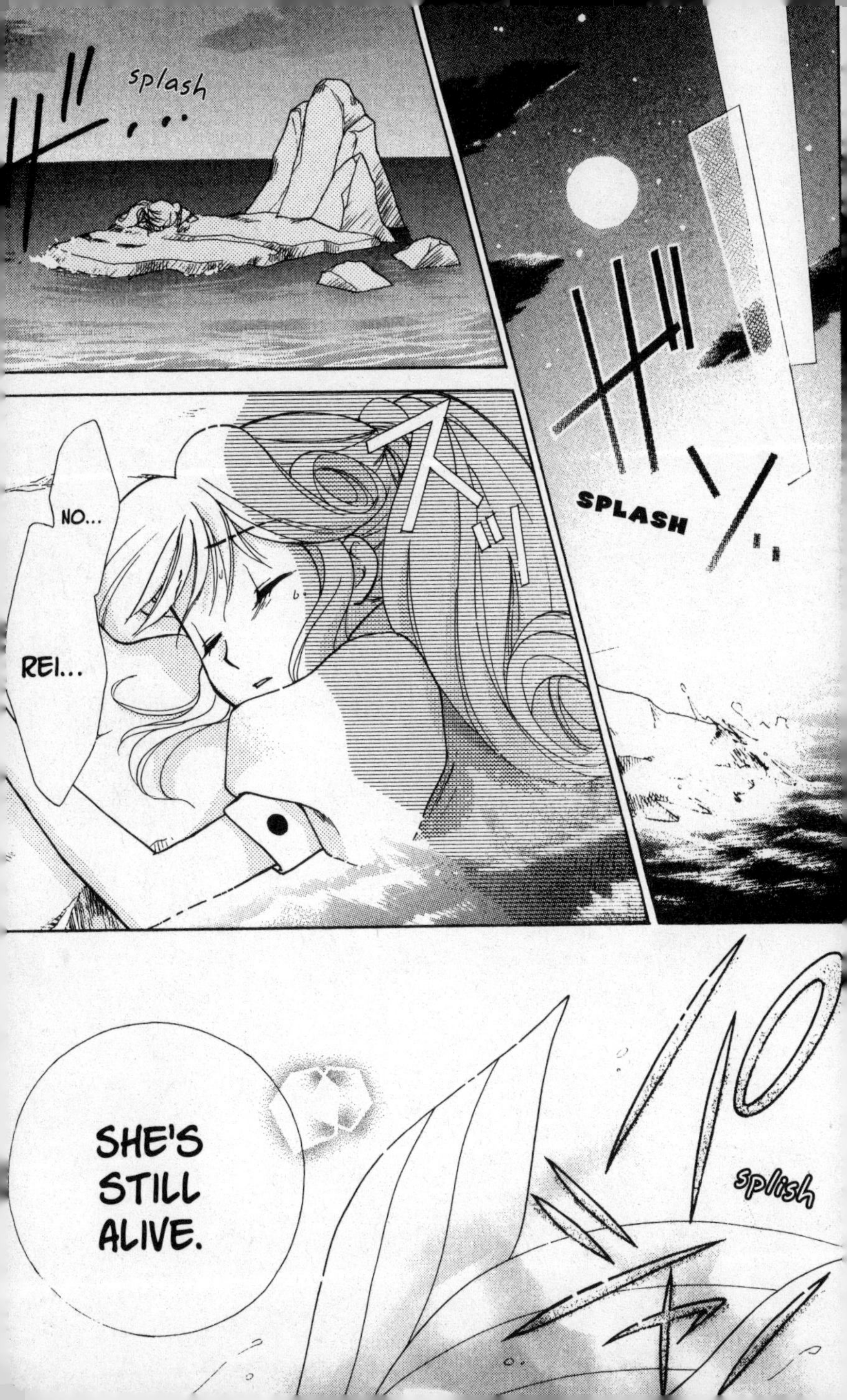
SPLASH
splash
NO...
REI...
SHE'S STILL ALIVE.
splish

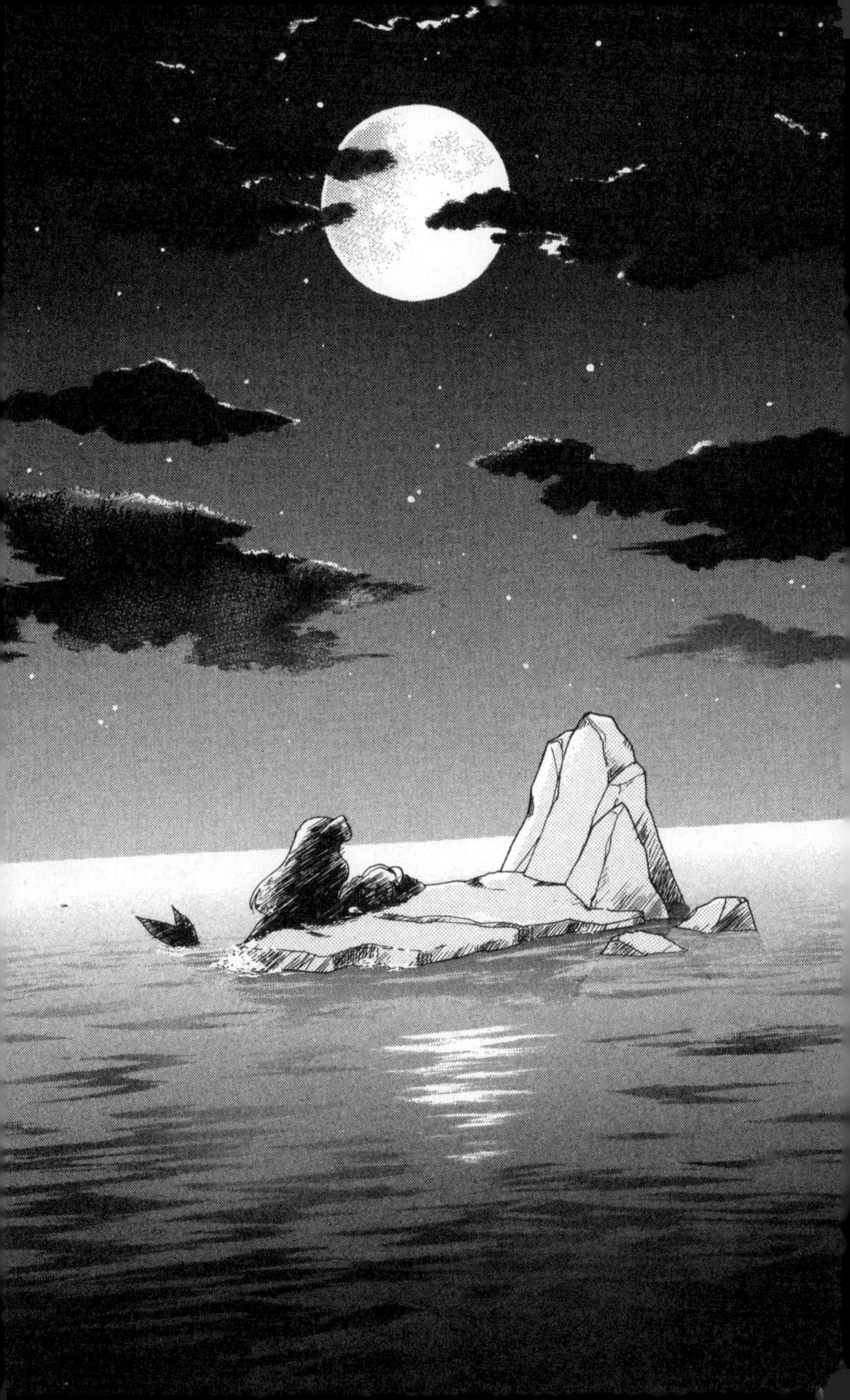

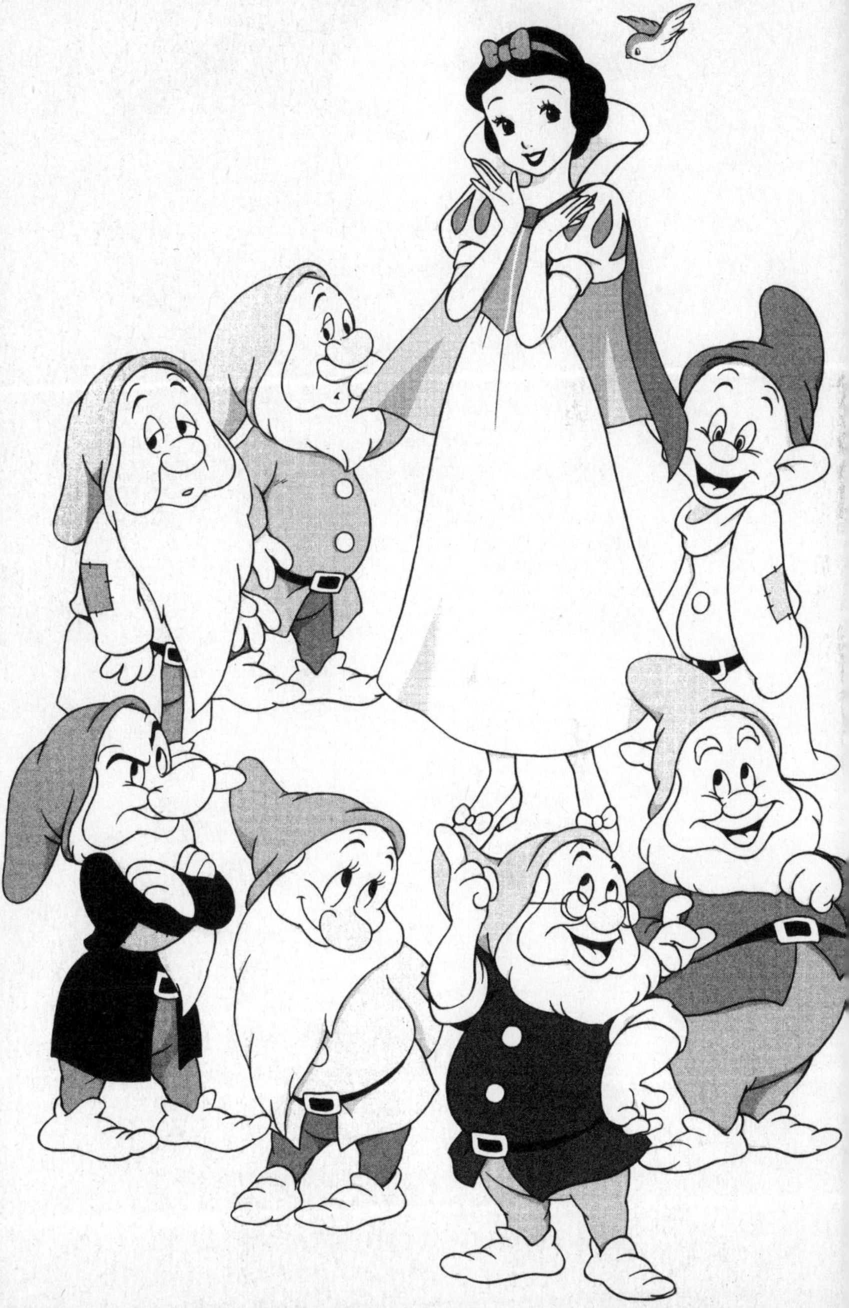

IN THE NEXT VOLUME OF

DISNEY

Kilala
Princess

A giant wave washes Kilala and Rei
into the sea, where they discover
the magical world of the Little
Mermaid. At first, things seem
peaceful, but the ocean can
be a dangerous place...

JOIN KILALA AND THE DISNEY
PRINCESSES FOR MORE
ADVENTURES IN VOLUME 2!

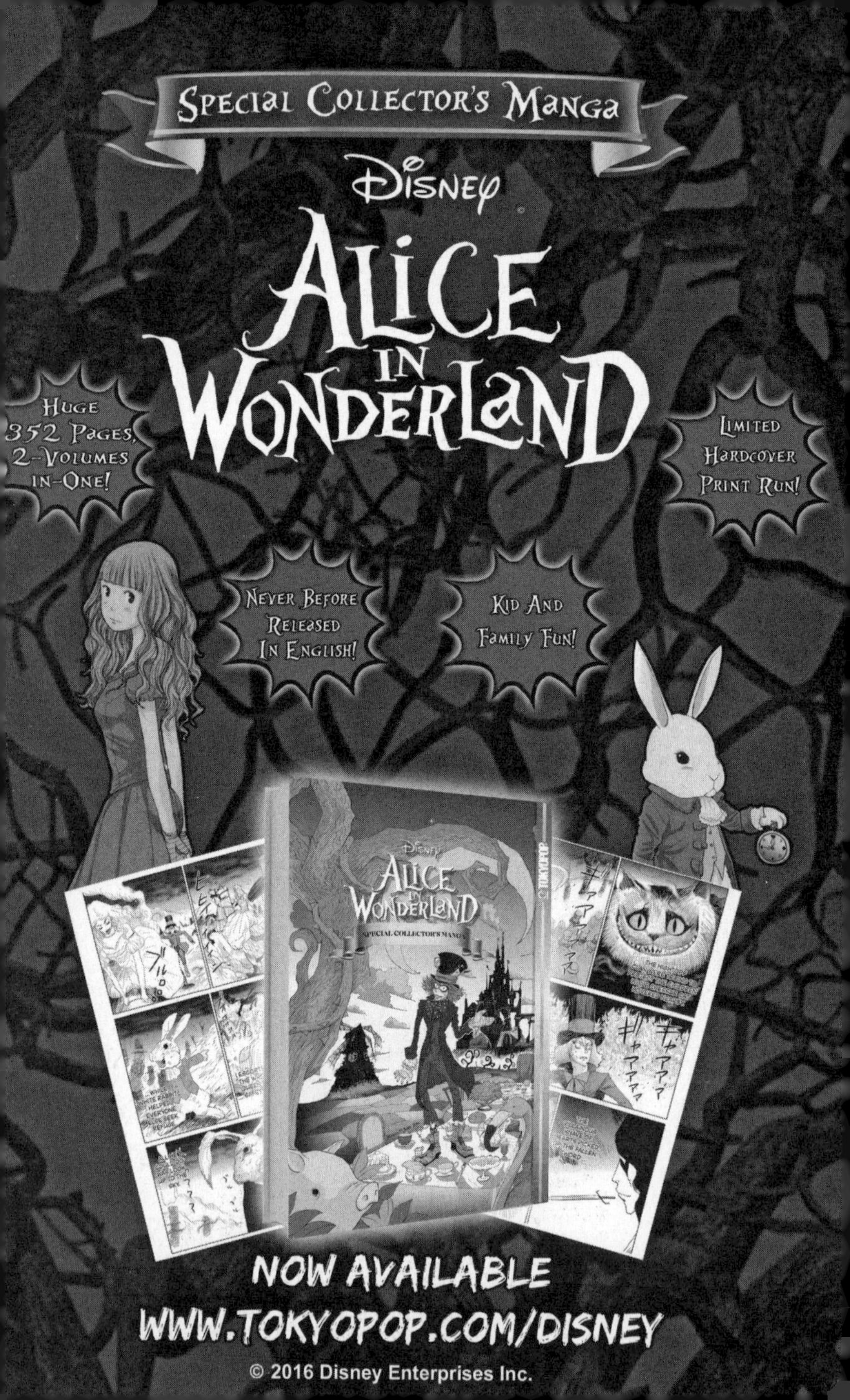
SPECIAL COLLECTOR'S MANGA
DISNEY
ALICE IN WONDERLAND
HUGE 352 PAGES, 2-VOLUMES IN-ONE!
LIMITED HARDCOVER PRINT RUN!
NEVER BEFORE RELEASED IN ENGLISH!
KID AND FAMILY FUN!
NOW AVAILABLE
WWW.TOKYOPOP.COM/DISNEY
© 2016 Disney Enterprises Inc.